THE SOCIAL FUNCTION OF SOCIAL SCIENCE

THE SOCIAL FUNCTION
OF SOCIAL SCIENCE

Duncan MacRae, Jr.

NEW HAVEN AND LONDON, YALE UNIVERSITY PRESS

Library of Congress catalog card number: 75-32282
International standard book numbers: 0-300-01921-1 (cloth); 0-300-02670-6 (paper)

Designed by Sally Sullivan
and set in Times Roman type.
Printed in the United States of America by
Vail-Ballou Press, Inc., Binghamton, N.Y.

11   10   9   8   7   6   5   4   3   2

To Edie and Amy

CONTENTS

PART II. THE ETHICS OF THE SOCIAL SCIENCES

5. Economic Ethics   107
    From the Old Welfare Economics to the New   111
    The Resurrection of Cardinality and Interpersonal
        Comparison   125
    Cost-Benefit Analysis   129
    Preference, Personal Welfare, and Ethical Judgment   138
    Imperfect Information: Freedom, Expertness,
        and the Information Market   145
    Induced Changes in Preference: Advertising
        and Education   150
    Types of Action Affecting Welfare   155

6. The Functions and Forms of Government   158
    Market Failure   160
    Types of Government Intervention   164
    Democratic Theory and Economic Concepts   167
    Democratic Forms and Political Market Failure   172
    Coalitions and Representation   181
    Welfare and Changes of Political Preference   186
    Representation, Ethical Judgment, and Deliberation   194

7. Changes of Preference: Learning and Therapy   203
    Preference Change in Economics and Learning Theory   206
    The Ethics of B. F. Skinner   211
    Ethical Criteria of Psychotherapy and Mental Health   218
    The Ethics and Politics of Preference Change   231

8. The Choice of Social Norms   237
    Social Norms   238
    Sociological Ethics: Normative Order, Science,
        and Opposition   243
    The Choice and Creation of Norms   251
    The Creation of Organizations   253
    Reciprocity and Symmetry in the Choice of Norms   257
    Justification, Ethical Argument, and Change of Norms   263
    Valuative Discourse and the Social Sciences   271

PART III. SOCIAL FRAMEWORKS FOR VALUATIVE DIS-
COURSE

PREFACE

In 1939, J. D. Bernal's *The Social Function of Science* was published. He argued then, as I do now, that science should serve human welfare, not simply scientists' satisfaction or the discovery of truth as an end in itself. He also favored the pursuit of general and fundamental findings in science, but with a greater concern for their use than "pure science" would dictate; this is also my position. For these similarities, I hope I am justified in using and amending his title.

In other respects, however, my approach will differ from Bernal's. He based much of his analysis on a particular diagnosis of the place of science in the social, economic, and political system and judged that socialism was superior to capitalism for its application. I shall not present such a diagnosis here but shall be concerned only with directing academic activities toward practical problems, including such diagnoses. Social scientists should have much to contribute to social diagnosis and prescription; but my argument here is that these contributions should be guided by clear notions of social health, i.e., by ethical criteria.

Social science as a collective activity has given rise to diverse diagnoses of the role of science in society. Ideally, the factual differences among these diagnoses should be resolvable by scientific procedures. To resolve these differences, social scientists must gather evidence systematically, and admit the possibility of new evidence, about the characteristics of various social, economic, and political systems. It is their task to examine these questions deeply but not to claim final answers unless the evidence is conclusive. For purposes of practical action we may not be able to wait for as much evidence as a scientific theory requires. But social science, if it claims to be scientific at least in approach, cannot commit itself so irrevocably. The very requirement that social science be scientific makes it less available as the ideology of a revolutionary movement—but should also make it a less than perfect support for existing arrangements. For these reasons I do not attempt a systematic diagnosis of the position and use of social science in contemporary society but simply suggest a direction for our discussion and a framework within which that discussion might guide social science to greater social utility.

Bernal's title, and mine, imply a concern with the *desirable* function of science. But since Bernal's time, especially in sociology, the discussion of "functions" has been ostensibly limited to *factual* analysis of contributions that parts make to the whole. I am choosing the older usage of the term, which implies a more valuative and less positivistic approach.

Bernal's substantive analysis stresses influences external to science that shape its development. My analysis, however, centers on the university and its basic units—the disciplines. The dominance of the disciplines in American higher education has become so evident that some reformers have dreamed of education without disciplines— analogous to the classless society or to world government. My recommendations are less radical; they aim to use the framework of the disciplines to retain the value of expert investigation and criticism, while seeking a more intelligent orientation of universities *and* disciplines toward broader social values. I may thus seem to be engaging in academic discourse rather than facing the problems of the world itself. I do so in order to grasp the attention of academics—as members of disciplines and not simply as citizens or "intellectuals"—and direct it to problems of action and choice.

The results of social scientists' inquiries, like those of natural science, may be applied to practical tasks, but the function of social science need not end there. For social science—or some of its presently disjointed parts—also has the potential of inquiring about, and hypothetically asserting, ethical criteria for practical choice. The discussion, criticism, and elaboration of these criteria can perhaps elevate social science to a role in which it offers greater guidance to society than it now provides. Yet once we acknowledge this possibility, we must immediately qualify it. The role of philosopher-king, or of technical aristocracy, is neither adequately provided by the sciences nor tolerated by the citizens in contemporary democratic societies. Social science can supply partial advice to decision makers, but for informed citizens, who are the ultimate decision makers in a democracy, it can

provide not only analyses of particular policies but also general education. This education must constantly direct our attention to the risks of
undue influence by the educated in their own behalf. It must consider
the political and democratic responsibility of the educated, and the educational system. It must provide informed citizens, who perhaps by
their own efforts will become better informed. And it must listen to
those who have learned in the world of practice, while guarding its
communications from the inexpert and the uninformed. These are not
easy tasks, even to define, but they are the tasks to which I address
myself here.

The "ethical hypotheses" discussed here are likely to have parallels
in the work of political philosophers of earlier times, which I do not
discuss. Readers who are conversant with the history of philosophy
will undoubtedly consider this a gap in the argument, and indeed, my
failure to do justice to them is a departure from the scientific norm that
one should cite the previous literature. My only excuse is that, had I
tried to include that literature, the gestation period of this book would
have been even longer than its actual twenty-five years. I hope that
this deficiency—as well as deficiencies in my citation and analysis of
the work of the social sciences—will be remedied in other works and
by other persons.

Another problem of my argument is that while it is addressed
largely to specialists in the various social sciences, it cannot easily
meet each specialty on its own terms. Each discipline properly defines
its own sphere of expertness and protects it through the criticism that
trained persons direct at one another. To speak to four or more such
disciplines, each on its own terms, is obviously difficult. For this
reason I have limited my discussion to four social sciences and omitted
others (for example, anthropology); but the four I have chosen appear
to me to permit the development of important issues in a coherent
fashion.

A further difficulty that I encounter in entering into the discourse of
each discipline is that I am dealing not with its central scientific core
but with a valuative component that is to some extent unofficial or
unrecognized. The references chosen are not only from the scientific
literature, but also from the "house organs" of the disciplinary associations and works intended for popular consumption—especially in

psychology, where I have made use of Skinner's *Walden Two* and *Beyond Freedom and Dignity*. While a more conventional approach might be to exorcise this valuative content in the name of science, to deny its existence, to "unmask" it from a radical or critical perspective, or otherwise to trace its social, psychological, or philosophical sources, I wish only to bring it out into open and reasoned discussion on its merits.

My aim is to encourage valuative discussion among the disciplines. Readers who are members of a particular discipline may well judge that my discussion of their own discipline is inadequate, while that of the other disciplines is unnecessarily complex. A remedy for both these faults is for the reader to continue the discussion with his colleagues or fellow students in other disciplines. The question I am addressing is, How should the university be structured in order to perform its proper functions in society? This is a question that no individual discipline can adequately answer. The modest structural change that I propose for the university cannot be undertaken intelligently without communication among the disciplines. The task is to recombine existing specialties to form new ones. In this task, some competence that combines various existing disciplines is required. Even if I have fallen short of the standards of particular disciplines, my effort must be judged not simply in terms of these preexisting standards, but in relation to the task.

I should like to thank the following persons who have kindly made suggestions for improvements of parts of the manuscript as it developed—but who are not responsible for its faults: James Begun, Joseph Ben-David, Thomas Blau, Alan Emdin, Robert Entman, Richard E. Flathman, R. F. Hafer, William R. Keech, E. Wood Kelley, Robert C. Kelner, Paul F. Kress, Joseph Morrissey, John S. Nelson, Jeffrey Obler, Mancur Olson, Thomas I. Ribich, Donald D. Searing, Edward Sharp, Edward A. Shils, Eugene Smolensky, Jürg Steiner, Maxine Stern, John W. Sweeney, Jr., and two anonymous readers for the Yale University Press. Numerous discussions with colleagues and students, both at Chicago and at Chapel Hill, have also touched on the issues involved. I am also indebted to the William Rand Kenan, Jr., Fund for assistance in preparation of the manuscript, to Gert Rippy for her care in typing it, and to Judith Heimlich for assistance with the index. The encouragement and support of my wife, Edith K. MacRae, has been of the greatest value in this long enterprise.

I am grateful to the following journals for permission to adapt earlier articles for inclusion here:

Minerva for "Science and the Formation of Policy in a Democracy," April 1973 (Chapter 2);

The American Political Science Association for "Scientific Communication, Ethical Argument and Public Policy," *American Political Science Review*, March 1971 (Chapter 4);

Public Choice for "Normative Assumptions in the Study of Public Choice," Fall 1973 (Chapters 5 and 6);

The University of Chicago Press for "Utilitarian Ethics and Social Change," *Ethics*, April 1968 (Chapter 8);

The American Sociological Association for "A Dilemma of Sociology: Science Versus Policy," *The American Sociologist*, June 1971 (Chapter 8);

The American Political Science Association for "Social Science and the Sources of Policy: 1951–1970," *P.S.*, Summer 1970 (Chapter 9);

Sage Publications for "Policy Analysis as an Applied Social Science Discipline," *Administration and Society*, February 1975 (Chapter 9).

PART ONE | SCIENTIFIC DISCOURSE AND ITS GOALS

1 SPECIALIZED KNOWLEDGE AND PRACTICAL CHOICE

A set of academic specialties known as the "social sciences" have grown and established themselves in American universities during the twentieth century. They have evolved from an earlier form of social analysis, less specialized and recondite, by imitating the natural sciences. The leaders of these disciplines, who have taken them along this path, have hoped thereby to gain more certain knowledge and broader social support, not only for the understanding of man and society but also for their improvement.

A major impetus to the growth of the social sciences has been the hope that they would eventually aid in the improvement of man's condition. This is a reasonable hope. But in imitating the natural sciences, many social scientists have subscribed to a widespread contemporary justification for natural science—that the most effective way to promote useful discoveries is to study uniformities in nature and society as if we were studying them for their own sake. This cultivation of fundamental social science is seen as a postponement, or an investment, which will ultimately yield important returns for human welfare.

By this sort of reasoning, many social scientists have become convinced that the most effective path to useful application lies through objective research and theory construction, free from the complications of ideological and philosophical dispute. They have thus developed distinct technical terminologies and methods of research, specialized journals, and programs of graduate instruction. Through these devices they have separated the discourse of specialists from that of the general public, and the communications of the individual specialties from one another. The course of the social sciences during the past several decades has thus been guided by the model of natural science—however distant they may seem from it to natural scientists themselves.[1]

1. For a historical analysis of related processes in the development of natural science, see Ben-David, *The Scientist's Role in Society*. Natural scientists themselves may assert

The model of natural science has been increasingly criticized during the past decade, however, by both the general public and social scientists. Various critics now regard the single-minded pursuit of basic science as failing to cope with a deterioration in man's situation, whether this results from a perversion of power, a lack of foresight and guidance, or a decay of social order. They have associated natural science increasingly with a rampant and destructive technology and an excessively mechanistic use of man's capacities.

Some social scientists have enlarged these criticisms and directed them at the dominant trends in their own disciplines. The most conspicuous of these criticisms in recent years has attacked not only the alleged involvement of social science with a power structure seen as undemocratic, exploitative, and misguided, but also scientific methods themselves. A contrasting philosophical critique sees modern philosophy and social science as based on error and recommends the return to earlier philosophical foundations with the abolition of the distinction between facts and values.[2] But whether in the name of humanism, phenomenology, existentialism, radicalism, or classical political philosophy, most of these criticisms would drastically reduce the use of technical methods and terminology by social science in order to bring the study of man nearer (in their view) to man's needs or his nature.

Even those social scientists who wish to emulate natural science also see practical action and valuation as conflicting with the development of scientific knowledge. This group would prefer to go still further in methodological rigor and sophistication. They would purge the technical vocabularies of the social sciences more completely of implicit valuations as well as of ambiguities and would direct attention to theoretically significant rather than narrowly practical problems. Such a program, though more confidently supported several decades ago, is still regarded by many as a means to reduce dissension, establish general propositions, and even ultimately to serve practical ends.

In these disparate arguments there is a single polar opposition:

---

valuations concerning society or nature that are characteristic of their particular disciplines, but they rarely do so in scientific journal articles. On their valuative "fringe associations," see chapter 3 below.

2. For an analysis of the first of these tendencies from the perspective of the second, see Cropsey, "Radicalism and Its Roots."

science versus valuation.[3] The critics of science, who see it as incapable of guiding its own development, would bring values to the fore by repudiating the methods and the rigor of science, at least in the study of man and society. Others assail the claim to objectivity as a sham, concealing conservative values. The defenders of a rigorous social science, on the other hand, would cleanse its discourse of valuative implications in order to seek the certainty of natural science.

I shall argue here that there is another path to follow; that reliable scientific knowledge of man and nature is an important resource for policy choice but can coexist with rational ethical discourse; that some of the values of science may be transferred to this ethical discourse; and that scientific propositions and ethical assertions, while clearly distinguishable, may be fruitfully combined in academic disciplines concerned with the study of man and society.

The ethical discourse that I propose would be more explicit, and more concerned with general principles, than most expressions of values that now appear in the literature of the social sciences. This literature does indeed include many valuations; but except for political philosophy it involves very little systematic valuative *discourse*. Insofar as valuations are embodied in journal articles that present empirical research, they are largely limited to use of "secondarily evaluative" terms, which have a factual meaning as well as a valuative one.[4] "Gross national product," "participation," "social mobility," and "mental health" are among the numerous terms of this type. Studies of empirical relations between such variables cannot easily be related to questions of general principle concerning the good life, the good society, or the best regime.

Imitation of natural science has thus restricted much of the discourse of the social sciences to relations among terms in their factual meaning. The valuative meanings of these terms cannot be analyzed in their

3. The terms "valuation" and "ethics" will refer, throughout this book, to assertions that acts are right or ought to be done, that things are good, or the equivalent. We shall refer interchangeably to "valuative" and "ethical" discourse as embodying such assertions. We do *not* include in this domain the factual assertion either that the speaker prefers a state of affairs or that a particular social norm exists. For the latter type of factual assertion we shall use the term "normative" (a sociological usage), although economists use this term for the assertion of valuations.

4. See Hare, *Freedom and Reason*, p. 25, and chapter 4 below.

own right in the same literature. The social science discipline that contains the most systematic ethical discourse—economics—tends not to recognize welfare economics as an ethics and hamstrings the discussion of maximizing social welfare with unnecessary positivist limitations. For similar reasons, it would be difficult for sociologists to analyze the conditions for optimum social mobility.

The quest for general causal relationships often allows social scientists to study value-laden topics, but in ways that have little relation to questions of right action. Coleman has pointed out that much research on general social problems is not very relevant to policy problems and merely reflects an "unhealthy symbiosis" between researchers and powerless sponsors of research. Similarly, the field of political sociology embodies values but is largely irrelevant to policy choice because of our difficulty in changing "the social bases of politics." [5]

The scientific study of society, I shall argue, need not try to copy physics, chemistry, and biology in every respect. But in so arguing, I do not wish to join the contemporary opposition to scientific method in social science; rather, I shall contend that an additional valuative subject matter should be explicitly related to the scientific analyses furnished by the social sciences, linking them together and joining them more meaningfully to the education of the citizen as well as to practical application.

In making this proposal I first encounter a verbal problem. In the social science disciplines it is frequently argued that the task of a "science" is to deal with factual questions, resolvable by observation, and not with the subjective and controversial realm of values. This argument, however, is often an effort to derive substance from words. Disciplines, whether they are called "sciences" or not, are organized systems of communication among trained persons and undergo modification through the contributions of those persons. These systems do not depend for their existence on dealing solely with empirical questions. I shall argue, therefore, that the "social sciences" cannot be barred from including valuative discourse simply because they now

5. Coleman refers to the "unhealthy symbiosis" in *Policy Research in the Social Sciences,* p. 22, and in this monograph he also elaborates the distinction between "discipline research" and "policy research"—a topic to which we return in chapter 9 below. "The social bases" is the subtitle of Lipset's *Political Man.*

happen to bear the name of "science." The question must be faced at a more fundamental level. Valuative and factual discourse can be combined either in existing disciplines or in new ones.

The problem, then, is whether it is desirable to combine a certain type of valuative discourse, which draws on the rationality of scientific communication, with the "social sciences." This is itself a valuative question, unanswerable on scientific grounds alone. It is of the same order as those questions that scientific societies confront when they decide how their organizational affairs should be conducted or whether to take collective stands on extrascientific matters. It also resembles some of the problems that a university department encounters when it considers a faculty appointment shared with another discipline. Such questions must be dealt with by existing disciplines, even though they extend beyond the disciplines' expert competence.

The potential gains from this change are of two kinds. First, the pursuit of objective knowledge can be joined with the valuation essential for practical choice. Reasoned discussion of ethical questions and of the goals of action can be combined with careful ascertainment of relevant facts and principles. Though not all ideological controversies can be resolved by appeal to facts, some can; and this resolution is easier if our discussions of ends and of means are together constrained toward rationality. I shall argue (though perhaps the case no longer needs to be made) that ethical discourse can be conducted rationally. In the social sciences, as in everyday discourse, we engage in valuations continually but unsystematically. We might with some effort eliminate these valuations; but in so doing we might deprive society of an important potential source of guidance. Thus we must combine with social science—introduce if necessary—some of the valuative discourse that might be conducted elsewhere in the university, as in departments of philosophy. We engage in it; we do so poorly; we cannot afford to discontinue it; therefore we must learn to do it properly.[6]

A second advantage of this change would be to provide connections, essential for practical application, among the separate social sciences. The basic disciplines are indeed often connected by problems of practical application, as when they are combined in the applied

6. A parallel argument was made three decades earlier by Myrdal in *An American Dilemma*, pp. 1041–1064.

sciences. But some of the gaps between them might also be bridged by
a common valuative discourse. In this way, the combination of skills
and judgments that we require to deal wisely with practical problems
might be more complete.[7]

As for the costs of such a change, I shall argue only that they are
tolerable, and probably less than its benefits. Some possible costs
derive from a lessening of certainty in the discourse of disciplines
whose assertions are still none too certain; an enlargement of the basic
notions as to what constitutes reputable, publishable work; and a possible politicization and internal controversy in the university, where
greater consensus might otherwise have been possible. But a central
part of my argument will be that valuative discourse need not bring
with it all the dangers that some anticipate, if is is conducted rationally; it need not be subjective, emotional, or ideological in the
sense of commitment to predetermined conclusions.

Scientific Disciplines as Closed Systems

The growth of the natural sciences, and the consensus within each
of their specialties as to what problems are important, have been attributed not only to their careful study of the natural world but also to
the fact that they constitute closed communities whose members write
and speak primarily for fellow specialists. At any one time such a
community, represented by its gatekeepers, judges what topics are
then relevant and in what terms they may properly be discussed. In the
longer run, new members may enter such a community when they
have acquired the relevant knowledge, vocabulary, and skills, typically available through graduate study in a discipline.

The closure of such a communication system permits a sharp focus
by its members on problems that are collectively judged to be important.[8] The scientist must communicate his findings first to colleagues
in his specialty, not to the general public. He is praised or criticized by

---

7. See Charlesworth, ed., *Integration of the Social Sciences Through Policy Analysis*. In chapter 9 below we consider "social production functions" as potentially interdisciplinary causal models centered about valuative dependent variables.

8. Kuhn, in *The Structure of Scientific Revolutions*, refers to these problems as
"puzzles."

these colleagues in terms of criteria peculiar to this expert group. This praise and criticism direct him to certain types of problems and methods rather than others and require him to communicate his findings in certain ways. This form of organization has furthered the growth of the natural sciences and enhanced the expertness and precision of their internal criticism. It has been copied by the social sciences and has brought them similar advantages.

The modern American university is dominated by these disciplinary communication systems. Research and instruction are largely controlled by departments, which correspond to national or international associations of persons working in the corresponding disciplines. Professors are rewarded by their universities for activities that gain esteem in their disciplines. Activities directed to other disciplines, or to the public, are largely irrelevant to their career advancement. If in addition, professors' other activities offend the moral or political views of important segments of society, they may suffer disadvantages, though their right to employment will be defended by members of their disciplines.

The division of academic labor into the specialized domains of the disciplines may perhaps be justified on the ground that a larger task should be divided into parts. The quest for knowledge is thus separated from outside political controversy,[9] and knowledge itself is divided into specialties. When division of labor occurs, those who work in a particular part of the system can then concentrate on manageable goals.

My argument for discourse among the disciplines is thus a call back to a "synoptic" view of valuation,[10] reexamining the larger context within which the division has occurred. Division of labor is most easily justified if it has been planned and is constantly under review. The harmonious cooperation of the parts of society is not so assured as that of the organs of a biological organism. If a society requires guidance by its leaders and its citizens, they must somehow acquire a larger perspective. As Whitehead pointed out, "Each profession makes progress, but it is progress in its own groove. . . . The remainder of life is

9. See Price, *The Scientific Estate,* ch. 5.
10. Such a view is criticized in Braybrooke and Lindblom, *A Strategy of Decision,* ch. 2.

treated superficially, with the imperfect categories of thought derived from one profession." [11]

Thus the same closure that provides advantages for scientific research also has disadvantages for the *application* of scientific knowledge. If scientists are motivated to speak and write primarily for one another, this organization of rewards does not guarantee that their findings will be applied practically. The scientist who seeks only the esteem of his colleagues may be indifferent to the practical consequences of his work, neither seeking to benefit society nor taking responsibility for harmful uses of his findings. He may be uninterested in checking the accuracy of applications of science that do not contribute to the advance of basic science. And he may communicate only with those other scientists whose work relates to his own through fundamental, rather than applied, problems.

The application of science must therefore be carried on elsewhere than in the basic science disciplines. Among the other institutions that now contribute to this function are the market, the political system, and the various arrangements for teaching applied science in the university. The market and the political system are expected to define the values to which science and other resources are directed; the applied sciences and professions define relevant problems, distinct from those of basic science and often regrouping basic specialties, and set some of the norms that circumscribe professional practice.

There remains a gap, however, in the relation of the university to these institutions. The applied sciences typically convey scientific information to decision points through the employment of persons who are trained for special careers—either in organizations, like engineers, or in professions such as medicine. This system supplements the communication systems of basic science and makes its findings more widely available. But insofar as it contributes to decisions made by the economic system (through production) or the political system (through policy decisions), it does not necessarily channel needed information to the consumer, patient, or voter. The consumer requires expertness to judge the claims of competing products; the voter requires it even more, if he is to judge among policies that are still more complex and

11. Whitehead, *Science and the Modern World,* pp. 196–197. The possibility of a "mixed-scanning" approach, alternating between larger and smaller perspectives, is suggested in Etzioni, *The Active Society,* ch. 12.

remote from his daily experiences. Applied science thus tends to aid the producer of goods, services, and policies more than the consumer or citizen.

In addition, each particular applied science centers its work about norms and goals peculiar to its domain of practice. The ethical assumptions of medicine, engineering, social work, and psychotherapy, for example, are disparate and largely unrelated; each professional ethic concerns what a different group of specialists should do. Whereas the basic sciences exclude valuative discourse, the applied sciences include it only in highly specific contexts.

Thus the university, even though it trains some of its graduates for applied work, fails to embody reasoned valuative discussion of the more general problems shared by particular applied fields. Contemporary philosophy has not gone far enough in relating such discourse to policy choice and factual knowledge about society; [12] to provide this combination may therefore be the responsibility—and the opportunity—of the social sciences.

If reasoned valuative discourse is to find its connection with the social sciences, it must link them together in general terms while drawing on the specific contributions of each. It must have relevance to practice without being drawn destructively into the controversies of practical choice. It must strive to maintain rationality in a realm that is not anchored in reproducible observations. And it must clearly distinguish the discourse of experts from that of laymen, while avoiding an elitism that would make applied science politically irresponsible. For all these problems, which involve assessing the advantages and disadvantages of autonomous, self-contained communication systems, the experience of the natural sciences is relevant. We must therefore examine both the ways in which scientific discourse is constrained into closed systems and the existing institutions outside these systems by which it is applied.

The social constraints or norms [13] that govern communication in the natural sciences are relevant to our argument in three ways. First, we

12. There may be a tendency among moral philosophers to concentrate on questions of deontological ethics, which do not require knowledge of social science.

13. Merton refers to the "ethos" of science, as a combination of values and norms; see his *Social Theory and Social Structure* (1968 ed.), p. 605. Storer separates "norms" and "values" in *The Social System of Science*, pp. 76ff. For a more detailed discussion of norms, see chapter 8 below.

must consider science as a source of objective ascertainment of matters of fact, and ask how its objectivity is influenced by these norms. Second, we must examine the relation between these norms and practical application, including the relations both among separate specialties and between specialized knowledge and the general knowledge of the informed citizen. Third, we shall consider certain aspects of scientific communication as models for ethical discourse.

If we asked a practicing scientist to describe the standards of his discipline, he would probably first refer to its firm foundation in repeatable observations or experiments. To these he might add the quest for powerful and elegant inferences from these observations. Further questioning might lead him to stress certain characteristics of the communications themselves. A concise summary of these norms is given by Parsons:

> The basic norms of scientific knowledge are perhaps four, empirical validity, logical clarity or precision of the particular proposition, logical consistency or precision of the mutual implications of propositions, and generality of the "principles" involved, which may perhaps be interpreted to mean range of mutually verified implications.

Ziman has seen these norms as contributing to the public character of scientic knowledge. They bear more on the process of verification and testing than on that of initial discovery.[14]

These norms, governing the propositions asserted in the literature, are mentioned (though usually passed over rapidly) by sociologists of science. Merton notes "the relevant definition of knowledge: empirically confirmed and logically consistent predictions." Barber refers to the same norms in saying that "Science exists only when rational thought is applied to what we may call 'empirical' ends." Storer refers briefly to "objectivity" and "generalization." Ziman stresses the precision of formulas used to convey scientific knowledge.[15] And al-

14. Parsons, *The Social System,* p. 335; Ziman, *Public Knowledge;* Kuhn, *op. cit.;* Kaplan, *The Conduct of Inquiry.*
15. Merton, *op. cit.,* pp. 595–606; Barber, *Science and the Social Order,* p. 33; Storer, *op. cit.,* pp. 80–81; Ziman, *op. cit.,* p. 45.

though the emphases are somewhat different, the various writers all seem to agree on these norms but to dismiss them as relatively obvious.

The social sciences have also benefited from applying these norms. Repeated arguments have been made for the value of establishing the truth of matters of fact objectively and publicly and of summarizing these facts in general theories. The stress on reporting one's findings in public, written statements; the insistence on describing experiments so that they can be repeated; and the requirement that new findings be justified as regards their significance in relation to the literature—all these norms relate to the process of winnowing the relevant from the irrelevant, the solidly based from mere speculation, and insure that the original contributions chosen will be public property in the discipline.

The study of man and society can benefit from these norms not only in the possibility of objectivity and some generality in factual matters, but also in a possible model for valuative discourse. Moreover, the conjunction of these two types of reasoned discourse—involving general matters of fact and general principles of valuation—may provide a central core of discourse uniting various applied fields.

The norms we have considered so far concern scientists as *individuals*—their relation to the empirical world and their reports about it. A less conspicuous, but no less important, set of norms regulate scientists' *interactions* with one another. Well-known to any practicing scientist (though perhaps less so to the undergraduate student) is a system of interpersonal relations, gatekeepers, and attitudes toward the literature, as well as a relation of the scientific discipline to the outside world, which have been extensively studied by sociologists of science.

This second set of norms, regulating interactions, are less clearly expressed by scientists in their day-to-day activities, but they are no less real. Scientists' activities are coming increasingly to be seen as collective rather than simply individual. An earlier view of the scientist's work saw him as interacting chiefly with nature in the laboratory and establishing the truth by observation and reasoning. But a series of writers in recent decades—sociologists, historians, and scientists themselves—have stressed the social interactions and communication processes among scientists in a given specialty and the constraints that these processes exercise on the work of the individual scientist.[16]

Scientific disciplines may be regarded as largely closed social systems with particular norms and organizational structures. These norms and structures coordinate communications among many members who work largely independently and who are not organized in an overall hierarchy. The resulting communications are constrained so as to concentrate work on major problems, to cumulate knowledge and avoid duplication, and to favor certain (but not all) types of criticism and innovation.

The norms that regulate interactions in these communities—to different degrees in different disciplines—are of two principal kinds. First, they stress the public evaluation of one's research by one's fellow scientists, particularly in his discipline or specialty. This evaluation by the scientific community takes priority when it conflicts with outsiders' evaluations—whether personally generated publicity, a reputation enhanced by the mass media, sales of textbooks, or popularity with students. It takes priority over personal profit, in that inventions or articles contributed for a fee do not ideally enhance a scientist's standing. It also takes priority over other criteria of status—political or religious authority or the scientist's nationality, ethnicity, or social class origin.

Second, they stress a peculiar combination of originality and conservatism, summarized in the phrase familiar to doctoral candidates, "a contribution to knowledge." Here the stress on originality constitutes part of what Merton has called "organized skepticism" [17] and distinguishes science from static, closed systems of ideas that simply maintain themselves through socialization and social control. But there is also an important expectation of continuity with past findings. This combination of innovation and conservation is summarized by Polanyi, who points out that if a scientific contribution is to be accepted it must meet the tests of plausibility, scientific value, and originality. He then notes that "Both the criteria of plausibility and of scientific value tend to enforce conformity, while the value attached to original-

---

16. In addition to works previously cited, see Hagstrom, *The Scientific Community;* Polanyi, "The Republic of Science"; and Popper, *The Open Society and Its Enemies,* ch. 23.

17. Merton, *op. cit.,* chs. 17, 18.

ity encourages dissent. This internal tension is essential in guiding and motivating scientic work.'' [18] The value of originality must be modified when we later extend some of these norms to ethics and the criticism of public policies. In ethics it will involve the same quest for possible inconsistencies as is followed in examining scientific theories, but it will not place a premium on discovery or on innovation for its own sake. In policy criticism, novelty will be easier to attain but generality more difficult because of the continual change of policy problems over time.

The closure of a scientific discipline has been supported as a means of distinction between the competent and the less competent; between solvable scientific problems and the disputes of ideology and philosophy; and between the subject matter that can be mastered by one group of specialists and the domains of other groups. In some closed systems of discourse, however, closure can lead to stagnation. Some of the artificiality and rigidity that might result from this subdivision of knowledge is compensated by the development of new scientific disciplines that form from time to time to cope with new problems and discoveries. But we shall also see that when members of a discipline write about their ''social responsibilities'' they typically do so within the closed social system of a discipline and the identities they derive from it. [19]

The social sciences, like the natural, are divided into largely closed specialties, but it is less obvious that different social sciences deal with completely distinct problems. The social science disciplines have developed distinct vocabularies for the study of man and society, but occasionally members of two disciplines deal, apparently unknowingly, with problems and concepts that are closely related even though separated by disciplinary paradigms. [20] Conceivably this duplication could be reduced by a greater stress on empirical verification aimed not only

18. Polanyi, *op. cit.,* p. 58. See also Kuhn, *op. cit.*

19. See MacRae, ''Careers, Science, and Politics,'' and chapter 9 below. Insofar as these identities derive from socialization in graduate school and in later life, perhaps they may be more easily changed than identities and values implanted in early childhood.

20. See the section on the economic approach to preference change in chapter 7 and the discussion of Musgrave's concept of ''merit wants'' in chapter 5, fn. 69.

at elaborating general theories, but also at testing their limits, by multiple methods.

But a more serious problem related to the ambiguous status of the social sciences is their interpenetration with the discourse of the informed citizen. The valuative discourse which they retain overlaps with that of the citizen, but so too does much of their factual vocabulary. Human beings sharing the language and culture of the investigator may be subjects of research and objects of policy and at the same time spectators and participants in policy formation.[21] Thus the social sciences not only contribute terms to everyday discourse, as the natural sciences do, but also derive more of their language from everyday usage.

This "underdeveloped" status of the social sciences, and the overlap of their discourse with that of the citizen, provides opportunities as well as problems, as it permits alternative possibilities of development. The reforms that we shall propose, including the introduction rather than elimination of valuative discourse, are still possible in the social sciences far more than in the natural sciences.

Science as Servant of Market and Organization

The generation and testing of knowledge in closed scientific communities, while it has advantages for the accuracy and organization of that knowledge, may still not be an optimal arrangement for its application. If we are concerned with the use of knowledge rather than simply with its generation, we must ask how these self-contained parts are to be combined. Practical problems rarely lie neatly within particular basic disciplines or specialties.

The evolution of the scientist's role since the early nineteenth century has involved a simultaneous development of careers, technical discourse, and group autonomy. Rationality and expertness have been purchased at the expense of reduced interrelation among specialized domains of knowledge. Some such interrelation remains for scientific reasons alone, as is illustrated by the combination of genetics and X-ray crystallography in Watson and Crick's discovery of the structure

21. In this respect, the study of foreign cultures or subordinate groups has a greater appearance of objectivity.

of DNA.[22] But the combination of competences required for dealing with practical problems cannot normally be generated by the motive of scientific discovery within the basic disciplines.

We therefore require roles and social structures to supplement that of the scientific specialist as regards the application of his knowledge. One such structure is that of general education. In addition to the prestigious function of generating and publishing new knowledge, the university also educates late adolescents and young adults. An important aspect of this education is the transmission of fundamental and practical knowledge from specialists to society at large, through its application by the university's graduates.

But if the university trains only the young, decades may elapse between their training and the later opportunities that some will have to make major decisions. In the meantime, if they have learned well, they may have educated themselves in other ways that prepare them for these responsibilities. For this, the university may have no concern. Its responsibility may be simply to teach the most fundamental and lasting principles and skills, to instill the desire to learn further, and to allow the graduate and his associates to do the rest.

There are, however, two direct links between the knowledge developed in the university and organizations and persons who apply it: the flows of information and of trained personnel. The first of these involves the direct provision of practical recommendations by the faculty to persons outside. Faculty members serve as consultants, write popular articles, and enter into contracts for applied research, in ways that draw on their expert knowledge. In a libertarian sense, these activities may be seen as private choices of the professor, selling his free time in the market, and not to be scrutinized by the university or his discipline. Alternatively they may be criticized as detracting from his salaried duties or creating commitments to special causes.

These practical activities are governed by the standards of the market more than those of the scientific discipline. If the market functions properly, consultants who have given useful advice in the past will be in demand in the future. But for large and novel policy choices, advisers whose word is esteemed are often those who have gained pres-

22. Ben-David, op. cit.; Watson, The Double Helix; Polanyi, op. cit., p. 59.

tige in their specialties through research; this prestige is not always based on the broad combination of skills that the problems require.[23] Nor is the critical discourse of the research community brought to bear on these advising activities. Even if we set aside the necessary confidentiality of some advising relations, the practical advice that *is* public is not reviewed as carefully by university specialists as is the research in their disciplines. As applied, rather than fundamental work, it eludes the attention which the prestige system directs to fundamental discoveries.

A second, and quantitatively more important, link between the specialized knowledge of the university and outside application is provided by careers in applied science. Schools of engineering, medicine, and other applied sciences and professions train their graduates to work in combinations of specialties that relate to well-defined tasks for which roles and markets exist. The applied scientist is usually employed in an organization, although in medicine he expects to be a free professional. He can receive scientific information from the literature of the scientific disciplines, possibly filtered through periodicals in his own applied field.

This link between basic science and practice, through careers in applied science, has several advantages. It transmits information rapidly, relative to the general education of the citizen, since the engineer or physician is generally better connected with the developing scientific and technical literature than is the informed citizen.[24] It insulates the scientific community from outside influences, since the basic scientist need not communicate his findings directly to laymen or court their favor, except to obtain research resources. And insofar as the expert discourse of the sciences excludes discussion of the goals to which their findings should be put, this linkage leaves the setting of goals to other subsystems of the society—chiefly the economic and political systems.

23. The disparity is especially striking among consultants who are professors of basic science, less in applied fields.

24. This is not to deny that obsolescence is an important problem for engineers; see Perrucci and Rothman, "Obsolescence of Knowledge and the Professional Career." But in spite of this problem, the engineer has advantages over the informed citizen for new information in his specialty. The citizen's information may come, however, from science reporting in the media and from popular science periodicals.

The transmission of scientific information through careers in applied science also permits some combination of the various types of knowledge that enter into practical decisions. The scientist who works on practical problems in an organization must consider exigencies such as schedules and deadlines, the chance of failure of his materials and the need for testing his designs, and the general structure of goals within which his organization works. The skills and resources that an organization commands, the features of competing products, and political or legal restrictions on certain alternatives are extrascientific considerations that affect the success of public or private applications of science. Not only the scientist, but also his employer or the policymaker he advises, combines these types of information. The employer must learn enough technical detail to make use of scientific advice, by either prior technical training or learning on the job.

But the ultimate justification of the goals served by careers in applied science depends on the proper functioning of the economic or political system. When science is applied in organizations, these goals derive from the employing organizations and their managers. If the employer is a private firm, then its goal is presumably to make profit from sales, given the constraints of the initial purpose of the firm and the skills and commitments of its personnel. These commitments, of course, derive in part from the choices that its employees have made to work there rather than elsewhere. But once the firm's function and purpose are set, they guide the particular applications of science.

A similar relation obtains between the firm and the consultant or the researcher agreeing to a contract. A process of negotiation takes place, in which the researcher and the client try to maximize attainment of their respective goals. The researcher, if he is a basic scientist, may try to pursue the goals of his discipline, and to work on problems of theoretical significance. He may also try to persuade the client to redefine his *practical* problem and show him how to attain an underlying practical goal more efficiently.[25] But for the most part the client's practical goals do not conflict with scientific goals, except as (from the scientist's perspective) they waste resources, compete for the re-

25. See Rossi,"Researchers, Scholars, and Policy-Makers," p. 1157; Merton, *op. cit.,* pp. 442ff., 624.

searcher's time, or risk making his report less intelligible to his fellow scientists.

The setting of goals in this way can be justified if there is reason to believe that the organizational client—or the economic or political system of which it is a part—is contributing by its action to the general welfare.[26] But insofar as the firm or organization brings about consequences that are not reflected in the market, these consequences may not be incorporated in the firm's goals; similar problems exist for governmental organizations. Thus an employee who is concerned about harm to the general welfare through "external costs," such as atmospheric or water pollution, imposed on others by his employer may be fired for his trouble.[27]

By the same token, a chemistry professor who works on problems of atmospheric pollution may find that his university considers such work irrelevant to his function as a teacher and researcher in chemistry. Or even if his university places an official valuation on applied work—as for "public service"—he may still find that the university, as an institution valuing its survival, is more likely to reward "public service" that leaves major organizational interests unchallenged than applied work that discovers and publicizes activities by its major donors or supporters which are detrimental to the general welfare.

When organizational goals are set by the market, therefore, there is some question as to who may properly criticize the effects of the working of the market, and under what conditions. The academic economist may diagnose abstract conditions for "market failure" (see chapter 6) and be rewarded for it professionally. If he uses this abstract readoning to point out that firms significantly related to his own university are engaging in market practices that depart from the ideal, he may be considered indiscreet. If he is an employee of such a firm and makes his criticism public, he may lose his job. A similar problem arises for the government employee who publicizes cost overruns by his agency.

26. For a functional analysis of the relation between organizational goals and societal goals, see Parsons, *Structure and Process in Modern Societies,* ch. 1. Definitions of the general welfare are a major theme of this book. Later in this chapter we consider in more detail this exchange relation between professional values and the society's values.
27. See Nader, "The Scientist and His Indentured Professional Societies."

The market for applied scientific work reflects demand not only in the short run, but also in the longer run, through the definition of specialties. Specialized training in applied science can be developed in the universities only for those occupations in which employment is predictable. New varieties of applied science develop gradually, reflecting technologies such as those of nuclear or aerospace engineering. But for novel or ephemeral problems, only the preexisting categories of knowledge are available. Persons who wish to practice a new applied specialty, if they are to be recognized, thus sometimes try to fit into preexisting categories. Experts in policy choice sometimes fit uncomfortably into the role of "social scientist," to the discomfiture of other social scientists.[28]

So far we have primarily considered the application of science through organizational careers in the private sector, which is presumably regulated through competition and the profit motive. Government, however, constitutes another important channel through which science is applied. In one view we might expect the failures of the market to be compensated by government. Demands not met in the market may enter the political system and lead to production of collective goods, regulation of the economy, and compensation for damages. The allocation of productive resources that results from market action may be modified by taxation and subsidies, as well as by government provision of goods and services. The distribution of income may be altered by directly distributive policies. Such compensatory actions might lead to a greater confidence on the part of the scientist that he could allocate his work resources to industry, government, or professional service in the market, on the ground that the overall system allocates resources in accord with the general welfare.

Insofar as the scientist is confident that his services will be directed by the market to beneficent use, he may then leave "policy" decisions to others. In applied work he may limit his attention to the client's requests and to the by-products they provide for basic science, while ignoring the effects of the application itself.[29] The individual scientist's judgments of the value of these effects are then relegated to a category of "preferences," presumed to be personal and irrational.

28. See Benveniste, *The Politics of Expertise,* pp. 10, 19.
29. Merton, *op. cit.,* p. 442.

This view of value judgments has been supported both by the positivistic philosophy which has reigned in the social sciences (see chapter 3) and by a prevailing confidence, in America in the recent past, in the beneficence of the economic-political decision system.

This confident justification has, however, been questioned increasingly in recent years. The satisfaction of the "American business creed" with the working of the economy was first supplanted after the 1929 depression with a greater emphasis on governmental intervention. Keynesianism gained ground, at least temporarily, in government circles. The "managerial strand" of the creed came to see more legitimate functions for government.[30] The increasing influence of technology was seen by some as reducing the effectiveness of market mechanisms, because of the difficulty for consumers and producers to anticipate the long-run social consequences of their choices;[31] but similar problems also arise in the functioning of democratic political systems.

In the late 1960s, a parallel criticism developed in many democratic nations with respect to the working of representative political systems. The preferences of the public were seen as being shaped by political and economic decision makers, rather than as guiding and controlling these elites. The makers of international and technical policies were seen as pursuing courses of their own, relatively free from popular control. Especially in the United States, involvement in the Vietnam war called forth an increasing criticism of the working of representative institutions. A "radical" criticism contended that their failures were due to insufficient democracy; this was joined to an increasing concern for the welfare of dispossessed and unrepresented groups in domestic politics.

This criticism might possibly lead to a more rigorous rethinking of the foundations of democracy and representation in their various forms. I shall suggest (chapter 6) some directions that this analysis might take—though my argument will begin not with radical criticism but with the extension of economic reasoning to political institutions.

---

30. Sutton et al., *The American Business Creed*, pp. 189–192.
31. See Chase, "Politics and Technology."

The Sciences and the Informed Individual

The social institutions of basic and applied science both preserve the autonomy of basic science and permit expert knowledge to be applied. This expert knowledge is applied to the productive functions of large organizations or to professional (for example, medical) care by individual practitioners. The decisions based on this knowledge eventually affect the individual consumer or voter.

But if the persons ultimately affected are not expert purchasers—such as wholesale clothing buyers or buyers of steel for automobile manufacturers—they are likely to have only a limited competence in making the choices that confront them. They cannot ordinarily afford the time, effort, or expense to become expert on all the choices they face. Conceivably an authoritarian system might relieve them of the effort of decision by reducing the amount of choice available, and even in a competitive system there are ways of lessening the burden of choice. But those affected are still at a disadvantage relative to the organizations or professionals that provide the services and products and to the applied scientists whom these organizations employ.

This advantage due to superior knowledge is not necessarily exploitative. The physician's knowledge is presumably used only to relieve the patient's complaints, and the ideal competitive system is supposed to satisfy consumer demand. In the political system, the possibility of exploitation is perhaps greatest, and the departure from its ideal functioning most likely, when there is a wide discrepancy in information between leaders and citizens.[32]

But even for individual market choices there are reasons to consider expending public resources to improve the consumer's information. Not only might the cost be compensated by more efficient allocation of resources and consumption in the market, but consumers can also use this information in collective action, telling others about the merits of products and services and transferring such judgments into the political realm through lawsuits or interest group activity. In addition, some of the functions performed by experts might be transferred to con-

32. We return to this problem in chapters 2, 6, and 9.

sumers—self-diagnosis and hygiene in medical treatment and, in general, the "productive" functions of consumption activity.[33] Education plays a part in increasing the "efficiency of consumption" as well as furnishing human capital for production, but the effects of education also extend into the political realm.

The gains from educational specialization, which are realized in occupational skills and which scientists try also to transfer into the political realm through specialized extradisciplinary associations,[34] are less easily transferred to consumption. Nevertheless, if we consider the cost of training experts and the difficulty of adapting their recommendations to the needs of particular clients (for example, physicians' house calls), it may sometimes be more efficient to transfer some of their information resources to consumers. Moreover, we cannot easily assume that this information market will operate optimally, for in an environment where advertising cultivates an uninformed certainty consumers may not always realize their need for information.

If the individual judges products or policies as they affect himself alone, he may still be informed in several different respects. He can learn, as we have indicated, about qualities of the product or policy itself. But as a possible substitute, he can learn about the purveyors of *bundles* of goods or policies—as in the case of the reputations of department stores, political parties, or candidates. He can also learn that he needs information or that certain sources of information will be accurate, suit his tastes, or be intelligible to him. And in a still different respect, he can learn that if his preferences, tastes, or capacities were changed to resemble those of certain other persons he would consider that altered state preferable to his present state.

All these judgments concern the individual as consumer; even political choices, considered from this perspective, resemble market choices. But he may also make choices (especially in politics) for the general or group welfare, and it is important to distinguish this basis of choice from *personal* welfare.[35] The individual as *citizen* (in a view of citizenship that extends beyond the "consumption" of policies) may

33. See Becker, *Economic Theory,* pp. 45–48; Lancaster, "A New Approach to Consumer Theory."

34. We treat these "fringe associations" in more detail in chapter 3.

35. See chapters 5 and 6.

become enlightened about the general welfare and about means to it. He will then have to consider not only information about means to known ends, such as his personal welfare, but may engage in reasoned argument about ends and the meaning of "welfare."

The Professions and Their Values

Side by side with the scientific disciplines and departments in most universities are schools for instruction in professions such as law, medicine, engineering, social work, city planning, and public administration. Professionals are concerned with practice, and especially when they serve patients or clients independently of organizations they set their own goals and terms of work through codes and norms of professional conduct.[36] Conceivably we might expect the professions, because of these codes, to be the source of general values for social criticism and policy choice. The professions make greater claims on society for respect and autonomy than do other occupations. In return, they make public commitments to larger societal values such as health or justice, which might be a basis for general judgments among public policies.

Important limits are set on a profession's values, however, by its relation with the larger society. The members of any occupational group are likely to formulate justifications and explanations for their activities, addressed to outsiders.[37] These justifications, because of an exchange relation with the rest of society, not only explain the value of that occupation, but also set limits on what it may justifiably do.

Professions are distinguished from other occupations in that they explain and justify their activities in terms of "disinterested" motivation rather than direct self-interest.[38] They claim the right to treat a

36. The lesser independence of organizational scientists and professionals is brought out in Kornhauser, *Scientists in Industry,* and in Perrucci and Gerstl, *Profession Without Community*. Professionals who teach in professional schools, less vulnerable to client demand, can sustain the collective values of the profession more easily; see Barber, "Some Problems in the Sociology of the Professions," p. 21. Limitations on practicing professionals' mutual control are analyzed in Freidson, *Profession of Medicine*.

37. Dibble, "Occupations and Ideologies."

38. Parsons, "The Professions and Social Structure," p. 35.

client (patient, parishioner) in view of their superior knowledge, unintelligible to laymen, without exploiting this situation for personal gain. The professional claims an authority based on technical competence acquired through training and justified by a standard higher than that of the professional person as an individual. The authority based on technical competence, however, is "functionally specific," that is, applicable only in a restricted and appropriate domain.[39] This claim is made by the profession collectively; in order to make it, the profession typically cultivates internal solidarity and the external appearance of consensus. Such a claim carries with it a presumed responsibility on the part of the profession to regulate itself. As Simpson puts it, "It is as if the profession had struck a bargain with society, agreeing to develop its knowledge and provide services in return for freedom from imperative control."[40]

The relation between a profession and the public is reflected by its public justifications. As Dibble points out,

> Lawyers espouse causes in return for money, fight with each other in public, and then leave the courtroom together as friends and colleagues. Since laymen do not act that way, the attorneys' peculiar performance is suspect.
>
> The legal profession explains this parochial behavior by showing its relationship to ecumenic goals. In the long run, it contends, justice is best served if each party in a dispute has the best advocacy it can command.[41]

The competitive relationship between litigants, with counsel, thus finds justification through its analogies to the economic system. In a precapitalist system or a communist system, where competition was less esteemed as a general social mechanism, adversary practices in the law might receive less support. The internal norms of subsystems of a society must bear some relation to those of the society at large, if the members of the subsystem are to be able to justify their activities

39. *Ibid.,* p. 38.
40. On solidarity, see Hughes, "Professions," p. 3. On the bargain with society see Simpson, "Imperative Control, Associationism, and the Social Order," p. 261.
41. Dibble, *op. cit.,* p. 230.

in terms of values shared with outsiders who are members of the larger society.

A profession or occupational group is likely to become involved in general political or persuasive efforts when its particular values—those it claims to contribute to society or those on which its activities depend—appear threatened or related to problems of society. But another requirement for a feeling of "social responsibility" is the feeling that members of the group can *influence* that aspect of the world. Thus, as Galbraith has pointed out, the doctrine of corporate social responsibility may have arisen from the possibility that individual corporations could exercise some control over socially relevant aspects of production.[42] Under the classical model of the competitive market, they could not and need not do anything other than seek profit. This type of mobilization or involvement by a profession, however, is likely to be sporadic. Individual professions will become involved only when their special expertise and values are in question; in this respect they will resemble particular interest groups.

Members of a profession also sometimes try to mobilize the profession as a group in the service of general ethical or societal goals. Alternatively, acting individually rather than collectively, they may practice "public interest" law or medicine or "advocacy planning," in the interest of the disadvantaged. Such efforts may be tolerated by the profession when they fall within the customary range of free individual choice. But if they seem to compromise general public support for the profession, they are likely to be resisted by senior members who are concerned with the profession's reputation in society; even if they succeed (as in academic governance in Germany), they may indeed reduce society's support for the institution in question. These selective emphases within a profession thus confront resistance, as practicing professions thrive on unanimity—on the public impression of lack of internal dissension.

The valuative involvement of professionals also suffers from limitations as regards the *generality* of the ethical stance taken. The typical basis of claims of social responsibility revolves about what one should do "as a scientist," "as a physician," "as a lawyer," and so on.

42. See Galbraith, *The New Industrial State,* pp. 136–137.

Physicians may be concerned about the delivery of health services, but less about public health measures. These perspectives limit debate to actions of which a particular profession is capable (individually or collectively), but they also take for granted the "organizational essence" of the profession itself.[43] The alternative questions whether the profession should exist, whether it should continue in its customary activities or change them, thus receive less attention. The ethical standards and alternatives with which members of a profession face questions of public policy are thus unavoidably narrow. The citizen, the public official, or the young person choosing an occupation faces larger questions.

Our analysis so far suggests limits on the involvement of professions such as law and medicine in the advocacy or inculcation of *general* ethical principles. They may well develop further the implications of notions such as those of justice and health respectively, and the norms of legal argument may support reasoned discourse more generally. But the condition of solidarity and consensus, seemingly necessary to support their claims of respect and autonomy, runs counter to the pursuit of general systems of values. The social sciences, although subject to some similar limitations, have latent value systems that are more general than those of the professions and thus may have an important role to play in general valuative discourse.

The Tasks of the Social Sciences

The problems created by specialized knowledge derive largely from the advance of natural science and technology, but we are concerned here with problems and opportunities faced by the social sciences. We have connected social science with natural because, in the first place, the social sciences have tried to imitate the natural. The connection results, secondly, from the fact that the problems that seem to derive from natural science and technology cannot be solved without consid-

43. Halperin, *Bureaucratic Politics and Foreign Policy,* pp. 28–40. The very solidarity of the profession leads to a particular concern on the part of one's professional colleagues when one *leaves* a profession (Hughes, *op. cit.,* p. 3), and this may extend to departure from its perspectives. A similar lack of generality of the latent ethics of the disciplines will be our concern in chapters 5–8, but the limitation there results more from the concepts used than from the roles within which action is considered.

eration of economic and political structures and human reactions to technology. And thirdly, social science itself has technological applications.

For all of these reasons, we shall advocate the development of ethical discourse that may provide more intelligent guidance for societal choices, in close cooperation with the social science disciplines. This guidance is needed for choices that involve the application of natural science, social science, or both together. But we advocate its introduction in connection with the social sciences because it would be less welcome in basic natural science, less useful in philosophy, and less rational if introduced only in domains of discourse nearer to everyday life.[44]

The social sciences aim at reasoned understanding and prediction of human behavior. They aim to supplement or replace intuition with systematic and disciplined observation, which is particularly important in anticipating the consequences of large-scale policy choices. They also measure variables that often come closer to the human values affected by policy choices than do the variables of natural science and technology.

There are, however, other types of knowledge relevant to practical decision, which may both compete and cooperate with that of the social sciences. Much of the knowledge we use in both personal and occupational life, and which supplements social science in policy choice, is highly specific to persons and circumstances. But there are also roles other than that of the social scientist that involve general discussion of man and society. One is that of the "intellectual" as contrasted with the academic. Noting the self-contained character of the scientific disciplines, and the choice of problems on terms set by one's colleagues, Jencks and Riesman have advocated a role for the intellectual who is an amateur:

> The term "intellectual" refers to an amateur role. . . . Intellectual questions grow out of reflection on experience, are asked by all sorts and conditions of men, and are answered . . . in ways that

44. Conceivably ethical discourse could also be developed in applied fields making use of natural science, such as operations research, systems analysis, engineering, and the health sciences.

make sense to such men. . . . Moral and political questions that cannot be resolved by research and do not yield to cooperative investigation are almost by definition outside the academic orbit. The protagonists of an intellectual argument, on the other hand, are expected to be "interested parties." Heated debate is respectable for intellectuals, since the outcome of their argument is expected to have personal as well as professional consequences." [45]

This intellectual role has often been adopted by persons who are also social scientists. It is expressed in books that I shall cite in analyzing the latent ethics of the disciplines. But lacking the organized control of a discipline, it is less rational and less cumulative.

Jencks's and Riesman's aspirations for academic discourse on valuative questions seem too modest, and their assumption that it includes heated debate and personal involvement, too restrictive. I shall argue that we must be concerned with the general interest and must try to discuss major practical questions with clarity and consistency, following our stated principles to their logical conclusions. For these purposes, even if agreement is difficult, rules for communication are vital. Thus the "personalization" of such communication, and its withdrawal from the norms of rational discourse, seem to encourage heated and irreconcilable debates.

Another set of alternatives to social science exists in other parts of the university itself—chiefly in the humanities. The humanistic tradition is actually expressed *within* the social sciences in the one subdiscipline where explicit valuative discourse is conducted: political philosophy. A forceful argument for a humanistic approach, in opposition to the "methodism" of contemporary political science, has been advanced by Wolin.[46]

In the humanistic disciplines and in the law we find alternative claims to deal with man's problems that antedate the social sciences and do not easily yield place to them. The relation between the social sciences and these fields may well require that social scientists learn from them, rather than simply ignore or advise them.

The alleged antithesis between science and valuation presses the

45. Jencks and Riesman, *The Academic Revolution,* pp. 242–243.
46. Wolin, "Political Theory as a Vocation."

social sciences between two images: that of closed groups of natural scientists and that of more open groups of humanists. An earlier generation of social scientists followed the first model; much contemporary criticism urges the second. Within each discipline, a radical position tends to favor openness to other disciplines and to less established views, as opposed to the norms of closure and of experts' dominance. The association of this openness with "humanism" may, however, be more pronounced in disciplines other than the humanities themselves.

Even though there are important aspects of practical knowledge and valuation that extend beyond the sciences, it is essential that we seek the greatest possible contribution from the sciences to remedying the problems we have considered. To deal with science, judge it, and control it requires some contact with it, and one cannot easily achieve this properly without scientific training. The coexistence of the sciences with the humanities in higher education permits us to ask whether they can be combined more effectively.

We shall therefore try to combine specialties in two ways. First, we can make use of diverse links among the specialties as they now exist. But second and more important, we can try to combine *within* individual disciplines (old or new) the consideration of valuative and factual questions; and this can be done most effectively in the areas now known as the "social sciences."

2 RECONCILING SCIENCE AND DEMOCRACY

The layman, in trying to regulate his personal affairs, faces a disparity between his own competence and that of specialists; as citizen of a large modern democracy he faces still greater problems of this kind. As citizen he must judge many questions remote from the competence that he learns for his everyday activities. The increasing involvement of science and technology in these questions intensifies the citizen's problems of judgment and makes them more difficult than the analogous problems he faces as a consumer. This difficulty has been related largely to natural science but increasingly relates to social science as well.

The citizen in a democracy is also led more obviously than the consumer to engage in valuative discourse. As a consumer, he may feel that the preferences and values he already possesses (his "tastes") are not properly matters of debate but that his task is simply to gratify them efficiently—whether through consumption or through household production. His discussion of goods and services with his fellow consumers is thus largely limited to the appropriateness of these means to the satisfaction of tastes that they may share. But as a citizen he may discuss collective choices with others whose personal tastes or needs differ from his own and engage in reasoned argument as to what should be done. He may also discuss the justifiable ways in which public policy should respond to their different needs, or the needs of others, on the basis of valuative principles.

Science Versus Democracy

Both the complexity of public choices and the relevance of valuative discourse to these choices lead to apparent conflicts between the values of science and democracy. Insofar as these choices depend on expert information, the values of science require that this information be introduced and judged by qualified experts rather than by the general public. The values of democracy, however, require that ultimate power be lodged with the public.

The conflict between expertness and popular rule is an ancient one. But in our time it assumes a distinctive character because of the nature of science and public attitudes toward it. Science makes a narrower claim than other types of expertness or wisdom. Because it is divided into closed communication systems, the experts in one field are not necessarily the same as those in another and cannot easily judge one another's expertness. The self-contained character of scientific communities also leads to difficulty in our defining and respecting the role of the generally informed citizen relative to that of the expert.[1] In addition, the scientist's expertness in policy realms is expected to relate to means rather than ends. When he moves outside the domain of means, as when he moves outside his specialty, he may be challenged on political grounds without receiving collective support from his colleagues.

The public is also more critical of scientists and experts than in earlier times. Science is one of the few domains in which experts can claim to decide better than a popular majority, but this claim is limited in scope. Recent years have seen a decline in an earlier faith in science and (at least in highly developed societies) a disillusionment with technology. Thus while science is more necessary for public decisions, it also meets increasing criticism. The standards of democracy sometimes conduce to suspicion of scientists as an elite who may influence policy toward special goals or values that do not coincide with the general welfare. Alternatively, the concern of science with means rather than ends leads some critics to see the effects of science as unplanned and uncontrolled and to advocate its closer guidance through representative institutions.[2]

The standards of science and democracy may conflict on three types of questions, which I shall state briefly and then discuss. First is that of "policy for science," which chiefly affects scientists themselves in their research, teaching, or professional practice but does not generate

1. Schutz, "The Well-Informed Citizen"; Lindsay, *The Modern Democratic State,* pp. 276–268.
2. See Habermas, *Toward a Rational Society.*

major conflicts in society at large. Though groups other than scientists who are affected by "policy for science"—taxpayers, students, patients—may contest the claims of scientists in their own work, these contests affect relatively limited interests in society. A second type of question, more important for our present discussion, is the intervention of "science *in* policy," [3] where expert advice can relate to policies affecting many persons other than scientists. Thirdly, the data of science and some of its norms may enter into the evaluation of the democratic process itself. A major theme of this book is that ethical discourse can be conducted in ways analogous to scientific discourse; in elaborating this theme, we shall treat the ethical justifications of democratic institutions. [4]

"Policy for science" concerns policies primarily affecting science itself. In the allocation of research support, scientists have favored delegating government decisions to groups of relevant specialists ("peer review") on the ground of competence. This delegation has been qualified by the counterclaim that the expenditure of public funds must be authorized by the public or its representatives. [5] In addition, the rival claims of various specialties must be reconciled in terms that transcend the individual specialties. [6] But even with these conflicts of values, the arena of "policy for science" has been less politicized than arenas in which science directly affects large numbers of nonscientists. Like other "distributive" policy questions, [7] it chiefly involves small segments of the public who are relatively well informed (though also interested parties) on the issue.

In "policy for science," one justification for support of science has

3. Brooks, "The Scientific Adviser," p. 76. The interrelation of the two categories is stressed, however, in Reagan, "R & D: Suggestions for an Allocation Framework."

4. See chapters 4 and 6. Although scientific data are relevant to our judgment of the possibility and results of various policies, the aim of this book is to further a certain type of discourse but not to prescribe its outcomes in detail, many of which depend on the results of future research.

5. There are conflicts between these claims, especially in America. See Daniels, "The Pure-Science Ideal and Democratic Culture"; Shryock, "American Indifference to Basic Science During the Nineteenth Century"; Price, *The Scientific Estate,* p. 92.

6. See Weinberg, *Reflections on Big Science,* for a comparison of the claims of the various sciences for research support, and Machlup, "Are the Social Sciences Really Inferior?"

7. See Lowi, "American Business, Public Policy, Case-Studies, and Political Theory."

been that it is a cultural pursuit valuable in itself. Thus it has been argued that a variety of such pursuits should each be governed by the separate standards of those who participate in them.[8] The adherents of this view might favor social representation through a plurality of groups and their elites, so as to permit culture-preserving and culture-creating elites to do their work insulated from the influence of the less informed general citizenry. This view, however, is more persuasive as a justification of the pursuit of science for its own sake than in specifying the place of science in the formation of public policies. Its argument is sometimes extended to support freedom and diversity of sources of criticism and analysis of public policy, on the ground that a single source would be too easily corrupted; but if we are ever to set limits to these diverse influences, or allocate scarce resources among them, we require more general valuative principles to reconcile their claims.

A politically more significant type of question on which the values of science and democracy can conflict is that of "science in policy"—that is, public policy affecting aspects of society other than science. Democratic governments make use of science in many types of policies. They employ it both as direct sponsors—in nuclear armament, health services, welfare programs—and as regulators of the private sector—controlling foods, drugs, the environment, and the effects of economic changes. And insofar as expert knowledge of political processes exists, governments may themselves be reformed by its guidance.

This type of question involves applied science or technology. Some scientists might try to distinguish basic science from technology and deny responsibility for technological applications. Current public attitudes, however, do not allow scientists to justify so easily their search for truth apart from its technological consequences. Science and technology are criticized together in the name of democracy or human values.[9] A "technological society" is seen as dominated by large organi-

8. For discussion of this "pluralist" view see Shils, *The Torment of Secrecy,* Chap. 7; Selznick, *The Organizational Weapon,* pp. 276–281; and, in opposition, Rogin, *The Intellectuals and McCarthy,* ch. 1.

9. Ellul, *The Technological Society;* Marcuse, *One-Dimensional Man;* Roszak, *The Making of a Counter Culture;* McDermott, "Technology, the Opiate of the Intellectuals."

zations, which fragment and restrict the lives of workers and citizens. And although this point was made by nineteenth-century critics of the Industrial Revolution, it is pressed upon us with especial force today. Science and technology have been linked with threats to privacy, with militarism, and with environmental chaos—consequences that affect both democracy and the values that democracy purports to serve. To some critics, the fault is in the proliferation of devices that affect the lives of ordinary citizens yet are difficult for them to comprehend or control.[10]

The connection between science and technology in the public mind has also been fostered by spokesmen of science, who have linked the two in appeals for support. After World War II, large segments of the public were successfully convinced that beneficent technological applications flow automatically from basic research. The connection between the two is now seen less as one of progress and beneficence, however, and more as one of a technology running wild, uncontrollable unless science itself is controlled. We are thus led to connect technology with science as we focus attention on "science in policy."

As we move from the realm of "policy for science" to that of "science in policy," we find ourselves drawn more toward a critical discussion of potentially conflicting valuative standards. The pluralist justification of science as a cultural activity tacitly allots to each cultural sphere its own standards and justifies their protection against overarching standards, including those of popular rule. In considering policies that affect society at large, however, we cannot simply take the goals of science as a source of definition of societal goals. Science applied to societal policy must be seen as a means to the better or more effective accomplishment of ends external to its own activity. In this perspective, "science for science's sake" is irrelevant.

It is here that we encounter the third type of question on which the values of science may conflict with those of democracy. Not only the findings of science, but also its procedures of discussion may have bearing on the value systems of democracy. There is a latent conflict between certain values implicit in scientific discourse and our actual practices in valuative discussion, including the justification of science

10. See Morison, "Science and Social Attitudes."

and democracy themselves. I shall argue in later chapters that much discussion of these questions falls short of the standards of clarity and consistency that scientists would require of their own theories and hypotheses.

In the realm of policy-related valuative discourse—the central concern of this book—lies a potential relation between social science, natural science, and ethics. Many of society's problems result from insufficient guidance of applied natural science. The social sciences have tried to imitate basic natural science with modest success. But the very modesty of their success, by leaving latent valuations in their literature, leaves open the possibility that they can combine the scientific study of society with ethical discourse. This combination may in turn provide guidance for the application of both natural and social science.

Social Structures for Science in Policy

The problems of "science in policy" are defined by policymakers in terms of societal standards and not simply the standards of the scientific specialties. We live in a society in which it is widely contended that the public at large should control the government's policies. Even though this control is modified by many representative and advisory institutions, in the last analysis the public is expected to rule. But the relations between policies and their consequences are often so complex that it is difficult to argue that the public is competent to rule. Thus science and technology seem to have exacerbated the problems of democracy by increasing both the *complexity* of the problems that large modern political systems face and the *inequality* of competence between scientists or technologists and other citizens.

Among the remedies put forward for this conflict of values, the simplest are those that favor science over democracy or vice versa. If we were to favor science, we might simply assert the superiority of expert information and judgment where it conflicts with the judgment of the public—a "technocratic" approach. The precise implications of such an approach are not clear, however, since scientists claim expertness only on matters of fact and not on valuations. Some would propose that valuations be determined democratically and that science decide only on the means to them, but this proposal is not easy to implement. If the public votes only on general valuative principles, it must then leave to expert interpreters the task of telling whether particular policies accord with one value or another. And if it votes on concrete policies, the public itself must judge whether these policies are in accord with its values.

Scientists might go farther and claim to propose policies in areas where the values sought seemed obvious (peace, clean air, human survival, economic growth). In this connection scientists sometimes advocate the entry of their professional associations into political arenas as pressure groups—perhaps under the rubric of "social responsibility." But if their pressure should be successful, as it has often been for the American Medical Association, we should still have to ask whether their influence had served the general welfare or simply the interests of scientists—a question that must always be raised for elite rule.[11] And since counterpressures must also be expected, this type of action risks erosion of the support that scientists possess as spokesmen for an objective truth superior to particular interests.[12]

We might, on the other hand, favor democracy, in the form of direct rule by the citizens. In the diagnosis of the "technological society," not only is technology criticized from this perspective, but one proposed remedy has been "participatory democracy," as distinguished from existing institutions. Forms of government, private or public, in which individuals generally affect decisions more and feel closer to them are expected to realize the value of democracy more fully. The hierarchy of decision processes, the dominance of experts, and the inaccessibility of decisions to ordinary people who are affected by them are attributed to science and technology and are to be reduced by an increase in democracy.[13]

But we shall set aside remedies that favor one value—science or democracy—at the expense of the other and shall examine in more detail the possibilities of reconciling the two. Among the remedies that remain, some stress the complexity of the problems and seek to simplify them. Thus if technological developments could be slowed, citi-

11. Dewey, *The Public and Its Problems,* p. 206.

12. Haberer, *Politics and the Community of Science,* p. 303. The politicization of science and the university is also discussed in chapter 9 below.

13. See Habermas, *op. cit.,* pp. 72–74; Carroll, "Participatory Technology."

zens might conceivably learn more easily to cope with the political problems that derive from them. The unintended consequences of military technology and the garrison state,[14] and the unnecessary development of products for the civilian market with "external costs" [15] not taken account of by the market, have drawn criticism on this score. If we could imagine a slowing of development of weapons technology, perhaps policies for both international arms control and civilian control of the military could be subject to broader popular discussion. Similarly, the external costs imposed by the use of automobiles, including traffic congestion and atmospheric pollution, might be better understood by the public if the increase in the use of automobiles had been less rapid.

Alternatively, systems of decision making might be broken down into separate units or "decoupled" in order to make the problems of governing these systems less complex and more intelligible to the layman.[16] Federalism and decentralization to regions or urban neighborhoods have been proposed as means to reduce the size of decision units. Technical functions such as health services have been included in these proposals. Under some conditions, however, the government of smaller units is less democratic or less just than that of larger ones.[17]

Changes in internal decision-making processes that provide more direct feedback loops are sometimes proposed for local or organizational government; these have included participatory democracy and codetermination—as in German industry. Such changes are open to criticism, however, from several points of view. Dahrendorf has criticized codetermination on the ground that it undermines party conflict at the national level. But another problem of local feedback loops in a complex society derives from the possible effects of political decisions on persons outside the system, analogous to the economic "externalities" that escape the calculation of the market.[18] These occur for na-

14. Lasswell, "The Garrison State and Specialist on Violence."
15. See chapter 6 for further discussion of this concept.
16. MacRae, "Some Political Choices in the Development of Communications Technology."
17. McConnell, *Private Power and American Democracy.*
18. Dahrendorf, *Society and Democracy in Germany,* ch. 11; Olson, "The Principle of 'Fiscal Equivalence.' " We discuss these effects further in chapter 6.

tions in their foreign policies, but also for decision-making units smaller than the nation, such as states, communities, or organizations. The creation of separate governmental units in high-status suburbs has been a kind of areal decoupling that has intensified metropolitan problems for city residents. For reasons of this sort, the problem of political externalities has sometimes led to proposals for *larger* governmental units. Thus the decoupling of decision systems requires consideration of external effects as well as the simplification of complex decisions.

Other proposals for reform stress the problem of inequality of competence. A conventional remedy for this problem is to raise the effective competence of major decision makers by the use of technically trained consultants or staff. The various branches of government may engage experts temporarily to supply information (for example, as consultants or witnesses), but the effective competence of the decision maker is raised more by his employment of his own staff. The employment of experts in either staff or consultant roles is normally associated with the distinction between means and ends. Experts are expected to be competent in choosing means, but the ends of organizations are to be chosen—in principle—by political representation or the market.[19]

Science and the Informed Citizen

In this "engineering model," [20] the employment of applied scientists in organizations permits the rapid communication of new technical knowledge to decision centers, insofar as the scientists learn of new developments and the organization makes use of them. But in spite of its effectiveness in the use of scientific knowledge, it may also transmit the scientists' own values to points of decision, and it ultimately places decision making in the hands of the leaders of the employing organizations. These organizations are in turn regulated or controlled by the working of the political system or the market, but this channel of transmission of scientific information does not serve particularly to educate the consumer, the citizen, or even political

19. D. K. Price, *op. cit.*, p. 95.
20. See Janowitz, "Sociological Models and Social Policy."

elites (such as legislators or leaders of voluntary associations) who are
concerned with general governmental policies.[21] Such arrangements
may be tolerable if the political system is not democratic, but even in
such a system it is important for decision-making elites to acquire
some competence in judging scientific and technical policy. In a society that considers itself democratic and that wishes to control the possible biases of experts toward special interests or values, general scientific education must extend more widely.

General education in science has been advocated as partly playing
the same role as classical education in an earlier epoch and providing
part of a general intellectual training for prospective leaders and informed citizens. This education must include social as well as natural
science. But if it is given only to the young, much of it will become
obsolete by the time they attain influence in society.[22] Education in
science must therefore be supplemented by the general diffusion of information and the scientific education of adults.

One might imagine that elected officials could be given some scientific training. They cannot easily receive this training after election,
however, because of their other responsibilities; before election the
group destined for such office cannot easily be identified. If politicians
are drawn from a generally educated public, without a selective bias
toward special interests, then perhaps they can bring a moderate degree of scientific information to public office. As a result of this type
of education, for example, the pool of scientific knowledge available
to a legislative body in constituting its science-related committees
might be greater, and the members of these committees could then ap-
point their staff and evaluate the testimony of witnesses with greater
discrimination.

The diffusion of scientific information affects not only the relations
between experts and citizens, but also the relations among experts in
various specialties. Policy advising typically requires a broader range
of knowledge than particular basic-science disciplines afford. Interdisciplinary training, general education, and applied fields that combine

21. Shils, "The Calling of Sociology," p. 1420; Janowitz, "Sociological Models
and Social Policy." The system may not merely leave the citizen ignorant, but also
misinform him; see Galbraith, "Power and the Useful Economist."
22. Lippmann, The Phantom Public, pp. 26–27.

basic sciences are all necessary. Scientists who are to work on environmental problems must possess some knowledge of chemistry, biology, engineering, medicine, economics, and politics; those concerned with urban housing should be able to combine the economics and technology of housing with urban politics and sociology.

A central role in the democratic control of technical decisions must be that of the "well-informed citizen." Schutz distinguished among the expert, with clear and distinct knowledge of a limited field; the man in the street, who knows recipes that are adequate for practical purposes; and the well-informed citizen, "who considers himself perfectly qualified to decide who *is* a competent expert and even to make up his mind after having listened to opposing expert opinions." The expert lacks this last competence because he is "at home only in a system of imposed relevances—imposed, that is, by the problems pre-established in his field." [23] This was Schutz's way of indicating the limitations of the closed communication systems of specialized sciences.

It is important for us to realize the need for informed citizens, as distinguished from specialists. But Schutz, in his analysis of this problem, did not say how the well-informed citizen is to be educated. Conceivably formal education may contribute to his development; alternatively, we might rely on the educative functions that have been attributed to democratic participation.

The undergraduate college education required by the citizen is of a different sort from the basic-science specialization aimed at preparation for graduate school, and even students who specialize in one field require a broad competence in others for their roles as citizens. This broader education also differs from preprofessional training, which though interdisciplinary is aimed at careers, and from majors in the humanities, which though nearer to the citizen's perspective deal less with science. But the provision of this broader education may be more effective if the faculty members who provide it can find rewarding careers other than those provided by the basic-science disciplines and graduate schools. Possibly interdisciplinary graduate schools for policy training can provide a partial substitute; in training society's potential

23. Schutz, *op. cit.*, pp. 466, 474.

leaders, they would somewhat resemble the medieval universities' training of students for roles of practice and authority.[24] But undergraduate training in policy analysis might also encourage the criticism of these leaders' policies by informed citizens who choose their own valuative perspectives.

In the college education of the informed citizen, a central problem then concerns the relations among the disciplines. In putting the problem in this way we assume that disciplines will continue to exist, that is, that college and university instruction will be organized through departments connected with national disciplinary associations; that careers in teaching and research will be guided by judgments of competence in well-defined subject-matter areas; and that disciplinary associations will provide national markets for their members. But we must also ask whether existing disciplines might be modified, new ones added, and skills such as those of teaching and policy training incorporated into their criteria of performance.

An argument parallel to Schutz's was made by Shils. He noted first that

> One of the major features of American intellectual life in the present century is the attrition of the "educated public." The emptiness and the specialization of education are its major causes. . . . The critical and solicitous care for the whole in the proximate future must be the charge which American intellectuals take on themselves, if American society is not to become the victim of the parochial preoccupations of specialized technological experts. If academic social scientists and free lance publicists or amateur social scientists are not critics on behalf of the whole society over the reasonably foreseeable future, no one else will be.

He saw a weak tradition of this sort of thought but considered that "What it lacks above all are organs through which its rhetoric can be formed by expression and its judgment sharpened by dialogue."[25] I

24. Ben-David, *The Scientist's Role in Society,* pp. 46–50. Training in policy analysis is discussed further in chapter 9 below.

25. Shils, "The Intellectuals and the Future," pp. 13–14. It has also been suggested that the creation of an educated citizenry be the function of certain colleges rather than of all; see Parsons and Platt, "Considerations on the American Academic System," pp. 522, 514–515.

concur, but differing somewhat in emphasis I propose that this dialogue be sustained by adapting to it the social structure of the disciplines that leads their members to pursue certain interests more than others and that protects the autonomy of their discourse against inexpert and irrelevant claims.

Even if we are able to educate undergraduates as prospective informed citizens, we still face the problem of motivating them to learn and participate after they leave college. If a student becomes a policy analyst, inside or outside the university, he may be led to participate as part of his career. But this participation, however valuable, may not go far beyond the "engineering model" that involves only persons hired as experts. Perhaps the possibility of checking the experts will be increased if they differ publicly and intelligibly among themselves, but the public or the officeholders who judge among them must then also be competent.

We look, therefore, to competition within and among groups of experts to foster the needed debate and scrutiny of alternative policies. But beyond these groups of experts, can there still be an adequately informed citizenry? Among political leaders, we might look either to professional politicians or to wealthy amateurs.[26] Apart from these, the role of the informed citizen appears more diffuse. A general increase in the attention and skill devoted to public affairs may occur, if education fosters it, and a broadening of the scope of concern by group leaders, from their own groups' interests to a wider understanding of other groups and issues, may also be a manifestation of informed citizenship.

In the formation of the informed citizen or the educated public lies a particular opportunity and responsibility of the social sciences. Their very difficulty in detaching themselves from the vocabulary and the perspectives of the citizen suggests that they may also communicate to him more easily than the natural sciences. The communication between technical adviser and client or administrator partakes of this problem, of course, but it does not in itself serve to educate the public. An alternative would involve more direct interchange between scien-

26. See Weber, "Politics as a Vocation."

tists and citizens or between social scientists and the persons they study.[27]

When we evaluate higher education, it is important to stress the formation of informed citizens. Two of the most conpicuous criteria now used—the output of research and the earnings of graduates—turn our attention away from this function. Insofar as new specialized knowledge is useful, and insofar as the market for graduates reflects its usefulness, then these two criteria are plausible indicators of the effectiveness of transmission of knowledge to policy through the careers of applied scientists. The two markets—one partly nonmonetary, for elegant scientific discoveries, the other monetary, for applied scientists—reward individuals and organizations for their contributions to the generation and transmission of information.

But the education of informed citizens involves "external effects" and cannot so easily be evaluated in market terms. It involves not merely the diffusion of information and skills that may be used to satisfy given preferences, but also the possible inculcation of values relevant to the functioning of society, economy, and political system—values that may include an intelligent consideration of the general welfare as well as personal or group interest. For this reason, even if we are not sure what sorts of education will best serve to produce informed citizens, we must recognize that some of the conventional evaluative criteria risk ignoring their education altogether.

Representative Science

In trying to cope with the conflicts between science and democracy, we considered first the possibility of simplifying the problems themselves; then the improvement of the "engineering model" of policy advice by supplying expert advisers to decision-making organizations; and third, education of informed citizens, drawing as much as possible on the diverse resources of the university.

But there is still another way to cope with this conflict. The risk of technocracy lies in the possibility of uncontrolled power held by an

27. Habermas, *op. cit.;* Janowitz, "Sociological Models and Social Policy." See also chapter 8 below.

elite and devoted to special values or interests rather than to the general welfare. We have sought the education of the citizen in order to control technology, but we can also consider reducing the biases of technologists as a group, through their selection and training. If those who apply science to policy bring to that task values and judgments beyond their strictly scientific competence, they may possibly improve the resulting policies but may also make them worse.

In the application of science to policy, scientists may recommend policies that derive not only from their expertise, but also from valuations they bring with them from their membership in a particular society or particular groups in that society [28] or from valuations incidental to their disciplines or to science generally. Their national allegiances may blind them to the welfare of foreigners. Their membership in higher social strata may render them insufficiently sympathetic to the problems of the poor in their own society. Their membership in a particular discipline may lead them to stress values that coincide with the central concepts of that discipline. And certain general features of the norms or attitudes of scientists may also introduce bias into policy formation: an excessively optimistic rationalism, a disregard for consultation of those affected by policy, or a stress on specialized rather than general viewpoints. All these may on occasion be desirable.

Conceivably these extrinsic valuations could be dealt with through the education of the scientist. Prospective scientists might be trained like Plato's Guardians, with special attention to their character. They might be required to work periodically with other social strata as a form of continuing education, as in contemporary China. Or they might be trained to a strict neutrality in matters of valuation, so as to fulfill the applied-science ideal of dealing only with means and not with ends.

If these extrinsic values cannot be eliminated, then perhaps we should strive for "representative bureaucracy." [29] But we cannot stop there, for in public life generally scientists are also expected by others

28. See Sewell, "Inequality of Opportunity for Higher Education."
29. See Kingsley, *Representative Bureaucracy;* Subramaniam, "Representative Bureaucracy: A Reassessment"; Krislov, *Representative Bureaucracy;* as applied to science, Eckert, *Wissenschaft und Demokratie,* pp. 50–54; and to medicine, Freidson, *Profession of Medicine,* pp. 372–373.

to speak for the universal value of truth. Nobel laureates, for example, even when speaking on matters remote from their specialties, receive more credence than the average citizen. Thus it may be necessary that each discipline contain an adequate representation of various groups affected by the policies to which its knowledge relates. It may be valuable to have a number of distinguished members who are (for example) blacks, women, or Republicans.

Such a proposal for representation of social groups, however, encounters difficulties. The very bases of representation are matters of political controversy, and the groups granted representation at one time might exclude other groups that were later more important. Nor can we be sure how a person's origin will influence the values he carries with him into positions of influence; some will embrace their groups of origin, others reject them. And if we discard the notion of group representation and substitute that of representative political orientations or opinions, we are implicitly rejecting the possibility that some judgments of policies might be more soundly or rationally based than others.

To identify certain bases of policy judgment as superior and see that they are represented, even if it should be feasible, would implicitly favor expertise over democracy; it simply applies a concept analogous to "expertness" to the use of these bases of judgment. Like the "engineering model" of policy advice, it accepts certain differences of power and tries to associate knowledge—or, by extension, virtue—with positions of power. If we took this approach, we should in effect be redefining democracy as an aristocracy of the educated or a democracy of experts.

Valuative Discourse and the Redefinition of Democracy

Examination of the scientist's role in democratic policy formation thus leads us to ask more precisely what democracy entails. We are led to examine democratic institutions as means to the attainment of other ends beyond democracy itself—ends to which both science and democracy may be means and in terms of which the conflicting claims of science and democracy may be reconciled.

The problem of redefining democracy is raised by the proposition that there are inescapable limitations in the competence of some segments of the public, which make it undesirable for them to participate equally in policy formation. The weakest part of this proposition, of course, is that some existing disparities may be removable rather than inescapable. Participation may have·educational effects, and "freezing" a disparity in participation may prevent the leveling of existing disparities.[30] Secondly, we must recall that the question of competence in "elite" and "mass" is not restricted to scientific knowledge but extends to other sorts of knowledge as well.

Schumpeter argued that democracy consists in competitors for leadership presenting themselves to the popular vote and that the voters cannot be expected to understand all the complexities of policy or control it in detail.[31] And several survey studies of voters' knowledge and attitudes have led to doubt as to voters' competence to meet the standard of rationality that may have prevailed in John Stuart Mill's time.[32]

Given these characteristics of the ordinary citizen, some writers have proposed pluralism as a remedy for inequality of knowledge. An essential ingredient of the pluralist solution is a set of elites within a variety of interconnected associations or groups. These elites are expected to refine, reconcile, and channel those groups' political demands.[33] This proposal is closely akin to the "engineering model," except that it works through private associations rather than government and has usually been advanced in support of an existing situation rather than for reform of it.

A related modification of the root notion of popular rule is the widespread assertion that democracy resides more in the carrying out of certain procedures than in any ascertainable power relations. Thus the subjection of officeholders to popular elections with a universal fran-

30. Bachrach, *The Theory of Democratic Elitism,* p. 45; but cf. Cropsey, "Conservatism and Liberalism," p. 56.

31. Schumpeter, *Capitalism, Socialism, and Democracy,* ch. 22; see also Lippmann, *The Public Philosophy,* p. 19.

32. Mill, *Utilitarianism, Liberty, and Representative Government,* pp. 218–227; Berelson, Lazarsfeld, and McPhee, *Voting,* ch. 14; Daudt, *Floating Voters and the Floating Vote;* Converse, "The Nature of Belief Systems in Mass Publics"; Key, *The Responsible Electorate.* Related problems, provoking even more heated debates, revolve about possible differences in citizen competence that may be genetic in origin.

33. Kornhauser, *The Politics of Mass Society,* chs. 1–4.

chise is seen as a criterion of democracy, as long as the choices of the public are not overtly constrained and certain freedoms are preserved.[34] But if the public's choices are in fact constrained, even in its own interest, by nominating procedures or by the persuasion of public and private leaders, how are we to judge this? It is easiest simply to call the resulting system "democracy" and avoid the problem. But the harder choices require us to discriminate carefully among various forms of government in which the public has more and less independent influence.

Our efforts to resolve the conflicts between the values of science and democracy in questions involving "science in policy" have led us repeatedly to problems of ethics or valuative discourse. The values of science alone were insufficient to deal with these questions. When we considered the role of the informed citizen, we touched on social criticism and criteria of relevance that might involve reasoned valuative discourse. The extrinsic valuations that scientists make when they give advice on matters of policy might also be made more disciplined and explicit if they were shaped in reasoned discourse that was part of the scientist's training. And the possibility of redefining democracy has led us again to inquire about more general systems of values within which the values of science and democracy might be reconciled.

Thus science may also conflict with democracy not only in "policy for science" and "science in policy," but also in a third area. The findings of science may indicate conditions under which the practice of democracy is difficult and may themselves undermine confidence in the workability of democratic institutions. As regards biological differences among individuals, the possibility that scientific research might lead to the discovery of systematic differences in innate capacity for political participation has been resisted. Research alleging to discover racial differences in ability has been sharply criticized, with respect to both the rigor of its methods and the motives of its authors. In the analysis of electoral behavior there have been findings that seemed to challenge the view of a rational and participant electorate and stimulated debate as to whether an ideal model of democracy is realizable.

Not only the findings, but also the procedures of discussion of

34. Mayo, *An Introduction to Democratic Theory,* ch. 4.

science may have bearing on the value systems of democracy. There is
a latent conflict between the values of clarity, consistency, and generality implicit in scientific discourse and our actual practices in valuative discussion, including the justification of science and democracy
themselves. Much discussion of these questions falls short of the standards of clarity and consistency that scientists would require of their
own theories and hypotheses.

Thus a still more significant problem concerns the possible subjection of the ideals of democracy themselves to penetrating logical analysis, such as science prescribes for its own theories. We are increasingly aware that the gratification of consumers' economic "demands"
has led in advanced societies to the phenomenon of a "harried leisure
class," [35] as well as of a debt-ridden middle and working class. We
see in this phenomenon not only a chaos of demands and "needs,"
but also a creation and manipulation of demands by means of advertising as well as by the rivalry of a competitive and mobile society. We
ask then, "What *should* the consumers demand?" This question leads
to a reexamination of the desirable directions for education and public
communication.

The same question can be asked about the economic notion of satisfaction of existing preferences through democratic politics. As televi-
sion propaganda increasingly dominates our election campaigns, mobi-
lizing some remote segment of our attitudes in support or opposition to
a candidate (or to his "image"), we wonder whether popular rule
indeed involves an aspect of ourselves that is worthy to rule. We ask,
then, how the shaping and learning of citizens' attitudes and information *should* take place. We cannot, of course, advocate the "freedom"
that would correspond to uncaused or random attitudes, but knowing
that the public's political information and attitudes can be shaped to
some degree by education, mass communications, and campaigns, we
must ask through what processes they *ought* to be shaped. In asking
this question, we become aware of the intrinsic conservatism of a
procedure of choice that selects these processes "democratically"; by
slighting the role of education and leadership, it holds public choice
close to an existing state of opinion within an existing group. Demo-

35. Linder, *The Harried Leisure Class.*

cratic processes of choice render it especially difficult to create a social system with a new and perhaps superior system of values and preferences. They do not prevent change; the conservatism of democracy may produce not a static society, but a change in an unknown and unanticipated direction, like unintended oscillation in a feedback system. The effects of this conservatism can still be felt even if the "democracy" of market and political system is produced by the actions of an elite that manipulates images to appeal to existing popular tastes or prejudices.

We are thus led to inquire about the rationale of democracy. Is it to be justified as a system that optimally combines individual values, as in welfare economics? Or is it a system providing for maximal consultation of citizens, so that policies will be supported and conflict minimized? Or could it conceivably correct the values of its citizens and lead them to prefer other policies, other goods, and other styles of life than those they had thought they wanted?

These questions take us into a realm between welfare economics, valuative political theory, and the ethics of other social sciences. They lead us also to ask *which* of an individual's existing preferences ought to be combined in a social aggregation system and which ought not. They lead, then, to a morally and politically oriented critique of welfare economics and its political extensions, making use of its technical sophistication but transcending the disciplinary bias of economists that preferences are to be taken as given.

The conservative bias of democracy is also reflected in another fundamental set of valuative choices: those concerning criteria of *membership policy,* or the possible alteration in the composition of deciding groups. Who shall *be* "the people," whose rule is democracy? This question encompasses the alteration of the geographical boundaries of the political community and its subdivisions: policies for migration, immigration, incarceration, and deportation; policies for the granting and deprivation of citizenship to residents; policies governing birth and (in extreme cases) death; and policies for the alteration of the genetic characteristics of the citizenry.

The criteria of democracy—of rule by the people—sharply limit the decisions that can be taken on such matters. A selfish version of democracy, justified on market principles, seems least fit for them. It will tend to perpetuate the characteristics of the existing majority, whether desirable or undesirable. Officeholders may seek security by increasing the homogeneity of their constituencies. Migration, if governed in this way by politics, may increase local homogeneity and neglect the interests of outsiders. Perhaps there is also a more moral and enlightened type of democracy that can be expected to consider the interests of outsiders, but its theory will have to be elaborated on other grounds.

The greatest problem that science poses for democracy, therefore, arises from the scientist's continual quest for general principles. This quest leads us to the critical logical examination of the cluster of values that define democracy. What do they entail? Where do they conflict? To what other ends may they be considered means? The very discussion of these questions risks being undemocratic in at least one sense, if it is conducted by persons whose values are not representative of those of the general public. Yet if we are to examine whether a political system functions properly, or whether changes are needed, we must first be clear about what proper functioning *is*.

But this is also a problem for science. For in the marriage of rationalism and empiricism that gave birth to modern science, the empirical component is not the only important one for questions of public choice. Ethical and valuative questions can be discussed rationally, and philosophers are doing so. But the rational conduct of valuative discussion—dealing with problems that affect and involve science as deeply as those we have considered—need not be isolated from science in a separate division of the university. To separate valuative questions from science is perhaps to strengthen pure science, but also to weaken applied science by making it totally dependent for its guidance on unreflective standards and modes of valuation. The values that guide the application of science are thus deprived of the rational component that is so essential to science's own internal functioning.

Scientists—or academic and professional groups that include scientists—still need to incorporate centrally into their own valuative discourse the rationality that they value in the conduct of science itself. They may attempt to do so by an appeal to mankind at large; [36] but if

36. See Feinberg, *The Prometheus Project.*

they have the support of the university and of academic disciplines in the effort, they may find the task less difficult. If rational valuative discourse is more closely tied to education in science, the foundations of experts' policy advice may be sounder, and they may more easily connect means with ends. But if it is also tied to general education, informed citizens may be better able to assess the advice of experts.

Conducting valuative discourse in accordance with the pattern of scientific discourse, which pays particular attention to clarity, consistency, and generality, we may narrow the range of possible ethical systems. A consensus that is reached rationally may lead to more consistent and practicable political decisions; this same limitation of admissible ethical foundations may also constrain the diversity of inconsistent individual ethical systems, such as we apply in the multiple roles of everyday life.

The problems of reconciling science and democracy have led us first to examine the ways in which science is applied to public decisions. In the education of the informed citizen, we have argued that a special role can be played by social science—but only if it can modify its definition of itself as "science." At the same time, we have been led to ask about the possibilities of democracy itself and the further values that it serves. Both these lines of inquiry—about science and about democracy—have led us to the systematic analysis of the standards on which democracy rests. Our task in the following chapters will be to build a foundation that can serve for this type of analysis.

3 POSITIVISM AND THE DEVALUATION OF ETHICS

The discourse of the social sciences falls short of the needs of policy guidance, not only because it is specialized, but also because it involves a deliberate effort to escape from valuation. This effort follows the example of the natural sciences, which have progressed by freeing themselves from common sense categories that have both factual and valuative meanings. Such categories, like those of ideologies, lead us to link valued symbols together and to separate them from disvalued symbols, blinding us to causal relations between valued and disvalued things.[1] Both Galileo's espousal of the heliocentric theory and Darwin's connection of man with lower organisms did violence to religious views that gave a special status to the earth and man. In social science, a similar development has taken us away from notions that "good causes good" or "evil causes evil," allowing us to see connections such as that between competitive striving and crime in America. An effort to free our concepts from valuative connotations might thus aid us to see some aspects of the world more clearly. But such a vocabulary cannot by itself serve as an adequate guide to action.

Valuative discourse in the university is extremely difficult to justify within the natural science disciplines, as it has little relation to their concepts and problems. The social sciences, however, have continued to use many terms, both old and new, that combine factual and valuative meanings;[2] their discourse thus still has much in common with that of the informed citizen. A major effort in the social sciences in recent decades has been to cut this tie and to distinguish expert social-scientific discourse from the discourse of everyday life. Yet both citizens and rival professions (such as the law) claim the right to criticize social science, raising the question whether this separation should and can be complete.

1. See Abelson and Rosenberg, "Symbolic Psycho-Logic."
2. See chapter 4 below.

The role of the informed citizen [3] requires not only understanding of specialties in order to compare their claims, but also a capacity for valuative discourse. Those alternative theories of democracy that regard voters as "merely objects whose votes are sought at election time," [4] even if they should be true, do not fully respond to this need. Even if some citizens should be unable to grasp the issues that confront them, there must be others able to choose among candidates and policies through reasoning, criteria of choice, and evidence. Mere sympathy or antipathy for particular personalities may be a realistic basis for citizens' choice, but it is not a *justifiable* basis for the conduct of public affairs.

The potential guidance that the social sciences might offer in this respect has been curtailed, however, by their rejection of systematic valuative discourse. This rejection derives not only from the model of natural science, but also from the influence of logical positivism—a philosophic doctrine claiming to interpret natural science, which has pronounced valuative discourse to be "meaningless" other than as an expression of personal emotions. The effect of this doctrine has gone far beyond the justifiable *distinction* between factual and valuative statements to eliminate reasoned valuative discourse from almost all of social science. It was proper to eliminate propositions that purported to be testable empirically but were not. But the dismissal of ethical principles from the recognized discourse of the social sciences has left these disciplines without sufficient guidance in dealing with the valuative problems of policy choice.

The rejection of systematic valuative discourse by the contemporary social sciences is not easy to trace to its sources. It has been preceded by a persisting tendency in philosophy to separate and devalue ethical discourse. The logical separation of factual and valuative assertions found forceful expression in the work of David Hume, and beginning in the 1920s logical positivists took the radical view that valuative assertions were "meaningless" or were to be dismissed as "metaphysics." But several decades earlier, Weber and Pareto had also ad-

---

3. And the role of the representative in particular; see chapter 6.

4. Weber, *The Theory of Social and Economic Organization*, p. 408. This statement parallels Schumpeter's theory in *Capitalism, Socialism, and Democracy,* mentioned in chapter 2 above.

vocated a strict separation between facts and values. Their
formulations have contributed to the dominant stance of contemporary
social science, which has clearly excluded systematic valuative discourse.

It is also possible that influences outside of science or philosophy
have contributed to this exclusion of valuative discourse. A value-
guided social science would not only enjoy less internal consensus
than a value-free one, but might also be open to attack if its values
threatened major interests in society. Some have argued, therefore,
that the effort of social science to be value-free results from social scientists' desires for support and prestige. Others have argued that social
science could gain more support if it were more directly useful to society. But even though the effort to be value-free can have sources *outside* the intellectual development of a science, internal and philosophical tendencies may also have played an important part.

or credibility [handwritten margin note]

The Antecedents of Logical Positivism

The philosophical position—or family of positions—known as
"logical positivism" has several tenets. It involves a theory of empirical knowledge as derived from the impressions received by the senses;
with this we need not be concerned. But it also involves the "designa-
tion of any synthetic sentence which is not ultimately verifiable
through perceptions as . . . 'meaningless.' " [5] This doctrine may
well have influenced the development of the social sciences.

The devaluation of ethics can be imagined to have taken place in
two stages. First was the separation of the valuative realm from the
factual—a separation that we shall accept, even though some have
challenged it. [6] Second was the elimination of valuative considerations
from the central activities of the disciplines studying society. [7] Conceivably this deemphasis could occur as part of a fruitful and cooperative division of labor—say, between the social sciences and philoso-

5. Brecht, *Political Theory,* p. 175.
6. The perspectives that deny the separation include those of Plato, Marx, and the
pragmatists. See Strauss, *Natural Right and History;* Goodwin, "The Historical-
Philosophical Basis for Uniting Social Science with Social Problem-Solving"; and references to pragmatism later in this chapter.
7. They remain in "fringe" activities, which we shall discuss later in this chapter.

phy. A division of labor has occurred, but at the cost of cooperation. Although we shall not attempt here to trace the development of philosophy beyond positivism, the subsequent importance of analytic philosophy and the study of ordinary language do not seem to have filled the gap.

The separation of fact and value may be observed in the development of natural science. Galileo's victory over the Ptolemaic view of the solar system was not merely the overthrow of a scientific paradigm, but a challenge to a theological world-view closely related to men's lives and the authority of the Church. Newton's effort to see God's will in the elegant uniformities of the universe, though no longer a challenge to orthodoxy, still linked fact and value. But as the communication systems of scientific groups separated themselves from external influence, the justification of science in terms of external values declined. In Poincaré's time, the esthetic values provided by scientific research seemed the only justification for the scientist's activity. But even in Newton's writing, an unwillingness to attempt to answer the unanswerable was reflected in his phrase, "hypotheses non fingo." He was pointing out, not that he abstained from hypotheses in the modern sense, but that he did not make assertions about underlying "metaphysical" entities such as the cause of gravitation, which were unnecessary to explain his observations.[8]

In parallel with the move of natural scientists away from a theological frame of reference was the formulation by philosophers of the clear distinction between fact and value. The antecedents of this separation date back to the Middle Ages,[9] but one of its most famous statements is that of Hume:

> In every system of morality . . . I have always remarked, that the author proceeds for some time in the ordinary way of reasoning . . . ; when of a sudden I am surprised to find, that instead of the usual copulations of propositions, *is,* and *is not,* I meet with no proposition that is not connected with an *ought,* or an *ought not.* . . . [A] reason should be given, for what seems altogether incon-

8. Santillana, *The Crime of Galileo;* Ben-David, *The Scientist's Role in Society;* Poincaré, *Science and Method;* Brecht, *op. cit.,* part I; Singer, *A Short History of Science,* p. 254.

9. Kolakowski, *op. cit.,* ch. 2.

ceivable, how this new relation can be a deduction from others, which are entirely different from it.[10]

Such a separation of fact and value, as we have suggested, freed the natural scientist from searching only for those factual relationships that supported valuative systems. It opened the way for him to discover the complex and elegant web of relationships that constitute modern natural science. A pervasive value of natural scientists has thus come to be ethical neutrality in their work. Under this rubric we may classify several more specific values: the expectation of disinterestedness in the scientist's motivation; [11] the choice of problems on theoretical rather than practical grounds; and the definition of science so as to exclude ethical questions.

Thus the development of natural science freed its concepts from the constraint of valuative categories. But the increased prestige of scientific discourse did not eliminate efforts to link it with ethics; rather, this prestige was accompanied by increasing efforts, outside the realm of scientific communication itself, to base ethics *on* science. In spite of Hume's distinction between "is" and "ought," the effort to move from observation to valuation has been a persisting one. Numerous ethical criteria proposed by scientists thus fall into the class that G. E. Moore called "naturalistic ethics," whose conclusions were purported to be established "by means of empirical observation and induction." [12]

Both Bentham and Mill apparently engaged in naturalistic reasoning in their support of utilitarianism; they connected happiness with the good, on the ground that happiness was in fact sought by human beings. Bentham wrote that "Nature has placed mankind under the governance of two sovereign masters, *pain* and *pleasure*"; and Mill wrote, "the sole evidence it is possible to produce that anything is desirable, is that people actually do desire it." [13] This type of argu-

10. Hume, *A Treatise of Human Nature,* Book III, Part I, Section I.
11. Merton, *Social Theory and Social Structure* (1968 ed.), pp. 612ff.; Barber, *Science and the Social Order,* pp. 131–132.
12. G. E. Moore, *Principia Ethica,* p. 39.
13. Bentham, *An Introduction to the Principles of Morals and Legislation,* p. 1; Mill, *Utilitarianism, Liberty, and Representative Government,* p. 32. But Goldsworth contends that Bentham was not a naturalist; see his "Bentham's Concept of Pleasure."

ment, linked to psychological hedonism, has unnecessarily linked utilitarian ethics to notions of motivation and preference, a point to which we shall return (chapter 6) in discussing the economic notion of "utility."

By the nineteenth century we find a variety of philosophical interpretations of science and meaning, of which some anticipate the devaluation of ethics, others attempt the leap from "is" to "ought" in naturalistic fashion, and still others (less influential) leave open the possibility for a meaningful but nonscientific realm of ethical discourse.

The most direct forerunner of logical positivism was the physicist Ernst Mach, who maintained Hume's distinction and reduced knowledge to experience.[14] But also during the latter part of the nineteenth century, naturalistic ethics derived from Darwin's discoveries became more prevalent. Herbert Spencer was among the leaders in the propagation of social Darwinism. At the turn of the century, the sociologist Lester Ward criticized Comte and Spencer for considering ethics a science, but he himself espoused a form of utilitarianism without presenting grounds for it or a basis for arguing about it.[15] The more recent development of ethical assertions by scientists, however, has come to coincide more closely with the concepts of their individual disciplines, as we shall see later in this chapter.

Another philosophical interpretation of meaning, unrelated to naturalistic ethics and linked only later with positivism, was that of pragmatism. Although one aspect of this philosophy was to deny the separateness of facts and valuations, another was to endow valuative statements with meaning, and thus to avoid the excesses of positivism which characterized them as meaningless.

Pragmatism has been associated with the general notion that meanings and actions are to be tested by their practical consequences. But this notion leaves much undecided in the realm of ethics, for a given set of consequences may be evaluated according to various ethical standards, and mere observation or prediction of consequences is insufficient for the judgment of right actions—however much it may contribute to that judgment. The pragmatist avoidance of distinct ethi-

14. See Kolakowski, *op. cit.,* pp. 114–121.
15. Ward, *Applied Sociology,* p. 317.

cal statements is illustrated by Dewey's notion that ends and means
form an unending continuum.[16]

A closer look at the position of the pragmatic philosopher Charles
S. Peirce, however, reveals elements of his thought that stress the
meaningfulness of ethical statements. Peirce was particularly concerned with the criterion according to which the *meaning* of an expression was to be determined. As Kolakowski summarizes Peirce's view,
"To find out whether a statement means anything, we must ask how
and whether it affects our actions and expectations." [17] The effect on
our expectations is closely related to the cognitive aspect of meaning
and may be related to the scientist's or the positivist's criterion of
meaning. But the additional realization that meaning can relate to our
actions leaves the way open for meaningful statements that dictate particular, specifiable acts as right or wrong, better or worse. In this sense
an ethical or valuative statement can have a clear meaning.

Feibleman also interprets Peirce's approach to ethics as specifying
meaning in this way:

> The maxim of pragmatism can be translated into the moral sphere
> by qualifying it. We can say that in order to ascertain the ethical
> meaning of an intellectual conception one should consider what
> practical consequences to conduct might conceivably result by ne-
> cessity from the truth of that conception; and the sum of these con-
> sequences will constitute the entire meaning of the conception. . . .
> But since this pragmatic conception is couched in terms of *conceiv-
> able* consequences, it reaches "far beyond the practical." [18]

We shall follow a similar approach to the meaning of "ethical hypotheses" in the following chapter.

By the first quarter of the twentieth century, however, the foundations were laid within social science for a stress on facts at the expense
of valuations. As Arnold Brecht suggested, the notion of science was
narrowed at about the turn of the century by "methodological scru-
ples." Valuative contributions were no longer considered part of
"science."

16. Dewey, *Theory of Valuation*.
17. Kolakowski, *op. cit.*, p. 151.
18. Feibleman, *An Introduction to Peirce's Philosophy*, p. 377; The maxim, without
the word "ethical," appears in Peirce, *Collected Papers*, vol. V., p. 6.

The principal tools of science qua science, [scholars] found, were observation of facts, measurement, and logical reasoning. Anything that could not be done with such tools should not be presented under the pretense of being scientific but be frankly put forward as the personal opinion of the writer, or as a piece taken out of a religious creed, or as a tentative assumption, or the like. . . . The withdrawal of science from ethical value judgments on purposes and means has established a *scientific void*.[19]

A major figure in this development, whose work has been taken as a landmark by supporters and critics alike, was Max Weber.[20] Weber was acutely conscious of the limitations of valuative assertions, and even though he recognized the possibility of reasoning about ethical matters his strictures on the subject seem on the whole to have discouraged it. He refers frequently to the difficulty of reconciling systems of valuation that differ in their ultimate premises, and when this high goal is recognized as unattainable the entire enterprise tends to be abandoned.

We are far removed, then, from the view that the demand for the exclusion of value-judgments in empirical analysis implies that discussions of evaluations are sterile or meaningless.

But the scientific treatment of value-judgments may not only understand and empathically analyze (*nacherleben*) the desired ends and the ideals which underlie them; it can also "judge" them critically. This criticism can of course have only a dialectical character, i.e., it can be no more than a formal logical judgment of historically given value-judgments and ideas, a testing of the ideals according to the postulate of the internal *consistency* of the desired end.[21]

It is precisely this formal judgment of consistency that we wish to promote. We can agree with the logic of Weber's argument and yet dispute its tone and its apparent consequences. In a sense, the subsequent chapters of this book are devoted to elaborating the possibilities if this mode of discourse is taken seriously.

19. Brecht, *op. cit.*, pp. 4, 7.
20. See Weber, *Methodology of the Social Sciences;* Brecht, *op. cit.*, p. 215, Strauss, *op. cit.*, ch. 2.
21. Weber, *op cit.*, pp. 14, 54.

The circumstances of the German university in 1917 seem to have been reflected in the initial pages of Weber's *Methodology of the Social Sciences*. The introductory essay in that volume stresses the limitations of academic discussion. It considers valuation in negative rather than positive terms. It denies the tenability of a distinction between partisan and nonpartisan value judgments. It stresses the individual character of the judgments that one makes about the universities:

> Those who . . . assign to the universities . . . the universal role of molding human beings . . . will take a different position than those who believe . . . that the academic lecture-hall achieves a really valuable influence only through specialized training by specially qualified persons.

It expresses a fear of the use of the lecture platform—which is considered influential and authoritative—for "personal prophecy." And it suggests that professorial promotions were going to prophets rather than to scientists.[22] All this reflects a particular historical situation—one that may well occur again, but which needs to be contrasted with our own.

In 1918 Weber delivered the two lectures that were later published as "Politics as a Vocation" and "Science as a Vocation." In the former he praised the responsibility of the political leader (as against the bureaucrat) and discussed various types of ethics, but in the latter he dealt with the limitations of the scientist's role. The study of " 'inconvenient' facts," and even the critical analysis of the consequences of democratic and nondemocratic forms of government are permitted in the classroom. But the goal is clarity: to "force the individual, or at least [to] help him, to give himself an *account of the ultimate meaning of his own conduct.*" Dedication, but dedication to a personal "demon," is the most that can be sought.[23]

Weber has left to American social science a legacy of abstention from choice of values. One aspect of this legacy has been the detached

22. *Ibid.*, pp. 1, 3, 4, 9. The status of the "prophetic mode" of sociology is a major theme of Friedrichs's *A Sociology of Sociology*.
23. Weber, *Essays*, pp. 145–147, 152, 156.

study of configurations of values, or of value-laden phenomena, such as Weber himself conducted in his study of world religions. A second, however, has been an approach by social scientists to the threshold of policy choice without their venturing over it. Many have thus seen their practical role in society as providing means to external ends or telling actors how to attain their own goals.[24] Some take these ends from clients who pay for their services. Others seek them in the decision processes of democracy or in public opinion surveys. Still others feel that underlying values can be discovered in discourse with clients who represent the public interest and that the analytic skills of the social scientist, while not actually entering into the valuative realm, can guide the client (or society) toward feasible and consistent means to its ends. It is paradoxical, however, that the Weberian approach does not provide social scientists within the university any principles on which to judge the appropriateness or reform of their *own* activities; in these terms, the university can be guided ultimately only from outside.[25]

In the years after Weber's death, his work was less remembered in Europe than in America. But, interestingly, it has also been taken in Germany as a source by the school of "critical rationalism" which has developed in recent decades and which *is* concerned with valuative criticism. One of its leaders, Hans Albert, has argued at length for the consistency between Weber's writings and the practical application of social science.[26]

A second influential figure in the development of a value-free social science was Vilfredo Pareto. Although he included value judgments in some of his writings, he analyzed the issues involved, judging by analogy with natural science that the use of ethical principles in economics had no scientific validity. Like Weber, he was interpreted by subsequent writers as favoring the total exclusion of ethical principles from social science, whereas in actuality he may not have gone this far.[27]

24. See Helle, "Knowledge and Action in Sociological Theory"; Coleman, "Policy Research in the Social Sciences," pp. 8–9.
25. Easton, *The Political System* (1971 ed.), p. 359.
26. See Dallmayr, "Toward a Critical Reconstruction of Ethics and Politics"; Albert, *Traktat über Kritische Vernunft*, pp. 62–67.
27. See Tarascio, *Pareto's Methodological Approach to Economics*, p. 47.

Positivism and Ethics

Over and above these antecedents, logical positivism itself has made a major contribution to the present value-free standard in the social sciences. The positivist conception of science and of knowledge, developing in the early part of the twentieth century, "denies cognitive value to value judgments and normative statements." [28] We shall be concerned primarily with the problems that this position raises for ethics, rather than with the positivists' theory of scientific knowledge.

Logical positivism involved an effort to establish firm grounds for knowledge and to state them systematically, taking natural science as a model. The work of Ernst Mach was taken as a point of departure by the Vienna Circle, a group of philosophers and scientists meeting in Vienna in the 1920s and 1930s. The effect of their work on the social sciences was similar to that of the simple imitation of natural science, but it became more extreme through a particular interpretation of natural science.

One of the clearest statements of a position taken by this group with respect to ethics was made by Carnap in 1932: "In the domain of *metaphysics,* including all philosophy of value and normative theory, logical analysis yields the negative result *that the alleged statements in this domain are entirely meaningless."* [29] But followers of this perspective were led from the devaluation of ethical discourse to occasional ethical statements in opposition to reasoned ethical argument. An expression of this view may be found in Hans Reichenbach's *The Rise of Scientific Philosophy* (1951), in a chapter entitled "The Nature of Ethics." The following sequence of statements conveys the trend of his argument:

> The modern analysis of knowledge makes a cognitive ethics impossible: knowledge does not include any normative parts and therefore does not lend itself to an interpretation of ethics.

> If the word "necessary" is to mean anything comparable to logical necessity, then there can be no moral necessity.

28. Kolakowski, *op. cit.,* p. 7.
29. Carnap, "The Elimination of Metaphysics Through Logical Analysis of Language," pp. 60–61 (in Ayer, ed., *Logical Positivism*).

The ethical axioms are not necessary truths because they are not truths of any kind. Truth is a predicate of statements; but the linguistic expressions of ethics are not statements. They are directives. A directive cannot be classified as true or false; these predicates do not apply because directive sentences are of a logical nature different from that of indicative sentences, or statements.

And he proposes the principle:

Everybody is entitled to set up his own moral imperatives and to demand that everyone follow these imperatives.[30]

The opposing demands, he suggests, should be resolved democratically, and we are democrats because we have been brought up so. His notion of politics is that of a democratic resolution of conflicts of volition, where neither the merits of various volitions nor those of political regimes are amenable to reasoned argument.

The consequence of such a view—as Reichenbach explicitly states later in the chapter—is to deny philosophy, or systematic discussion, any rightful place in reasoning about moral issues. And it is precisely this denial, with its persuasive rhetoric, that must concern us. We might better say, with the earlier Wittgenstein, "Whereof one cannot speak, thereof one must remain silent." [31]

An influential contribution to this tradition was Ayer's *Language, Truth and Logic*. Ayer styled himself a "logical empiricist," distinguishing his position from that of the logical positivists on grounds related to the theory of knowledge. But he shared their sharp attack on metaphysics and on the attempt to know transcendent realities: "We may . . . define a metaphysical sentence as a sentence which purports to express a genuine proposition, but does, in fact, express neither a tautology nor an empirical hypothesis." By including only those sentences that purport to express propositions, he exempts poetry from his criticism but attacks the activity of philosophers who deal with metaphysical questions. As a result of this approach, Ayer claimed to "complete the overthrow of speculative philosophy" and to be "in a

---

30. Reichenbach, *The Rise of Scientific Philosophy*, pp. 277, 279, 280, 295.
31. Wittgenstein, *Tractatus Logico-Philosophicus*, final section.

position to see that the function of philosophy is wholly critical." [32]

These critical assumptions and instruments are brought to bear in a chapter entitled "Critique of Ethics and Theology." He attacks the argument that " 'statements of value' are genuine synthetic propositions" (that is, that they convey meaning beyond that deriving from definitions and logic). He argues that "in so far as statements of value are significant, they are ordinary 'scientific' statements; and that in so far as they are not scientific, they are not in the literal sense significant, but are simple expressions of emotion which can be neither true nor false." [33]

Ayer then raises for ethical argument the alternative standards of analytic and synthetic knowledge. He shows that common ethical notions cannot be sustained as analytic (logical truths or tautologies), since their contraries are not self-contradictory. He goes on to argue that the specification of an ethical system, giving precise meanings to ethical terms in relation to observation, would not allow reasoned argument about ethics:

> We are not of course denying that it is possible to invent a language in which all ethical symbols are definable in non-ethical terms, or even that it is desirable to invent such a language and adopt it in place of our own; what we are denying is that the suggested reduction of ethical to non-ethical statements is consistent with the conventions of our actual language.
>
> Another man may disagree with me about the wrongness of stealing, in the sense that he may not have the same feelings about stealing that I have, and he may quarrel with me on account of my moral sentiments. But he cannot, strictly speaking, contradict me. For in saying that a certain action is right or wrong, I am not making any factual statement, not even a statement about my own state of mind. I am merely *expressing certain moral sentiments*. And the man who is ostensibly contradicting me is merely expressing his moral sentiments. So that there is plainly no sense in asking which of us is in the right. For neither of us is asserting a *genuine proposition*.

32. Ayer, *Language, Truth and Logic* (2d ed., 1946), pp. 41, 44, 45, 48. Initially published in 1936.
33. *Ibid.*, pp. 102–103.

We can now see why it is impossible to find a criterion for determining the validity of ethical judgments. It is not because they have an "absolute" validity which is mysteriously independent of ordinary sense-experience, but because they have no objective validity whatsoever. If a sentence makes no statement at all, there is obviously no sense in asking whether what it says is true or false. And we have seen that sentences which simply express moral judgments do not say anything. They are pure expressions of feeling and as such do not come under the category of truth and falsehood. They are unverifiable for the same reason as a cry of pain or a word of command is unverifiable—because they do not express genuine propositions.

Ayer contests G. E. Moore's position that we do in fact argue about questions of value, by claiming that such arguments deal not with the "wrongness" of ethical feeling, but with "the facts of the case." He challenges the reader "to try to construct even an imaginary argument on a question of value which does not reduce itself to an argument about a question of logic or about an empirical matter of fact." [34] I shall argue in the following chapter that this approach, like Weber's, is not incorrect but that the pessimism engendered by its phrasing narrows our notion as to the content and possibilities of ethical argument.

The most extreme positions of the logical positivists have subsequently been qualified in a variety of ways. Moritz Schlick, the leader of the Vienna Circle, also elaborated a naturalistic ethics that blended factual analysis into utilitarianism.[35] Ayer, in the introduction to the 1946 edition of his book, admits that his points did not require the espousal of an emotive theory of ethics; that "the common objects of moral approval or disapproval are not particular actions so much as classes of actions"; and that in ethical arguments there can be disagreement without formal contradiction. In view of this last observation, ethical argument can involve elements other than logic or factual statements. "One may, for example, call [the other persons's] attention to certain facts that one supposes him to have overlooked." And it is "also possible to influence other people by a suitable choice of emotive language"—though whether this is legitimate argument or il-

34. *Ibid.*, pp. 105, 108–109; emphasis mine.
35. Schlick, *Problems of Ethics.*

legitimate manipulation remains to be specified. But these means have limits, and they do not go to the "truth" of the matter, as "the question of truth or falsehood does not here arise." [36]

The group of logical empiricists who gathered together to publish the *International Encyclopedia of Unified Science* appeared in some ways also to represent a more moderate position with respect to ethics. A listing by Joergensen of their forerunners indicates that their common concerns included not only the unity of science, but also "eudaemonism." Two volumes of the encyclopedia were devoted to ethical questions. But in practice their ethical perspective was represented by Abraham Edel and John Dewey, neither of whose approaches seems to have led to active and reasoned ethical discussion. [37]

Social Science and the Assertion of Values

The logical positivists' view that ethical statements are meaningless represented one extreme of a spectrum of views that were held on the subject during the first half of the century. Weber's position, as well as that of Karl Popper, was more moderate. Yet the net result of these views seems to have reinforced the tendency of the social studies to call themselves "sciences" and to confine themselves to factual matters, while at the same time weakening the concern of philosophers with ethics.

The widespread acceptance among social scientists of the notion that valuative assertions are improper in their disciplines has led them to apply a characteristic vocabulary and set of categories to valuative assertions. I shall argue in detail later that the valuative aspects of secondarily evaluative terms (combining factual and valuative meanings) are used unsystematically in the social science literature. But behind this usage there are also certain almost subliminal assumptions that pervade discussion of valuative questions.

First, there is a general tendency to regard valuative assertions as

36. Ayer, *op. cit.,* pp. 21, 22.
37. *International Encyclopedia of Unified Science,* vol. II, No. 9, Joergensen, "The Development of Logical Empiricism," p. 6; No. 3, Edel, "Science and the Structure of Ethics"; No. 4, Dewey, "Theory of Valuation." On Dewey, see also Kolakowski, *op. cit.,* pp. 163–165.

reflecting the "personal preferences" of the speaker. For example, Lasswell writes: "The word 'policy' is commonly used to designate the most important choices made either in organized or private life. We speak of 'government policy,' 'business policy,' or *my own* policy,' regarding investments and other matters." Is it an accident that the three examples he gives provide only the choice between policies of major societal institutions and those of individuals? Could an academic discipline or profession (for example, economics, engineering, or medicine) provide the basis for a policy in a particular domain? Or could a policy be derived from utilitarianism or democratic theory? Merton, writing in the same volume, discusses the roles of the scientist-adviser in the choice of problems: "As a 'socially oriented' scientist, he will explore only those policy alternatives which do not violate *his own* values." [38] Why just "his own" values? Why not a political philosophy, a professional code of ethics, or one or more ethical systems elaborated through reasoned criticism? Again we are dealing with a passing remark, and we cannot be sure how seriously to take it for purposes of criticism. But it is in such passing remarks that ethical discourse and its potential results are characteristically dismissed. The literature of social science is replete with them, and I shall cite more in later chapters.

The individualistic framework in which valuations are tacitly placed is also revealed by a peculiar terminology used by economists. The formulation of criteria under which "social welfare functions"—a type of ethical system—are specified typically characterizes them as imposed by despots, dictators, or individual social scientists. [39] This assimilation of valuative discourse to the given, unsystematized, and undebatable tastes of the consumer encourages the neglect of systematic discourse, within the political and educational systems of a society, concerning the relative merits of various valuative standards and judgments.

A second aspect of this discourse is the assumption that valuations are not only personal but also "preferences." In this aspect also, the influence of economics has been considerable. Personal preferences, in

38. Lerner and Lasswell, eds., *The Policy Sciences*, pp. 5, 302. My emphasis.
39. See for example Samuelson, *Foundations of Economic Analysis*, p. 221; Musgrave, *Fiscal Systems*, p. 12.

this perspective, are to be expressed only as ordinal rankings. There is indeed a sense in which a complete ordinal ranking of possible states of the world would give all the information that an ethical system contained. But if we could speak of ethical systems only in this way, we should be paralyzed in our practical dealings. This problem has been recognized by those economists who make policy recommendations, and for this reason they have devised additive criteria such as the gross national product or costs and benefits.

This usage goes back to a movement in economics in the 1930s, which included the penetrating criticism by Lionel Robbins [40] of the previous mixture of factual and valuative discourse in economics. It was carried forward in Hicks's *Value and Capital,* which demonstrated the superfluity of "utility" as a concept in the explanation of consumer behavior and the sufficiency of indifference curves—a point that Pareto had also made earlier. [41] A final step in this sequence, particularly relevant to subsequent economic approaches to politics, was taken in Arrow's *Social Choice and Individual Values.* The demonstration that cardinal utility was unnecessary to the analyses of economic science, and that the combination of ordinal or ranked utilities could not be made under "self-evident" axioms, led to an impossibility theorem. These two blows, administered within economics but felt throughout the social sciences, have contributed to the devaluation of ethical discourse.

A direct connection between these developments and the influence of the Vienna Circle has been pointed out by Alexander:

> When young Lionel Robbins, as he then was, returned to the London School from the Vienna of the twenties with his head stuffed with positivism, he administered a shock to Anglo-Saxon economics from which it has not yet recovered. . . . Interpersonal comparisons of utility were out and Pareto optimality . . . was in. Today the elementary textbooks authoritatively tell us that economics is limited to the investigation of the consequences of economic actions. Whether the consequences are good or bad is a matter for the

40. Robbins, *An Essay on the Nature and Significance of Economic Science.* For the influence of Weber and Pareto on Robbins, see Tarascio, *op. cit.,* pp. 47–48.

41. Pareto, *Manual of Political Economy,* pp. 393–394; Stigler, *Essays in the History of Economics,* pp. 117–128.

citizen to decide—not for the economist. How such a judgment is arrived at, the textbooks do not say. It clearly cannot properly be derived from a study of the consequences of economic actions.[42]

Parallel tendencies and problems have arisen within sociology. The effort to attain a value-free scientific discourse has been effective. Techniques and research methods have been developed systematically, and the valuative concerns of some of the founders of the discipline have been left by the wayside. This tendency was criticized as early as 1951 by Bendix, who was able to regard the discipline from a European perspective. More recently, a crescendo of criticism from radical sociologists has denounced the scientific model. But while the radicals' diagnosis of capitalist society has converged on a Marxian perspective, their notions as to how truth is to be confirmed and tested reveal less clear agreement.[43]

American political science has undergone a similar evolution. During the 1920s and 1930s, leaders of the discipline argued as to whether a value-free stance was desirable. After World War II, the study of political behavior gained in importance, though valuative approaches remained as important aspects of the discipline—sometimes concealed in the study of the history of political philosophy.[44] Schumpeter's reduction of the democratic "ought" to the behavioral "is," though a creative contribution, may have resulted in part from his affiliation (as an economist) with the Vienna Circle.[45] Today, in parallel to a movement of radical criticism, the field of policy analysis is growing in importance, though political scientists who study policy formation are divided between objective observers and advocates or choosers. The more general field of policy analysis that we shall discuss in chapter 9, however, is an interdisciplinary one.[46]

Psychology became scientific even earlier. Although William James combined empirical study with moral philosophy, a rigorous scientific

42. Alexander, "The Impersonality of Normative Judgments," p. 55.
43. See MacRae, "A Dilemma of Sociology," esp. pp. 3–4; Friedrichs, op. cit., pp. 72–75; Bendix, Social Science and the Distrust of Reason.
44. See Somit and Tanenhaus, The Development of American Political Science, ch. IX; and, on sociology, Friedrichs, op. cit., ch. 4.
45. Brecht, op. cit., p. 182.
46. On the inadequacy of political science alone for this task, see MacRae, "Sociology in Public Policy Analysis."

psychology was developing in Germany in the late nineteenth century under the leadership of Wundt. This approach spread in the United States and was eventually reflected in a rigorous value-free theory of learning and behavior. But a contemporary leader in this field, B. F. Skinner, has extended his work in a valuative direction. We shall deal with this work, together with the ethics of psychotherapy, in chapter 7.

Psychotherapy, in contrast, has never claimed to be indifferent to values, though at times it has concealed them under the cloak of medicine and health. The methods of clinical psychology also serve the values of therapy. Since Freud's day, many psychoanalysts have worked toward broadly conceived human values and have related their field to history and literature, resisting the technical specialization of the sciences.

Valuation on the Fringes of the Sciences

We are thus left largely with a notion of applied science—both natural and social—which serves the values of others. This service may appear worthwhile and libertarian when it is described as avoiding unanticipated consequences or aiding others to realize their values, or it may appear biased in its goals when social scientists are criticized as "servants of power." [47] Natural scientists have sometimes seen the mere selling of their services in the market as insufficient. They have argued in the name of "social responsibility" that they had valuable knowledge that the market did not demand or that, having created weapons of mass destruction, they should work to harness these forces for human benefit.[48] As human beings, and as possessors of the optimistic rationalism that is also associated with natural science, they have not always been able to live for the progress of science alone. But however they might have wished to act on these social and political questions, they have usually had to act outside the confines of their disciplines.

When scientists are drawn to policy advocacy and valuation that

47. Baritz, *The Servants of Power.*
48. Gilpin, *American Scientists and Nuclear Weapons Policy,* p. 26; Friedrichs, *op. cit.,* pp. 114ff.

their disciplines do not permit, and when they bring to these activities some of the skills and knowledge of their disciplines, they face a conflict. The ways in which they respond to it, both separating and combining factual and valuative discourse, provide indirect evidence of the social structure of their disciplines. The central norms of a group or organization are often revealed by the group's response to deviance or the limits it sets on tolerable behavior. Thus when the fact-value distinction is embodied in the organized structure of disciplines, a study of efforts to circumvent it can be especially informative.

When members of a modern academic discipline become interested in valuative or policy problems, they have several alternatives. One is to join as individuals with political groups, without seeking to connect their status as academics or specialists with these activities. The basis of organization of these groups is typically a political program or an ideology, not an academic discipline.

A second alternative is to work as an applied scientist for an organization serving values that the scientist supports. The influx of scientists into government work in World War II was in considerable measure of this kind. The move of young lawyers into the Civil Rights Division of the Justice Department under the Johnson administration was similar. But when authority and establishments come under criticism, this alternative is less conspicuous.

A third alternative is to try to combine in some degree the activities of one's specialty—publication, research, and teaching—with orientation to valuatively significant topics. This type of activity is sharply limited, however, by the exclusion of ethical discourse from the professional communications of the natural sciences and by its devaluation in the social sciences. These limits are maintained by the gatekeepers of the disciplines and supported by large bodies of members who approve of them.

There is, however, one way of engaging in valuative discourse without abandoning one's identity as a member of a discipline and of retaining some of the expertness of the discipline in the valuative realm. This is to deal with valuative meanings attached to central *concepts* of the discipline's own theory. The transfer of such concepts into the valuative realm is common both in the naturalistic ethics that draw their inspiration from science and in quasi-empirical sub-disciplines in the social sciences, such as welfare economics. Natural scientists have proposed ethics of evolution, ecology, survival, and thermodynamics,[49] in addition to addressing more specific problems such as those of environmental pollution, conservation, energy resources, population, and the world food supply. Analogous ethics in the social sciences will be a major theme of chapters 5–8 below. But this transfer of concepts from science to ethics produces a fragmented set of "specialist ethics," corresponding to the interests and theoretical structures of particular disciplines, and hinders the formulation of general ethical systems. An example of this hindrance, which we consider in chapter 5, relates to the *scientific* inappropriateness of interpersonal comparison of utilities, which is not properly a restriction on using such comparison in ethical systems.

The use by sociologists of the category "social problems" as both a valuative category and an observable entity creates similar difficulties. The necessity to start from the society's definition of "social problems" or "social issues" points to a problem that Strauss highlighted in his criticism of modern social science. He suggested that "the logic on which the new political science is based may provide sufficient criteria of exactness; it does not provide objective criteria of relevance." But he also noted that "intelligent and informed citizens distinguish soundly between important and unimportant political matters," although "in the words of Burke, '. . . the generality of people are fifty years, at least, behind hand in their politics.' " [50] He suggested, therefore, that the problems considered important by *some* citizens may properly be taken as important for political scientists to study, but the latent democratic bias involved in the notion of "social problems" provides an inferior criterion for judging what problems are important.

The incompatibility of ethical systems among social science disciplines is illustrated by the difference between the economic ethic of satisfying preferences, regardless of their source, and the ethic of Skinner, which stresses the modification of preferences by reinforce-

49. See for example R. B. Lindsay's "thermodynamic imperative" in Margenau, *Ethics and Science*, p. 83.
50. Strauss, "Epilogue," in Storing, ed., *Essays on the Scientific Study of Politics*, p. 317.

ment.[51] The diversity among these "specialist ethics" is all the more apparent if we also consider the naturalistic ethics associated with the natural sciences.

Groups within a disciplinary association may consider that they have particular knowledge and responsibility related to a particular area of public policy.[52] They may begin to meet together at the annual meeting of their association. A natural extension of this activity is to form a "fringe association" that meets together with their professional association. Such has been the Federation of Atomic (now American) Scientists, the Society for the Psychological Study of Social Issues, and the Society for the Study of Social Problems. Such an association may publish a journal, and in the latter two instances its contents may conform to scholarly standards, so that it is part of the corresponding disciplinary literature. Though such journals do not ordinarily include philosophical analysis, they have in some measure combined concern for value-laden issues with disciplinary respectability. Case studies of the development of these journals and associations would give interesting information about the possibility of enlarging valuative discourse in the social science associations. Their leaders have undoubtedly encountered limits on the scope of their valuative activities, as well as risks of external criticism and internal factionalism, that have jeopardized the existence of their organizations.[53]

This combination of published contributions to a discipline with concern for valuative questions is impossible in the basic natural sciences, as well as in the social sciences when the author's contribution does not involve research. For speculation and the advocacy of policies, an increasing number of policy-oriented journals have been founded that are directed to informed citizens rather than members of a discipline. They contain few footnotes and are not taken seriously in the evaluation of their authors' standing in basic disciplines. From the

51. Skinner, *Walden Two* and *Beyond Freedom and Dignity;* we discuss this question further in chapter 7.
52. To some extent their notion of responsiblity may be subsumed under systematic ethics through the notion of a "social production function," which we discuss in chapter 7.
53. See Skura, "SSSP, Valuative Discourse and the Ambivalence of Sociologists." The effort to combine prestige in a discipline with valuative concern has been criticized by Coleman, however, as relatively useless to policy; *op. cit.,* p. 22.

viewpoint of the discipline's internal stratification system, contributing to such journals is at best a harmless diversion. Inclusion of citations to these journals on an author's bibliography is unlikely to influence his colleagues or his academic superiors to regard him more highly as a scholar. The time spent on these activities, though it may be a public service, is not a service to the author as a member of a discipline.[54]

It may be questioned whether contributions to journals aimed at the informed citizen *should* add to the author's stature in his discipline. But if *some* forum does not exist in which public and private motives conjoin to promote reasoned ethical discourse on public policy, this discourse may not be cultivated sufficiently. Our task in the following chapters will be to propose intellectual bases for this discourse, illustrate its possible content, and propose social structures that will encourage it.

54. The attainment of office in a professional association can, however, enhance his standing, and contributions to disciplinary "house organs," which address one's fellow scientists on matters outside their expertise yet of concern to them, lie somewhere between the two.

4 ETHICAL ARGUMENT AND THE NORMS OF SCIENTIFIC COMMUNICATION

Many of our difficulties in guiding the applications of science might be reduced by dealing with them systematically in the university. If we could discuss various alternative systems of valuation and their implications for policy choices, we might provide better foundations not only for academic and scientific discourse about means to these values, but also for the discourse of informed citizens.

If we are to deal with valuative questions in close relation to the social sciences—and indeed to deal with them in the university at all—we must justify the claim to some expertness and generality. If valuative assertions are regarded as mere expressions of individual emotion, without rational content or meaning, that claim is untenable. If, on the other hand, they are expressed in discourse that includes precise definitions, clear logical implications, and specifiable relations to our knowledge of the consequences of acts, then valuations may well have a justifiable place in the university, in close association with the social sciences.

Ethical Discourse in the Social Sciences

The social sciences now include—indeed, are pervaded by—valuations. The values involved range from approval or disapproval of specific states of affairs to the more general evaluation of alternative regimes in political philosophy. These values are largely compartmentalized along the lines of the conceptual schemes of particular disciplines.

Social scientists are often guided by valuative considerations in their choice of research problems, even though these considerations may lead away from the sort of guidance by paradigms that is common in natural science.[1] In addition, in spite of their ostensible quest for value-free discourse, social scientists continually use valuative terms in the statement of the problems and findings of their research. The characteristic process by which these valuations are introduced involves what Hare has called "secondarily evaluative terms." [2] Words like "industrious" or "courageous," he points out, normally have a prescriptive or evaluative meaning as well as a descriptive one. Some well-known terms of this sort in various social sciences include "stable democracy," "development," "per capita welfare expenditures," "real national income," "social mobility," "personal adjustment," "mental health," and (in a negative sense) "prejudice." We might perhaps add Marx's use of "exploitation" and "surplus value." Each of these terms has a valuative connotation, though with care we can speak of it as though it did not; but it also has a descriptive meaning, which corresponds to empirical observations and to usage in a disciplinary literature. Because of the descriptive meaning of such terms, propositions involving them are considered legitimate in the corresponding discipline, while the researcher can feel at the same time that his work is relevant to values with which he is concerned.

This indirect introduction of valuative terms, though it departs from the ideal of pure science,[3] does permit the scientist to exercise some choice in treating policy problems. It is insufficient for reasoned analysis of policy, however, because these secondarily evaluative terms are not related systematically to one another, or to primarily evaluative terms such as "good" and "right." It allows social scientists to deal with isolated aspects of policy, but not with coherent programs connecting various policies that relate to different secondarily evaluative terms. The narrowness and compartmentalization of disciplinary factual knowledge is thus compounded, for policy purposes, by a fragmented and unsystematized valuative vocabulary.

Some of the discourse of the social sciences is (at least in intention)

1. See Kuhn, *The Structure of Scientific Revolutions* (1970 ed.), p. 64. A complementary argument, that the social sciences are and should be guided by fundamental intellectual concerns, is presented in Riecken, "Social Sciences and Social Problems."

2. Hare, *Freedom and Reason*, p. 25. Little, in his *Critique of Welfare Economics*, p. 71, also distinguishes between pure descriptions, pure value judgments, and combinations of the two.

3. The argument for removing valuative discourse from social science has been made, e.g., in Kemeny, "A Philosopher Looks at Political Science."

free of ethical or valuative statements; other parts of it are more valuative, and a few explicitly involve discussion of ethical principles. The problem as to what norms should govern this ethical discussion is a continuing one; it has been recognized increasingly by philosophers in the last few decades, and the positivistic enthusiasm for clearing out metaphysical rubbish has given way, at least in ethics, to a renewed search for means of rational discussion.[4] This renewal of concern is a sign of health as regards the potential relation between the university and society. But in order for this concern to realize its full potentialities, it must be shared at least by the social sciences and perhaps by other disciplines as well.

If social scientists wish to engage in systematic valuative discourse, they must discard some of the assumptions involved in their treatment of it in the past. One source of difficulty is the assumption that evaluations are to be considered chiefly in light of their origins early in the evaluator's life history.[5] This approach not only transmutes the "ought" into an "is"—a doubtful advantage—but inclines social scientists to think of valuations as discrete and specific, rather than systematically organized. Insofar as we put forward particular value judgments on this basis, they will risk being inconsistent and restricted to the matter at hand.[6]

If we require consistency on the part of each evaluator, the policies recommended by any such system will be more coherent. But human fallibility may still leave errors in these individual systems, and even a highly systematized ethics, subscribed to by only a single individual, may have little effect. For both these reasons it will be useful if proponents of these individual systems compare them with one another by systematic critical procedures.[7]

Within the social sciences, the opportunity for such discourse is

4. See, for example, Flathman, *The Public Interest,* pp. x–xi; Gunnell, "Reason and Commitment"; Hunter, "The Possibility of a Rational Strategy of Moral Persuasion."
5. See Lasswell, "Policy Sciences."
6. This view leads to the same deemphasis on consistency as does intuitionism; see Rawls, *A Theory of Justice,* pp. 34ff. A parallel criticism is Lowi's advocacy of "juridical democracy" in *The End of Liberalism,* pp. 290–291.
7. The requirement of internal consistency is similar to Rawls's requirement of "reflective equilibrium," *op. cit.,* pp. 45–51; to Sidgwick's approach, as noted by Barry in *The Liberal Theory of Justice,* p. 5; and to Raiffa's requirement that personal preferences be rendered consistent, in *Decision Analysis.* The requirement of critical comparison resembles that of Albert in *Plädoyer für kritischen Rationalismus,* p. 16.

greatest in political science. This discipline has customarily included explicitly valuative discourse under the rubric of "political philosophy" or "normative political theory." I shall propose to extend this type of discourse through a set of rules for its conduct, related to the rules governing scientific communication, which may encourage reasoned discussion of the ethical foundations of public policy. Related problems have been considered by political thinkers of the past and are now discussed by philosophers. But while we can draw on this discussion, it is especially important to connect systematic ethics with policy-oriented research.

I shall propose to *model* ethical discourse on certain aspects of the discourse of natural science but to *conduct* it in close connection with the social science disciplines.[8] The norms we shall consider for ethical discussion are analogous to those that govern the discussion of scientific theories or hypotheses. Central to them will be the requirement, for a particular realm of interdisciplinary communication, that before anyone enter into ethical argument he first render his own ethical system clear, consistent, and general—modifying it in detail if necessary. This is analogous to the requirement in science that, before one tests a system of hypotheses, he must render them consistent. Argument deriving from such a system will be free from one common weakness of ethical argument: reliance on a collection of vague and mutually inconsistent principles that can be used for ad hoc rationalizations rather than genuinely pointing to a single clear implication in a particular case.

I shall first weigh the advantages and disadvantages of this approach, in comparison with linguistic usage in everyday life, science, law, and policy analysis. I shall then specify the proposed norms more precisely and review some types of existing ethical systems that might confront one another in this type of argument. Chapters 5–8 will present and compare ethical positions characteristic of various disciplines. The central discipline for this purpose will be economics, since its ethical discourse (even though not always recognized as such)

---

8. The rules of discourse I shall propose, although they have close parallels with those of scientific theory formulation, might also have been drawn from fields such as logic or law. The parallel with science is chosen in order to appeal to the reader who esteems scientific discourse, as well as to exemplify these norms in concrete detail.

is more systematic and precise than that of any other social science discipline.

If I am to make this proposal, I must specify ways in which ethical discourse can rise above the usage of everyday life and attain a certain degree of rationality. We can see the necessary transformations most clearly by contrasting the prevalent style of valuative discourse—in social science and in everyday life—with its alternatives.

Everyday Linguistic Usage

Valuative assertions in much of the discourse of social science have been made in passing, as it were, and thus without close attention to their clarity and consistency. As a result, they have some of the characteristics of the use of language in everyday life—a usage that is vague and contains numerous potential contradictions, especially in contrast with scientific usage.

In everyday usage, words and sentences are interpeted with the aid of information about their context, that is, about the speaker's past history, his motives, his present circumstances, and his relation to the audience. This type of interpretation is commonly used in both factual and valuative discourse. In everyday discussion of facts, we may be armed with a variety of approximate principles that apply in *ceteris paribus* fashion but would not do for scientific discussion of the same subjects.[9] In ordinary discussion of ethical matters, we also typically apply a variety of rules concerning right and wrong, but without advance specification as to what is right in situations where they conflict. By allowing flexibility in the meaning of words or statements, we manage to preserve the form of the statements themselves; we can thus feel more confidence in familiar statements, but at the cost of not being able to derive from them clear choices of policy.[10] The precision

9. "Scientific usage" and "everyday usage" are actually polar types; between them lie many actual types of discourse with various degrees of regulated precision. The distinction between science and common sense is discussed in Nagel, *The Structure of Science,* pp. 1–14.
10. This flexible persistence of everyday factual assertions is noted in Nagel, *loc. cit.;* a similar persistence in the valuative symbols of ideologies is noted in Sutton, Harris, Kaysen, and Tobin, *The American Business Creed,* pp. 264, 391.

of scientific usage, on the other hand, might require us more often to reject these statements or to modify them explicitly.

The discourse of everyday life has been studied extensively by Garfinkel, who has characterized some of the typical practices involved in everyday communication and interpretation. One such practice he refers to as "et cetera," that is, the assumption that a general principle carries with it the provision, accepted by members of the communicating group, that one can never enumerate *all* conditions under which the principle applies; there will always be others that can be added later. A second he denotes as "unless": a principle is expected to hold unless some later unspecified conditions obtain—the naming of the conditions, and the acceptance of their legitimacy, being reserved for a future occasion and the possible bases of exception being unnamed in advance. A third is "let it pass": an apparent exception or violation of a principle is observed, but it is not viewed as a true exception, for reasons that are sufficient to the participating group.[11]

Participants in a communication system typically carry with them a stock of implicit conditions for interpretation of messages or statements and for the generation of "legitimate exceptions." A trivial example is suggested by Bittner: "When inside a church, one normally uncovers his head, but it would be distinctly foolish to remove one's cast if one's skull were recently fractured."[12] Similar qualifications surround the exercise of political rights. In scientific discourse, interpretation of this kind also sometimes occurs: for example, the departure of a result from expectation may be small, the experimenter unskilled (as seen after the event), or the circumstances (as seen afterward) inappropriate for a true example of the principle to be observed.[13] But even though such interpretive principles are sometimes necessary, even among scientists, the normative regulation of scientific discourse reduces their incidence considerably. This possibility of

11. Garfinkel *Studies in Ethnomethodology,* ch. 1. This work derives in part from that of Alfred Schutz, a bibliography of whose work is given there in chapter 2.

12. Bittner, "Radicalism and the Organization of Radical Movements," p. 930. In law and philosophy, this property of principles is known as "defeasibility."

13. An example of interpretive work of this kind in natural science was the interpretation of the results of the Michelson-Morley Experiment as "zero ether drift" when initially they revealed a small non-zero value. See Polanyi, *Personal Knowledge,* pp. 12–14.

constraint may be due partly to the fact that science is practiced "on the side," apart from the practical considerations of everyday life.[14] The separation between the research laboratory and the world of practice, or between the academy and the world of political controversy, finds some justification in this relation between the separateness of science and its autonomous regulation of its discourse.

These studies of the transactions of ordinary life are both similar and dissimilar to the work of ordinary-language philosophers. They are similar in that they avoid the artificial for the real and focus on the domain of the commonplace. They differ, however, in the degree to which they see everyday discourse as a model from which significant conclusions can be drawn. In ordinary-language philosophy, it is sometimes considered that careful reflection on the usage of words will reveal a clarity of meaning that will be instructive—even refreshing in comparison with the artificiality of previous work in philosophy. Garfinkel's work, however, stresses another aspect of the procedures of everyday life: that they are intrinsically different from the ideal procedures of science, involve meanings that are subject to continuous modification, and are immersed in a context with a past history and a future perspective.

The rise of ordinary-language philosophy has helped to rescue ethical discourse from the neglect it suffered in the heyday of positivism and has stimulated linguistic analysis in legal and political philosophy.[15] It has not, however, always conduced to the development of new and more precise linguistic usages. Most linguistic philosophers (perhaps like Socrates in the Platonic dialogues) consider that the close examination of languages as they *are* used is both necessary and desirable for a clear understanding of words. The languages to which they direct attention, however, are not usually the technical ones created by natural or social scientists. Still, terms from these technical languages move into ordinary language, whether through the spread of technical devices or through the publicizing of specialists' categories such as "power structure." It seems hard to justify excluding these

14. See Bittner, *op. cit.*, p. 931; Kuhn, *op. cit.*, p. 164.
15. For an introduction to this approach see Chappell, ed., *Ordinary Language*. Applications to law and politics include Hart, *The Concept of Law;* Pitkin, *The Concept of Representation;* and Flathman, *op. cit.*

new elements of language from study, except for the difficulty of mastering multiple specialties. But once we study them in comparison with previous usage, it is only one step further to ask which is *better* to use and under what circumstances.

In defense of a position similar to mine, Mates has argued that the dialogue intended to discover the meaning of a word can often alter that meaning. Cavell, in reply, has suggested that the contextual specification of a meaning can end in a finite time and that its end point may be a set of specified rules or directions.[16] My view here is simply that we should make every effort to write down those rules or directions for applying terms before we enter into a serious argument about the ethical foundations of policy.

My position differs from both that of Garfinkel and that of the ordinary-language philosophers, in that it stresses the artificial reconstruction of meanings of words—not limitless or arbitrary, but departing from the meanings of everyday life if these meanings need to be changed. In another sense my position is intermediate between the two just described. It sees the contextual limitation of everyday meanings as partly remediable by the norms of scientific communication and thus departs from the pessimism that one might derive from Garfinkel's approach. On the other hand, it sees the meanings of everyday discourse as intrinsically ambiguous and its principles as potentially contradictory. It thus despairs of the efforts to discover clear and consistent meanings of major terms in social science and ethics from everyday usage. They are to be created, not simply discovered. Yet if clear and consistent meaning for "right" or "ought" *could* be found in everyday usage, it would not be barred from discussion by the rules I propose.

The Guidance of Discourse by Norms of Communication

The linguistic usage of ordinary life is constrained by a complex system of norms, and the uses of words in the published discourse of an academic discipline are further constrained. But the valuative

16. Mates, "On the Verification of Statements About Ordinary Language," Cavell, "Must We Mean What We Say?" reprinted (the latter in revised version) in Chappell, ed., *op. cit.* The relevant pages in this volume are 73 and 89.

aspect of the discourse of the social sciences, which is less constrained than their factual discourse, requires still further guidance or regulation. As models for such guidance we may consider more highly regulated realms of discourse such as those of science or law. These types of discourse stand apart from the discourse of ordinary life in several attributes such as the use of precise definitions, stress on written rather than oral communication, and limitation of meaning to what has been specified in advance. They exemplify general rules of reasoning but embody them in particular human associations.

In considering science in this way, we single out another of its diverse aspects for attention. For various purposes one may consider its empirical reliability, the elegance of its theories, its progress and change, or the compartmentalization of its specialties. But for the guidance of ethical argument, its most relevant feature is that it constitutes a regulated realm of discourse. In such discourse, a statement can be given a precise and delimited interpretation by any of a large body of hearers or readers, without being supplemented, interpreted, or explained. For example, a scientific article published by an unknown but properly trained author can direct the activities of similarly trained readers so that its assertions are testable in their laboratories. And while the testing procedure cannot be reduced to the determinacy of a computer program, it still involves a high degree of "predictiveness," that is, identification of a specified set of activities and observations from written directions.

This degree of predictiveness is attained in scientific discourse because in any scientific discipline there exists a group of trained specialists who communicate with one another about a special subject matter, largely in writing, under particular normative constraints. Such a group uses a specialized vocabulary and syntax—in its ideal form mathematical or logical. The propositions they assert are set off from context. Specific citation of previous work combines with precision of definition to reduce the chance that similar propositions will be phrased in different terms without systematic relation to one another. The procedures to be used for identifying an instance of a concept are also specified in precise ways known to readers who have been properly trained. These constraints on communication, having proved useful in the natural sciences, have been proposed for the social sciences as well. The social sciences have thus been led, in varying degrees, to state more of their hypotheses in formal propositions and mathematical expressions.[17]

A different but related type of constraint is observed in legal discourse. A codified body of law, together with a specialized profession whose members interpret it, allows a type of predictiveness that might not exist under other forms of the administration of justice.[18] Thus rational law, like the hypotheses of science, provides a relatively precise directive as to how forms of words are to be applied in particular situations. And even though this precision is not complete, it is far greater than in ordinary discourse that is unaided by such systematic bodies of codified material known to groups of experts.

Discourse that is regulated or constrained in these ways should not, however, be expected to be perfectly objective, in the sense that it could be reduced to a computational algorithm. The aspiration to a completely objective scientific language would be utopian, even within disciplines whose communication is most highly constrained and "predictive." In the law, for example, while codification and professional training have taken us far from the intuitive judgments on particular cases in simpler societies, students of legal reasoning still argue forcefully that computerized justice is both impossible and undesirable.[19] And in statistics, the domain of objective decision procedures, Tukey has argued that the good investigator's judgment, particularly when choosing among clearly formalized techniques of analysis, is frequently superior to inflexible decision procedures.[20]

A second qualification concerning the development of such constrained systems of ethical discourse is that the precision required may take time to obtain. Short-run practical decisions may have to be made within a different realm of discourse—linked to ethical theory, never-

17. See Kruskal, ed., *Mathematical Sciences and Social Sciences*.

18. See Rheinstein, ed., *Max Weber on Law in Economy and Society*, chs. 8. 9. 11. Legal terms, however, can change in meaning in a way that scientific terms cannot. The analogy between the legal community and a scientific community, as a justification of valuative discourse, is pointed out in Ward, *What's Wrong with Economics?*, ch. 15.

19. On "Khadi-justice" see Rheinstein, *op. cit.*, p. 244. On legal reasoning see Gottlieb, *The Logic of Choice*, p. 16; Hart, *op. cit.*, pp. 125–127; Levi, *An Introduction to Legal Reasoning*.

20. John W. Tukey, in lecture at the University of Chicago, June 12, 1969; personal communication, January 23, 1970.

theless, as applied science is to fundamental science. A separation of roles between basic and applied science has long been recognized. In the relations between science and government, this parallels Price's "spectrum from truth to power"; [21] but it need not and should not be at the same time a distinction between value-free and value-guided discourse.

A third problem related to precision in ethics is that even if we could clearly specify the conditions under which one state of affairs was better than another, we might have difficulty knowing whether these conditions were met in the real world. This is a common problem for ethics of consequences; many social groups try to deal with it by stating that certain acts or policies are right or wrong *regardless* of their consequences. In political science, this difficulty has encouraged a stress on the value of observable political *processes* rather than on the less certain outcomes of policies. The emphasis on political processes has been accompanied in recent analyses of the American political system by a doctrine that the interrelations of groups tend to produce beneficent results through a sort of "invisible hand" mechanism. But as Schick has pointed out, the process approach and the accompanying pluralist outlook have been unnecessarily apologetic for "outcomes resulting from the established process." [22] For this reason, an effort toward precision in the evaluation of policy seems worthwhile.

The Norms of Scientific Communication

We wish to transfer to valuative discourse some of the norms that a well-organized scientific community imposes on its own communications. The norms that we wish to transfer are those that are explicitly held by scientists but exclude (as inapplicable to ethics itself) the important requirement of repeatable empirical tests. We therefore stress logical clarity, logical consistency, and generality, [23] whose meaning I must now explain. To these we add another preva-

21. Price, *The Scientific Estate,* ch. 5.
22. Schick, "Systems Politics and Systems Budgeting." The process approach is advocated in Lindblom, *The Intelligence of Democracy.*
23. Parsons, *The Social System,* p. 335. See also chapter 1 above.

lent norm: that each contributor to the literature take into account what has gone before and not capriciously restate or contradict previous contributions.[24]

Our first concern is with the norms that impinge on the individual scientist or scholar in reporting his work, rather than with those that connect a community of scholars. I shall later propose the development of such a community, overlapping the various social sciences, but I am now concerned with norms governing a single communication that might enter into such a larger system.

To advocate the transfer of the norms of science to other domains implies that these norms have contributed to desirable features of scientific communication. But this argument requires a distinction between empirical discovery, on the one hand, and the coordination of the activities of scientists, on the other. It is only the latter advantage that we hope to transfer.

Even in natural science, the norms we shall consider are more important for communicating discoveries than for making them initially. Individual scientists in every generation might be able to repeat the discoveries of their predecessors independently with equal inspiration, with no particular provisions for scientific communication. But the cumulation and interrelation of these discoveries, and the guiding of scientists in distant laboratories to the same crucial problems in a given period, require precise and impersonal communication that defines the important problems and tells how the previous results have been reached. The norms of scientific communication may thus be justified not simply as a key to scientific progress, but also as an orderly means of coordinating the activities of persons in various parts of the world and of building on the findings of the past.[25]

The problems of applying these norms in ethics are considerable, as actual ethical discourse often departs from them widely, and the reference point of objective observation is absent. Nevertheless, these problems are mitigated by a possible restriction of ethical discussion. In clarifying our ethical systems and comparing one with another, we

24. The conservative aspects of this last norm are brought out in Kendall, "The Open Society and Its Fallacies," p. 979.
25. See Ziman, *Public Knowledge*.

can restrict ourselves to a realm of "pure ethics" by assuming that we have all the necessary information about the choices under consideration. Ambiguities and conflicts in ethical systems can thus be examined with the aid of real or hypothetical choice situations in which there need be no disagreement as to the facts. The ethical systems thus refined can then be applied to real problems of practical decision; there we shall be confronted with the usual problems of characterizing a situation, or of predicting the future, but these problems will not contribute to the ambiguity of the ethics itself.[26]

This separation of ethical argument from the establishment of facts is both logically convenient and well adapted to the specialization of closed domains of academic discourse. I am proposing it within an organization of the disciplines that would bring ethics and science far closer together than they now are, but other proposals have gone farther toward merging the two domains. Easton has proposed that valuative discourse be conducted through the comparison of ideal political systems, embodying factual and valuative arguments together.[27] Dewey's approach, which in this respect resembles Marxism, views valuation as immersed in action rather than as amenable to abstract discussion.[28] And Mannheim characterized a separate "theory of ends" as embodying the particular perspective of the liberal-democratic bourgeoisie.[29] Thus the separation I propose is not the only way to connect valuations and factual information about society in policy choice, but it does derive from an analogy with theoretical and experimental natural science.

We take natural science as an example, therefore, not to banish ethical discourse from social science, but to encourage this discourse under constraints similar to those of scientific discourse. The con-

26. This approach is also proposed in Rescher, *Distributive Justice,* p. 19. A similar distinction is made in Levi, *op. cit.,* p. v, between appellate cases and those that pass through the fact-finding stage of the trial court. A descriptive account of legal or ethical reasoning would have to include the latter, but there may still be advantages in setting off the ascertainment of facts for separate consideration. We shall practice this separation below, especially in chapters 6–8, in an effort to avoid factual controversies about the actual features of polity, personality, and society.

27. Easton, *The Political System,* pp. 230ff.

28. Kolakowski, *The Alienation of Reason,* pp. 163–165.

29. Mannheim, *Ideology and Utopia,* pp. 108–110.

straints that I propose are for trained academic specialists, not necessarily for the practitioner or the layman.[30] There are certainly many
occasions when the everyday style of communication is more econom-
ical, less embarrassing, and esthetically more pleasing than scientific
communication about the same matters. But a major function of the
academy and its disciplines is to deal in general principles that *direct*
our attention to particular matters and do not simply adjust themselves,
with a flexible ambiguity, to new situations.

We now define the norms of scientific communication more fully,
by contrasting them with their opposites. "Clarity" refers to the capacity of a verbal or symbolic expression to indicate precisely those
observations or actions to which it would and would not apply, independently of the speaker, the listener, or subsequent explanation.
"Consistency" refers to the capacity of a set of principles to withstand
searching scrutiny and to reveal no instances in which its implications
are contradictory.[31] "Generality" refers to breadth of application,
perhaps in relation to economy of expression if this latter norm of scientific theorizing is to apply.

For our present purpose, the opposite of "clarity" is dependence on
context.[32] A word or sentence whose meaning is continually contingent on a succession of explanations related to the particular speaker
and audience, their past histories and their intentions, is highly dependent on its context. If a scientific experiment apparently contradicted a
general hypothesis, but we were able to remove this contradiction by
reinterpreting the hypothesis, the interpretation would be dependent on
the context. While such reinterpretations do occur in the exact sciences, the principles of reinterpretation in those disciplines are less
peculiar to the occasion and more clearly known in advance than in
everyday usage. In the social sciences, the opportunity for particular
reinterpretations is greater.

The opposite of consistency would appear to be inconsistency. But

30. They may, however, affect the discourse of practitioners or citizens through education.
31. See Popper, *The Logic of Scientific Discovery,* pp. 91–92.
32. I ignore further differences such as that between ambiguity and vagueness. The
clarity of scientific propositions does depend on an educational context shared by a community of specialists but much less on the extended verbal text in which an equation is
embedded.

inconsistencies are less evident when they are concealed in the indirect implications of a set of principles. The assertion of a statement, followed immediately by its opposite, is an obvious inconsistency, but what about such an assertion a hundred pages later in a book? Or an assertion which according to dictionary definitions (not superseded by special definitions in the text) would negate an earlier assertion? Or—and this is the most important condition—a principle whose implications in some particular case, not brought explicitly to our attention, contradict those of another principle used in the argument? The scientific norms involved here are those of precise formulation and of seeking out extreme or limiting cases to put our principles to a severe test.[33] They assume that principles apply without restriction, unless restrictions have been explicitly stated in advance. We accordingly require ethical argument to seek out the most difficult cases, even hypothetical ones, and to assume that stated principles apply to them. This is the opposite of a procedure common in everyday life: to refrain from seeking out exceptional cases until they are presented to us and then to explain or justify the exceptions with ad hoc principles, themselves drawn from a repertoire of principles not systematically constrained to consistency. It is also the opposite of the practice of the U.S. Supreme Court, which avoids ruling on general principles when it can resolve a case by more specific ones. These customary practices no doubt reduce dissension, but for the fundamental (and properly "academic") ethical discourse that underlies policy, they seem inappropriate.

If we are to test the consistency of a set of principles by seeking difficult cases and latent conflicts, the principles themselves must be clear. The possibility of multiple interpretations must be minimized, for if they exist, we cannot easily discover those cases in which principles conflict and require modification. The principles must also be general, so as to cover the widest possible range of actual or conceiv-

33. Precise formulation is taken for granted in the theories of natural science. In economics this requirement has also been transferred to ethics; Rothenberg notes that a function of welfare economics is "to seek to resolve . . . inconsistency in values," in *The Measurement of Social Welfare,* p. 327. In sociology, the norm of consistency is stressed in the construction of formal models; see Duncan, "Path Analysis: Sociological Examples," p. 7. The seeking out of hard cases is also a central theme of Popper's argument in *The Logic of Scientific Discovery.*

able situations and at the same time to increase the chance that we will discover inconsistency among them.

A Normative Meta-Ethics

The rules which I shall specify for ethical argument, modeled after the norms of scientific communication, may be considered a normative meta-ethics. Typically, meta-ethics deals with problems of higher abstraction involved in ethical discourse, such as "What is the logic of moral reasoning and of reasoning about value?" [34] But while discussion in this field usually limits itself to analysis and observation, I wish to *prescribe* certain rules for the conduct of ethical argument; in this respect I am asserting valuations analogous to the prescriptive norms of science. [35] These rules themselves require justification or at least persuasion, but to avoid an infinite regress and get on with the job, I simply appeal to those who esteem this type of discourse to join in.

The rules I propose are as follows:

1. Ethical argument is to be conducted between the proponents of ethical systems that are specified in writing in advance; we shall call such systems "ethical hypotheses." [36] This specification is intended to support the norm of clarity and can include definitions specified in ways other than those of ordinary usage, statements of principles set off from context, and logical or mathematical symbols. We consider the case of only two discussants at a time, though the procedures may be generalized.

2. Each discussant shall have equal opportunity to argue for his own system, and against the opposing one, by pointing out presumed

34. Frankena, *Ethics,* p. 79.

35. A disparity between the two has been noted and criticized in Alan Gewirth, "Positive 'Ethics' and Normative 'Science' ' ''; see also his "Metaethics and Moral Neutrality," and Lenk, "Der 'Ordinary Language Approach' und die Neutralitätsthese der Metaethik."

36. This term has been used by many other writers to indicate the tentativeness of ethical formulations; some have also stressed their clarity and consistency. For Bentham's usage see Baumgardt, *Bentham and the Ethics of Today,* pp. 529–530, 571. For its use by pragmatists see Feibleman, *op. cit.,* p. 367, and Brecht, *op. cit.,* p. 194. A similar notion was expressed in Einstein, *Relativity–A Richer Truth,* foreword.

shortcomings in the other system.[37] These shortcomings can be of several kinds:

    a. Lack of generality. The proposed system fails to apply to a choice about which both discussants have moral convictions [38] and to which the critic's system does apply.

    b. Internal inconsistency. The proposed system makes contradictory prescriptions in a situation suggested by the critic, in which the critic's system is self-consistent.

    c. Inconsistency with presumably shared moral convictions. The proposed system makes a prescription which, in a specified "conflict situation," conflicts with moral convictions presumably shared by the discussants, while the critic's system does not lead to such conflict.

We shall refer later to these bases of argument as the rules of *generality, consistency,* and *convictions,* respectively. It is expected that an internally consistent ethical system, specified in this way, will not be consistent with all the particular moral convictions of its proponents; the aim of this procedure is to test whether the system must be modified, or whether particular convictions must be suppressed, as a basis for further argument.

    3. After each such opportunity to present conflict situations, the proponent of the ethical system under criticism shall decide whether he wishes to alter his ethical system or make the choice dictated by it.[39]

    Ethical argument conducted in this way resembles some argumentative procedures that have been proposed previously and differs from others. Ayer argued, for example, that ethical argument reduces to

37. The symmetry and reciprocity here reflect a general feature of social norms, discussed in chapter 8 below.

38. By "moral convictions" I mean any beliefs that can be expressed in terms of "ought," "right," or their equivalents. A rule requiring generality is relevant to the controversy about cardinal economic welfare and interpersonal comparison; see Harsanyi, "Cardinal Welfare, Individualistic Ethics, and Interpersonal Comparisons of Utility." The problem of lack of generality is also treated in Rescher, *op. cit.,* p. 18.

39. In practice it is important to see the ways in which ethical systems might be altered. If argument takes place while Rawls's "reflective equilibrium" is being reached, we might expect gradual changes ramifying through a system. But if the opposing systems are fully crystallized, changes may occur only in all-or-none fashion. See Kress, "The Web and the Tree."

factual and logical argument, if it has any meaning at all. These two elements do both enter under our rules. The possibility of contradictory prescriptions relevant to the rule of consistency may result not only from logic, but also from empirical conditions. An inverse relation between two policy variables that produce the same effect, or scarcity of resources that makes it difficult to attain two goals at the same time, impose such restrictions. But this factual relation concerns intermediate or lower-level goals used in practical decision making as surrogates for the more general desiderata specified in ethical systems.

The basic "data" of this sort of argument are particular shared ethical convictions. When the disputants diverge radically in these convictions, agreement may be impossible. Moral convictions are simply not as invariant among persons as the observations of science. Minor disagreements, embedded in a broader context of agreement on general values and modes of argument, may be resolvable by the disputants' modifying their own convictions. This process of changing one's valuations or moral convictions blends into the general social processes by which we acquire and change values. Thus in actuality, ethical argument (more broadly conceived) may involve persuasion, role playing, education, manipulation, seduction, or coercion. We must recognize that these processes occur and that the norms of particular societies also change historically, but the type of argument proposed here does not include all possible processes of change.

The variation among individuals' values derives from many sources, but even in a perfectly integrated society it might not disappear. A large, complex social system, with many tasks to undertake, might well develop social differentiation, or factoring of tasks. In order for participants to be motivated to perform these particular tasks, they might have to be especially devoted to their tasks. And for some of the norms of the society, if there was considerable motivation for deviance, it might be socially necessary to instill them as absolute prohibitions. Thus it is not surprising that diverse ethical convictions exist and that they are resistant to change.

The status of these ethical "data" is an important point of controversy when we set the terms of ethical argument. One widespread view, which I reject here, is that they are to be treated like scientific data and that ethical theories must accord with them or account for them. This tacit premise appears, for example, in an argument by Hart: "Even in a modern society . . . , calculations of harmfulness to others do not *account for* the importance attached to moral regulations of sexual behavior." [40] It has also been used by Rawls: "It is doubtful whether the effect on the practice ever weighs in the particular case; certainly it cannot *account for* the strictness of the obligation where it fails to obtain. It seems to follow that a utilitarian *account* of the obligation to keep promises cannot be successfully carried out." [41]

The same sort of assumption appears in Graaff's analysis of the bases of theoretical welfare economics; in connection with the agreement required on social welfare functions, he writes: "Can [such a function] be *formed?* That is to say, can we somehow distill the various ethical beliefs of the members of a community into a consistent system, suitable for our purposes and capable of telling us how to 'add' one man's welfare to another's?" [42] The position implied in our rules is rather that expressed by Smart: "[In] ethics should we not typically test particular judgments by means of general principles, instead of, as in science, typically testing general principles by means of their practical consequences?" [43] Meehan also suggests that

> A well-developed ethic will be built around a central core of purposes, assumptions, postulates or principles that can serve as a yardstick for judging the acceptability of other proposed principles or purposes. Any principle or standard, once accepted, limits the acceptability of other principles, given the rule of contradiction. When principles conflict one or another must give way.

He prefaces this remark with the statement that "The goal of the discussion [in the book] is to bring normative discussion and choice under rational control." However, he departs from our proposed meta-ethics (as well as from the procedures of welfare economics) earlier when he writes, "Value judgments refer to genuine empirical situations. Hypothetical or imaginary cases cannot be judged." [44]

40. Hart, *op. cit.*, p. 170. My emphasis.
41. Rawls, "Two Concepts of Rules," pp. 15–16. My emphasis.
42. Graaff, *Theoretical Welfare Economics*, pp. 10–11.
43. Smart, "The Methods of Ethics and the Methods of Science," p. 346.
44. Meehan, *Value Judgment and Social Science*, pp. 138, 137, 43.

A principal reason for instituting these rules is to eliminate a common tactic in ethical argument, which appears to militate against consistent ethical systems but in fact derives from an inconsistent basis. This tactic is to point out that a proposed ethical system conflicts, in a particular situation, with a shared moral conviction. But since it is unlikely that all these shared moral convictions can themselves be reconciled with any consistent ethical system, this tactic gives the critic an unfair advantage. Once it is recognized that criticisms must themselves be justified in terms of a consistent system, the excessive requirements implied by this type of argument will be removed.[45]

Ethical systems are not often compared in the way I propose; ad hoc criticism, based on particular convictions rather than on a consistent system, is far more frequent. The consistent formulation of ethical systems sharply restricts the bases of criticism; examples are various ethics of maximization or hierarchies of principles with strict orders of precedence. The central concepts of such systems may vary; for example, properties of states of affairs ('goodness'), of acts ('rightness'), or of persons ('virtues') may be stressed.[46] But whatever central concept is chosen, other valuative terms must be related to it in a determinate way. One of the chief tasks in formulation of an ethical system will thus be a reduction in the multiplicity of independent valuative terms.

Whether this is an advantage may be debated. Many elements in the Western tradition of political thought run counter to my proposals—from Aristotle's admonition not to try to specify ethical terms too precisely to the tradition of rights that are considered to be plural

45. See Rawls, *A Theory of Justice,* pp. 34–40, on intuitionism. We not only expect the dictates of the moral conscience to be mutually contradictory but continue to suspect this even when the dictates of a discipline are superposed on them. Thus I shall contend (chapter 5) that Arrow's "impossibility theorem" is a special instance of this general phenomenon, in which economists' convictions about cardinality, interpersonal comparison, and proper professional conduct play a central role. The observation that particular moral convictions, as we have learned them, or "sympathy and antipathy," ought not be an ultimate and unshakable criterion for judgment of ethical systems was made by Bentham in *Principles of Morals and Legislation,* pp. 15–17. See also MacKaye, "Convictionism and Non-Convictionism."

46. See Abraham Edel, *Science and the Structure of Ethics,* pp. 50ff. The possible emphasis on characteristics of persons might also direct our attention to ethical systems prevalent among psychologists or psychotherapists.

absolutes. My argument has derived more from the values of science than from that tradition, but it is aimed, of course, at remedying a major defect of past approaches based on science.

I propose to emulate scientific discourse, therefore, in imposing on ethical systems an uncommon degree of clarity and consistency. I do this by admitting into ethical argument the consideration of hypothetical choice—situations designed to expose the latent contradictions in ethical systems or their conflicts with the particular ethical convictions of their proponents. But this insistence on generality is not merely an academic diversion. It may increase the applicability of ethical systems to future problems, as well as those widely recognized at present. In an age of social and technological change, it is especially important to anticipate future problems before they give rise to major dislocations.

The parallel between this proposed type of argument and the internal criticism of science is not, of course, complete. In addition to the different role played by the "data" in the two realms, my proposed argumentation also lacks the premium on originality found in science. In the proposed ethical discourse, only the refinement and reconciliation of existing valuations is to be conducted. The participants may seek new relations among them, but they do not seek new "data" as the scientist does. The elaboration of the implications of given ethical systems, as in theorems of welfare economics, may constitute original contributions, but novel discoveries like those of empirical science are not to be expected.[47]

Having stated the rules I propose for ethical discourse, I shall proceed in part II to elaborate and compare some existing ethical systems from the social sciences that give promise of internal consistency and thus of entering into the proposed argument. Such a selection cannot be exhaustive but may serve as an invitation for proponents of other views to advance other systematic formulations. The bases of other such "ethical hypotheses" undoubtedly exist in the literature of social

47. This carries with it a possibility of eventual decline of innovation in ethical discourse; see Ben-David, *The Scientist's Role in Society,* pp. 28–30, 38, on the stagnation of Greek and Confucian philosophic discourse. If, however, the constantly changing problems of policy choice are combined with ethics, as I propose in chapter 9, the problems will at least be different.

science and philosophy, and some, like legal systems, may be complex and detailed rather than simple in form. I shall emphasize ethical systems closely related to the social sciences. This emphasis leads to several biases of selection. First, the ethical systems considered will be linked to the conceptual schemes of particular disciplines; I see this as a shortcoming, to be reduced by their mutual confrontation.

A second bias relates to my omission of ethics of rights, duties, or other justifications based on the rightness of actions in themselves and apart from their consequences. These ethical justifications are of the "deontological" type, in distinction to "teleological" arguments, which deal only with the consequences of acts. Although this type of argument is widespread in philosophy, political science, and ordinary discourse, it appears to resist systematic and consistent formulation. The rules I have specified therefore militate against arguments of this type, insofar as they derive from a set of unsystematized rights or duties. Some readers may consider this a shortcoming of my rules; others, of deontological ethics.[48] We thus deal with ethics of consequences, or teleological ethics. Even if deontological ethics could be formulated consistently, social scientists would have far less to do in judging rightness or wrongness under them. Under this constraint, the ethics of social science compare not merely acts but the expected states of the world that result from them.

Individualistic and Relational Ethical Systems

A third bias in my choice of ethical systems is toward "individualistic" systems, in contrast to "relational" systems.[49] Individualistic ethical systems, in this sense, are based on values associated with individuals (choices, experiences, personal development, etc.), combined into a "social welfare function"; discussion of ethical systems of this type has been conducted largely in philosophy and economics, though some has also taken place in political science.[50] Relational

48. See Braybrooke, *Three Tests for Democracy.*
49. Ethics of consequences might also include holistic supraindividual goals, such as social cohesion or cultural persistence.
50. I use "individualistic" in a very different sense from that employed in Buchanan and Tullock, *The Calculus of Consent,* pp. 11ff. Bergson has proposed that social welfare functions be compared in philosophic criticism; see his *Essays in Normative Economics,* p. 47.

ethical systems consider the basic elements of the good or of welfare to reside not simply in individuals' preferences or experiences, but in relations such as those of power (in a negative sense), freedom, or reciprocity between individuals.

Individualistic systems thus include various forms of utilitarianism, with its notion of sums of happiness over persons. They also include the Pareto criterion, which is indifferent to distributive considerations or the relative welfares of individuals. In chapters 5–8 we shall compare only systems of this type. Insofar as relations or comparisons between individuals are viewed as producing values or disvalues that reside in particular individuals, these effects may be subsumed under individualistic ethics. Thus many external effects (in economics), comparisons with reference groups, or norms that may be formed (in sociology) can be treated in this way.

Even if the basic elements of good or welfare are associated with individuals, it is also possible to combine them in a social welfare function that includes relations between the welfares of various individuals. Thus in an ethic of distributive justice, Rescher considers the standard deviation of the distribution of individual welfares as a negative contribution to the social welfare function, and Rawls's difference principle concentrates attention on the least favored persons. A general family of ethical systems, based on individual "utilities" but varying between simple utilitarianism and Rawls's difference principle, has also been described by Alexander.[51]

In Rawls's presentation of the theory of justice, both his meta-ethical notion of "reflective equilibrium" and his substantive ethics deserve serious consideration by social scientists.[52] Rawls's position does not arise from the concepts of empirical social science but has much in common with a tradition in political philosophy. He also compares his theory of justice with utilitarianism, and this comparison deserves to be considered in parallel with those we shall make here.

Our subsequent discussion will be concerned more with alternative definitions of the good, or of welfare, for individuals than with the relations between individual welfares in social welfare functions.

51. Rescher, *op cit.*, pp. 33, 35; Rawls, *op. cit.*, pp. 75ff.; Alexander, "Social Evaluation through Notional Choice."
52. Rawls, *op. cit.*, and see MacRae, "Justice, Normative Discourse, and Sociology."

These alternative definitions of individual welfare correspond to the central valuative concepts of various individualistic ethics. Any consistent ethical system, if it includes various value terms, relates them to one another in a precise fashion; one way to accomplish this is by defining them all in terms of a central function or quantity which is to be maximized. When this approach is used, there is effectively only a single scale on which acts (or states of affairs) are compared. The base values for such scales vary among various versions of individualistic ethics.

The Benthamite criterion of "happiness" designates one type of value, presumably related to the *experiences* of individuals,[53] though Bentham's addition of a hedonistic psychology, taking pleasure and pain to be central motives as well as valued qualities, confused the issue by implying that motives, or choices in advance of action, were simply equivalent to experiences felt afterward. An alternative type of value is that of *choice* or *preference,* which differs from "happiness" in stressing more the opportunity of the individual to make his own mistakes. An ethics of preference is perhaps more egalitarian in its implications, less likely to lead to technocratic solutions, than is an ethics of happiness. On the other hand, the sovereignty of individual preferences is likely to elevate unreflective choice to the level of reflective or expert choice and to deemphasize education and leadership.[54]

Within economics, the special field of welfare economics has developed and is centered about the choices of individuals rather than their experiences. Since choices are central to the analysis of economic behavior, there is a certain disciplinary convenience in assuming that choices or preferences are the proper elements to be considered in policy evaluation. We shall treat this field in detail in chapter 5. Economists have also contributed to the development of cost-benefit analysis, in which monetary values for various individuals are combined in ways that preferences cannot be. The resulting systems of valuation tend to be specific to the problem at hand, whether it be the evaluation

53. A systematic argument for the location of intrinsic value in experience was made by Lewis in *An Analysis of Knowledge and Valuation;* see esp. p. 387.
54. The distinction between preference and welfare is discussed in Braybrooke, *op. cit.,* pp. 121–145.

of military alternatives, water resources policy, or educational policy. The underlying principles are more general, however, and we shall compare them with other ethical systems in chapter 5 as well.

Relational ethical systems are those that find their basic elements of value in *relations* between individuals, such as power, freedom, or reciprocity; we assume that these are ultimate values, rather than merely means to individualistic values. To apply such ethical systems to particular choices we must consider values deriving directly from relations between individuals rather than values associated with individuals separately. Although I shall not treat such systems in the chapters that follow, reciprocity is an important element in social norms (chapter 8). The basic notion that persons similarly situated should be treated similarly and should treat one another similarly is an important feature of norms and of ethics generally. It is thus a significant ingredient of many ethical arguments that might be conducted under my proposed rules.

It is not always clear, however, whether reciprocity enters as an aspect of meta-ethics or of substantive ethics. My proposed meta-ethical rules explicitly place the participants on an equal footing, by allowing reciprocal criticism. Similarly, the formation of a social contract may be seen, as in Rawls's "original position," as a preliminary process through which we must pass in order to arrive at a substantive ethic. But it is difficult to show that reciprocal meta-ethical procedures will inevitably lead to substantive ethics that are reciprocal or egalitarian. The Hobbesian social contract, giving rise to a powerful sovereign, is one counterexample.

Notions akin to reciprocity have, however, entered into a number of relational ethics. To illustrate this type of ethic, I may suggest several that have been formulated, so that they might be compared under my meta-ethical rules. These examples, although related to political philosophy, do not do justice to the history of this field, whose existence provides an important legitimation for valuative discourse in political science. It is to be hoped that ethical arguments under my proposed rules will include the ethical positions of major political philosophers, either as they themselves stated their views or as others have interpreted them.

One type of relational ethical system that might enter these comparisons was presented by Dahl in *A Preface to Democratic Theory*. In this volume he presented systematic versions of justifications for various aspects of democracy. The central terms in these justifications are sometimes relational and sometimes individualistic. For "Madisonian democracy," he considers the central term to be "tyranny," a relational term; for "populistic democracy," it is "equality" [55]—a relation between the preferences of individuals. In the latter case the base value is individualistic. The condition of equality provides a basis for interpersonal comparison and converts a system otherwise resembling Pareto-type welfare economics into a more generally applicable one. Dahl takes another step in this direction later when he examines the implications of considering preferences that differ in "intensity"— a possibility that also leads toward a cardinal and Benthamite ethics. The problems of converting any such general ethical system into evaluations of particular political institutions are formidable, but they are not our concern here. Rather, I wish to stress Dahl's comparison between particularly relational values and more nearly individualistic criteria. This debate, again, confronting political and economic ethics, might be conducted according to the rules I have proposed.

A second relational ethical system is that proposed by Bay in *The Structure of Freedom*. In this volume he proposes three definitions of aspects of an individual's freedom: (a) degree of harmony between basic motives and overt behavior; (b) the relative absence of perceived external restraints on individual behavior; and (c) the relative absence of unperceived external restraints on individual behavior.[56] To be discussed according to our rules, these three values would have to be reconciled with one another, but our present purpose is to illustrate the types of central values that have been proposed in ethical systems. The first of Bay's three values is akin to certain values that have been proposed by psychologists and relates primarily to personality structure. The second and third are more relational; to assess their attainment requires examination of the constraints placed on individuals by one another.

A third ethical system of this type has been proposed by Gewirth.[57]

55. Dahl, *A Preface to Democratic Theory*, pp. 6, 37.
56. Bay, *The Structure of Freedom*, pp. 83, 88, 95.
57. Gewirth, "Categorial Consistency in Ethics."

On the basis of a logical argument—a meta-ethics different from the one I propose—he puts forward the "Principle of Categorial Consistency [PCC]: Apply to your recipient the same categorial rules of action that you apply to yourself." More specifically, "(1) In acting toward a recipient do not coerce him, that is, do not make him participate in the interaction with you against his will, or involuntarily, or against his consent. (2) In acting toward a recipient do not frustrate his purposes, that is, do not diminish or remove something that seems to him to be some good of his." [58]

These rules, like Bay's three definitions, need to be reconciled with one another; moreover, they are phrased in absolute terms rather than as matters of degree, so that in particular situations there might be no alternative acts, or several, that satisfied such principles. But as Gewirth later elaborates them, they have the character of an ethics of maximization: "The PCC puts a premium on freedom and on mutual accommodation of wants or purposes; these have an obvious application in the socio-political sphere as the principles of consent and of common good or public interest." [59] In addition, he interprets his ethic in a spirit akin to rule-utilitarianism: "Any particular act must be in accord with the PCC unless the act is in accord with a specific rule which itself is in accord with the PCC." [60] Thus we see in outline another ethical criterion, relational in its concern with consent and mutuality, emphasizing freedom but less concerned than Bay's ethic with intrapsychic freedom.

This enumeration of relational systems suggests some potential lines of argument under our meta-ethical rules, beyond those to be analyzed in chapters 5–8. We now return to the comparison of "ethical hypotheses" more closely related to the concepts of various social sciences. This comparison, if it has any prospect of increasing the generality of these ethical systems, must be based on moral convictions shared by persons in various disciplines rather than on the narrower framework of any one discipline. It may thus lead to greater consensus through the reconciliation of differences among ethical systems, but failing this, it can at least clarify these differences.

58. *Ibid.*, p. 292.
59. *Ibid.*, p. 297.
60. *Ibid.*, p. 298.

PART TWO | THE ETHICS OF THE SOCIAL SCIENCES

5 ECONOMIC ETHICS

Having argued for systematic ethical discourse in the social sciences and proposed a meta-ethics within which it can be conducted, we must now show how it might proceed. Ideally, an argument should take place between representatives of various views who present rival "ethical hypotheses" and modify them under one another's criticism. The result would be a continuing process in which genuinely different positions were advanced and defended, and the workability of our proposed meta-ethics was given a serious test. As a step in this direction, I shall present several ethical positions, drawn from various social sciences, in the next four chapters.

The central set of positions will be those of valuative economics ("normative" as economists use the term); these are significant both for their importance in public policy formation and for their conformity to our meta-ethical rules. We shall consider three basic types of economic ethics: the "old" welfare economics, employing a notion of "utility" in Benthamite fashion; the "new" welfare economics of Pareto optimality, supplanting the "old" in the 1930s and constricting its generality; and cost-benefit analysis, reintroducing interpersonal comparison but running counter to widespread moral convictions regarding equity or justice. After comparing these types with one another I shall develop a general line of criticism applicable to all of them, based on the distinction between preference and welfare.

The second set of positions might be taken by a political scientist sympathetic with the potential contributions of economic reasoning to his discipline but critical of the valuative foundation of this approach. The application of economic reasoning to politics tacitly transfers the economic ethic to politics as well. We shall first note that the substantive values of this ethic, embodied in the notion of "market failure," extend our analysis of political forms to numerous specific choices that might otherwise be ignored. But in the political domain we shall also see potential conflicts between the economic ethic and some of our moral convictions regarding the roles of representatives, administrators, and others who assume roles related to the common good or general welfare. The chief argument introduced by the political scientist will thus be an extension of one made in the economic realm: that the notions of preference and welfare must be freed from the semantic connection made by terms such as "utility."

The third set of ethical positions will be drawn from psychology, with stress on learning and therapy. Their common feature will be stress on change of preferences; in this respect they suggest the lack of generality of the economic ethic and point to a possible dialogue between the disciplines. This classification of learning and therapy together, which we make to facilitate the contrast with economic ethics, deemphasizes certain important differences in the conceptualization of human behavior and personality, as between Skinner and Freud.

The fourth set of ethical positions will be that of a sociologist who sees that the concepts of his own discipline, when translated into the ethical alternative of changing social norms, fill certain gaps in the previous argument. They not only call attention to the possibility of social contracts—small as well as large—but also raise questions regarding the limits of applicability of the scientific perspective in view of our reciprocal relations with our fellow human beings.

The meta-ethical rules I employ will be primarily the rule of generality of applicability of an ethical system and the rule concerning the inconsistency of a system with shared moral convictions. We shall deal with systems presented in writing and shall select systems, for the most part, that satisfy the rule of consistency. It will sometimes be difficult, however, to associate each criticism based on generality or convictions with an explicit alternative ethical hypothesis advanced by the critic, as our rules would require.

Throughout my exposition of these ethical positions, I shall repeatedly employ a simplifying procedure. Pairs of ethical systems, which differ only in certain respects but are similar in others, will be chosen for contrast. I choose these pairs in order to highlight the particular types of argument to be expected, which will be fewer than if systems differing in many aspects were compared. Thus I first contrast several

types of economic ethics, which differ in important details but are all
open to similar criticism from outside the economic perspective. We
then consider an economic approach to politics, suggesting both its
generality relative to process-oriented democratic theories and its vul-
nerability to arguments concerning representative roles and the general
welfare. The psychological ethic I first choose for attention, that of
learning theory, resembles that of economics in dealing with a multiplicity of distinct behavioral tendencies or preferences. And even
when we consider the more complex ethical systems characteristic of
psychotherapy, I again stress notions such as that of ''externalities,''
in order to indicate possibilities of greater ethical generality that may
be attained by discourse among the disciplines. My final ethical concern, with choice of norms, is not specifically paired with one similar
system but raises issues relevant to all the preceding ethics. This
simulated argument will of course reveal fewer irreconcilable differences than a real one, as well as conform more easily to our meta-
ethics.

Each of the ethical approaches we shall consider is centered about
variables that enter into the theories and research of the corresponding
discipline but which also have valuative connotations. Because of the
self-contained character of academic disciplines, however, there is insufficient recognition of the need to combine these valuative connotations in an inclusive ethical system. For this reason, the relations between causal variables in one discipline and the values stressed by
other disciplines are often slighted. Thus the influence of the economic
system on social norms and personality is a topic that is largely lost in
the interstices between the disciplines. Conversely, the study of the influence of learning and therapy on general systems of preference satisfaction, such as markets, is also hindered by a disciplinary gap. The
increasing introduction of economic reasoning into political science
and sociology helps to bridge some of these gaps, but it is a largely
unilateral effort, and corresponding corrections to the economic perspective are also needed.

The implicit ethic of each of these disciplines stresses one aspect of
what might be a larger system. Economics deals with the satisfaction
of existing individual preferences and the systems of exchange that
satisfy them. Political science, insofar as it escapes from the economic

perspective, deals with those roles and institutions in which responsible citizens and public officials may be expected to consider the general welfare; perhaps for this reason political science contains more explicit valuative discourse than any other social science. Psychology—especially in its relations with education and psychotherapy—is concerned with the changes that may be produced in preferences and in their structure in individuals' personalities; it thus supplements the assumption of economics that preferences are to be taken as given. Sociology is concerned with social norms, and a related ethical emphasis is on joint action undertaken to change them.

Among these systems, the ethical positions of economics stand out because of their high degree of formalization. They specify in precise detail, with the aid of mathematical notation, what policy is to be chosen in any of a wide range of choice situations that come within their domain. They do so consistently, in terms of a single principle from which particular instances are deduced.

The two types of economic ethics with which we shall be principally concerned are those of welfare economics and cost-benefit analysis. Welfare economics, in its main contemporary form, considers the conditions under which the satisfaction of at least one individual's preferences can be increased without reducing the satisfaction of any other individual's preferences—the Pareto criterion.[1] Cost-benefit analysis, on the other hand, directly compares the welfare consequences of a policy, in monetary terms, to the individuals affected.

Welfare economics is not simply an ethical theory, but an integral development of valuative decision criteria together with inferences from positive economics about the consequences of policies. Its contributions include, first, a formal apparatus for relating the preferences of individuals to notions of collective welfare; and second, through the findings of positive economics, the systematic consideration of the reactions of actors to a policy that affects them.

In the second aspect, it is the scientific findings of economics rather than its ethical postulates that are the distinctive contribution. Economics has been more successful than the other social sciences in sys-

---

1. Reviews of this field for noneconomists have been presented in Zeckhauser and Schaefer, "Public Policy and Normative Economic Theory," and Bish, *The Public Economy of Metropolitan Areas.*

tematically considering the indirect effects of intervention in systems. Some of the characteristic choices that economists have analyzed—taxes, tariffs, regulation—involve prediction of this sort. They examine whether compensatory arrangements will take place among private parties, modifying the immediate and intended effect of regulation.[2] They consider whether the regulation of one parameter in an economic system will change others, as when rent control slows housing construction, or a minimum wage moves resources toward automation. In the case of particular tariffs influencing the flow of international trade they consider the secondary effects as well as the immediate.[3]

Contemporary welfare economics, in its valuative aspect, may be considered as a family of ethical systems whose primitive term is "preference." In describing it in this way, we stress the valuative aspect more than many economists would.[4] Not only the strengths of the field, indicated above, but also some of its philosophical weaknesses derive from its close connections with the concepts of positive, scientific economics. Welfare economics is often portrayed as a positive science that merely helps individuals in economic systems to attain their own preferences in a situation of scarcity. A prevailing societal ethic that supports the market and exchange contributes to the noncontroversial—and thus nonvaluative—appearance of the field. But a recognition that the field is basically valuative will allow us to examine its underlying assumptions from the perspective of the other social sciences and of philosophy. We shall thus be led to examine the claims, within economics and outside, of cardinal welfare measures and interpersonal comparison and of distinctions between various sorts of preference.

From the Old Welfare Economics to the New

One way to approach these questions is to examine the history of the field. Initially it was closely related to Benthamite utilitarianism,

---

2. Johnson, "The Economic Approach to Social Questions," p. 3; Okun, *The Political Economy of Prosperity*, p. 5; Coase, "The Problem of Social Cost."
3. Lipsey and Lancaster, "The General Theory of Second Best."
4. We return below to the question of just what "preference" embraces. Little, in *A Critique of Welfare Economics*, concludes (p. 267) that the terminology is normative.

which with a naturalistic tendency connected the desirable with people's existent desires.[5] Thus for a number of nineteenth-century and early twentieth-century economists it was only a small step to write of "utility" as a measure of both usefulness and motivation. Some recognized that preference (motivation) might occasionally diverge from satisfaction later experienced but judged that in economic activity the two would coincide sufficiently closely that they might be equated. Pareto was ahead of his time in defining distinct concepts of utility (usefulness) and "ophelimity" (quality of being preferred) in the 1890s.[6] But a dominant formulation until at least the 1920s assumed utility to be characterized by a cardinal number, comparable among consumers, which measured both the satisfaction derived from the consumption of given quantities of goods and the consumer's relative preference for them.

The subsequent evolution of economics, however, has taken it far from this simplistic conjunction of value and motivation. More than any other social science, economics has divested itself of controversial valuative concerns during the past half-century and has developed a self-contained, technical professional discourse. This change follows the characteristic pattern of development of the natural sciences.[7] The scientific career has been institutionalized. Disciplines have become separated from one another and from the discourse of the layman or amateur. Technical discourse, careers, and training required for entry are among the indicators of this development. Important advances in quantification and mathematical formulation in economics have accompanied these structural changes and have defined the methods and problems of the discipline more precisely.

Throughout this development, leading economists have come less and less to be contributors to other disciplines. Adam Smith, John Stuart Mill, and Pareto all made such outside contributions. Frank H. Knight recognized that a competitive economy can shape our personal-

5. This stage is described in Little, *op. cit.*, pp. 6–13. On naturalistic ethics see chapter 3 above.

6. For example, Pareto, *Cours d'Économie Politique,* vol. 1, p. 7; Stigler, *Essays in the History of Economics,* ch. 5.

7. See Ben-David, *The Scientist's Role in Society;* Stigler, *op. cit.,* ch. 3.

ities.[8] Schumpeter's alternative theory of democracy is also well known as a contribution to "pluralist" political theory. But leading economists today are more likely to concentrate on the development of the powerful tools of economic analysis within their own field or, if they venture outside, to do so by extending economic theory and methods to other fields such as political science and sociology. This extension has led to some of the economic approaches to politics which I shall discuss in the next chapter—carried out not only by economists themselves but also by political scientists. But unlike the work of earlier contributors, it is narrowly centered about economic concepts rather than relating them to the concepts of other disciplines.

The development of economics has thus led to the choice of problems on grounds internal rather than external to the discipline. Economists can now turn more easily to clearly defined and neatly solvable problems in their field rather than to the problems of society—assuming that their colleagues, and eventually society at large, will acknowledge the correctness of their choice. When they do venture into other subject matter, or into practical policy advice, it is with the aid of the conceptual machinery that their discipline has developed internally.

In 1920, Pigou could write that "It is not wonder, but rather the social enthusiasm which revolts from the sordidness of mean streets and the joylessness of withered lives, that is the beginning of economic science." [9] Such a claim would scarcely be made today by a leading economist—in spite of increasing criticism of the underlying assumptions of the discipline. Economics is seen primarily as a positive science. Its occasional use of terms such as "better off" or "optimality" is seen as resting on assumptions so obvious as not to be valuative at all.

Among the major contributors to this exclusion of obvious value judgments from economics was Lionel Robbins, who emphasized that interpersonal comparison of utilities has no scientific status:

> Now, of course, in daily life we do continually assume that the comparison can be made. But the very diversity of the assumptions

8. Knight, "The Ethics of Competition."
9. Pigou, *The Economics of Welfare*, p. 5.

actually made at different times and in different places is evidence of their *conventional nature*. In western democracies we assume for certain purposes that men in similar circumstances are capable of equal satisfactions. . . . But, although it may be convenient to assume this, there is no way of proving that the assumption rests on *ascertainable fact*. And, indeed, if the representative of some other civilization were to assure us that we were wrong, that members of his caste (or his race) were capable of experiencing ten times as much satisfaction from given income as members of an inferior caste (or an "inferior" race), we could not refute him.[10]

Robbins' strictures reflected the influence of logical positivism.[11] He correctly distinguished between scientifically ascertainable matters and those decided by convention or consensus, but this distinction carried with it an unnecessary depreciation of valuative discourse.

Not only interpersonal comparison of utilities, but also cardinal measurement of utility or welfare was denied scientific status. Only those variables necessary to account for consumer choice were admitted. Consumer choice was at best related to comparisons made by each individual consumer, but this did not require a measurable "utility." Rather, whatever function the individual consumer maximized could be subjected to a monotonic increasing transformation without affecting his choices. Only the loci of constant value of such functions—indifference curves or surfaces—had operational significance.[12]

After the stronger valuative overtones were removed from the study of consumer behavior in this way, the question was again raised as to the status of value judgments about the welfare of society. These judgments were seen by Bergson as introduced from outside positive economics in the form of a "social welfare function." Various mathematical welfare functions could be postulated by economists (or others if they could master the symbolism) to express their personal judgments as to the ingredients of society's well-being. But by expressing these functions in general form, Bergson was able "to show what their max-

10. Robbins, *An Essay on the Nature and Significance of Economic Science*, p. 140. Emphasis mine.

11. Alexander, "The Impersonality of Normative Judgments," p. 55.

12. Hicks's *Value and Capital* was a major contribution to this argument, but Pareto had stated it earlier as in his *Manual of Political Economy*, pp. 393–394.

imization implied for observable economic variables." [13] Analogously to the preference system of the individual, a social welfare function contained no more information than an ordering of various social states. [14]

This formulation of the problem, like Weber's statement of the relation between factual and valuative discourse, seems to have discouraged economists from actually setting forth and debating their proposed "social welfare functions" as anything more than arbitrary personal preferences. That which was not knowable scientifically could not be subjected to reasoned argument. Thus discussion was restricted to what could be said without controversial, and apparently arbitrary, elaboration of these functions in detail. General classes of social welfare functions could be expressed with elegance and parsimony, but this abstraction diverted attention from particular functions that might be more relevant for ethical argument or practical application.

In the perspective provided by our meta-ethics, these social welfare functions might be examples of ethical hypotheses, which could be compared and evaluated in view of their proponents' ethical convictions. But if this comparison were to take place, the rival systems would first have to be specified in sufficient detail that specific implications could be drawn from them. For this purpose, not only explicit statement, but some codification and simplification would be necessary. A general class of mathematical functions, or an imagined ordering of all possible states of the world, though useful for some general discussion of social welfare functions, is of extremely limited use for either ethical argument or policy guidance.

The same process of making decision criteria ("objective functions") specific and usable, which we are recommending for ethical argument, has actually been pursued in the field of decision analysis. Its purpose there is to guide important decisions by individuals or

13. Bergson, "A Reformulation of Certain Aspects of Welfare Economics." The appraisal of Bergson's contribution is from Samuelson, Foreword to Graaff, *Theoretical Welfare Economics*, p. vii. These functions are ordinarily formulated in static terms, as depending instantaneously on the quantities of goods possessed by individuals. But they may be extended to dynamic problems by taking into account changes in possessions and their relation to expectations.

14. Samuelson, *Foundations of Economic Analysis*, p. 228.

firms. This development provides a useful example of formalization together with specificity, even though it is not precisely within either economics or ethics. Although the preferences and choices of the individual are ordinarily taken as given in economic analysis, Raiffa has proposed a procedure for rendering them more consistent.[15] When an individual confronts a sequence of choices involving risk, with later choices depending on the results of earlier ones, he can choose so as to maximize his own expected return. And unlike the consumer in economic analysis, who is expected to choose automatically, a chooser trained in Raiffa's procedure may revise his preferences for complex alternatives in a systematic procedure that includes judgment of the values and probabilities of various possible outcomes. This procedure illustrates the possibility of rendering one's own preferences more systematic and explicit. Its application to ethics arises, however, only when the choices in question are aimed at some goal or value that can be justified in ethical terms, rather than at the chooser's personal welfare. When applied to ethics, it corresponds to the expression of a social welfare function in explicit and concrete form.

Within economic discourse, however, argument about the relative merits of social welfare functions was not permitted. In the absence of agreement—or even discussion—of these stronger valuative judgments of social welfare, all that remained was the criterion of Pareto optimality.[16] This corresponded to a state of affairs in which no individual could be made "better off" (in terms of his preferences) without another's being made worse off. Pareto, like Robbins, recognized that we compare daily "the sensations of men of a same society, and sometimes of different societies." He considered these comparisons to rest on judgments of similarity between persons who do not depart far from an average.[17] But the more scientific part of his argument, embodied in the criterion of Pareto optimality, eliminates such interpersonal comparisons.

The result of this criticism was a setback for the naïvely naturalistic

15. Raiffa, *Decision Analysis.* We here appeal to a possible argument by decision theorists against theoretical welfare economists, based on different meta-ethical convictions.
16. Pareto, *Manual of Political Economy,* p. 261.
17. Pareto, *Cours d'Economie Politique,* vol. II, pp. 46–51.

ethics of the "old" welfare economics and its replacement by the weaker inferences of the "new" welfare economics, which sought conditions for the optimization of variables that could be measured (in principle) within the definition of "positive economic science." [18] But the Pareto criterion as an ethical system is easily assailable under the rule of generality, in comparison with a system such as cost-benefit analysis, as it says nothing about those choices through which one person gains and another loses.

This change from the "old" to the "new" welfare economics, though a step backward as regards the rule of generality, was nevertheless a response to the rule of convictions. The chief conviction to which it responded was that only scientifically ascertainable matters were meaningful—a meta-ethical conviction held by economists and deriving from logical positivism. As the discipline of economics became a more nearly closed system, its discourse became more impervious to valuations introduced from other aspects of its members' lives. The result (the "new" welfare economics) was an ethic closely linked to the scientific concepts of the discipline—and typically regarded as not an ethic at all.

A major contribution of the "new welfare economics" has been a theorem that under certain assumptions "the equilibrium conditions which characterize a system of competitive markets will exactly correspond to the requirements of Paretian efficiency." [19] In this approach, relative prices or shadow prices are determined by considerations of marginal rates of substitution between commodities, and an extensive maximization problem is solved. In principle, the solution of this problem sets values of prices, wages, and the employment of factors in production.[20] The standard set by this theorem constitutes a base against which less than optimal market performance can be compared; from such comparisons there arises a notion of "market failure," which we shall consider in the next chapter in connection with the pos-

18. A historical analysis of these developments is given in Rothenberg, *The Measurement of Social Welfare.*

19. Bator, "The Anatomy of Market Failure," p. 351. Paretian efficiency is sometimes distinguished from "optimality" on the basis that the former deals with preference, the latter with welfare; see Alexander, "Comment," in Margolis, ed., *The Analysis of Public Output*, pp. 24–25.

20. Bergson, *op. cit.*

sible allocation of decisions between the market and the political system.

A second consequence of the approach taken in the "new welfare economics" has been the separation of relatively noncontroversial from more controversial problems. The optimization problem is typically divided into two parts: (a) the allocation of resources, goods, and services, in accordance with a price system, for efficiency; and (b) the distribution of income (or wealth) among persons.[21] The latter problem, unsolvable without interpersonal comparison of some kind, is treated separately from the establishment of prices. Whether this separation is politically possible in the real world, or desirable, is another question.

The strengths and weaknesses of the new welfare economics are illustrated by Arrow's *Social Choice and Individual Values* (1951). Mathematical elegance, noncontroversial assumptions, and faithfulness to the assumptions of the discipline were all combined—unfortunately for welfare economics—in a *negative* finding, the "impossibility theorem."

The aim of welfare economics has been to state conditions under which one or another state of affairs is better in terms of the preferences of the individuals affected. From a notion of ordinal preference and the Pareto criterion, this line of reasoning has led to numerous interesting conclusions as to the desirability of various sorts of intervention in market systems. It does not, however, lead to a complete ordering of states of affairs; if state A is higher in the preferences of some persons than B, and lower in the preferences of others, this criterion lacks the generality to compare the two states.

The problem Arrow considered was that of specifying a procedure that would yield a complete ordering of states of affairs, rather than a partial ordering, on the basis of any given set of individuals' rankings of these states. The logical apparatus he developed is equally applicable regardless of the basis on which individual preferences are reached. In analyzing democratic decision processes one can include individuals' preferences about matters that do not affect them but which they judge to affect the welfare of others; for other purposes one

21. See Musgrave, *The Theory of Public Finance,* ch. 1, which also includes the function of stabilization.

may wish to consider only preferences concerning the chooser's welfare (a distinction I elaborate later in this chapter). Although Arrow explicitly refused to distinguish types of preferences in his analysis, the distinction will be important for ours.

Arrow initially called the function he was seeking a "social welfare function" but later referred to it as a "constitution," in view of the broader consensual basis that it might have. He distinguished these two interpretations, respectively, as "the welfare judgments of any single individual . . . unconnected with action," and "a rule for arriving at social decisions . . . agreed upon for reasons of convenience and necessity without its outcomes being treated as evaluations by anyone in particular." [22] This is a useful distinction, but still fails to include the topic of our argument here: ethical systems. An ethical system is more than a system of personal preferences, because we can try to persuade others to subscribe to it; our meta-ethical rules are designed to guide that persuasion. In the course of ethical argument, various ethical systems may be held by various segments of a political community. Each such system, if developed precisely together with empirical causal judgments, may lead its adherents to advocate certain policies. It thus provides the basis for a set of judgments that are more than personal but less than societal. If such an ethical system is of sufficient generality, it may even lead its adherents to advocate a certain constitution. A constitution actually adopted may be a compromise among segments of society. Arrow's assumptions for his analysis (listed below) appear very weak and therefore seem appropriate for a constitution, but as we shall point out, his first assumption is strongly limited so as to conform to the convictions of present-day economists—a restriction unnecessary for citizens' debate.

Arrow required that a social welfare function, or constitution, be subject to a set of apparently reasonable assumptions. [23] Procedures such as majority vote or vote by summed numerical rankings of alternatives, though used in practice, fail to meet these requirements completely. The assumptions, in nontechnical terms, were:

22. Arrow, *Social Choice and Individual Values*, pp. 23, 106; "Public and Private Values," pp. 13–14.
23. Arrow, *Social Choice and Individual Values*, ch. III, gives the initial formulation of the axioms; a later restatement is given on pp. 96–100.

1. *Individual and social preferences as rankings.* Individual preferences, and the corresponding social preference, must be expressed as complete rankings of alternative social states; for any two states, one must be preferred to the other, or they must be considered equivalent. Individual preference rankings can assume all logically possible orderings.

2. *Positive association of social and individual values.* If a given alternative rises in the preference rankings of some individuals, and does not fall in any such rankings, it must not fall in the social ranking.

3. *Independence of irrelevant alternatives.* The social ranking of a given set of alternatives must not be affected by changes in individual rankings of alternatives outside this set.

4. *Citizens' sovereignty.* If all individuals prefer alternative x over v, the social preference must also be for x over v.

5. *Nondictatorship.* No single individual's preferences shall always determine the social preference and determine it irrespective of the preferences of other individuals.

From these weak and apparently (to economists) obvious assumptions, Arrow concluded by logical analysis that *no* social preference function satisfying them all could in general be found. This negative finding has been extremely influential.

In a sense, the problem that Arrow posed was that of rendering an ethical system consistent; his reasoning thus exemplifies the metaethical rule of consistency. The axioms or ingredients that he chose, however, seemed so weak and noncontroversial that some observers have not regarded them as valuative at all.[24] Moreover, Arrow himself rejected certain *other* assumptions (to which we shall return) as "value judgments." He thus evidently did *not* regard his axioms as having this character. I have phrased them in more valuative form than Arrow did; the term "must" or "shall" appears in each here and indicates its valuative content.

Arrow's first assumption has probably seemed the least valuative of all. Derived from the positivistic notion of science, it appeared to rest simply on the restriction of *meaning* to those concepts that enter into

24. Walsh, "Axiomatic Choice Theory and Values."

scientific propositions. Arrow's acceptance of the positivistic view of science—not merely distinguishing facts and values, but considering valuative assertions meaningless—is illustrated in his second chapter on "The Nature of Preference and Choice":

> The viewpoint will be taken here that interpersonal comparison of utilities has *no meaning* and, in fact, that there is no meaning relevant to welfare comparisons in the measurability of individual utility. . . . During the entire controversy, the proponents of measurable utility have been unable to produce any *proposition of economic behavior which could be explained* by their hypothesis and not by those of the indifference-curve theorists. Indeed, the only *meaning* the concepts of utility can be said to have is their indications of actual behavior, and, if any course of behavior can be explained by a given utility function, it has been amply demonstrated that such a course of behavior can be equally well explained by any other utility function which is a strictly increasing function of the first. If we cannot have measurable utility, in this sense, we cannot have interpersonal comparability of utilities a fortiori.[25]

In the second edition of the book, he restates the point:

> Only observable differences can be used as a basis for *explanation*. In the field of consumers' demand theory, the ordinalist position turned out to create no problems; cardinal utility had no *explanatory power* above and beyond ordinal.[26]

But this notion of the meaningful is unnecessarily limited. Social conventions such as laws or the order of the letters of the alphabet may be established and may have precise practical significance, without figuring importantly in the generalizations of any scientific discipline. The very recognition that we are engaging in ethical argument frees us from this restriction.

An alternative position that he also elaborates in the second edition is that interpersonal comparisons may conceivably be given empirical meaning through the introduction of otherwise "irrelevant" alterna-

25. Arrow, *Social Choice and Individual Values*, p. 9 (emphasis mine).
26. *Ibid.*, p. 109 (emphasis mine).

tives.[27] If there were a social convention or consensus that a particular good or stimulus made equal contributions to the welfare of different individuals, then one or more elements of this sort might serve as a yardstick for cardinal interpersonal comparisons. Thus we might consider rejecting both Assumption 1 (rankings) and Assumption 4 (irrelevant alternatives). But under our proposed meta-ethics, we may wish to reject some such convictions in order to formulate an ethical hypothesis of more general applicability. Much of the commentary on Arrow's theorem, to be discussed in the next section, revolves about the problem of modifying one or another of his axioms in order to obtain more general social preference functions. This modification of apparently self-evident assumptions or ethical convictions is precisely what we suggested in chapter 4 would be required if moral convictions (and, in this case, convictions about meaning) were to be summarized in a consistent ethical system.

Valuative assertions have been regarded in two principal ways by welfare economists. The "old" welfare economics was characterized by a naïve naturalism in which it was assumed that "utility" could be ascertained objectively or that aspects of experience were known to constitute the good. An example of this is Pigou's assertion that "the elements of welfare are states of consciousness and perhaps, their relations." [28] In the "new" welfare economics, such valuative assertions were considered to be nothing more than personal preferences, arbitrarily chosen and not susceptible to systematic justification. From this assumption, it was concluded that one could not really discuss them or that at most one could assert personal preferences as to social welfare functions and then deduce their consequences. On one occasion Samuelson has extended the basis of such functions to the consensus of the family as a consuming unit, but not to larger groups or societies.[29]

The naturalistic ethics of the "old" welfare economics was too little concerned with the foundations of ethical assertions. The "new" wel-

27. *Ibid.*, pp. 112–114. See also Arrow, "Public and Private Values," p. 19.
28. Pigou, *The Economics of Welfare* (1932 ed.), p. 10.
29. Samuelson, "Social Indifference Curves," p. 10. Rothenberg, *op. cit.*, ch. 13, goes farther and considers choices of the society as a whole. In part he views the process of reaching social consensus as a detached observer of given social mechanisms, but he also stresses the "power" (generality) and consistency of ethical systems in a way that parallels our meta-ethics.

fare economics, however, was too little aware of the possibility of rational ethical discourse and thus could not easily descend from abstract classes of welfare functions to the particular agreements necessary to formulate and evaluate policy choices. Between the two types of discussion lies the possibility of arguing rationally about particular welfare functions. The assertion of these welfare functions would then be grounded neither in science nor in mere personal whim, but in this rational discourse and in whatever increase in consensus might result.

There is, however, another way to introduce valuative assertions into the discourse of welfare economics: through the use of axioms or postulates that appear to command such general assent as to be self-evident. If, as in geometry, one can derive new and interesting conclusions from such axioms, the theorems and derivations leading to them are considered contributions to the literature. This method has been used by Arrow and others and has several advantages for contribution to the literature of a discipline. It permits technical refinement of logical procedure, in a way that oral argument does not. It addresses a large and impersonal body of readers, rather than a particular opponent. And in practice it makes use of axioms or assumptions that are relatively noncontroversial, so that even if it is valuative it does not appear extremely so. The greatest accomplishment in this sort of exercise, of course, is to draw surprising and even controversial conclusions from apparently obvious assumptions. This approach is somewhat akin to the meta-ethical rules proposed here, which at first glance do not require any particular ethical outcome but may in fact constrain ethical discourse considerably.

Arrow's remaining assumptions (other than the first) have this weak valuative character. That they do may be shown by imagining situations in which we should judge it right to assume the opposite. We might imagine some individual so mistaken, or evil, that his preferences should be reflected negatively in the social choice (#2); some alternative which, though "irrelevant," is nevertheless required as a yardstick for interpersonal comparison (#3); some matters on which all the members of a particular group are in error as to how to further their own welfare or the general welfare (#4); or instances in which only one member of the group possesses the knowledge of how collective welfare should be furthered (#5). I do not wish to argue for these

opposite principles, of course, and cite them only as possible exceptions. But the mere fact that they can be entertained illustrates that Arrow's assumptions are not logically necessary.[30]

The basic formal assumption of Arrow's analysis—that cardinal
welfare and interpersonal comparisons of welfare were meaningless—
had restricted the valuative judgments of welfare economics to the criterion of Pareto optimality. The semantic problem that led to this cur-
tailment of valuative discourse was the collapsing of preference (a
concept of positive economics) and welfare (a valuative concept) into
the same valuative term, "utility." Because these two meanings were
locked into the same word, the justifiable scientific strictures on the
usage of "preference" were improperly extended to the "welfare"
component of the term.

It was clearly seen by economists as early as the 1930s that this limitation of the meaning of "utility" sharply restricted their capacity to
make judgments as to what policies were preferable to others. They
were indeed concerned with the desirability of general ethical systems.
The criterion of Pareto optimality failed to apply to the many real-
world choices that made some persons better off and others worse.
Problems of equality, transfer, and redistribution of income seemed to
be excluded from consideration. The inapplicability of the "new"
welfare economics to these problems led to efforts to remedy its lack
of generality. There has thus been a continuing effort to discover other
assumptions that would extend the scope of welfare economics with
some collective support from the discipline.

Some British economists asked whether one could justify the repeal
of the corn laws, even though landlords were worse off as a result.[31]
One effort to cope with this difficulty was the proposal, by Kaldor and
by Hicks in 1939, that a hypothetical possibility of compensation be
considered. Thus a policy would be considered desirable if the gainers
could afterward compensate the losers and thus achieve a Pareto-type
improvement—even though the compensation was not actually
required. It was soon pointed out by Scitovsky, however, that this criterion of compensation was complicated by its reversibility—that is, in

30. See the citation of Ayer in chapter 3 above, after fn. 33.
31. Mishan, "A Survey of Welfare Economics, 1939–59," pp. 219ff.; Little,
op. cit., ch. VI; Rothenberg, *op. cit.*, chs. 3–4.

some instances the losers might be able to bribe the gainers not to carry out the policy in the first place.[32]

The criterion of hypothetical compensation did not explicitly introduce interpersonal comparisons of utility, as it was formulated in terms of monetary transfers rather than subjective variables.[33] Since that criterion was proposed, there have also been other efforts to strengthen the weak types of valuative statements that can be derived from Pareto optimality or that seem to be allowed by Arrow's impossibility theorem. One approach to Arrow's theorem has been to argue that in practice—or under certain conditions—individual preference rankings are unlikely to assume all logically possible orderings.[34] Should this be the case, decision procedures might be formulated that would be adequate for practical purposes. An alternative approach has been through the analysis of transfers that are willingly undertaken by the donors, that is, "Pareto optimal redistribution." [35] Such analysis is relevant to the scientific consideration of how transfers are in fact made or how they might be made without leaving anyone lower on his preference scale, but its contribution to analysis of ethically "optimal" transfer policy is largely illusory. As I shall indicate below, it combines indiscriminately preferences that relate to the chooser's social welfare function and those that relate to his personal welfare.

The Resurrection of Cardinality and Interpersonal Comparison

The major line of criticism of Arrow's conclusion has centered on his assumption that cardinal utility and interpersonal comparison were meaningless. These aspects of utility or welfare are closely interrelated, since one of the simplest ways of formulating interpersonal

32. Kaldor, "Welfare Propositions of Economics and Interpersonal Comparisons of Utility"; Hicks, "The Foundations of Welfare Economics." Scitovsky, "A Note on Welfare Propositions in Economics"; Arrow, *op. cit.*, ch. IV; Samuelson, "Evaluation of Real National Income." Scitovsky was in effect invoking the rule of consistency against the Kaldor-Hicks ethical hypothesis.

33. See, however, Baumol, "Community Indifference," p. 46.

34. Tullock, "The General Irrelevance of the General Impossibility Theorem"; Black, "On Arrow's Impossibility Theorem." This approach and others are reviewed in Riker, "Voting and the Summation of Preferences."

35. Olsen, "A Normative Theory of Transfers"; Hochman and Rodgers, "Pareto Optimal Redistribution"; Zeckhauser, "Optimal Mechanisms for Income Transfer."

comparison would be by specifying a relation between cardinal utilities for two persons.[36]

One alternative to the purely ordinal notion of utility was put forward by Von Neumann and Morgenstern, who introduced cardinal measures through probability mixtures of particular alternatives to form new alternatives. This approach to cardinal utility has been used in numerous subsequent analyses. Such a scientific basis for cardinal utility may have mitigated the positivistic meta-ethical convictions against it and changed the possible arguments under the rule of convictions. But by itself it provides no basis for interpersonal comparison, since an individual's choices among probability mixes of alternatives would remain the same even if his cardinal utility function were subjected to a linear transformation.[37]

A stronger alternative to Arrow's conclusion has involved explicit relaxation of one of his axioms. Some writers have proposed alternative welfare functions (ethical hypotheses) that explicitly make use of "irrelevant" alternatives. One such approach to interpersonal comparison of "utilities," based on purely factual observations, has been proposed by Coleman on the basis of exchanges of votes among individuals engaged in collective decisions. The strategic preferences expressed in such interaction incorporate the participants' intensity of preference, and thus provide a basis—at least in principle—for a stronger notion of individual utility or welfare. Coleman argues that nearly all social decision rules allow for the expression of relative intensities of preference. He goes on to say, however, that "when it is possible to express such intensities, . . . the elimination of an 'irrelevant' alternative, though it be very low in his ordering, may change the rational individual's behavior." The introduction or elimination of alternatives *does* affect the bargaining situation in a legislature and in this respect violates Arrow's assumption concerning "irrelevant" al-

36. See Goodman and Markowitz, "Social Welfare Functions Based on Individual Rankings," p. 262. The problem is relevant even to an ethic that stresses the welfare of the least favored groups in society, since these groups have to be identified and compared with others.

37. Von Neumann and Morgenstern, *Theory of Games and Economic Behavior,* p. 25. For choices involving a given set of persons, each individual's function might be modified by an arbitrary additive constant, analogous to the multiplicative constant in DeMeyer and Plott, "A Welfare Function Using 'Relative Intensity' of Preference." But for population policy the additive constant is important; see Rawls, *A Theory of Justice,* pp. 161ff.; Rothenberg, *op. cit.,* p. 192.

ternatives. Alternatives of this kind are introduced by the legislators themselves and do not appear to reflect the whims of the observer. But they may be introduced for strategic reasons and thus may not on reflection conform to our ethical convictions as fully as "yardstick" alternatives specified in the conventions of an ethical system.[38]

There remain a number of approaches that introduce interpersonal comparison through use of axioms or assumptions that do not derive from empirical science alone. Some of these axioms appear relatively noncontroversial, while others, such as the use of monetary values in cost-benefit analysis, are controversial but originate in the world outside the analyst's judgment and thus attempt to circumvent the accusation that the analyst is merely imposing his personal preferences on policy choices.

Goodman and Markowitz have proposed an alternative set of axioms, also differing from Arrow's in that certain "irrelevant" alternatives are considered in the formulation of a social welfare function. They demonstrate that under certain assumptions the sum of ranks constitutes the only possible social welfare function.[39] The justification for this approach as an ethical system lies in its generality in dealing with questions beyond Pareto optimality. The authors also consider it plausible that a larger difference in ranks corresponds to a greater difference in intensity of preference. However, even if intense preferences deserve special consideration, we cannot be completely sure that the intervening alternatives are not near-duplicates in their positions on some imagined scale of value. This criterion, like Coleman's, allows the collective choice to be influenced by alternatives that have a special degree of "irrelevance," in that we have no notion of their substantive content in advance. Such a procedure may be acceptable as a practical voting rule, but in ethical discussion it may be argued that an effort to reach substantive consensus on "yardsticks" is preferable.

One can also consider interpersonal comparison after first assuming

38. Coleman, "The Possibility of a Social Welfare Function." On irrelevant alternatives see pp. 1106, 1111. Our reference to ethical convictions involves the corresponding meta-ethical rule, in favor of an alternative class of ethics discussed later in this section. See also chapter 6, fn. 44.

39. Goodman and Markowitz, *op. cit.* This sum is also known as the Borda count or Borda function. See Grofman, "Some Notes on Voting Schemes and the Will of the Majority"; Fishburn, The *Theory of Social Choice*, pp. 163–167.

that cardinal measurement is possible for individual utility functions, game payoffs, or loss functions. In this case only their comparison (not their measurability) is in question. A number of writers have proposed sets of axioms that assume cardinal utility for individuals, introduced "irrelevant" alternatives as yardsticks for interpersonal comparison, and arrived at notions of social welfare as a sum of individual welfares.[40] The choice of "yardsticks," and empirical procedures for defining them, involves both social conventions and problems of measurement. Some may be more appealing, as ingredients of ethical hypotheses, than others; for example, the assumption that the highest or most preferred choice of an individual is to be set to a value of 1.0, and the lowest at 0.0, is open to the criticism that the standard is arbitrarily changeable. The standard of "arbitrariness" here is not simply that the judgment is unscientific, but that it is not governed by reasoned argument and may affect choices in ways unrelated to what we would consider the welfare of those involved, in view of our initial convictions concerning "welfare."

These proposals for interpersonal comparison seem, however, to have had little impact on the literature of welfare economics. There may have been an increasing recognition that valuative or conventional judgments are meaningful, but this does not make them part of "economic science." Economists recognize that practical problems demand interpersonal comparisons, made on ethical or political grounds and thus imported from outside the discipline. But the doors of the discipline have been closed to discussion of these valuative criteria. Perhaps such discussion will become possible through internal dissidence or through relations with other disciplines.

Outside theoretical welfare economics, however, there have been numerous applications of economic reasoning to practical decisions, using assumptions far stronger than Pareto optimality. The measurement of economic growth by indices such as the gross national product (GNP) has the merit of providing a complete ordering of states of the

40. Fleming, "A Cardinal Concept of Welfare"; Hildreth, "Alternative Conditions for Social Orderings"; Kemp and Asimakopolos, "A Note on Social Welfare Functions and Cardinal Utility"; Luce and Raiffa, *Games and Decisions,* pp. 145–150, 345–353; Theil, *Optimum Decision Rules for Government and Industry,* pp. 341–348; Pattanaik, *Voting and Collective Choice,* p. 146; J. L. Simon, "Interpersonal Welfare Comparisons Can Be Made."

economy, even though it neglects questions of distribution. The computation of national income involves a more direct comparison of individuals by means of a monetary yardstick and is used practically in spite of some theoretical difficulties.[41] And a criterion used increasingly in recent years for the assessment of public projects, cost-benefit analysis, also makes use of monetary comparisons that in effect compare individuals.

Cost-Benefit Analysis

Although the basic data of theoretical welfare economics are the preferences of individuals, the exigencies of practical decision have led to the use of prices in their place. Thus if we wished to compare the effects of two government policies on an individual and could estimate the amounts of goods each would produce for him, we could estimate his preferences for the two policies in terms of prices and quantities of the goods he received. If he experienced costs as well, we could subtract them and estimate his preference for the policies in terms of their net benefits. The resulting analysis of benefits and costs could be considered an applied form of welfare economics.[42]

We might, therefore, use prices to estimate preferences, but without interpersonal comparison of benefits or costs. These monetary comparisons *within* an individual's preference system would resemble some of the earlier notions of cardinal utility. The use of a common monetary yardstick, however, leads almost automatically to the addition and subtraction of monetary benefits and costs across individuals. The "benefit" value of a monetary unit, though "irrelevant" in Arrow's sense, is taken by consensus to be equal among all the persons af-

41. Samuelson, "Evaluation of Real National Income." Modification of the GNP to bring it nearer to a monetary measure of welfare has been proposed in Nordhaus and Tobin, "Is Growth Obsolete?" But a general underlying problem is that if prices differ among the alternative states of affairs being compared, an indeterminacy similar to that of the Pareto criterion results.

42. At this stage we have not yet considered the "consumer's surplus," the excess above the market price that he would be willing to pay, or the effects of changes in prices and incomes. The connection of prices to preferences has led Harberger to refer to cost-benefit analysis as a form of "applied welfare economics"; see his "Three Basic Postulates for Applied Welfare Economics." We shall ordinarily refer to theoretical welfare economics as discussed above, however, as "welfare economics."

fected. This assumption, customarily made in cost-benefit analysis, has the convenience of being "objective" (outside the analyst's control), and it allows us to add quantities of goods or money without knowing just who receives what goods. The result is an ethical hypothesis similar to that of GNP maximization, far more generally applicable than that of Pareto optimality and thus superior on the rule of generality. Insofar as the choice between two policies affects a subsystem of the national economy, cost-benefit analysis is a special case of a more general ethic of "net national benefit." If the choice ramifies further in its effects, some of these can be considered by including the notion of "opportunity costs," that is, the costs of alternative policies foregone.

Cost-benefit analysis thus attempts to judge the desirability of proposed government projects by estimating their expected monetary costs and benefits and maximizing the net benefit. It assumes that the decisions are to be made by government rather than by the market, as it is used when the market is incapable of making these decisions optimally. But it assumes at the same time that if the costs and benefits are decomposed into elementary parts (for example, transportation costs in the case of a new road or subway, prices of crops in the case of water resources), the corresponding values and disvalues may be represented by prices set by competitive markets for the goods or services which are those parts. The preferences of individuals affected by a proposed project are thus assumed to be summarized by market mechanisms that respond to the preferences of producers, consumers, and investors. Alternatively, they may be inferred from estimated "shadow" prices or by survey questions about monetary valuation.[43] The benefits and costs of a project are assumed to be the same for all, rich or poor, who receive the same goods or who pay the same taxes. And the evaluation of later as against present consumption—which here enters importantly while not explicitly considered in theoretical welfare economics—is assumed the same for all, young or old, as measured by a common discount rate.

43. See J. L. Simon, "Some Principles of Practical Welfare Economics." Assessment of evaluations through surveys might also include respondents' evaluations of sudden change or risk of change.

The monetary yardstick of cost-benefit analysis is the same as was used in the Kaldor-Hicks compensation principle; in neither approach is it required that compensation be actually carried out.[44] The problems of possible inconsistency that were debated for the compensation principle do not seem to be mentioned for cost-benefit analysis, perhaps because it deals only with minor interventions in the economy or because it is seen only as a rule of thumb for advising decision makers rather than an ethical criterion.

Although formally we can treat cost-benefit analysis as an ethical hypothesis, it occupies a somewhat different place in political decisions from either an ethics for general use or an electoral system. Its results are to be *communicated* to decision makers, who are expected to add ingredients of their own. Costs and benefits are *attributed* to particular persons affected, but these persons are not ordinarily surveyed nor do they participate in the determination of these figures. These persons, if they are voters, may use the analysis as an ethics; they may vote for the political officials who listen to the economist's advice or read the analysis in the newspapers before voting on a referendum. But cost-benefit analysis does not attempt to take account of political preferences, which are partly ethical but in some ways duplicate the preferences underlying the analysis. One economic view is that cost-benefit analysis is not primarily intended for citizens.[45]

Cost-benefit analysis is used to evaluate projects for which it is assumed that other decision procedures must supersede the market. In these decision procedures the economist plays the role of an expert consultant (to elites or informed citizens) but does not design the nonmarket decision procedures involved. Thus we do not typically conduct cost-benefit analyses of constitutions or electoral systems. But when we turn (in chapter 6) to the evaluation of political institutions in quasi-economic terms, we must then decide whether to follow the model of theoretical welfare economics or that of cost-benefit analysis.

44. Mishan refers to this criterion as "potential Pareto improvement"; see *Economics for Social Decisions,* pp. 14–17.

45. See Bergson, *Essays in Normative Economics,* pp. 37–38, expressing a view with which he disagrees: "The problem is to counsel not citizens generally but public officials." But this distinction seems to imply that citizens' decisions are selfish and that only the official is "neutral ethically." We return to this distinction in chapter 6.

The former leads to abstract analysis in terms of preferences, the latter to empirical estimates of welfare.

Cost-benefit analysis has arisen from a confluence of several streams of thought concerned with the allocation of public funds among alternatives that could not be adequately compared by the market. One of these streams is a long-standing interest by public administrators in evaluating the allocation of funds in relation to their benefits, and not merely from the perspective of economizing.[46] The trend from this older attitude toward consideration of benefits, and toward grouping budgetary categories in relation to function performed, was also stimulated by the increasing proportion of public spending in the national economy, by the use of fiscal policy to guide the economy, and by a management orientation expressed in the 1949 Hoover Commission report. There was also a general intellectual line of descent from welfare economics to "planning programming budgeting" (PPB). But the tendency of theoretical welfare economics toward formalism and concern with Arrow-type problems led budgetary decision makers to go beyond its limitations.

A second and distinct line of development came in the analysis of military alternatives and is associated with the names of Secretary of Defense Robert McNamara and of researchers at the RAND Corporation. Although it is difficult to place monetary values on strategic advantage or lives lost, numerous cost-effectiveness analyses have been conducted in which costs of weapons systems have been measured against their performance. This approach was introduced into the Defense Department under McNamara, then diffused during the Johnson administration to other departments, where it met some of the other streams.[47]

A third line of development is exemplified by a 1950 analysis of river basin projects that drew together and systematized the general approach. The assumption that costs and benefits will be measured in terms of prices is there stated clearly:

46. For examples of the stress on economizing, see Schultze, *The Politics and Economics of Public Spending*, pp. 10–11; Fenno, *The Power of the Purse*, p. 105.

47. Schick, "The Road to PPB: Stages of Budget Reform"; and Hitch and McKean, *The Economics of Defense in the Nuclear Age*.

The values placed on "goods and services" through the exchange process afford one means of measuring the degree of want-satisfying power attached to those goods and services by those who participate in the exchange. Most of the effects of projects involve goods and services which are readily evaluated in terms of market prices. Some effects of a project, however, such as improvement of health and enjoyment of recreation, have not been customarily evaluated in the monetary terms used in the market system. Furthermore, it is recognized that the values attached to goods and services in the market may not always reflect accurately the want-satisfying power from a public viewpoint because of various influences such as subsidies, tariffs, price supports, and imperfect markets as reflected by surplus commodities. . . .

Despite the limitations of the market price system in reflecting values from a public viewpoint, it is concluded that there is no other suitable framework for evaluating the effects of public works projects in common terms.

. . . Prevention of loss of life, improvement of health and provision of facilities for recreation should be evaluated in monetary terms as fully as possible.[48]

These principles have been widely applied; one detailed example concerns their use in evaluation of a proposed underground railway in London.[49]

The central theme that connects these approaches, for our purpose, is the application to practical problems of an "ethic" that measures advantages and disadvantages of action in monetary terms. The fact that this is actually being done—by economists among others—shows that the "impossibility theorem" has been circumvented without the need for philosophical considerations or meta-ethics such as we have advanced, although these considerations are still relevant to criticism of it. Cardinal utility measurement and interpersonal comparison have

48. Federal Inter-Agency River Basin Committee, *Proposed Practices for Economic Analysis of River Basin Projects,* pp. 6–7.
49. Foster and Beesley, "Estimating the Social Benefit of Constructing an Underground Railway in London."

both simply been carried out, with no questions asked. The need to decide whether "to allocate x dollars to activity A instead of activity B" overcame the reservations of welfare economics.[50]

Cost-benefit analysis is closer to practical decision than is theoretical welfare economics, but the two can still be criticized and compared within our meta-ethical framework. In a sense, cost-benefit analysis is the application of a particular "social welfare function," constructed not from preferences, but from prices as a substitute. If a dam is to be built, the economist by calculating costs and benefits arrives at a particular sort of "preference" for or against its construction. This "preference" is a judgment of collective welfare and has no necessary connection with the dam's effects on the economist's own welfare. His "preference" for building the dam, as compared with other policies, thus has a different status from the preferences of the individuals affected.

The economist conducting cost-benefit analysis is forced not only to consider the collective welfare, but also to be more systematic in his analysis than the individual voter might be. He typically considers not only the costs and benefits of the project, but also the alternative uses to which resources might have been put. This approach calls to our attention the alternative acts with which a given act must be compared. It exemplifies the notion that any ethical choice may be considered as a choice among available alternative acts.

The use of monetary valuation in cost-benefit analysis, although it provides generality for this ethical system, may be criticized on several scores. An important criticism derives from the fact that it ignores possible differences in the welfare that we might judge to be produced for different individuals by the same amount of money.[51] The problem of income distribution effects has been considered by Weisbrod, who suggests ways for analysts to include them. He proposes that benefits and costs to different population groups—classified, for example, by race and income—be tabulated so that policymakers can take them

50. Schick, *op. cit.*, p. 45.
51. Maass, "Benefit-Cost Analysis: Its Relevance to Public Investment Decisions," p. 213. The problem, within our meta-ethics, is to propose another ethical hypothesis that is responsive to our convictions concerning vertical equity. A recent review of problems in cost-benefit analysis is Haveman and Weisbrod, "Defining Benefits of Public Programs."

into account, and he does this—in a preliminary way—for several actual water-resource projects. Similar reasoning has been followed in cost-benefit analysis of higher education.[52]

Another way to consider distributional values would be to include in cost-benefit analyses, as a matter of routine, alternative assessments based on several possible functions of income or wealth—for example, a logarithm of income.[53] But before proposing these functions, social scientists must play a part in the societal discussion that seeks consensual bases for them. In this debate, they might call attention to the progressivity of taxes that have been adopted, or to the relations of other welfare indicators, such as measures of happiness,[54] to income. Initial research on this topic may not be regarded as a contribution to basic social science, but once published it would provide subsequent cost-benefit analysts with a basis, other than their personal preferences, for presenting results based on such welfare functions.

Cost-benefit analysis is also likely to ignore benefits or costs that cannot easily be assigned monetary values, even though its practitioners often extend the domain of monetary valuation by ingenious computation of equivalent prices. An example of this difficulty is the effort to estimate the monetary value of loss of life, in connection with policies concerning health or the prevention of accidents. An initial approximation often used is the expected income stream of the person in question during the remainder of his life. But among the additional factors that must be considered are the bias of this criterion in favor of males and those with high salaries and the relative importance of death and anxiety about death.[55]

52. Weisbrod, "Income Redistribution Effects and Benefit-Cost Analysis"; Windham, *Education, Equality and Income Redistribution.* The calculation of separate welfare functions for separate population groups is not, however, the same as a consistent ethical hypothesis.

53. This approach is followed in Greene, Neenan, and Scott, *Fiscal Interactions in a Metropolitan Area,* ch. 3, which includes three "marginal utility" functions of income (Y) and their implications: K, K/Y, and K/Y^2. Numerous other functions might be considered, embodying negative utilitarianism, an anti-poverty ethic, distributive justice, etc. In comparing such functions we should be applying rule (2c) of our meta-ethics, concerning convictions.

54. Bradburn, *The Structure of Psychological Well-Being;* the data on p. 45, for example, suggest a step function. And see Easterlin, "Does Money Buy Happiness?"

55. Schelling, "The Life You Save May Be Your Own"; Zeckhauser, "Processes for Valuing Lives."

A further problem concerns whether the value of a commodity to the consumer is adequately reflected in its price, since even the rational consumer is expected to equate it with price only at the margin. There has been, however, an aspect of cost-benefit analysis that attempts to take this "consumer's surplus" into account.[56]

Another important line of criticism of cost-benefit analysis concerns its discounting of future benefits and costs to obtain their "present value." Much discussion of the proper relative weighting of future returns suggests that it should be strongly guided by actually prevailing rates of interest.[57] Yet it is possible that in ethical terms we might wish to support the judgment that the economy's valuation of the future is wrong—for example, too low, in terms of the rule of convictions. Our decisions about this discount rate can affect our valuation of governmental activity in an important way.

When one considers political scientists' analysis of the values embodied in the founding of a constitutional regime, or in the preservation of free regimes, one wonders whether the two realms of discourse can even meet. Cropsey specifically points out that the value of a regime may far exceed that of the persons who embody it at one time, because of the extreme difficulty of re-creating it once it is destroyed. But Baumol also recognizes that the action of the free market can lead to irreversible and extremely costly changes.[58]

Economists may thus wish to derive from society's values a "social discount rate" different from the interest rate available in the market. This rate may be attributed to individuals, acting on behalf of society, or to a collective valuation. Samuelson refers to the long-term interest rate as equal to "the subjective rate of (planner's) time preference."[59] He regards such valuations on the planner's part as subjective and individual but at least does not expect them to be based exclu-

56. See Dupuit, "On the Measurement of the Utility of Public Works"; Harberger, "Three Basic Postulates for Applied Welfare Economics: An Interpretive Essay."

57. Baumol, "On the Social Rate of Discount." Such considerations are natural as long as the decision maker can postpone a policy option, invest the funds that would have been used for it, and then use the augmented funds to exercise the option later.

58. Cropsey, "The Moral Basis of International Action," p. 81; Baumol, op. cit., p. 801.

59. Samuelson, "The Two-Part Golden Rule Deduced as the Asymptotic Turnpike of Catenary Motions," p. 89. Alternatively, the discount rate might be set collectively by a legislature, for example.

sively on consumer or investor preferences. Alternatively, Landauer
contends that "A great historical mission which the individual attributes to the community" may permit a distinction between "private
and public time preference." "If this sense of mission is strong
enough, it may sustain the rationality of large present sacrifices for the
sake of a distant future in spite of Tullock's objection that '. . . the
next generation is going to be wealthier than we are. . . .' " [60] Although Landauer's argument is sometimes as much behavioral as ethical ("explaining the operation of the sense of national mission" in the
USSR), he raises important questions.

A deficiency in economists' discourse about the social discount rate
is in its lack of explicitly valuative argument. Thus the difference in
perspective between constitution makers and economic water-resource
planners results in part from the lesser discount rate assumed by the
former. The typical assumption in economics is that valuative considerations have to be introduced from sources outside the discipline,
such as the planner's personal preferences (a datum) or a societal sense
of mission. In either case, the potential valuative discourse is short-cir-
cuited.

For ethical discourse, we cannot be content with an allegedly factual
"social discount rate." For the preservation of regimes, institutions,
or irreplaceable resources, ethical considerations may properly lead to
the use of lower discount rates than those prevailing in the market. Indeed, it can be argued that the proper social rate of discount is zero.[61]
But conceivably in other matters we are too much disposed to save
rather than to enjoy, and thus higher rates should be set.

Cost-benefit analysis encounters difficulties not only as regards its
justification, but also as regards its feasibility of calculation. In feasibility, however, it should not be considered inferior to other ethical
systems, but rather as providing advance guidance to them for the time
when they, too, encounter the realities of practical policy choice. Thus
cost-benefit analysis also encounters objections from decision makers

60. Landauer, "On the Social Rate of Discount: Comment," pp. 917–918; Tullock,
"The Social Rate of Discount and the Optimal Rate of Investment: Comment," p. 334.
61. Rawls suggests a zero discount rate to promote justice between generations; see *A
Theory of Justice,* p. 295. See also Solow, "The Economics of Resources or the
Resources of Economics," p. 9.

who are accustomed to less explicit choice procedures. More to the point, perhaps, are the objections that it encounters from interests harmed by it, especially when the degree of harm and the alternative allocation of resources are spelled out more explicitly than before. As Schmid writes,

> I was speaking with a certain Senator's aide about a water project the Senator was interested in for his state, but which was not in the President's budget. I asked if the Senator would be interested in a systems analysis that would show that his project was better than the poorest project now on the President's recommended budget list. The aide indicated he would not use such information even if it were available, since it would put the Senator in the uncomfortable position of causing some other identifiable and specific Senator to lose.

In other instances that he cites, participants have objected to the formal presentation of alternatives in order to reduce the incidence of disappointed expectations. "No Congressman appreciates an agency that gets his constituents stirred up and divided over several alternative plans." [62]

The major arguments we have considered concerning welfare economics and cost-benefit analysis deal with formal procedures for satisfying given preferences, rather than with the nature of preference itself as an ethical concept. But even if some particular measure of cardinal welfare or "intensity of preference" is incorporated in an ethical hypothesis, we shall still have to compare this quantity, as a basis for ethical choice, with intensities or measures of other sorts.

Preference, Personal Welfare, and Ethical Judgment

One virtue of studying welfare economics as an ethical hypothesis is that its formal apparatus applies over a variety of ethical assumptions about what is to be maximized. Once we choose between the cardinal

---

62. Schmid, "Public Appropriations Structure and Performance: The Case of PPBS in Water Resources," pp. 18, 20. Here we encounter an inconsistency among the meta-ethical convictions that an ethic be public and precise in its implications yet applicable in practice.

and ordinal positions—or choose a function by which to combine individual "welfares" into "social welfare"—then many of the theorems we derive within this framework are transferable to a class of similar ethical systems. But we must now turn our attention to various specific desiderata proposed by economists and others to which this formal apparatus might be related.

Even among economists there has been some divergence of opinion as to just what it is that should be maximized. It has been necessary, of course, to maintain the assumption that preference and welfare are closely related, if not identical, in order to examine conditions under which the market maximizes a valuative criterion. Early writers such as Pareto and Pigou explicitly stated that this was an approximation but that they considered it largely valid for consumers' market choices. Subsequent writers have increasingly assumed that preference satisfaction was the task at hand and have been concerned with formal than with substantive considerations in evaluating mechanisms of market or collective choice.

Yet even within the domain of "preference," distinctions may also be drawn as to just what *criteria* are to be used in counting certain preferences as more relevant to "social welfare" than others. In the study of consumer preference, economists do not ordinarily look beneath preferences or choices and distinguish types of them according to the reasons on which they are based. But the transfer of this indiscriminate notion to ethics is open to criticism. As Brandt expresses it,

> Some choices are motivated by the prospect of enhanced *personal welfare* (this may include the happiness of children, etc.), whereas others are motivated by considerations of *moral principle*. . . . But a person's following a moral principle need not maximize his utility; for him it may be a serious sacrifice. [63]

In *Social Choice and Individual Values,* Arrow made a similar distinction between "tastes" (corresponding more nearly to personal welfare) and "values" (including judgments based on moral principle).

63. Brandt, "Personal Values and the Justification of Institutions," p. 27. This criticism was addressed to Arrow's views in a symposium, and Arrow seems then to have agreed with it; see his "Public and Private Values." More general questions as to what is being maximized are also raised in Cropsey, "What Is Welfare Economics?"

Yet he refused to distinguish them in the definition of his problem, because this decision would be "a value judgment":

> In general, there will . . . be a difference between the ordering of social states according to the direct consumption of the individual and the ordering when the individual adds his general standards of equity (or perhaps his standards of pecuniary emulation). We may refer to the former as reflecting the *tastes* of the individual and the latter as reflecting his *values*. The distinction between the two is by no means clear-cut. An individual with esthetic feelings certainly derives pleasure from his neighbor's having a well-tended lawn. . . . Intuitively, of course, we feel that not all the possible preferences which an individual might have ought to count; his preferences for matters which are "none of his business" ought to be irrelevant. [But] the decision as to which preferences are relevant and which are not is itself a value judgment which cannot be settled on an a priori basis. From a formal point of view, one cannot distinguish between an individual's dislike for having his grounds ruined by factory smoke and his extreme distaste for the existence of heathenism in Central Africa. There are probably not a few individuals in this country who would regard the former feeling as irrelevant for social policy and the latter as relevant, though the majority would probably reverse the judgment. I merely wish to emphasize here that we must look at the entire system of values, including values about values, in seeking for a truly general theory of social welfare.
>
> It is the ordering according to values which takes into account all the desires of the individual, including the highly important socializing desires, and which is primarily relevant for the achievement of a social maximum. The market mechanism, however, takes into account only the ordering according to tastes.[64]

Arrow's distinction between bases of preference is commendable, but from an ethical perspective we may criticize his decision to disregard it in his aggregation process. Such a distinction does indeed involve value judgments, but in an ethical hypothesis it may involve them. I shall argue below (in advancing an alternative ethical hypothe-

---

64. Arrow, *Social Choice and Individual Values*, p. 18. See also his "Little's Critique of Welfare Economics," p. 927, for a stronger statement.

sis) that both bases of preference are relevant to social choice, but that "tastes" are more properly aggregated, while "values" concerning the general welfare are more properly debated and discussed.

His omission of this distinction from his aggregation process may alternatively be regarded as suitable to the task, not of devising a social welfare function, but of devising a democratic decision procedure. Such a decision procedure would resemble actual voting procedures in that they combine judgments of personal welfare and general welfare in unknown proportions; if we regard voters' preferences as analogous to consumers' preferences, we do not look beneath them for their bases. But one of our major arguments in chapter 6 will be that a democratic system of this sort might not produce maximum welfare and that we might recognize this possibility if we formulated our notions of welfare more clearly. The economic ethic that fails to distinguish among types of preference thus finds itself allied with a democratic ethic that sees process as an ultimate good, but in contrast to them we may consider ethics that treat democracy as a means to the furtherance of an explicit notion of welfare that is more nearly in accord with our ethical convictions.

Subsequently, Arrow has seemed more willing to distinguish between types of preferences, even though the distinction involves value judgments:

> Yet in the cases that students of criminal law call "crimes without victims," such as homosexuality or drug-taking, there is no direct relation between the parties [those who do it and those with moral feelings about it]. Do we have to extend the concept of externality to all matters that an individual cares about? Or in the spirit of John Stuart Mill, *is* there a second-order value judgment which excludes some of these preferences from the formation of social policy as being illegitimate infringements of individual freedom? [65]

But in this argument he is still seeking to "find" his "second-order value judgment" rather than to construct an ethical hypothesis.

Economists refer to influences of this sort, whether related to moral feelings or material effects, as "external effects" of one person's ac-

65. Arrow, "Political and Economic Evaluation of Social Effects and Externalities," p. 16. Emphasis mine.

tivity on the satisfaction of another's preferences. Such effects impinge on the other without his voluntarily participating in a transaction such as sale or compensation. The view that Arrow contends the majority of us feel intuitively, however, would include in a welfare aggregate the external effects of well-tended lawns or factory smoke but would tend to *exclude* the external effects produced in observers by heathenism, homosexuality, or drug-taking. The presumed distinction among these examples is that in the former instances satisfaction and dissatisfaction are produced, whereas in the latter moral feelings are involved. In actuality the two sorts of feelings are mixed and difficult to discriminate, but in principle we may imagine situations in which welfare and moral feeling (or judgment of others' welfare) vary independently.

The difficulty here is that, in terms of widespread moral convictions, we do not evaluate all external effects on preferences alike. For this reason welfare economics that views all preferences alike, even though in conformity with some of the convictions of economists, is open to criticism under the rule of convictions. We must thus view the question as to which external effects are relevant to welfare as subject to ethical argument, rather than expecting to resolve it on a scientific basis or to discover a solution as consensual as Arrow's axioms. Mishan sees these judgments more clearly as ethical:

> Economists . . . might wish to distinguish . . . between external effects that are a source of "legitimate" satisfaction or grievance, and those that are not. Among the latter are the resentment or envy felt by some people at the achievement or possessions of others. . . . Once ethics are brought into external effects in this way, the question of which effects are to count and which not must, in the last resort, depend on a consensus in the particular society.[66]

But reasoned ethical argument can be used in arriving at such a consensus.

I am thus led to suggest a class of ethical hypotheses that some readers may consider superior to that of undifferentiated preference satisfaction. I propose that only individual *welfares* be combined in

66. Mishan, *Economics for Social Decisions*, p. 90.

social welfare functions and that not all preference satisfaction be considered relevant to the welfare of the person whose preferences are involved. I speak here of a class of ethical hypotheses, because particular hypotheses that make this distinction may still differ as to where they draw the line between "relevant" and "irrelevant" externalities. It is this class that we shall emphasize in chapter 6, in distinguishing legislators' welfare *judgments* from their personal welfare.

The separation of "welfare" from "preference" is therefore an indispensable terminological condition for further discussion of these topics.[67] In fact, we must separate three conceptually distinct bases for ranking states of affairs in relation to any individual:

a. His *preferences* for these states, as regards his anticipated personal satisfaction. This is *not* synonymous with his preferences as they result from all his sources of motivation; it corresponds more nearly to Arrow's "tastes." Insofar as we assert that it is desirable for preferences *of this sort* to be satisfied in the main, then we will seek social decision systems that respond particularly to the individual's preferences as self-interested consumer.

b. His *personal welfare* resulting from these states. This is a category of valuative criteria corresponding roughly to "needs"; it is *not,* however, to be inferred directly from preferences, nor to correspond perfectly to them, unless the conditions for correspondence are specified.[68] These conditions affecting the relation between preferences and welfare include both valuative assertions (for example, that the satisfaction of informed preferences is or is not the good) [69] and factual conditions (such as the existence of adequate information).

c. His *judgment* as to the furthering of the *general welfare,* or the public interest, or the welfare of some collectivity, corresponding to

67. This distinction for the individual was made, for example, by Pareto (ophelimity vs. utility), *Cours d'Économie Politique,* tome II, p. 3; and Pigou (desires vs. satisfactions), *The Economics of Welfare,* pp. 23–26.

68. Brandt, *op. cit.,* pp. 29–30.

69. In addition to ethics involving preferences or various functions of income, a definition of "welfare" distinct from preferences can take us from the realm of "want-regarding" ethical principles into that of "ideal-regarding" principles; see Barry, *Political Argument,* pp. 38ff. In economics, the notion of welfare as distinct from preferences is incorporated in Musgrave's notion of "merit wants"; see Musgrave, *op. cit.,* p. 13. See also Braybrooke, "From Economics to Aesthetics: The Rectification of Preferences."

the states of affairs being compared. Judgments of this sort have been distinguished by economists from personal preferences, although they are often attributed primarily to particular persons making constitutional "welfare judgments" rather than to citizens at large.[70]

The first of these three bases of ranking—preferences for personal satisfaction—enters into the market through consumer choice. It may enter into voters' choices, but it is less clear that voting *should* be decided on this basis. Rankings on the second basis—personal welfare—may be aggregated by an observer in applying an ethical hypothesis; and a ranking on the third basis, if rendered precise, can *constitute* an ethical hypothesis but need not be of the individualistic or aggregative type.

The distinction between the first two—individual preference and welfare—has been obscured by their combination in the term "utility." [71] A similar confounding of meanings can occur in the term "interest" as when groups are presumed to seek their own interests but also to benefit when these are obtained. The differences among these three meanings are more pronounced, and more important, in the citizen's or the representative's choice than in the consumer's. The first two differ because the citizen's choice involves appraisal of complex policies that affect him only indirectly; the third is a distinct ingredient of many political choices, especially those of the representative.

But even in economics, there are several reasons for distinguishing personal welfare from preference:

1. Individual consumers may not be adequately informed as to the consequences of their purchases. These may be short-run effects if the information from the initial communications (for example, advertisements) that generated the preferences is supplemented by purchase and use, which then lead to altered consumer behavior. But longer-run consequences of consumption that are unknown to the comsumer at

70. This is done for example by Bator in "The Simple Analytics of Welfare Maximization," p. 29n, when he distinguishes a person's W (welfare)-function from his U (utility)-function. The former relates to his role as "citizen." But Bator is skeptical whether empirical inferences can be made about W-functions except through actual choice of societal policies. See also Arrow, "Public and Private Values," p. 13; a similar distinction is attributed to Colm in Musgrave, *op. cit.*, pp. 87–88.

71. See Braybrooke, *Three Tests for Democracy*, pp. 122ff.

the time, such as the effects of foods and drugs on health, also need to be considered as aspects of economic welfare.

2. Individuals (even if informed) may act so as to decrease, or at least not maximize, their satisfaction or welfare, even when considering only the consequences of purchases to themselves. This is clearly true in the case of some habit-forming drugs, but the broader question whether individuals have psychic conflicts and seek to harm themselves, or whether they devote sufficient resources to their own education and development of new capacities, must also be raised as a critique of consumer sovereignty.

3. Individuals may also act altruistically by taking into account the presumed welfare of others. The consequences of these types of acts to the actor may not be simply related to his preference or desire to perform the acts. In particular, an altruist may choose or prefer an act that we would ordinarily judge to *decrease* his personal welfare—a possibility that we could not easily describe in terms of a circularly defined "utility." He may thus, in terms of welfare, engage in transactions that lead to a "consumer deficit" as well as a consumer surplus.

4. Most generally, the two distinct realms of discourse—science and ethics—in which "preference" and "welfare" are respectively used make it unreasonable to restrict the definition of "welfare" as we would the definition of "preference." The two concepts may thus have different formal properties. Whereas economic preference (or preference in other domains) may not be ascertainable other than as an ordering relation, we may be able to formulate more satisfactory ethical hypotheses if "welfare," as a variable in an ethical system, is expressed as a cardinal number comparable among persons.

Imperfect Information: Freedom, Expertness, and the Information Market

We have proposed a type of ethical hypothesis that distinguishes between preference and welfare and suggested that not all preferences *ought* to be aggregated in a social welfare function—contrary to Arrow's (1951) catholicity. But the distinction also raises the converse question: ought we to consider aspects of welfare that are not reflected

in preferences? One such aspect is welfare that is not correctly anticipated by the chooser, even though he intends to choose in view of his
own anticipated satisfaction; his information may be inadequate.

The question of imperfect information is often brushed aside, however, with arguments similar to those of Graaff:

> We have already defined a man's welfare map to be identical with
> his preference map, which indicates how he would choose between
> different situations if he were given the opportunity for choice. Let
> it be said at once that most people would probably want to regard
> this as a definition of welfare *ex ante,* rather than *ex post;* and that
> most people would probably feel that the latter is the more signifi-
> cant concept. It is, however, very hard to think of defining welfare
> *ex post.* We could, of course, simply assume that the observing
> economist knew what it was, or that we had a lie-detector and could
> question people to find out if they were better off yesterday than the
> day before. But neither of these assumptions is very helpful, and if
> we want to make any progress we shall have to be content with wel-
> fare *ex ante.* To pretend that we can distinguish the two concepts in
> practice, and for people other than ourselves, leads very rapidly to a
> paternalist approach—not only to group welfare, but to individual
> welfare itself.[72]

Graaff's statement reveals valuations of "progress" in economic analysis and of libertarianism to an unquestioning degree. But his distinction between *ex ante* and *ex post* raises the question whether welfare
can be judged not only before and after choosing, but also before and
after changing one's preferences themselves.

The two ethics of "welfare *ex ante*" (that is, preference) and "welfare *ex post*" may be compared under the meta-ethical rules I have
proposed, chiefly the rule of convictions. When comparing them we
may set aside questions of cardinality and interpersonal comparison
and focus on the qualities that will be fostered by each ethic, as well
as the types of power relations in society that each might imply. We
consider first the problem of information needed for consumers' decisions and in the next section the possibility of changes in preferences.

72. Graaff, *op. cit.,* p. 33.

The ethics of preference would presumably decentralize consumer decisions as far as possible—leading to a negative income tax in place of resources channeled by "experts" who judged what was "good for" the recipient. Thus *even if* a food-stamp program gave preference to certain foods for health reasons, or if the social worker did know what was good for the persons served, these judgments would not be allowed to intervene in the consumer's choice. An ethic of welfare *ex post* might allow such intervention.[73]

The issue is of course broader than this, as we have posed it so far only for beneficiaries of welfare programs. Those in our society who earn their own income *are* allowed to dispose of it with the same freedom that would be accorded to recipients of negative income taxes. True, they have been prohibited by law from purchasing certain drugs or foods deemed harmful and from purchasing "intoxicating liquors" between 1919 and 1933. But otherwise they have considerable freedom of choice among goods and services offered on the market, within their ability to pay. If one argued that consumers sometimes did not know what was good for them, he might extend the ethic of welfare *ex post* to consumers generally, rather than merely to those receiving government aid. The arguments in favor of an ethic of "welfare *ex post*" over an ethic of preference are illustrated by health-related issues such as provision of health care, diet, medical examination and preventive medicine, and the environment. Some prevalent ethical convictions favor providing services in these areas even to persons who do not demand them or who have become accustomed to situations that observers would consider undesirable.

The counterargument for an ethic of preferences also has important political aspects. Closely related to it is the argument that consumers should have more control over the economic system. Economists such as Graaff who advocate an ethic of preference consider the alternative to involve paternalism. Advocates of collective consumer influence, however, tend to argue that market processes are not sufficient to satisfy preferences. The free-market advocates ask in reply, not what policy would be chosen in an instance in which we knew the conse-

73. On the distinction in practice between ethics of preference and welfare, see Braybrooke, *Three Tests for Democracy*, pp. 121–145. The role of the expert is criticized in Keith-Lucas, "The Political Theory Implicit in Social Casework Theory."

quences of acts for "welfare *ex post*," but how government will control the market if decisions are made under uncertainty by fallible human beings with political interests. This argument can be interpreted, in part, as an appeal to the criterion of actual anticipated consequences or "welfare *ex post*," on the ground that elite rule, monopoly, or tyranny may run counter not only to preference satisfaction, but also to welfare maximization in the longer run.

It is important, however, to be clear whether we are arguing that preference satisfaction or consumer control is a desirable ultimate standard or that it is a desirable and feasible decision procedure for attaining some other end. If the latter, we are free to consider modifications of an existing market system to further that other end. The argument then becomes an empirical one about the likelihood that monopoly, corruption, tyranny, and other consequences will result from the establishment of various institutions for social choice.

But when we consider either preference satisfaction or consumer control, we must ask whether consumers' preferences are well informed. If we depart somewhat from the criterion of preference *ex ante*, and ask under what conditions preferences are adequately informed so as to conduce to welfare *ex post*, we are led to analyze the production and distribution of information. Those aspects of advertising that relate to the furnishing of information have been analyzed systematically by some economists, even though they less often consider its effects on changes of preference.

Several economists who have analyzed the effects of advertising from an information standpoint have argued, counter to a widespread critique of advertising, that it often permits economies for the consumer. Stigler has noted that the variation among prices at a given time in a market provides rewards for the expenditure of effort in search for information about them. Benham has shown that the prohibition of advertising of eyeglasses in certain states has been associated with higher prices. Telser, countering the argument that brand loyalty reduces competition, has shown that in markets where advertising is a high proportion of sales—cosmetics, toiletries, and toothpaste—brand turnover among consumers is high.[74] From this finding one might

74. Stigler, "The Economics of Information"; Benham, "The Effect of Advertising on the Price of Eyeglasses"; Telser, "Some Aspects of the Economics of Advertising."

infer that advertising was less effective in determining preferences than some had thought, but it might also indicate that advertising in those markets does not convey an accurate expectation of the product.

Economists have also pointed out that there are devices for improving consumer information which themselves can be provided in markets. These include department stores, *Consumer Reports,* and political parties, all of which perform the function of providing a "brand name" that permits consumers (citizens) to judge a variety of particular goods (policies) at lesser cost in information seeking. In each of these cases, additional reasons and information relevant to the choice may be supplied (goods are displayed, performance tests are given, arguments are advanced), but the central symbol of the aggregate, once it is accepted, can be used to reduce the cost of information for consumers or voters.[75]

The general approach of these economic analyses has thus been to show that the market for information operates like other markets: that consumers are willing to pay to obtain information and that the market meets this demand. In these terms, we should perhaps not ask that more information be supplied, since the demand would seem to represent consumers' proper allocation of their scarce resources between information search and other activities.

We may nevertheless ask whether the market for information functions properly. Consumers may still spend too little on information, for several reasons. Even if information were a private good that could be sold at a given price to those who received it, we could not be sure that those who needed it would seek it out, since it is plausible that information *about* the information market is inadequate.[76] Consumer information may also be undersupplied by virtue of being a collective good, such that once it is available many can consume it freely. But at the same time, the sellers of consumer goods transmit unsought information to the public. Knowing that information about these goods will not be sought by all prospective purchasers, they pay to incorporate it

---

75. Downs, *An Economic Theory of Democracy,* pp. 100ff.

76. See Scherhorn and Wieken, "On the Effect of Counter-Information on Consumers." Arrow suggests that one remedy for sellers' information advantages over buyers is the creation of ethical codes such as those of the professions; see his "Social Responsibility and Economic Efficiency," pp. 313–314. "Need" here is a shorthand for "potential increase in welfare."

in other information media, such as those for news and entertainment, or to supply it in public places. Stigler suggests that this may also compensate for the fact that "the assimilation of information is not an easy or pleasant task for most people." [77]

Information furnished by sellers need not be of high quality, however; in addition it may alter preferences or create diswelfare directly through communication to persons who do not wish to receive it. For this reason the government sometimes enters as a regulator of the information market, as an enforcer of laws concerning truth in advertising or regulation of billboards. In the supply of *political* information, however, the difficulties of improving such a market are compounded by the involvement of government as an interested party.

The analogous problem of a political information market is also more difficult if citizens are expected to make judgments concerning the general welfare rather than simply their own welfare. In this case the optimal search effort may be greater than if only the searcher himself were affected. Political information, if it relates to the welfare of others besides the chooser, may be even more a collective good than consumer information.

Induced Changes in Preference: Advertising and Education

The proposed distinction between an individual's self-oriented preferences and his welfare has further implications that go beyond the problem of imperfect information. Even in a world of perfect information, where consumers could unerringly choose what they wanted, their welfare might still be greater if their preferences were different. A theoretical framework that takes preferences as given omits important factual problems, but it also leaves totally unanswered the question, "What should we prefer?" [78]

We are led, therefore, to consider and evaluate communications that change preferences or welfare, in accord with the rule of generality. An individual may be led by external influence to alter his preferences

77. Stigler, *op. cit.*, p. 222.
78. See Parsons, *The Structure of Social Action;* Gintis, "Neo-Classical Welfare Economics and Individual Development"; and Gintis, "Alienation and Power: Towards A Radical Welfare Economics."

concerning his own welfare or the welfare he receives from a given external state of affairs. He may also be led to connect his own welfare with the welfare of others—positively or negatively. And finally, he may be led to change his preferences for states of affairs as they affect others, without corresponding changes in his own welfare; this effect includes the results of deliberation about moral judgments or the general welfare and is particularly relevant to political choices.

Two major forms of communication in which preference might be altered have been analyzed by economists—advertising and education. In both, it is precisely the aspects involving changes of preference that are often neglected. Economic analyses of advertising have considered its effects on prices, competition, and effective capital investment, but for a general evaluation of advertising they must also be concerned with changes in preference.[79] In education, a major aspect studied has been the resulting change in productivity (human capital formation, with income as an indicator). Increased efficiency of consumption has also been considered. But changes in attitudes, especially in the moral and civic realms, are also important possible results of education.

In discussing welfare *ex post* and the information market, we considered studies of advertising that treated it in terms of its information content. If the information content was greater, the market presumably approached the ideal of fully informed preference satisfaction—provided we could incorporate information costs in the description of the ideal. In one sense this ideal is seen as the ultimate ethical good, and it would seem meaningless to measure the adequacy of a perfect market by any external criterion. Imperfect markets, however, or markets in which there is a long delay between choice and knowledge of the consequences of that choice, may be assessed by measuring their results. Thus the markets for health care and food may be as-

79. The related fields of psychological learning theory and therapy, treated in chapter 7 below, are even further from economic analysis. Some economists have indeed noted that preferences can be changed, even though this observation cannot easily be incorporated in their central paradigm. Galbraith notes in *The New Industrial State,* ch. XIX, that advertising decreases consumer sovereignty. Tullock, in *Toward A Mathematics of Politics,* pp. 2–3, notes that this neglect has even more serious consequences in politics than in economics, and Boulding has criticized "the immaculate conception of the indifference"; see his "Human Betterment and the Quality of Life." For a review of studies on the effects of advertising see Ferber, "Consumer Economics: A Survey," p. 1318.

sessed (at least in part) in terms of their influences on the actual state of health of a population, or the labor market may be assessed in terms of workers' productivity and satisfaction.

But the use of such external criteria seems all the more important if preferences may be changed. It is possible, for example, that advertising creates unnecessary anxiety in areas of life where the consumer's self-image can be linked to product preferences. In addition, the cumulative impact of advertising may be not only to supply information, but to increase demands beyond the level at which they can be realistically satisfied. A growth of material production may result but be accompanied by a constant level of economic striving and dissatisfaction. Similar effects may obtain in politics.

Yet advertising may also have the converse effect: it may not only influence demands and tastes, but also increase the satisfaction that consumers receive when they buy a product; products, like political leaders and policies, may acquire symbolic significance. The support that a government generates for itself by public statements and symbolic acts is not so often judged undesirable, but we need to judge the two by similar standards.

We must therefore examine, through research and valuative discussion, whether advertising creates welfare or satisfaction over and above the results of channeling goods and services to consumers. In the simplified view of critics of advertising, its communications sell shabby goods and create negative welfare by inducing consumers to buy products that they do not need and which are often unserviceable as well. Were this demonstrably so, then the manipulative aspects of advertising would find little justification. But suppose, on the other hand, that advertising did nothing to alter the flow of goods (as a political regime's public relations might conceivably operate), but simply aimed at convincing people that they were pleased with what they *had*. Would this possibly be a desirable result? And if not in a presently existing economic system, then would it be so under an alternative system?

Education, like advertising, both provides information and changes preferences. It is useful to consider the two together, so that our standards of judgment will be as general as possible. A major economic approach to the evaluation of education has been through the income streams received by educated persons, but it has also been suggested that the educated are more efficient consumers or are better prepared for the production that takes place in the family unit.[80]

In the educational process, preference structures may be changed in three aspects that are worthy of consideration. We may describe them positively, though the opposite effects might also occur:

a. The development and enhancement of tastes, so that the educated person may achieve greater welfare (satisfaction, appreciation) from given states of affairs. For example, in analyzing the state of the arts in American society, Scitovsky suggests that "the public would benefit from a more educated taste." [81]

b. The rendering consistent of tastes or preferences (with one another or with a situation considered as given), so that the educated person may efficiently seek his own welfare, insofar as he can appraise it correctly. This increase in consistency must be distinguished from education in skills permitting more efficient production or consumption. I refer here to actual changes in preferences, forming more consistent systems such as are used in decision analysis.

c. The "external" effects produced by education. For example, as Schultze points out, "programs to train the hard-core unemployed have additional benefits in terms of an improved social structure which cannot be measured simply in terms of added employment and income." An important aspect of "improved social structure" is the breadth of view and public-spiritedness of potential leaders or the "benevolence" of some members of the society toward others.[82] Or in another sense, if we may accept one of the findings of Coleman et al.,[83] the presence of abler and more highly motivated children in a school class produces external benefits for other students in the class. These benefits may of course be manifested in income; they need not be ignored by the market for graduates but are "external" in that the play of free choice alone in a voucher system might not provide them sufficiently unless the abler children were compensated. The same

80. See for example Windham, *Education, Equality and Income Redistribution;* Ribich, *Education and Poverty,* p. 9; Becker, *Economic Theory,* pp. 47–48.

81. Scitovsky, "What's Wrong with the Arts Is What's Wrong with Society."

82. Schultze, *The Politics and Economics of Public Spending,* p. 72; Boulding, "The Network of Interdependence."

83. Coleman et al., *Equality of Educational Opportunity.*

problem arises for a free urban residential market with neighborhood schools.

If we consider first the development and enhancement of tastes, questions of evaluation are simplified in two senses. First, we can consider the problem (as an approximation) as involving individuals separately, without externalities or political (collective) aspects of the decision. Secondly, we can consider over-time comparison of the experiences of the *same* individual (if experiences are our criterion), in retrospect—or by asking comparable questions before and after.[84] A variety of tastes and skills may thus be cultivated, but for illustrative purposes we can restrict our consideration to art, music, literature, and drama.

The development of these tastes may be a function of education, formal or informal. But note that the decision to develop them is to be appraised in terms of costs and benefits, as well as alternative uses of time and resources. The consideration of certain esthetic objects as "objectively superior" will then be replaced by a notion that such superiority may exist only as an average over persons, among whom capacities for appreciation vary. Moreover, experiments such as those of the BBC Third Programme need to be considered in terms of the conditions for voluntary choice of "high culture." We thus confront Bentham's issue of pushpin vs. poetry, but without taking an existing state of tastes for granted.

As a second approximation we encounter the question whether scarcity or prestige value ought to be attached to cultural goods and services. Conspicuous consumption (attending the Boston Symphony) and reports of it have status overtones. Original paintings are considered superior to reproductions or imitations (no matter how faithful) in terms of their scarcity, as are live performances in the performing arts. Perhaps valuations or preferences deriving from these sources will be neglected in certain ethics.

Still more important in education is the inculcation, at some point in citizens' and leaders' socialization processes, of valuation of general welfare as against personal or particular welfare. The problem of corruption in political representation is difficult to pose in a self-interested

84. James and Nordell, "Preference Transformations and Welfare Theory."

"economic" model of politics. We need additional evidence as to how leaders and citizens acquire their support for political "rules of the game" and the conditions under which the game benefits the general welfare or that of a governing group.[85] Nevertheless (as I shall argue in the next chapter) these "preferences" are of vital importance, and we cannot assume that they will necessarily be purchased in the educational market or adequately measured by the subsequent salaries of graduates. Indeed, the lack of concern with the development of the educated public or the well-informed citizen, to which we referred in chapter 2, is an indication of this type of market failure.

Types of Action Affecting Welfare

We have argued for ethical hypotheses that distinguish between preference and welfare and for consideration of preference change as a source of welfare. This argument enlarges the range of acts that we may consider for producing welfare and thus is consistent with our rule of generality. In this more general perspective, we may classify various types of action in social, economic, or political systems to increase welfare. We are concerned here with social policies, which, though realized through actions of individuals in the last analysis, are to be judged in terms of the general welfare rather than simply that of these individuals.

We must recognize, first, that according to most notions of welfare it is possible to enhance welfare through promotion of "economic" action aimed at the satisfaction of given preferences. Such benefits may be promoted by regulation of economic systems, as in the prevention of monopoly, or by refraining from interventions that unnecessarily distort the allocation of goods and resources that the market produces. Still in the economist's perspective, we may also increase welfare by redistribution or transfer of resources from one group in society to another. The economic perspective may also be extended to political choice, for (as we shall see in chapter 6) a number of valuative theories of politics are based on notions of choice and exchange analogous to those of the market.

85. See Melnik and Leites, *The House Without Windows*.

Second, we must also consider social policies that increase the consonance between individual preferences and individual welfare. If we restrict ourselves to the economist's notion of welfare *ex post,* this is to be done mainly by supplying information. Political parties and groups may also perform this function. But if our ethical hypothesis stresses another notion of welfare, then we may consider the change of preferences (for example, by education) in order to lead to that sort of welfare—such as the development of character or the philosophical life considered as an end. It is also possible to consider policies that adapt individual preferences to accord with feasible alternatives; one may thus consider reconciling preferences with the individual's "social production function." And finally, preferences may be changed in the direction of greater internal or *intra*personal consistency.[86]

Third, we may consider altering or conserving social structures (structures of norms) so as to maximize opportunities for welfare. This includes increasing the interpersonal congruence of preferences. As Olson has pointed out, this may occur either through agreement in preference (for collective goods) or through reciprocal differentiation of preferences permitting exchange, as in a market or division of labor. The aspect of most interest to moralists is the internalization of social norms in the personality, leading to an increase in personal preference for states of affairs that increase the welfare of others. This type of policy also includes modification of the existing alternatives— through changes in institutions, regulation (elimination or addition of alternatives), alteration of mechanisms for combining preferences, or other changes in material or social technology. One may also restructure the alternatives by changing the rules of a game to make it non-zero-sum.[87] Congruence among the preferences of various persons, or between the preferences of one and the welfare of another, can be sought through the creation of groups, communication links, or constituencies in which persons participate jointly.

86. See Bay, *The Structure of Freedom,* ch. 4. The notion of a "social production function" is discussed in chapter 7 below in connection with therapy. Schultze, in *The Politics and Economics of Public Spending,* pp. 57–64, uses the term to characterize the possible welfare outputs of social programs, but the notion may be extended to individuals' acts.

87. Coleman, "Political Money"; Wertheimer, *Productive Thinking,* pp. 127–136. The internalization of social norms is treated in chapters 7 and 8 below.

Fourth, we may consider population policies that increase or decrease the numbers of persons in the social or economic system. Such changes are extremely difficult to evaluate within an ethic of preference satisfaction. In a utilitarian framework, one is led to quite different population policies depending on whether he considers the average happiness ("quality of life") or the aggregate.[88]

Finally, social policy may be concerned with creation or maintenance of conditions under which acts of some of the above types can take place. Among these conditions is political or economic competition. For example, as Cropsey has pointed out, economic competition and private property may have been considered by Adam Smith to be conditions for political dissent.[89] In general terms, choices among political regimes, constitutions, rules, and policies may affect the attainment of ethical goals, including welfare. It is to these choices that we now turn.

88. See Rawls, *A Theory of Justice*, pp. 161–164.
89. Cropsey, *Polity and Economy*.

6 THE FUNCTIONS AND FORMS OF GOVERNMENT

Political institutions have been justified or criticized in terms of various criteria—their response to the wishes of citizens; the furtherance of goals embodied in their processes, such as participation; the promotion of the good life, freedom, or justice; the development of character; or the rights they sustain. But analysis and evaluation of political institutions are now being made increasingly in economic terms.[1] One economic approach, concerned with possible failures of the market mechanism, leads us to judge whether particular functions might be better performed through government intervention. But a second approach involves formulating models of government itself in economic terms—of the behavior of voters, group members, coalitions, political parties, legislators, and bureaucrats. This approach, like the first, leads us to ask highly specific questions about the appropriateness of particular governmental procedures. In both, therefore, the economic approach leads us to judge particular choices within democratic polities, which might not be judged in such detail by broad justifications of democracy as a regime. Both tend to neglect the choice among regimes, and both are open to some of the same criticisms we have made of economic ethics in the previous chapter. Some of these criticisms will in fact be strengthened when we examine the application of economic ethics to the less appropriate subject matter of politics. But for general ethical discourse, we shall argue that the approaches of economics and political science complement one another. The economic approach has some advantages under the rule of generality, and certain approaches of political philosophy have advantages under the rule of convictions.

The first of these two economic approaches leads us to consider

1. The philosophic foundations of liberal democracy, however, are closely related to those of the market economy; see Macpherson, *The Political Theory of Possessive Individualism*.

governmental action as a remedy for the failures of the market. In this view, the market should be allowed to make those types of resource allocations that it makes well, without the "distortion" that governmental intervention might produce. A principal function of government in domestic policy, other than assuring competition, would then be the redistribution of income so as to increase the degree of equity without impairing the allocation of resources that results from producers' and consumers' motives to economize.

From the perspective of political philosophy, such a view of government seems narrow. The discipline of political science still contains this valuative field, which encompasses the major political thought of the past. This tradition provides some of the legitimation for the enterprise of this book. Its ethics are more fully articulated than those implied in the concepts of the scientific study of politics. We shall relate one such ethical principle, that of the social contract, to sociological concepts in chapter 8.

We cannot, therefore, speak of an "ethics of political science" in the same sense as "economic ethics." Rather, modern behavioral studies of politics have been informed by an unreflective notion of democracy. Insofar as this notion has been refined, it has made use of economic concepts and assumptions. Together with political analyses by economists, it thus constitutes a second economic approach to politics, analyzing the operation of the political system rather than the deficiencies of the market. We shall trace out this second economic approach to politics as well, to see both its values and its shortcomings. We shall in effect follow our meta-ethical rule of convictions, indicating political situations in which the implications of economic ethics conflict with widespread moral convictions more than do those of an alternative ethics. The alternative ethics, introduced in chapter 5, is of the type that distinguishes judgments of general welfare from preferences related to personal welfare.

If we wish to apply the criteria of welfare economics to the activities of government, we must ask two major types of questions. We first ask what sorts of functions or activities are inappropriate for the market and thus perhaps appropriate for government. Second (in this perspective) is the paramount question of political philosophy: What sorts of procedural arrangements, or constitutions, are best for arriving at governmental decisions? This general domain of investigation corresponds to what Samuelson has called "welfare politics." [2] The first of these questions leads us to the economic analysis of market failure, and part of the second finds expression in efforts to model and evaluate political systems in economic terms.

Market Failure

A strength of the first economic approach lies in the standard it provides for allocating particular economic functions to government. A major theorem of the new welfare economics concerns the optimal allocative properties of a competitive economy. The theorem states that (under certain conditions) if each producer chooses an optimal combination of factors of production in view of his own profits, and if each consumer seeks to maximize the fulfillment of his own preferences, the price system will distribute goods in a Pareto-efficient fashion.

In this perspective, government intervention other than the simple redistribution of income or wealth must first be justified by "market failure"—that is, by the failure of some necessary condition of the theorem to obtain. If the market has no failures other than disparities in incomes, then this theorem leads economists to oppose certain kinds of intervention, such as tariffs, excise taxes, rent controls, minimum wage legislation, and rationing. It leads also to advocacy of a negative income tax rather than payments in kind if income is to be transferred, embodying the libertarian assumption that the poor should be allowed the same freedom of choice as the rich.

The "perfect market" model used as a standard in this theorem is a static equilibrium model. It says nothing about the rate with which a system adjusts to new external conditions, its possible oscillations about equilibrium, the disappointed expectations that result from economic fluctuations, the influence of changing tastes, or the welfare effects of changes in population. These are among the phenomena that must be incorporated in a model that furnishes a general criterion for choice in changing systems. Some efforts have been made to charac-

2. Samuelson, "The Pure Theory of Public Expenditure," p. 389.

terize a dynamic optimum as regards the growth of an economy.[3] But we must also consider the possibility of optima attained through oscillation, as in a "stable" two-party political system, if closer parallels between the performance of economic and political "markets" are to be found.

The criterion underlying this model defines welfare as preference satisfaction. It fails to tell us whether the wants or preferences to which the market responds are those to which it *should* be responding—a criticism that is significant for the market but far more important in the realm of political choice.

Basic to this theorem is the condition that producers' and consumers' decisions be made in terms of a price system, which guides the producer's combination of factors of production and the consumer's choice of quantities of goods. But if prices fail to indicate all the effects of these choices on others' welfare or diswelfare, the conditions for the theorem will not hold. If a producer imposes costs on another producer, or on consumers, by influences such as atmospheric or water pollution that are not reflected in prices, the market will fail to signal these costs, and the producer may be expected to produce too much. Conversely, if he conveys benefits to others that are not reflected in prices he receives, he will produce too little. Effects of this sort are known as external costs or economies, or as "externalities." Insofar as these or other conditions lead to a less than optimal allocation of factors and goods, one may speak of "market failure"—though there are numerous types and degrees of such failure.[4]

The ideal model of a competitive economy thus requires that each producer or consumer make choices independently of their consequences for others.[5] The producer's calculations are then not contami-

3. See for example Samuelson, "The Two-Part Golden Rule Deduced as the Asymptotic Turnpike of Catenary Motions."

4. Bator, in "The Anatomy of Market Failure," analyzes types of failure that can occur even when individual choices are errorless and well informed. The concept has since been extended; see Haveman and Margolis, eds., *Public Expenditures and Policy Analysis*.

5. This independence was referred to as "non-Tuism" in Wicksteed, *The Common Sense of Political Economy* (1935), vol. I, p. 180. See also Mishan, "A Survey of Welfare Economics, 1939–59," p. 204. This perspective neglects not only altruism but also malevolence; thus while some political scientists and psychologists are concerned with conflict resolution, few economists are.

nated by side effects of his production, and the consumer's contribute directly to the welfare of society. As long as a chooser does not help or harm others as a result of self-interested activities, his preferences may be expected to work through the market for a Pareto-efficient result.

Economists have illustrated this principle with numerous examples in which this condition of independence fails and in which external effects result from productive activities. These include the effect of one vehicle on others through road congestion, the benefit that immunization against disease confers on other persons, and the underproduction of apples because of the failure of a market system to consider the additional benefit that apple blossoms confer on beekeepers for the production of honey.[6] In all these hypothetical examples there is a nonoptimal allocation of factors of production because external effects are not reflected in the price system. Simple examples of this type facilitate discussion of the principles involved, but they also omit the ethical ambiguities relating to one person's moral feeling about another's activity, which we noted in discussing Arrow's notion of "values" in chapter 5.[7]

Certain types of market failure will be especially important for our further discussion. Monopoly or failure of competition can impair the functioning of the price system. The generation of costs and benefits (economies) not reflected in prices is another type of market failure, which can occur in two different ways. First, an actor engaging in one activity can jointly produce *other* "goods" or "bads" that impinge on other persons without pricing: pollution, noise, positive or negative esthetic effects, and possibly the pain associated with moral disapproval. Second, a producer of one good may automatically make that *same* good available to a number of consumers without their being chargeable for it or depleting the supply. The production of information, protection of a community against external threats, the creation

6. Knight, "Some Fallacies in the Interpretation of Social Cost"; Olson and Zeckhauser, "The Efficient Production of External Economics"; Meade, "External Economies and Diseconomies in a Competitive Situation."
7. Arrow's examples also involved external effects produced by consumers, which we shall treat further in chapter 7. An additional complication is the possibility that two or more external effects will compensate one another.

of attractive surroundings, and the creation of social norms are often of this type. Goods of this type are known as *collective goods*.[8]

In a restricted sense, "market failure" refers to departures from Pareto efficiency that occur even though producers and consumers are behaving as maximizing economic men. But by extension we may refer to other sources of "failure" of actual markets: the use of force, persuasion, or political action on the part of producers or consumers; inadequate information; dynamic rather than static departures from optimality; and departures from ethical standards relating the preferences of various individuals, such as that of equity. We shall refer particularly to problems of equity when we introduce the analogous notion of "political market failure" later in this chapter.

When the market fails to allocate factors or distribute goods optimally, a prima facie case can be made for collective action to set things right. And if the costs of private collective action are excessive, then such a case can be made for governmental action.[9] We are then led to ask, from this economic perspective, what types of activities might be appropriate for government.

The approach differs from that of political philosophy in treating the detailed functions of government before the form of the regime.[10] And yet the very assumption that a competitive market exists implies that the regime does not control that market other than to insure its operation. Prices may, alternatively, be set optimally by the calculations of a socialist government, but in this case we must ask what criteria other than the calculations of buyers and sellers would enter into the setting of these prices or what other functions the socialist government should perform. In general, however, this economic approach to government assumes a democratic regime. It gives rise to proposals for particular

8. Often called "public goods"; but this latter term creates the incorrect presumption that they are necessarily provided by government rather than privately. The distinction between external effects and collective goods is not a sharp one; a more elaborate typology is presented in Mishan, "The Postwar Literature on Externalities," pp. 9–14. See also Riker and Ordeshook, *An Introduction to Positive Political Theory*, p. 261. Social norms are treated in chapter 8 below.

9. See Buchanan, "The Institutional Structure of Externality."

10. See Cropsey, "What Is Welfare Economics?" Some political philosophers begin their argument with consideration of the good life and pass from this to consideration of the best regime.

types of government intervention, though it cannot evaluate all these interventions as elegantly as it evaluates the market.

Types of Government Intervention

To remedy market failure, government may conceivably intervene in the economy in various ways. It may rectify the allocation of factors of production by taxes or subsidies to particular industries or by regulation of production with respect to side effects such as working conditions or pollution. It may make laws to combat monopoly or regulate "natural monopolies" that result from increasing returns to scale. It may intervene in the information aspects of the market by regulation of advertising content or provision of information. It may specify which products can be marketed, in view of possible harm to the consumer from some products, or lack of genuine benefit from others, which he cannot properly anticipate. It may intervene more directly by allocating scarce resources (broadcast channels or parks) or by direct production of goods and services. And it may redistribute income directly by taxation and subsidies to individuals.

Governmental intervention may also concern the dynamic features of the economy, such as stabilization and growth. These features may be influenced by the control of interest rates or by the alteration of tax rates or rates of government spending. The policies that affect them cannot, however, be chosen on the basis of the static notion of "market failure."

The role of government may also extend beyond intervention in the economy to the creation of decision-making subsystems. These choices include the modification of governmental forms themselves, through the creation of new constituencies, committees, organizations, or rules. They include the creation of price mechanisms that add incentives or reduce externalities and thus render actual choice systems more like the ideal market: "effluent charges in pollution control; incentive contracts and subsidies in manpower training programs; efficiency-oriented reimbursement schemes in medical insurance programs" [11]—all involve governmental intervention in the structure of decision systems, without control of detailed allocations. French eco-

11. Schultze, "The Reviewers Reviewed," p. 47, and his *The Politics and Economics of Public Spending*. ch. 6.

nomic planning, and the use of tuition vouchers for educational services, also share this character of permitting individual choice under structured incentives. If we consider the possibility that government may create or modify decision systems in these ways, we can escape the artificial dichotomy between "synoptic problem solving," on the one hand, and "partisan mutual adjustment" in a given system, on the other.[12]

Governments may also create decision systems that do not involve individual decision or participation to the same degree as the market or the vote. This type of system involves observation of the individual's condition, behavior, or reactions, without requiring judgment or deliberation on his part, even in self-interest. Variables that can be used in such systems include individuals' health, education, and career advancement or indicators of the functioning of organizations or social systems, such as crime rates, traffic and transportation patterns, use of public facilities, and reactions to public policies or programs. In any of these cases, a feedback system may be devised such that information about the variable in question can be used to guide intervention in the system and to influence the variable. An example is the monitoring of traffic flow by pavement sensors or overhead observation and the setting of signal-light timing by means of the data obtained.

A distinctive feature of these "behavior-feedback systems" is the nonparticipation of the individuals affected. Their role in these systems is that of subjects rather than participants,[13] although they may have some latitude of choice rather than being coerced. But the design and operation of such systems is presumably subject to control by the political authorities, and if citizens participate in the choice of these authorities, they may be willing to assume the role of subject in subsystems. The interaction between system and subsystem may nevertheless affect character development or the general level of conflict in the society.[14] Insofar as these systems are judged to be useful, they may be cited in argument against ethical systems that consider participation an end in itself (rule of convictions).

The types of intervention listed above have been proposed (or cri-

12. Lindblom, *The Intelligence of Democracy.*
13. Almond and Verba, *The Civic Culture.*
14. See Dahrendorf, *Society and Democracy in Germany,* ch. 11, for a similar effect presumed to result from codetermination in industry.

ticized) by economists concerned with remedying market failures. The analyses that have led to these proposals or criticisms have begun with the ethic of Pareto optimality, modified at times by notions of equity or other ethical considerations. A virtue of these analyses, to which we have called attention, is their capacity to deal with specific policy choices within an existing regime. There are, however, other specific types of government action, involving changes of preference, to which a general ethics should apply; we shall later suggest some of these additional options in order to indicate the lack of generality of this economic approach.

The economic approaches of "welfare politics," and of the theory of public choice, have generally assumed a regime involving free universal suffrage and, within it, individuals who are free to conclude private bargains and form voluntary associations. Within this framework they allow us to compare governmental action with possible alternatives, including the working of the market as well as other private actions.

In place of the simple notion that governmental intervention is the remedy for market failure, we must therefore consider several alternatives. First is the possibility of private transactions that may lead to the same allocation of factors of production as government intervention would have produced. Coase gives an extensive list of examples in which one producer creates external costs to another and in which private compensation would lead to at least as good a productive allocation as government regulation, but he points out that questions of equity and justice, such as courts would consider, are ignored in this equivalence.[15]

A second type of private adjustment involves the formation of a social group or organization. The formation of a firm itself, or a combination of firms, may change external effects to internal, and if the resulting internal decision process is adequate, a type of market failure may be reduced.[16] A private association, whether a family or a cooperative, may also be formed to supply services to its members. And in the political realm, private associations may be formed at intermediate

15. Coase, "The Problem of Social Cost."
16. See Coase, "The Nature of the Firm"; Buchanan and Tullock, *The Calculus of Consent,* p. 50.

levels between the individual and government. Closely related to this type of private adjustment is the voluntary change of social norms, which may be affected by private as well as by governmental action.

The prima facie case for government intervention to cope with market failure is reduced not only by the possibility of private action, but also by a more objective view of the working of government itself. If government action is to be considered as an alternative, it should be considered realistically, rather than in an ideal or moralistic model; this was Downs's reason for attempting to construct an economic theory of democracy. Governments may produce nonoptimal distributions of goods and services, or external effects, as we shall consider below in connection with "political market failure." The regulatory activities of governments may derive from the concerns of particular firms and industries more than from a consideration of the general welfare.[17] But the same realistic criteria should of course be applied to the economy; the disproportionate influence of certain firms or industries in politics may possibly be attributed to economic concentration as well as to governmental shortcomings.

Democratic Theory and Economic Concepts

Most political philosophers' approaches to the evaluation of political institutions have been quite different from that of economists.[18] Political philosophy has long been concerned with the justification of one or another type of regime. In the contemporary Western world it gives special attention to "democratic theory," comprising those justifications offered for democratic institutions. These institutions themselves vary considerably in detail among nations, historical periods, systems, and subsystems, and conceivably an economic approach will permit us to compare and evaluate some of these various types. But the main

17. Downs, *An Economic Theory of Democracy*, pp. 282–283. A similar argument as to the inefficiency of majority vote for market-type decisions is made in Shubik, "Voting, or a Price System in a Competitive Market Structure." The problem of client-dominated regulation has been recognized by political scientists in studies of regulatory agencies but is also stressed in Stigler, "The Theory of Economic Regulation." See also Galbraith, *The New Industrial State*.

18. See Buchanan and Tullock, *The Calculus of Consent*, Appendix 1; Tullock, *Private Wants, Public Means*, p. 111.

concern of democratic theory has been with popular control itself and
with the procedures and guarantees that insure it.

The criteria by which democracy is judged or justified are diverse.
They include the valuation of democracy as an end which is itself to
be maximized; the valuation of certain processes such as deliberation; [19] and various relational as well as individualistic ethical criteria.
These relational criteria include rule or control by the people in general, distributive justice, freedom, and equality. The participation and
consent of the governed are also seen as values that it provides; and
Mill, among others, emphasized the development of citizens' character.[20] Criteria of rights and obligation have also been used in the justification of democracy.[21] Consideration of a social contract has been
developed by Rawls in distinction to a utilitarian analysis of government.[22] Conceivably these goals and standards are not all optimally
furthered by precisely the same forms of government.

The criteria of judgment that are of special interest within our meta-
ethics are those that can be formulated clearly and consistently and are
of broad applicability. Among these, a prominent type are those that
seek to maximize certain aspects of the consequences or end states that
result from our actions—including our choice of political regimes.
Aspects that may be stressed include the development of the citizens'
character or personality, their experiences, or the distribution of goods
and services. Criteria such as these may be connected with one another, or with those mentioned above, by presumed causal relations.
One of the important tasks of social science is to provide data that test
such relations and compare actual alternatives. Our discussion here,
however, will be limited to simpler hypothetical choices.

Many of the criteria used to justify democracy, like those of welfare
economics, are closely related to Benthamite utilitarianism. The utili-

19. Dahl, *A Preface to Democratic Theory*, p. 64; Hallowell, *The Moral Foundation
of Democracy*.

20. See Pateman, *Participation and Democratic Theory*. She points out (p. 349) that
Bentham was less concerned with the educational function of political participation. See
also Mayo, *An Introduction to Democratic Theory*, pp. 260ff.

21. See Dahl, *op. cit.*, p. 6, on Madisonian democracy; Mayo, *An Introduction to
Democratic Theory*, pp. 254ff. On the conflict between liberty and equality see Sabine,
"The Two Democratic Traditions."

22. Rawls, *A Theory of Justice*.

tarian movement was associated with the expansion of the British electorate in the Reform Act of 1832, even though Bentham had come to
be concerned with parliamentary reform only late in life. Both
Bentham and John Stuart Mill, in their views of political representation, were influenced by psychological hedonism and sought "to en-
sure that governors and legislators, in pursuing their own happiness,
will also maximize the happiness of the citizens as a whole." [23] Thus
Mill was led to support the Hare system of proportional representation,
although subsequent political scientists have questioned the value of
this system.[24] The connection between utilitarianism and radical politics was evidently not perfect, however, since Bentham adopted "an
attitude of hostile indifference" toward the French Revolution, and
Burke deduced "an anti-democratic political theory" from a utilitarian
philosophy.[25]

Although the economic approach to government has concerned only
detailed modifications rather than alternative regimes, it does employ
maximizing criteria based on the consequences of alternative arrangements. It has led not only to concern for what functions should be performed by government rather than the market, but also to consideration of variations in form *within* the general class of democratic
institutions. These include the choice of constituencies (in size and
function), electoral systems and voting rules, forms of representation,
and administrative structures.

Reasoning along these lines cannot be expected to justify "democracy"—or *any* particular form of government—without regard for the
particular circumstances of choice. Different answers may be expected, for example, for government of families, voluntary associations, educational institutions, and states. The nature of the issues
being considered (whether technical or not); the relation between the
voting constituency and the persons affected; the knowledge and competence of leaders and citizens and their concern for general or particular aspects of welfare—all are relevant conditions.

23. Birch, *Representative and Responsible Government*, pp. 55, 44–45.
24. Mill, *Representative Government*, ch. VII; MacRae, *Parliament, Parties, and
Society in France*, p. 259.
25. Halévy, *The Growth of Philosophic Radicalism*, pp. 164, 158. The use of utilitarian principles, unaided by rigorous empirical criticism, for rationalization was also
evident in Edgeworth's *Mathematical Psychics*.

Moreover, in the short run, the justification and viability of particular governmental forms depends on what the citizens and leaders expect of the regime. Important conditions have been set by prevailing "ideologies of representation" in Weimar Germany and more recently by the belief in participatory democracy.

There is, however, an affinity between the economic approach and a justification of democracy as against elite rule. If we stress the satisfaction of individuals' preferences rather than their welfare, we imply that only the individual himself has the right to judge what is good for him; experts or elites cannot claim to know better, even if they should expect the individual himself to admit later that they were right. A second parallel between the market and democracy lies in the expression of preferences in the vote, which has a formal similarity to the expression of consumer preferences. Thus the criterion of preference satisfaction has been prominent in both the economic and the political ethics of capitalist democracy—in the former, because preference is a key concept in the positive theory of consumer behavior; in the latter, because the determination of a person's "welfare" by others, independently of what he prefers, appears undemocratic and therefore undesirable. The egalitarianism of the vote, however, does not appear in welfare economics, insofar as the latter avoids interpersonal comparison.

A central value in democratic theory that may support a preference ethic is not only the abhorrence of tyranny, but also the notion that a certain type of "political rationality" resides in the gaining of consent and in the question of *who* has approved a policy, over and above who is affected by it.[26] This value may be nearly an ultimate one for some democrats, but it may alternatively be a means to the acceptance and implementation of policies whose ultimate rightness is judged on "welfare" grounds.

The extension of the approach of welfare economics to governmental institutions has often led to a stress on exchange and bargaining. In an ideal market, we may assume that consumers judge their own prospective welfare rather than the general welfare and that Adam Smith's "invisible hand" will take account of the welfare of others.

26. Diesing, *Reason in Society*. Consent also relates to the expectation of reciprocity, which we discuss in chapter 8.

The only normative influences that must bear on the individual are those that maintain the market, that is, protections against force and fraud.

The analogous approach to political systems assumes that citizens or groups also base their participation on their private welfares rather than on concern for the general welfare. A prevailing ideology of "interest-group liberalism" has expressed this notion. Coleman has suggested the creation of "political money" that will allow legislators to exchange votes more readily, and Tullock and Olson have also stressed the benefits ideally attainable from logrolling. Lindblom also sees the process of "partisan mutual adjustment" as operating somewhat in the fashion of the invisible hand and attaining results superior to those of "synoptic decision making." [27] An emphasis on bargaining and exchange also pervades Buchanan and Tullock's *The Calculus of Consent,* but in constitution making, they assume that the participant will consider himself in various possible positions under the proposed constitution and will thus consider interests broader than those he personally may have in particular items of legislation.[28] Niskanen, however, in an economic critique of bureaucratic functioning, warns of a possible bias in logrolling toward the interests of groups with a high demand for public services and of undesirable consequences from the self-interested motivation of bureaucrats.[29]

These models seem to require that the public be allowed, or even taught, to vote in terms of special or private interests and that legislators vote in terms of the interests of their districts.[30] An effort to vote in terms of the general welfare, from this perspective, might be expected at times to harm the general welfare. But in addition, the normative assumptions underlying the model would have to be maintained; force, fraud, and corruption would have to be avoided. Some of the problems that we have considered for economic ethics also arise here, but they are more difficult, and more important, in the political realm.

27. See Lowi, *The End of Liberalism;* Coleman, "Political Money"; Tullock, "A Simple Algebraic Logrolling Model"; Olson, "The Principle of 'Fiscal Equivalence' "; Lindblom, *The Intelligence of Democracy.*
28. Buchanan and Tullock, *op. cit.*
29. Niskanen, *Bureaucracy and Representative Government,* p. 145 and *passim.*
30. This view is criticized by Bay in "Politics and Pseudopolitics."

Democratic Forms and Political Market Failure

A second major economic approach to democratic institutions considers their outcomes and evaluates them for one set of institutional arrangements in comparison with another. This type of comparison is analogous to that between a perfect market and an imperfect market or between the states of affairs before and after the introduction of a tax. It typically deals with small changes rather than changes of regime, but it illustrates that alternative political arrangements can be compared in terms of precisely stated criteria. When one such political arrangement is inferior to a possible alternative in terms of its consequences, we shall then speak by analogy of "political market failure."

We speak of "political market failure" in order to stress certain analogies with the economic approach to market failure. A precisely formulated ethic of consequences is used to assess the differences in outcomes made by small changes in an existing system. A model of the system is used for this assessment; such a model may now involve the behavior of voters, groups, parties, or bureaucracies rather than producers and consumers. A comparison of static situations is made rather than a dynamic assessment. And the ethical criteria used are based on the preferences of voters or citizens; in discussing political market failure, we restrict ourselves to ethical hypotheses of this kind.

The analogy, however, is not perfect. In theoretical welfare economics, the single criterion of Pareto efficiency dominates the field; for political systems a variety of criteria (ethical hypotheses) have been used. And perhaps most important, no optimum equilibrium situation seems available for comparison.

A major difficulty in extending the "market failure" approach from economics to politics is that an ideal equilibrium situation is harder to define for a political system than for a market. If individuals are characterized by preferences, a state of affairs that is clearly most preferred by a group under a given decision procedure cannot always be found. This was the burden of Arrow's theorem; but its relevance here is to constitutions and electoral systems, not to the more determinate ethical systems by which observers may judge the working of political institutions. Not only may various criteria based on preferences be formulated, but if there is no obvious optimum a proposed change may be an improvement on our standard of comparison rather than a remedy for "failure."

Increasing attention has been devoted to finding the conditions for equilibrium in voting processes. The conditions for cyclical majorities, and their likelihood, have been analyzed. Possible restrictions on the form and variety of individual preferences have been considered,[31] reducing the problem to a less general one than that of market equilibrium, but comparisons of decisions reached under these conditions are still instructive.

A more determinate standard for comparison is possible if each consumer-citizen is characterized by a personal demand curve for collective goods, specifying how much he would consume at each given price. In this case, an aggregate demand curve may be constructed by addition of the prices that consumers would be willing to pay for each given quantity of the good. The resulting demand curve, together with a supply curve, determines an optimal level of supply, in terms of the same ethic used in the basic theorem of the competitive market. This approach has been used in Samuelson's pure theory of public expenditure, and an additive approach considering total net benefits has been used in Niskanen's comparison of alternative levels of supply of collective goods by bureaucracies under legislative control.[32]

From an economic perspective, the task is to compare real governmental decisions with real market decisions, in the knowledge that either can be imperfect. The illustrative policies compared are usually simplified and hypothetical, but they need not be ideal in a valuative sense and are expected to capture some of the deficiencies of real choice processes.

The "realism" that the economic approach suggests, however, stresses certain aspects of reality at the expense of others and indeed may cultivate them if it is widely believed to represent reality com-

31. See Pomeranz and Weil, "The Cyclical Majority Problem"; DeMeyer and Plott, "The Probability of a Cyclical Majority"; Kramer, "On A Class of Equilibrium Conditions for Majority Rule"; Kramer, "A Dynamical Model of Political Equilibrium"; Pattanaik, *Voting and Collective Choice*, ch. 4; Hansen and Prince, "The Paradox of Voting."

32. Samuelson, "The Pure Theory of Public Expenditure"; Niskanen, *op. cit.*, pp. 184–186. Earlier sources for this approach were Erik Lindahl and Howard Bowen; see Musgrave, *The Theory of Public Finance*, ch.4.

pletely. It rests on the assumption of "self-interest," which can be interpreted in two ways.[33] In one interpretation, self-interest simply reduces to the notion that actors maximize *some* goals, which may be as diverse as "tastes" for exploitation or charity, pushpin or poetry. In this case it is devoid of content except for the assumption that "more is better." In another interpretation, however, self-interest is exemplified by political parties' desire to win elections or to obtain more votes (perhaps up to the point of a winning coalition) or by politicians' desire to remain in office or bureaucrats' desire to maximize their budgets. These particular exemplifications tend to omit concern for others' welfare. Rules or norms surrounding the political game are also assumed, though merely as an inconspicuous framework for the play of interests: force, fraud, and corruption may thus be ruled out. Such a framework is assumed in economics as well, but these norms, as we shall suggest, are more important in politics.

In discussing political market failure, we shall begin by accepting these assumptions. We shall consider voters who know and seek their own welfare or legislators who faithfully seek the welfare of their constituents—no less and no more, neither their personal welfare nor the general welfare, unless the latter be served by an invisible hand. We shall then ask the extent to which, under various political arrangements, they succeed in maximizing the general welfare as defined by one or another ethical hypothesis.

The problems of assessing political market failure are illustrated by a simple example discussed by Davis and Hinich.[34] They assume that, with respect to a particular policy issue, two candidates' platforms (alternatives) can be characterized by points on a single dimension and voters' preferred policy positions by a continuous distribution on that dimension. A policy issue of this type might be the provision of a collective good by means of a uniform tax, each point corresponding to a

33. "Interest" connotes both motivation and welfare, but in the usage of the term the mixture of these ingredients varies.

34. Davis and Hinich, "A Mathematical Model of Policy Formation in a Democratic Society," pp. 180–182. The conclusion cited has been generalized in Hinich and Ordeshook, "Social Welfare and Electoral Competition in Democratic Societies." A somewhat different criterion for two-party competition is used in Hirschman, *Exit, Voice, and Loyalty*, p. 67n.

monetary level of provision. They also assume that all voters participate and that between two alternatives each voter votes for the one nearer to his own position. In this case, if one alternative is at the median of the voters' distribution and the other is not, the median alternative will win a majority over any other.

The authors also introduce a valuative criterion—the policies chosen by a "wise and beneficent dictator." He assumes interpersonal comparison and decides to minimize the sum of quadratic loss functions for all voters. Each voter is thus assumed to suffer loss proportional to the square of the difference between his own position and the position of the alternative chosen. On the basis of this criterion the optimum alternative can be shown to be the *mean,* not the median, of the voters' positions. When the "market" position defined by the median under majority rule is not equal to the mean, a simple example of political market failure occurs in terms of the assumed cardinal welfare function or ethical hypothesis.

This example illustrates the distinction between preference and welfare, even though the latter is found in the judgments of a dictator rather than in reasoned ethical discourse or in the decisions of well-informed citizens. The authors' working assumption that voters' preferences are given, and that voters' positions reflect personal welfare while only the dictator aggregates them, are characteristic of the economic perspective. But the dictator's judgments do involve cardinal welfare and interpersonal comparison, while the behavioral inference that the median is dominant does not.

Even if the mean and median coincided, political market failure could still result through limitation of the alternatives or operation of the electoral system. If the median policy could not be put forward, because of the action of gatekeepers, nomination procedures, or voting rules, then some other alternative could become the winning policy. In addition, if some voters voted in accord with their expected personal welfare while others did not, the decision might be displaced from the median. This could happen either through "stragetic voting" (as opposed to "sincere voting"),[35] under some procedural rules, or through

35. Farquharson, *Theory of Voting;* see also Grofman, "Voting Schemes and the Will of the Majority."

some voters' voting in terms of the general welfare, leading to an underemphasis on their personal welfares.[36] In addition, under plurality vote, the possibility of considering more than two alternatives in a single ballot can allow a nonmedian alternative to win if the opposition is divided.

The possibility that mean and median may not coincide has a parallel in a problem of geographical constituencies discussed by Olson. He considers the case in which benefits from a collective good reach only part of the constituency that provides it (by taxation) and refers to this situation as an "internality." Whereas in the case of externalities, outsiders are affected without having chosen to receive the effects, here some voters are expected to choose on questions from which they might properly be excluded. If a large number of persons are taxed and only a small number receive benefits, then in the absence of compensation the proposal will presumably be defeated on a majority vote in this constituency. Yet we might judge the net benefit to be increased if the proposal were passed and thus (by this criterion) that political market failure had occurred. One remedy would be to "set up a special local taxing authority" and to decentralize decisions to it.[37]

The problem posed here is also often treated as that of failure of a voting system to take into account "intensity of preference." [38] This concept arises only in the economic analysis of voting, not in the study of economic behavior itself. Its analogue in consumer behavior is the willingness to exchange a large increment of one good for a small increment of another, as reflected in a marginal rate of substitution or the slope of an indifference curve or the related demand function in relation to price. If the policies or goods under consideration vary only along a single dimension, a voter can prefer different quantitative positions (for example, levels of provision of a collective good with corresponding tax rates), and one possible "intensity" that can be as-

36. See Wolff, *The Poverty of Liberalism*, p. 35n.

37. Olson, "The Principle of 'Fiscal Equivalence,' " p. 482. Other examples of economic analysis of local collective goods are Pauly, "Optimality, 'Public' Goods and Local Governments"; and Smolensky, Burton, and Tideman, "The Efficient Provision of a Local Non-Private Good." Possible failures of democratic systems to yield results in accord with cost-benefit analysis are also discussed in Haveman and Weisbrod, "Defining Benefits of Public Programs," p. 175.

38. See Dahl, *A Preface to Democratic Theory*, ch. 4.

sociated with them is that of a personal monetary demand curve, as discussed above.

In political scientists' discussion of "intensity," however, the monetary yardstick for interpersonal comparison is not ordinarily used. In this case there is no analogue to price or marginal rate of substitution; and "intensity," if it figures in an ethical system, may have to be defined by fiat or consensus. "Intensity of preference," as the term is used in democratic theory, thus may well have an important valuative aspect.[39] It confronts the same problems of interpersonal comparison as does cardinal welfare. Its usefulness in scientific analysis cannot then be expected to justify a definition of the term that will have the properties needed for valuative discourse.

In the Davis-Hinich example above, we might ask whether some other scheme of voting would yield better results when mean and median differ. If voting were "sincere," we might ask each voter to state his preferred numerical level of provision of collective-good-plus-taxes and let the decision procedure be to take the average. But knowing this, the informed and self-interested voter would then "strategically" declare a position farther from the median in the direction of his own position; if limits were set on the extremity of such positions, all voters would tend to cluster at the two extremes. The information provided by these declarations would then be no greater than that provided by a simple dichotomous vote.

So far we have considered a single choice on a single dimension, made by voters directly rather than through intermediate groups such as political parties. We have also assumed perfect information and universal participation; the removal of each of these assumptions can give rise to a corresponding type of political market failure. In addition, the comparison of electoral systems provides another dimension of variation, but for simplicity we shall restrict our discussion largely to majority contests between two alternatives. The alternatives may be either individual policies or bundles of policies such as may be formed by

39. We have previously questioned whether "intensity" could be defined on scientific grounds alone, in discussing Coleman's social welfare function in chapter 5. Here we use the one-dimensional case as a "conflict situation" to question this meta-ethical notion further. See fn. 44 below; and Rae and Taylor, *The Analysis of Political Cleavages*, ch. 3.

platforms, ideologies, coalitions, or parties. The connection between particular policies may also be made by knowledge of the interrelations of their consequences; this knowledge can play the same role in the formulation of coherent collective choices as Raiffa suggested for systematization of individual choices.

If we depart from the condition of a unidimensional choice space, several lines of analysis are possible. One is to consider choices without respect to dimensionality at all. Another is to consider a single collective choice in a multidimensional space. A third, and the most interesting for our purposes, is to consider a group of voters faced with a *set* of particular decisions on different dimensions, to be made either in sequence or in bundles determined by coalitions among the voters.

The first of these lines of analysis, which avoids dimensions altogether, is that adopted in Arrow's theorem. But it has also been employed in an effort to justify the majority voting rule, using as a valuative criterion the probability that a representative (or average) voter will be disappointed by the result of the vote. This criterion is quantitative, and its minimization under specified conditions leads to the conclusion that majority decisions are optimal.[40] It involves interpersonal comparison but assumes that all those on the losing side of any vote suffer equal loss in terms of the ethical criterion used.

The second line of analysis, extension to multidimensional spaces, has proven difficult when undertaken in general terms. Kramer, reviewing the literature on the subject, concludes that "Cyclical majorities, or the absence of stable outcomes under majority rule are very likely the rule rather than the exception in problems involving voting over multidimensional choice spaces."[41]

In view of this possible instability, it may seem bold to consider interrelations between collective decisions on two or more dimensions. Nevertheless, some of the most interesting conclusions from economic approaches relate to the exchanges that may occur among voters faced with two or more decisions. It is axiomatic to students of the market

40. Rae, "Decision-Rules and Individual Values in Constitutional Choice"; Taylor, "Proof of a Theorem on Majority Rule"; Curtis, "Decision-Rules and Collective Values in Constitutional Choice." Note that according to this criterion political market failure would not have occurred in the Davis-Hinich example above.

41. Kramer, "On a Class of Equilibrium Conditions for Majority Rule," ms. p. 25. See also Sloss, "Stable Outcomes in Majority Voting Games."

that exchange between two persons can lead to benefits for both. This fact has led to stress on logrolling and exchange among citizens or legislators. Economists from Wicksell to Buchanan and Tullock have thus stressed the values to be expected from requiring, not majority rule, but unanimity as a condition for the making of certain collective decisions.[42] They assume that by requiring everyone to be consulted we can obtain a result similar to Pareto optimality and that the majority can no longer impose costs on the minority without compensation.

The distinctive feature of decisions in two or more dimensions is that otherwise separable decisions may now be linked together. Thus congressmen might have considered various degrees of expenditure on dredging a harbor in Massachusetts and on building a bridge in Arkansas. These matters might have come up for separate votes and each been defeated. They might also have been referred to state or local authorities, as Olson suggested, and been passed. But there is also the possibility of aggregating them, formally or informally, in compound proposals. If the aggregation is informal, they may come up for separate votes, and congressmen may seem to be engaging in strategic voting; that is, the Arkansas representative may vote for the Massachusetts harbor, even though his constituents will pay taxes for it and apparently receive nothing in return. But if we look at the reality rather than the forms, both congressmen may be voting on both proposals in an aggregate, and on this both are voting sincerely.

We thus consider a community, or a legislature, which confronts a number of possible decisions under a given electoral system or voting rule. The group is considered to be small enough for its members to know one another's preferences completely. It may aggregate these individual decisions into bundles and vote on a bundle by means of the voting rule in question. This type of voting is typical of logrolling on legislative decisions. It can also occur in voting for multiple candidates, but the analogy is closest if different candidates correspond to different policies that may be aggregated, for example, if they are running for distinct offices but connected by a "balanced ticket" or a rule of alternation.

42. Wicksell, "A New Principle of Just Taxation"; Buchanan and Tullock, *op. cit.* The workability of the principle is limited, however, by both transaction costs and strategic voting.

We then ask the conditions for political market failure when coalitions can be formed to secure approval for bundles of policies. The most frequent examples used to illustrate this process are those in which each item involves an "internality" and greatly benefits a few voters but imposes small costs on the rest.[43] If the net contribution of each item to the general welfare is positive—and if the items are truly on separate dimensions and do not interact—then the bundle of items will correspond to greater welfare than the status quo and will also receive more votes than any component item. If a voter prefers the bundle to the status quo, he will vote for it, but this decision implies only an *intra*personal comparison of values across the items in the bundle, not an *inter*personal comparison of welfares.[44]

Majority vote and logrolling may sometimes, however, lead to excessive government action, because of the exploitation of the minority by the majority. Buchanan and Tullock illustrate this with the case of a township inhabited by one hundred farmers, who must secure a majority vote in order to have local roads repaired, each road serving only a few farms.[45] Because each particular repair is automatically paid for by an increase in the real property tax, any proposal to repair one road by itself will be defeated. Majorities can be assembled by logrolling, however, and thus majority members can have the roads near them repaired with a subsidy from the minority. Because of this subsidy, or "external cost" to the minority, the level of repair that will be supported by the majority will tend to be excessive, just as in the case of external costs in the market. The standard of comparison here is not that of a political equilibrium, however, since any particular majority

43. Olson, "The Principle of 'Fiscal Equivalence' ", Buchanan and Tullock, *op. cit.*, pp. 143–144. "Benefit" is here defined in economic terms.

44. It is thus conceivable that a logrolling combination of items, even among actors well aware of the conditions for their own welfare, will provide less welfare to the group than another combination that would receive fewer votes. The multiplication of certain voters' welfare scales by a factor relative to others, such as might result from interpersonal "yardsticks," can change the interpersonal sums (e.g., matrix columns) without changing the intrapersonal sums (matrix rows). This "conflict situation" is intended to bring the meta-ethical rule of convictions to bear on Coleman's argument in "The Possibility of a Social Welfare Function."

45. Buchanan and Tullock, *op. cit.*, pp. 135–145; the majority they discuss is a coalition of minorities. Niskanen (*op. cit.*) suggests even greater excesses of bureaucratic production. See also Downs, "In Defense of Majority Voting"; Riker and Brams, "The Paradox of Vote Trading."

is not necessarily an equilibrium solution. Rather, the conclusion is based on the evaluation of collective goods in terms of the summed prices that consumer-taxpayers would be willing to pay. It is unclear whether such an optimum is attainable through *any* electoral system, unless farmers vote for the ethical ideal rather than for their individual welfares. But such a solution, as the authors point out, is in danger of being undermined by self-interested voting.

Gains of one group at the expense of another, through use of the power of government, can also occur in other ways. A majority can simply require transfers of resources from a minority, without any of the gains of exchange or production that result from self-interest in the ideal market. Such transfers can be exacted from either the rich or the poor, and the welfare consequences will presumably differ accordingly. If a governmental system permits active control by minorities, such transfers can also be effected by minorities. As Stigler has pointed out, the firms in an industry can use the powers of government regulation to restrict the entry of additional firms and thus decrease the likelihood of competition.[46]

This last example, however, moves away from the processes of the township or the legislature toward processes of representation in which lasting groups or organizations act as collective units in larger political systems. We shall now consider these group processes in more detail.

Coalitions and Representation

So far we have assumed that the principal relation among individual voters, other than their agreement to the norms of the political system, is exchange of votes or agreement to support a specified bundle of policy items. Such coalitions may be assumed to dissolve once the items in question are voted on. But especially in larger political systems, voters can also combine in more lasting groups or coalitions and remain in these groups for consideration of an indefinite number of items or decisions. The paramount group of this sort is the state itself; its formation, and the citizen's obligation to it, have been treated in political philosophy in connection with the notion of the social contract.[47]

46. Stigler, "The Theory of Economic Regulation."
47. The related topic of formation of social norms is treated in chapter 8 below.

Within the state, many lasting groups or collectivities play a part in politics. Most conspicuous are voluntary associations, political parties, and constituencies. Other types of groups, whose primary function is usually nonpolitical but which are sometimes politically important, include firms, governmental bureaucracies, and ethnic and religious groups.

The presence of such lasting coalitions, with members attached to them at least in part by normative commitment, gives rise to new problems in the assessment of political market failure. First, in this sort of group politics, disparity in size and effectiveness among groups can affect the equity of weighting of their members' preferences and welfares in policymaking processes. Second, a new type of judgment of collective welfare arises—that of *group* welfare or interest. And thirdly, the role of the representative, who stands for the group, forces us to consider the processes of deliberation that may alter his judgments of collective welfare. In this final respect, the economic ethic and the notion of market failure have particular shortcomings when applied to politics.

Each of these types of grouping may enter into processes of representation. For the individual member, such groupings may vary in their degree of "voluntariness," that is, in the ease or difficulty with which he may transfer his membership. Most difficult, after the state itself, are geographical constituencies; decreasing in difficulty are occupationally based groups, political parties, and other private political associations. Each such grouping may be represented by a single person, or a single issue position, in a larger decision process. The creation of a voluntary grouping may also involve norms, including elements of obligation or contract such as are associated with the state.

The formation of a group to consider an indefinite set of items collectively may occur for various reasons. First, the interests of the members may be such that, over a specifiable but indefinitely large class of decisions, they expect to agree.[48] Such expectations may arise from previously shared norms, culture, language, locality, or various social roles. Second, members of such a coalition may simply wish to gain power in general, without restricting it to particular matters; such

48. See Marschak, "Towards an Economic Theory of Organization and Information"; Rothenberg, *The Measurement of Social Welfare,* pp. 310ff.

motives are sometimes attributed to professional politicians in non-ideological parties.

Thirdly, the economy of information may be relevant. The devices we have mentioned (chapter 5) for economizing information for the consumer have their parallels in politics. But more serious problems exist for the voter, as the collective choices of the entire electorate do not necessarily conform to his own choices, and many of these collective choices influence him only indirectly, if at all.[49] The voter's information shortages are mitigated by various political institutions, including political parties and interest groups, which summarize numerous specific choices for him by relating them to more general symbols or ideologies.

At this stage of the argument, we shall treat the activities of these groups as based entirely on given preferences of their members—the economic approach.[50] Similar lasting groups—firms and groups of firms—also arise in economic systems and are usually treated by economists as coalitions based on self-interested calculations.[51]

The problem of political market failure in group politics is simplest when the representative is given a precise voting mandate by his group or constituency. In this case the election of a representative is equivalent to the choice of a position by the group on each issue. It is as though the group has formed a lasting agreement to vote alike but employs an internal decision process to determine what that unanimous vote in a larger system will be. A mathematical account of such decision procedures, of which the contemporary Electoral College is an example, has been given by Fishburn.[52]

In this case, an important type of political market failure that can result from individuals' joining into coalitions corresponds to inequity or disparity in power among them. In the extreme case a permanent

49. See Buchanan, "Individual Choice in Voting and the Market"; Downs, *An Economic Theory of Democracy;* Buchanan and Tullock, *op. cit.,* pp. 37–39.

50. Groups formed on any of these three bases, even if initially based only on self-interested calculation, may later develop internal norms; see Selznick, *Leadership in Administration,* on the development of organizations into institutions. The process of development of these norms involves preference change, not considered in the economic ethic.

51. See Coase, "The Nature of the Firm"; Alchian and Demsetz, "Production, Information Costs, and Economic Organization."

52. Fishburn, "The Theory of Representative Majority Decision."

majority coalition, acing in its particular interest, can continue to draw resources from the minority and use them for its own welfare—a state of affairs that sometimes, but not always, is to the detriment of the general welfare. It was from a fear of these disparities that Rousseau, and many later French political thinkers, disapproved of intermediate groups between the individual and the state.[53]

Such a disparity in influence among voluntary political groups is also seen as a problem by Olson.[54] He suggests first that insofar as participation in voluntary associations is costly, potential members will prefer to be "free riders" and allow others to generate the collective goods that such groups provide, while the free riders enjoy them without participation. Insofar as organizing effort is required, then, group activity for the production of collective goods will be insufficient. The coercive powers of government for tax collection can be used to prevent citizens from being free riders for governmental services. In certain private organizations, side benefits also serve to maintain membership. These side benefits may promote equity among groups, if used by mass-membership groups in contrast to more easily organized "special interest" groups consisting of a small number of firms.[55]

Even when such groups (for example, constituencies) are equal in size, the distribution of persons among them may still give rise to inequalities of influence among individuals. It is well known in the practice of legislative districting that the votes of a permanent minority faction in a district may be largely wasted.

In order to demonstrate that certain coalitions or arrangements for representation are inferior to others, however, and involve political market failure, we must not only show that the results differ from one case to another but relate them to a criterion of welfare. Here a very serious problem arises for abstract models. One group may have disproportionate power, exact transfers from others, or enjoy other advantages in a particular case, but these advantages do not necessarily diminish the general welfare. They may compensate for preexisting disparities. Moreover, in actual political conflicts, each group will

53. Rousseau, *The Social Contract*, Book II, Chapter III.
54. Olson, *The Logic of Collective Action*.
55. *Ibid.*, pp. 141–148.

tend to justify its own gains in relation to its own notion of the general welfare. Sometimes this justification may be refutable with reference to empirical causal assertions that it contains; at other times competing groups will simply propose alternate notions of the general welfare.

If we persist with abstract analysis, we are then driven to examples involving the choice of formal decision rules so as to reduce disparities in influence. We may try to analyze these rules without claiming to know just what groups will benefit from such disparities—haves or have-nots, ourselves or others.[56] In this perspective we typically consider disparities in power or influence as possible evidence of political market failure.

In addition to disparities in influence, the representation of individuals through large groups or organizations has been seen as disadvantageous to some participants. Coleman has suggested that the individual loses power in this way. Kornhauser and other advocates of social pluralism have argued that the individual's identity, as well as the extent and quality of his participation, may also be impaired when group structure is inadequate, but these problems go beyond the ethics of preference satisfaction and the economic approach to politics.[57]

An additional source of political market failure in representation is the possibility that voting within a group for members' best-liked candidates will produce candidates or proposals from the group that are too extreme to win in later contests. Coalitions agree not only to vote together, but to vote *for* particular positions in the larger groups of which they are parts. The positions of two coalitions may then compete for the support of voters whose positions lies between them. If a group's position is chosen by such "sincere" voting within the group, it may be located at the internal median and may not be near enough to the center of the larger group to win. Strategic voting in view of later contests, on the other hand, such as Downs attributes to political parties, may be more successful.[58] *If* the success of the group in question should correspond to the general welfare (for example, if it has suf-

56. This is the approach of Buchanan and Tullock, *op. cit.,* and of Rawls's original position.

57. Coleman, "Loss of Power"; Kornhauser, *The Politics of Mass Society.*

58. See for example MacRae, *Dimensions of Congressional Voting,* pp. 361–367; Davis and Hinich, op. cit., p. 201; Downs, *An Economic Theory of Democracy;* Coleman, "Internal Processes Governing Party Positions in Elections."

fered from an inequitable disadvantage), then we may also classify the result as political market failure.

So far in this chapter, we have in effect argued *for* the extension of economic ethics—recognized as ethics—to politics. The notion of political market failure, which directs our attention to detailed consequences of political arrangements in terms of their results, has advantages (in view of the rule of generality) over vaguer ethics that serve only to justify democracy in abstract terms. Because it is an extension of economic ethics, it may not of course be satisfactory to persons whose ethical convictions strongly support the values of justice, rights, or human perfection. It also lacks generality in failing to deal with choice of regimes. But its precision and apparent nonideological character have won increasing support for its use in political analysis.[59]

The economic approach to evaluation of political arrangements may also be criticized, however, from a standpoint similar to our criticism of economic ethics in chapter 5. This standpoint is that of a class of ethical hypotheses that permit interpersonal comparison but consider changes in preferences and distinguish among the chooser's preferences, his own welfare, and his judgments of collective welfare. All these issues arise in the economic evaluation of politics. Interpersonal comparison has been assumed in many of the examples cited earlier in this chapter. And as we shall now argue, problems of changing preferences and of judgments of collective welfare raise particularly acute problems for economic ethics when it is applied to politics.

Welfare and Changes of Political Preference

An economic approach provides insight into political institutions and directs our attention to important problems. But an ethic of preference satisfaction leaves unanswered the questions whether certain preferences are adequately informed, whether they *should* be satisfied, and whether some of them should be changed. Alternative ethical hypotheses, such as we proposed in chapter 5, might go beyond the assump-

59. See for example Ostrom, *The Intellectual Crisis in American Public Administration.*

tion of rational self-interest on the part of the individual and the corresponding ethic of preference satisfaction. In departing from that ethic, we also go beyond the notion of political market failure; criticisms of political systems based on the distinction between preference and welfare may point to failures of these systems, but they are not simply failures to respond to existing preferences.

We thus return to the criticisms of the economic ethic made at the end of chapter 5. We first distinguish the individual's preference from his own welfare, as in the economic notion of "merit goods." We then distinguish between the individual's preferences concerning his own welfare and his judgment regarding the general welfare.

If we admit the distinction between individual preference and welfare, we are led to consider political decisions that enhance the welfare of individuals even though they run counter to those individuals' preferences. These decisions will necessarily constrain those individuals or render them less free in the short run than they might otherwise have been. Examples of such decisions that are likely to conform with our convictions are compulsory education and the forceful removal of harmful foods and drugs from the market. More controversial examples are the legal enforcement of dominant religious and sexual norms.

A pluralistic perspective in politics has tended to assume that moralism in voting is undesirable, as it contributes to collective decisions an element of externality that ought not to be included in the result.[60] But since some morally derived views could conceivably be expressed as "ethical hypotheses" about the general welfare under our meta-ethical rules, we cannot automatically exclude them from political debate.

The argument against an unqualified ethic of preference satisfaction in politics thus rests on the same base as in economics. Not only may individuals be unaware of available choices that will promote their own welfare, but they may prefer one state of affairs to another on ethical grounds. These ethical judgments require deliberation and debate, not simply aggregation. If they are aggregated by the vote, this is a second-best procedure to secure consent and make necessary deci-

60. This is the same issue we raised in chapter 5 concerning Arrow's discussion of "crimes without victims."

sions, in the interval in which the more fundamental discussion continues.[61]

An example of this problem occurs in Buchanan and Tullock's discussion of road repair. They consider the possibility that there may be "a minority of farmers who feel very intensely that much more should be spent on road repairs [over the whole township] than the majority of other voters." [62] But should intense preferences about the money spent on other people's roads be heeded? The answer to this question involves ethical questions as to whether the community's welfare is being furthered, though they are concealed by the view that preferences are given and that the value judgments that distinguish among them are inadmissible.

The fundamental discussion that seeks the conditions for general welfare may be compared with that of a scientific community, in which disputes are settled by experiment and reasoning but not by majority vote. The task is of course far more difficult in the realm of values and policy. The goal of this discussion has sometimes been seen as an entity such as Rousseau's "general will," which is taken to exist and to be discovered. The notion of its existence, attributed to idealist philosophers, has sufficed to discredit this approach in the eyes of positivistically inclined social scientists.[63] There is, however, an analogy between the "general will" and citizens' consensual judgments of general welfare and between the "will of all" and a sum of cardinal utilities.[64]

It is in the realm of citizens' ethical judgments that the problem of misguided preferences, or of preferences that ought to be changed, is most acute. To assert that one's fellow citizens' preferences are misguided is of course doubly hazardous; one may be wrong in doing so and even if right may be met with hostility. But in this realm we

---

61. Compromise of fundamental philosophic differences through the vote is, however, considered a virtue of democracy in some theories. Aggregation of reflective moral judgments was also proposed by Rawls in "Outline of a Decision Procedure for Ethics,"p 196.

62. Buchanan and Tullock, *op. cit.*, p. 143.

63. See Arrow, *Social Choice and Individual Values*, pp. 81–86, and chapter 8 below.

64. Rousseau, *The Social Contract and Discourses*, p. 23. See also Russell, *A History of Western Philosophy*, pp. 698–699.

must nevertheless stress the deficiencies of an economic approach in relation to some of our ethical convictions. The consumer with insufficient or inaccurate information presumably harms only himself. The citizen with insufficient information—even when benefiting from the information economies of party or ideology—may nevertheless feel mistaken contentment in a situation that requires political change or channel misguided dissatisfaction into ineffective or harmful political movements.

The boundary between preferences for the chooser's welfare and ethical judgments about others' welfare, however, involves choice among ethical hypotheses. Individuals may prefer states of affairs in which others' welfare appears to be enhanced, particularly if they belong to the same group as the others.[65] Insofar as our ethical hypothesis considers the satisfaction of these preferences to contribute to the general welfare, then political acts that satisfy them would appear desirable. Thus the appointment of a popular member of an ethnic group to high political office may generate sympathetic feelings in a wide constituency. The satisfaction that the members of that constituency gain thereby is created symbolically, rather than by a direct change in the goods or services (in the ordinary sense) that they receive.[66]

Different ethical hypotheses, however, would evaluate such a change differently. Some might regard such an appointment as at best a symbol of material benefits in the future and would consider it to add nothing to the collective welfare. Others would regard the symbolic transaction as good in itself, either because it satisfied citizen preference or because it involved an experience deemed valuable. And in real political systems, much would depend in the longer run on what the citizens expected of such an appointment—whether it was seen as an "outcome" in itself or whether it was regarded as simply an advance indication of later tangible benefits.

Political institutions, like economic, may not only respond to individual preferences but may also alter them. They may do this in four

65. Boulding, "The Network of Interdependence"; Olson, "The Economics of Integrative Systems."

66. See Edelman, *The Symbolic Uses of Politics;* Moynihan, *The Politics of a Guaranteed Income,* pp. 152–153.

principal ways. (1) In the short run they may present policies, or
bundles of goods, that allow the individual chooser only combined alternatives rather than choices on individual items. (2) They may permit political persuasion to affect him. (3) Through the long-term influence of participation they may shape the participant's character, for
better or worse, and thus perhaps both his preferences and his welfare.
(4) They may directly enact policies that influence preferences.

1. The aggregation of particular preference alternatives into "policy
bundles" can constitute an alteration of these preferences, even though
at first glance it might seem merely the introduction of new objects of
preference and the removal of others. If the citizen favors or opposes
such a composite object, or possible policy aggregate, his attitude
toward it may come to apply to the component parts as well as to
the whole, thus changing his previous preferences for some of the
parts.

In the short run, typical political institutions that combine or aggregate particular alternatives into larger ones include interest groups,
political parties, and legislatures.[67] Such combination can conceivably
be justified on three grounds: (a) the formation of majorities, (b) the
economizing of information, and (c) the making of coherent policies.
For all these reasons, larger "bundles of goods" seem to be required
in political than in market choice. These three justifications lead different directions, however, as regards the voter's consideration of personal or general welfare. The first two, dealing with logrolling and information economies, are of the economic type: they seek aspects of
actual self-interested behavior that seem to conduce to welfare and try
to explain and enhance them. The third, however—creation of coherent policies because of the interdependence of the effects of individual
parts—requires that the voter seek to be informed and that he consider
the general welfare. It is this last criterion that especially calls forth
the qualities of the well-informed citizen or the well-informed representative.

But the linking together of decisions, while it eases the burden of
decision for the voter, also renders him less competent and sets him
farther from expertness in judging the alternative policies that result.
This complication, in turn, may heighten the role of parties, interest

67. See Almond and Coleman, *The Politics of the Developing Areas,* pp. 16ff.

groups and their leaders, and other elites. It may also turn us from mutual persuasion in the shaping of general-welfare judgments to a form of shaping that allots different roles to leader and citizen and asks only passive consent for policies rather than response of policies to prior preferences. The requirement of consent without deliberation implies a vote but may also imply the shaping of citizen alternatives—and perhaps preferences—by leaders.

2. A second general process by which individuals' political preferences are changed is political persuasion, as in campaigns. In one sense, campaigns reshape preferences for aggregated policies such as we have just discussed. But they can also influence attitudes on particular items apart from their aggregation.

These changes in political preferences are analogous to changes in consumers' preferences for goods. The democratic political system is seen as the locus of "citizen sovereignty" just as the market is seen as embodying "consumer sovereignty." But because preferences can change and be changed, we must ask some of the same critical questions about this view of the voter as about the consumer. We must thus ask whether an ethics of "citizen preference sovereignty"—or rather a view of democracy that embodies a more general ethic based on preferences—has anything to say about the ways in which political preferences are formed. Education and political advertising must be evaluated as sources of preference change. And unlike the case with the notion of "human capital," we cannot argue so easily that political education will be repaid primarily through the recipients' income. Thus an ethic of "citizen preference sovereignty" is open to criticism under our rule of generality.

With respect to political persuasion, we might well fear that support was being obtained in ways that had little to do with candidates' prospective policy positions. Schumpeter's theory of democracy explicitly accepts this possibility.[68] But in addition, past as well as prospective policies may be symbolically embellished or vilified and thus seen inaccurately by the voters. As long as incumbents are to be held responsible for their actions, we may require political "consumer research," or "truth-in-campaigning" laws, by analogy to features of advertising in the market. The problem is greatly complicated, of

68. Schumpeter, *Capitalism, Socialism, and Democracy*, ch. 22. Support for political authorities is discussed in Easton, *A Systems Analysis of Political Life*, p. 292.

course, by the fact that the bias of government in regulating political persuasion is likely to be still greater than in its regulation of the market.

It is well known that political or economic demands may affect policy (or products available) and thus reduce the initial demands.[69] Such assumptions have been included in models of political and economic systems. They may perhaps not have been tested rigorously, but they are recognized and on the whole accepted as desirable. On the other hand, the response of such a system through the modification of opinion or demand, as by political or economic advertising, *without* any corresponding change in tangible output, is often considered undesirable. Whether it is always undesirable is an open question for ethical discussion and research.

3. A third way in which political institutions may transform preferences is through the alleged long-term influence of participation. The contribution of democratic participation to character development has long been cited in support of democracy,[70] even though this relationship has seldom been tested. Conceivably, immersion of a citizen in one or another political system can affect not only the welfare (for example, satisfaction) that he receives from given states of affairs, but also his preferences. His concern for the welfare of other citizens may be developed through participation; one consequence of transferring particular functions from economic to political decision may be a long-run influence on citizens toward considering public rather than private criteria of choice. Thus we must allow for, and examine, the possibility that political and economic institutions are also educational.

4. A fourth way in which government can influence preferences is by the direct enactment of policies that do so. The possibility of such policies enlarges the range of possible government interventions that we considered above, beyond those aimed at remedying market failure. We referred there to the possibility that social norms might be

69. The terminology here is that of Easton, *ibid.,* pp. 384, 403, but not that of economics. In economic terms, a citizen's demand for production of collective goods may depend on the amount (or rate) of his previous consumption. Even when his demand *schedule* is not altered by political outputs, he may be moved along a demand curve to a point where he is not willing to pay as much (in political cost) for another incremental unit of output.

70. Mill, *Utilitarianism, Liberty, and Representative Government,* pp. 193–195; Mayo, *An Introduction to Democratic Theory,* pp. 260ff.

considered as collective goods, but the creation or modification of norms involves not only the satisfaction of preferences but also their change. Thus in addition to acting so as to satisfy preferences, government may also modify or maintain values and preferences. This possible governmental function includes:

a. Education—considered not simply as the creation of "human capital," but also as including the inculcation of civic virtue, intergroup understanding, and other qualities that provide external benefits.[71]

b. Creation and maintenance of norms, including not only new laws but also the conditions necessary for market transactions and for political as well as economic competition.[72] Here we stress the function of attitude or behavior maintenance (for those who conform) or change (for those who deviate), as against the simple provision of differential costs such as would be considered in an economic theory of crime.

These governmental functions, like those that cope with market failure, also require a particular sort of regime. Civic virtue is especially important in a regime where the citizens participate in government. A regime in which most citizens are expected to devote themselves exclusively to the private concerns of livelihood and family might require less civic education. The numbers and types of informed citizens required by different regimes are quite different. Similarly, consideration of the conditions for maintenance of political competition implies that such competition exists and should exist. A restricted electorate or an aristocratic regime would call for less general education, and perhaps less diffusion of normative principles concerning public policy, than would a democracy with broad participation.

The separation of preference from welfare is known to provide a point of entry for arguments against democracy and to raise the question of unwarranted control by minorities. As Schumpeter phrased it,

> To try to force the people to embrace something that is believed to be good and glorious but which they do not actually want—even though they may be expected to like it when they experience its results—is the very hallmark of anti-democratic belief.[73]

71. On these external effects, see Owen, "Education for Majority Voting?"
72. Tullock, "Entry Barriers in Politics."
73. Schumpeter, *Capitalism, Socialism, and Democracy,* p. 237. See also Flathman, *The Public Interest,* pp. 48–49.

But it is hard to agree with all the implications of Schumpeter's statement if it is taken literally. Insofar as our convictions support representative government rather than direct democracy, we may grant some discretion to representatives—as Schumpeter himself does in his revised theory of democracy. We may concede representatives the right to pursue unpopular policies between elections, in the hope that they will be vindicated in time—or by history if the electorate later repudiates them. And even if representatives should not "force" people to accept policies for their own good, they can try to persuade. Thus we elect representatives with some discretion but require them to justify their actions publicly.

Not only representatives, but also experts and elites are conceded some right to judge the conditions for others' welfare. Even in democratic regimes, scientists are permitted to judge some matters on which they are more competent than the general public. Conceivably some subgroup of a population may be able better to judge the general welfare than can the entire population. We know the dangers of this argument, related to the self-interest of any such group. But the improvement of collective decisions may involve the better use of scarce types of competence together with an enlargement of the competence of the public. And if policymaking elites and representatives are responsible to those whom they influence, the dangers of arbitrary control are less.

Representation, Ethical Judgment, and Deliberation

If the representative has some discretion, rather than a simple mandate, then a crucial problem arises for the economic model of politics. In our earlier analysis of economic preference and welfare, we distinguished among the individual's preferences, his welfare, and his judgments of the welfare of collectivities. The third of these categories— collective-welfare judgments—is of particular importance when we consider the actions of political representatives with discretion. It is here that the economic or "exchange" approach to politics encounters special difficulties.

When the representative has discretion, then the citizens' choice of representatives is distinct in its consequences from multistage voting on policy items. The representatives' discretion may then be exercised in bargaining for constituency interests, in deliberation with regard to the general welfare, or in service of their personal interests.

The analysis of group representation of this sort can be made most precise if the representatives are assumed to be legislators, voting under fixed procedural rules. The analogous characteristics of interest groups have also been analyzed, but the effects of organization of a large interest group are harder to formulate precisely.

Representative institutions such as legislatures are widely supported but run counter to the direct expression of citizens' preferences in government decisions. One justification (or explanation) for legislative representation may lie in the possibility of greater information on the part of legislators than citizens, as regards the expected consequences of public choices. Another may be the reduction in size of the collective decision unit to the number among which bargaining and vote exchange can take place without excessive cost.[74] Legislative assemblies may vary in many respects—size, terms of office, electoral systems used, constituency types, and the functions they are expected to fulfill. These characteristics may be chosen in terms of ethical criteria such as those based on preference or welfare, in view of the character of the social system within which the assembly is to operate; that system may itself vary in size, cleavages, political socialization, education, and pressures from its environment.

The model of exchange is plausible and often useful for both description and evaluation of interactions among citizens or among legislators. It is limited, of course, by the necessity of assuming norms within which exchange can be conducted freely and honestly—the limitation of force and fraud. But when we consider the relation between representative and constituent, or between a representative and other persons affected by his decisions, the normative assumptions we must make for an exchange model are far stronger. We must be sure that the representative, while acting in self-interest, is guided only by the interest he represents and not by personal interest or that of representatives as a group.[75] This problem arises for representatives of constituencies,

74. Buchanan and Tullock, *op. cit.*, p. 68.
75. These three types of "wills" of "magistrates" are distinguished in Rousseau, *The Social Contract and Discourses, op. cit.*, p. 51. The promises that a candidate makes in his electoral platform are analogous to a seller's promise to deliver goods with certain qualities at a specified price.

interest groups, or the public in general. As Rousseau described the problem,

> The will of . . . particular societies has always two relations; for the members of the association, it is a general will; for the great society, it is a particular will; and it is often right with regard to the first object, and wrong as to the second. An individual may be a devout priest, a brave soldier, or a zealous senator, and yet a bad citizen.

The converse difficulty was a major theme of Michels, who saw the socialist leader as failing to be a true socialist through his quest either for personal security or for votes.[76] Michels did not acknowledge that when the socialist leader sought bourgeois support he might be devoting himself to the general welfare—analogously to Marx's bourgeois elements who go over to the side of the proletariat.

In the analysis of group goals, several approaches have been followed. Downs considers the actor in question to be a political party rather than a person and assumes that parties can further their interests only in certain ways. He thus tacitly assumes that there are norms that prevent parties from receiving graft or benefiting in other ways than those allowed by the model.[77]

Merton's "functional" analysis of political machines seemed to assume that exchange had its benefits and that the constituent who received coal, food baskets, jobs, legal advice, and other services from the precinct captain was possibly even receiving more than he might under some other governmental arrangements.[78] Thus the virtues of exchange, through less than legitimate channels, were considered.

Coleman considers exchanges among legislators, but he simply assumes that the goals they serve are those of the constituency rather than personal goals. The embodiment of this model in a game is somewhat useful as civic training,[79] but a game that embodied different assumptions, also allowed by an economic model, might include secret

76. Rousseau, *A Discourse on Political Economy,* in *op. cit.,* p. 237; Michels, *Political Parties.*

77. Downs, *An Economic Theory of Democracy.*

78. Merton, *Social Theory and Social Structure* (1968), pp. 125–136.

79. Coleman, "The Possibility of a Social Welfare Function"; "Political Money"; "Collective Decisions."

committee votes in executive session, payoffs, and accounts in Swiss banks. Buchanan and Tullock consider in detail the possible relations between constituency interests and legislators' coalitions, but they too simply characterize legislators by the constituency interests they are assumed to represent. Their argument also considers a type of political market failure deriving from legislators' representing bare and biased majorities in their districts.[80]

This assumption that representatives automatically vote in accordance with the preferences of their constituencies—or that candidates' behavior consists simply in the statement of policy positions—is not merely an analytic simplification, but also risks blinding us to important valuative aspects of representation. We must examine carefully the conditions under which legislators will vote for the interests of their constituencies (whether district, party, group, or nation) rather than for their personal, material, or career interests. These latter interests manifest themselves not only in corruption, but also in the collective career interests of legislators as a group.[81] The possible formation of a coalition of representatives against their constituents has at times seemed a peculiarly French notion, but in the United States as well it has some basis in fact. Congressmen speak of certain rhetorical appeals that are restricted to constituents: "The main rule of the game is 'thou shalt not demagogue thy colleagues.' We acknowledge that a person does a little bit of demagoguery with his people, but snow is for the folks." [82] They agree on norms that gain support for incumbents as against potential rivals, such as those concerning private bills, pork barrel distribution, and gallery passes. They consider it normal to place members on committees that relate to constituency interests and will aid the members' reelection. This tacit mutual support by incumbent legislators tends to circumvent the value of *competitive* democ-

80. Buchanan and Tullock, *op. cit.*, ch. 16. The motivation of representatives is treated in more detail, from an economic perspective, in Curry and Wade, *A Theory of Political Exchange*, pp. 41–44, ch. 5; and in Frohlich, Oppenheimer, and Young, *Political Leadership and Collective Goods.*

81. See Heidenheimer, ed., *Political Corruption;* Mayhew, *Congress: The Electoral Connection.*

82. See R. de Jouvenel, *La République des camarades.* The Poujadist movement also attacked the *"syndicat des sortants"* (trade union of incumbent deputies). Quotation from Clapp, *The Congressman,* p. 13.

racy. It also creates significant policy biases toward producer interests at this second stage of representation.[83] And although other occupational groups also seek security, all such practices deserve critical scrutiny in terms of their consequences.

We are thus led, in describing or explaining the actions of legislators, to give particular weight to their informed judgments of collective welfare, arrived at through deliberation.[84] This emphasis seems more important for legislators (or representatives generally) than for the public at large, both because of the relation of trust and because of the expectation that legislators will be better informed and take a broader view than their constituents. In this respect, however, our reasoning parallels some of the pluralist arguments, for it seems to suggest particular faith in the interacting leaders of interest groups and in *their* judgments of the general welfare as against those of their constituents or rank and file. But it is also important that the rank and file be informed and that movements with strong mass support not be dismissed by definition as irrational.[85]

The representative's aims must be elevated not only above his personal welfare, but also often above that of his district. Service on committees, whether they concern general or special interests, ideally requires consideration of interests of the nation rather than the district.[86] And beyond the interests of the nation's voters, representatives may well consider the interests of persons affected but *not* represented: children, future generations, disfranchised minorities, resident aliens, and foreigners whose welfare will be affected by military or economic policies. Again ideally, this calls for the "virtual representation" that Burke considered. But note now that the bargaining model, based on constituency interests, must be rejected (even though Burke rejected it even for domestic policy). Legislative decision—and discourse—in

83. See Niskanen, *op. cit.,* chs. 14, 15.

84. The bargaining or exchange model has been criticized on this ground in Hallowell, *The Moral Foundation of Democracy,* in Tussman, *Obligation and the Body Politic,* ch. 4, and in Kendall and Carey, "The 'Intensity' Problem and Democratic Theory," p. 21. Deliberation may involve aspects of the social contract or of the formation of norms; see chapter 8 below.

85. See Rogin, *The Intellectuals and McCarthy.*

86. An analysis of the pursuit of district interests by a committee is given in Ferejohn, *Pork Barrel Politics.*

terms of notions of the general welfare is required.[87] A similar argument can be made for the fiduciary responsibility of public administrators, as contrasted with the self-interested model of the "bureaucrat."

Here we confront a major difference between the perspectives of economics and political science on human motivation. The economist's assumption that one individual makes decisions independently of the welfare of others (discussed at the start of this chapter) will not do as an exclusive maxim for the representative. When we consider recruitment into important representative roles, and the motivations of persons who must fill them, we must recognize the advantage to society of inculcating norms of social responsibility. The role of the representative requires them. The cost to society may be less if these motives are a substitute for material compensation (though perhaps this reasoning applies to the entrepreneur as well). And the presence of these norms will lessen the likelihood of corruption. The process by which this socialization occurs involves change in preferences. And it may require the support of such norms not merely by representatives, but also by the citizenry at large.

Thus while a number of spatial models of representation assume the position of the representative to be central in relation to his constituency,[88] the *mechanisms* for bringing this relation about transcend the motivation of economic man. Voters may well support candidates whom they perceive to be nearest to themselves in a choice space and thus may choose a representative whom they *perceive* to be at their median position, but this does not explain the conditions under which he will actually act in this way in his representative role, given the limitations on information flow to his constituency. The notion that representatives are motivated to follow this course solely by desire for reelection requires demonstration. When such motivation obtains, it may require the support of norms proscribing fraud, far more than in the economic domain.

Even if we grant that representation requires some modification of the economic or exchange model, we must still ask whether the model is adequate for direct democracy. Could a small political system of the

87. Buchanan and Tullock point out that consideration of the public interest is associated with disapproval of logrolling; *op. cit.*, p. 275.
88. E.g., MacRae, *Dimensions of Congressional Voting,* appendix C.

order of the *polis* or the town meeting conduct itself according to exchange procedures? Arrow has recognized the problems that the economic model encounters in political representation and sees that they extend to the citizens as well as the representatives:

> Political representation is an outstanding example of the principal-agent relation. This means that the link between individual utility functions and social action is tenuous, though by no means completely absent. . . . To some extent, . . . the voter is cast in a role in which he feels some obligation to consider the social good, not just his own.[89]

The norms appropriate for political discussion may vary depending on the matters about which decisions are to be made. Those decisions that involve the aggregation of small parts, each of which benefits a small minority, may call for self-interested bargaining. Those involving collective goods that are to be furnished more uniformly to all citizens may require discussion and voting in terms of the general welfare, if only to avoid free-rider problems. The distinction between these types of issues, and the difficult cases between them, will require greater clarity on the part of voters and representatives, as well as further investigation by valuatively oriented students of politics.[90]

Central to all these observations is the quest for *conditions* under which particular governmental forms—perhaps generally "democratic" in a broad sense but sometimes undemocratic in subsystems—are most appropriate. Thus the social structure (cleavages) and the values shared by the citizenry, as well as their political skills and habituation to particular institutions, will always be relevant.[91] So, too, will be the size of the polity and the objective problems confronting it (for example, pressures from the international system). The problem of choosing governmental forms has been stated in similar terms by political philosophers.[92]

It is with these conditions in mind that we must consider alternatives

89. Arrow, "Political and Economic Evaluation of Social Effects and Externalities,"p. 19.
90. See Rawls, *A Theory of Justice,* pp. 283–284, 359–360.
91. See Steiner, *Amicable Agreement Versus Majority Rule.*
92. For example Rousseau, *op. cit.,* pp. 35–42, 64ff., 89; Mill, *op. cit.,* pp. 218–227.

such as those among branches of government, federalism, bicameralism, separation of powers, and even the alternative of cybernetic-survey feedback for certain decision-making subsystems. Here, too, we consider the question as to the proper governmental forms within *subsystems* of a larger polity. Such subsystems include productive firms, voluntary associations, educational institutions, and semiautonomous organizations such as the parts of government that are influenced by particular interests under "interest-group liberalism." [93]

When we consider the desirability of democratic forms within a particular organization or subsystem of a larger polity, we must bear in mind not only a general ethical hypothesis, but also the characteristics of the particular organization. An educational organization may involve disparities in competence between teachers and students; an interest group may sometimes further its members' goals or the general welfare more effectively with less internal democracy. We must also consider the alternatives to internal democracy, such as external competition and withdrawal of membership.[94] We must consider the contribution that membership itself makes to the member's welfare, as compared with the contribution made by organizational decisions on the economy or polity. And finally, we must consider the degree to which the organization is self-contained in its effects; an organization with greater external effects may require control mechanisms that more fully consider the welfare of outsiders. Some of these same considerations are relevant to nations in the international system.

In analyzing the economic approach to politics, we first stressed the advantages that flow from the use of precise criteria of judgment (ethical hypotheses) for comparing detailed structural variations within democratic regimes. Larger alternatives such as the comparison of regimes themselves are less often treated by economists, but the general principle of comparing alterntives in terms of their expected outcomes can be extended to such choices.[95]

A major shortcoming of the economic approach, however, was revealed by our analysis of the role of the representative. Economic

93. Lowi, *op. cit.*
94. See Hirschman, *op. cit.*
95. See Dolbeare, "Public Policy Analysis and the Coming Struggle for the Soul of the Postbehavioral Revolution."

models of representative government must place limits on the selfish motives of the legislator if they are to be ethically acceptable. These limits reflect the need for normative regulation of representatives' actions. They also support the major modification of the ethic of preference satisfaction that we proposed in chapter 5: the distinction of collective-welfare judgments from preferences regarding the chooser's own welfare and the restriction of interpersonal aggregation to the latter. While some mechanisms of collective choice may perform this aggregation, others will involve deliberation concerning the general welfare and will involve both legislative debate and discourse among informed citizens. The process of deliberation involves both preference change and reciprocity among participants—topics to which we turn in the next two chapters.

7 CHANGES OF PREFERENCE: LEARNING AND THERAPY

Economic ethics, whether applied to the market or to politics, begins with the postulate that preference satisfaction is the good. Consideration of political choices as well as externalities has led us, however, to distinguish among types of preferences, some concerned with the chooser's own welfare and others with the general welfare. Consideration of education, advertising, and legislative deliberation led us also to stress that preferences can be changed and that the question how they should be changed is an important ethical problem that transcends the economic framework. The perspective of economic ethics can thus be criticized, in terms of our meta-ethical rule of generality, by proponents of ethical systems that encompass change of preferences.

An important potential source for this criticism of economic ethics can be found in psychology. While economic ethics neglects changes of preference, certain ethics held by psychologists give them a central place. Rather than taking preferences as given, these psychologists devote considerable attention to processes by which preferences, behavior, or personality characteristics are changed.

Psychology, as much as any other social science, has developed a scientific approach to its subject matter.[1] Thus, when we seek latent ethics in the discipline, we must rely largely on publications other than the major research journals for expressions of valuative positions. We shall select certain of these publications, either because they have drawn attention or because they aptly illustrate the ethical discourse that may take place between disciplines. But in spite of this selectivity—both on psychologists' part in expressing valuative viewpoints

1. See for example Misiak and Sexton, *History of Psychology*. Psychology is not simply a social science, as it involves physiology. Like other social sciences, it has become separate from its philosophical origins, but these origins are more closely related to epistemology than to ethics.

and on ours in choosing them—the common concern of various schools of psychology with preference change is characteristic of the discipline in contrast to economics.

The distinctive feature of psychological ethics—and of psychological models of man—in this respect is that they include the possibility of change in a person's behavior tendencies, or personality, so that after the change he will act differently in the same situation or environment. Such a model of man differs sharply from that of the economic demand curve, which implies that a consumer will continue to make the same choices among goods when prices, income, and the quantities he possesses are given.

But even though various schools of psychology consider the possibility of preference change, they differ considerably in the particular models they employ, in the corresponding types of action they consider, and in the values they seek in their latent ethics. These ethics are diverse as regards both ends and means. Their ends are as diverse as hedonism, perfectionism in the restructuring of personality, and harmony in interpersonal systems.

The simplest of these models, which we shall emphasize for its comparability with the economic model, may be found in learning theory; the discrete responses that are acquired or changed in this model correspond somewhat to the particular categories of demand in economics. But a variety of others also involve what an economist would consider changes in prefrences.

Most of the models of man used in psychotherapy differ from those of learning theory in dealing with personality as a system.[2] Not particular behavioral tendencies or attitudes, but a structure of needs and conflicts often rooted in early childhood, is seen as the cause of symptoms in these approaches and thus also as the focus of remedial action. Diagnostic categories such as those of the neuroses and psychoses occupy a central place in the choice among types of therapy: diagnosis precedes prescription and treatment. In all these respects the field of psychotherapy involves a depth of theory and of controversy that we deliberately deemphasize in order to stress questions of ethics rather

2. Behavior modification based on learning theory is also used in therapy, however.

than science. Freud's maxim, "Where id was, there shall ego be," [3] stressed the conscious control of one's own actions through insight into previously unconscious processes. Other therapeutic approaches seek to penetrate less deeply into the unconscious or attribute less importance to the influence of childhood experience and sexual motives.

The ethics of psychotherapy, like those of medicine, are largely concerned with the restoration of normal functioning; therapy is concerned with remedies for diseases or disorders. These ethics also have parallels, however, in values deriving from the study of personality for purposes other than therapy. Maslow and other advocates of a humanistic psychology have stressed the realization of man's full potential, a form of perfectionism; he was concerned with "peak experiences" as well as "synergy" in its goal of mutually advantageous interpersonal relations. [4] Erikson's developmental characterization of the unfolding of a sequence of possible virtues at different stages of life represents another set of goals for normal personality, extending beyond the problems of therapy. [5] And farther still from the role of the therapist, studies of the development of personality in childhood, and of the development of moral reasoning, have also suggested stages leading to a goal of maturity. [6] These types of goals have not always been associated with forms of therapy, nor have they been connected with the design of social policies, but they constitute bases for "ethical hypotheses" that might enter into the discourse we propose. [7]

3. Freud, *New Introductory Lectures on Psycho-Analysis*, p. 112. But Freud denied that psychoanalysis could support a *Weltanschauung* other than that of science (pp. 217, 248).

4. See Maslow, *Toward a Psychology of Being; The Farther Reaches of Human Nature*, ch. 14. Maslow's concern with objectively discoverable human needs was shared by Fromm, as expressed in *Man for Himself*. A general summary of this approach is Bühler and Allen, *Introduction to Humanistic Psychology*.

5. See Erikson, *Insight and Responsibility*, ch. 4.

6. See for example Piaget, *The Moral Judgment of the Child;* Kohlberg, "Development of Moral Character and Moral Ideology." But maturity itself, as the basis of an ethical hypothesis, may be criticized on the ground that it is not identical with moral conduct; this argument, which is consistent with our meta-ethical rule of convictions, is suggested in Hartmann, *Psychoanalysis and Moral Values*, pp. 73–74.

7. Two examples of works in which psychological theories have been incorporated in discussion of social and political alternatives are Bay, *The Structure of Freedom*, and Fromm, *The Sane Society*.

Preference Change in Economics and Learning Theory

The disparity between psychological and economic perspectives is so great that it will be useful to compare them directly, for scientific as well as for ethical purposes. We can clarify the difference in ethical perspectives by relating it to some of the scientific problems investigated in the two disciplines.

Among the ethics of psychology—and the concepts from which they derive—are some that are especially suited for comparison with the ethics of economics. These are the ethics and concepts that relate to discrete and specific tendencies on the part of the organism— behavioral tendencies or attitudes. Theories of learning deal with changes in these specific tendencies, in contrast to therapeutic or other theories that deal with personality as a system that interrelates such tendencies. The specific behavioral elements in learning theory resemble the specific categories of goods and services in the economic treatment of consumer demand.

The economic concept of "preference" seems to have close parallels in the psychological study of behavior and attitudes. Insofar as economists consider an internal state that precedes and guides choice behavior, this concept of preference [8] parallels the psychological notion of "attitude." But in each discipline there is also a school of thought whose adherents avoid mentalistic concepts and concentrate on the study of observable behavior. Both the psychological study of behavior (exemplified by Skinner) and the economic study of revealed preferences are concerned with an organism choosing between alternative states of affairs that affect it. The behavioral psychologist assumes that certain stimuli such as food, which an economist might say were "consumed" by the organism, reward or reinforce behavior. The economist defines a good or service for human beings as that for which "more is better." Each also assumes that there are aversive stimuli or situations: electric shocks for the experimental animal, work

8. Arrow treats "alternatives which could conceivably be presented to the chooser," in *Social Choice and Individual Values*, p. 11. He postulates a complete ordering of these alternatives (p. 13). Such a notion of preference clearly involves potential, rather than simply actual, choice.

for the economic man. The two domains might well be studied with common hypotheses and methods.

Yet while psychological learning theorists are concerned with the processes by which positive and negative reinforcement (reward and punishment) strengthen or weaken types of behavior, theoretical welfare economists largely ignore these processes. Learning theory, like other psychological approaches, assumes that communication, social rewards or punishments, and therapy produce changes in human behavior, but economists are often skeptical whether advertising really changes consumer preferences. Empirical questions are, of course, involved, but the paradigms of the two specialties seem so disparate as to lead to opposite assumptions about similar phenomena, with few efforts to synthesize them or reconcile them empirically.

The source of this difference may lie in the conceptual schemes, problem definitions, and dominant techniques of inquiry in the two specialties.[9] In behavioral psychology, the experimental student of learning observes the behavior of the organism over time, in a controlled environment, where he can clearly judge that its behavior has changed even though its environment and physiological drives have not. In economics, aggregate variables are typically measured in natural uncontrolled situations, where it can be argued that changes in consumer demand for a given product do not result from "true" changes in preference but are merely responses to a changing environment, for example, to changes in income or in the prices of other goods and services.[10]

A simplifying approach that has diverted economic ethics from concern with changes in preference is "comparative statics"—in Samuelson's phrasing, "the investigation of changes in a system from one position of equilibrium to another without regard to the transitional process involved in the adjustment." The centering of price theory about a "stationary economy" requires by definition that there be no

9. Contrasts among paradigms in the social sciences, even at a given time, illustrate Kuhn's points in *The Structure of Scientific Revolutions* at least as forcefully as do Kuhn's historical contrasts for the natural sciences.

10. The lack of experimentation in academic economics has also sometimes been a weakness of that discipline in giving policy advice. See Walter Williams, *Social Policy Research and Analysis*, pp. 129–132.

changes in tastes, as well as none in resources or technology. The difficulty of describing paths of movement of economic systems toward equilibrium "can be eliminated by postulating that the final equilibrium is attained immediately," as Stigler has written, "and this is a general practice among economists." [11]

Much economic treatment of the behavior of consumers and producers makes use of graphical representation of supply and demand to analyze the effects of exogenous influences that may move an economy from one state of equilibrium to another. The demand curves introduced by Alfred Marshall embody this characteristic. Demand is considered a single-valued function of price, as long as income and other prices remain unchanged. Thus to each price for a commodity there corresponds a given quantity demanded—regardless of the path by which consumers reached it. The multiple-valued demand curves that might result from the development or fluctuation of brand loyalty are excluded by the definition of this single-valued function. [12]

Comparative statics presumes that the short-run changes in behavior through which actors adjust to changing situations have come to an end (equilibrium) when observation occurs. Those behaviors (or preferences) that change rapidly in comparison to the time interval considered are treated as changing instantaneously, those that change slowly in relation to this interval are considered fixed, and intermediate rates of change are ignored. This assumption is more easily maintained because economists neglect the measurement of individual choice behavior over time and consider such measurement peripheral to the central domain of price theory. It is conceivable, of course, that a change from one equilibrium to another may result from changes in preference. [13] But such changes are difficult to incorporate in positive eco-

11. Samuelson, *Foundations of Economic Analysis,* p. 8; Stigler, *The Theory of Price* (1946 ed.), pp. 25, 29. A more cautious justification of considering tastes as fixed, for economic analysis, appears in the 1966 edition, p. 39. See also H. A. Simon, "Theories of Decision-Making in Economics," pp. 254–255. An alternative approach to modeling changes in opinions over time is illustrated by McPhee, *Formal Theories of Mass Behavior.*
12. See Hirschman, *Exit, Voice, and Loyalty,* p. 90. This phenomenon is analogous to hysteresis in the behavior of magnetic substances.
13. See Katona, "What is Consumer Psychology?" The problem of modifying central economic postulates through behavioral research is also illustrated in Cyert and Hedrick, "Theory of the Firm: Past, Present, and Future: An Interpretation." We might

nomic theory, other than as exogenous influences, and even more difficult to include in welfare economics.

This disregard of rates of change of preferences, in both the concepts and the measurements of economics, corresponds to an important difference between the economic and psychological ethics we are considering. Not only does economic ethics normally consider preferences as fixed; it considers preference satisfaction itself as the good, while it is by no means the ultimate good for the ethics of learning theory or of psychotherapy.

Economics is also concerned with dynamic phenomena, but these concerns do not carry over to welfare economics.[14] Moreover, the elements of economic dynamics that describe rapidity of response of the economy to exogenous variables include other possible rates of response than those involved in consumers' learning. In the dynamics of the "cobweb theorem," it is delays in the response of agricultural production to the market that enter.[15] In "psychological" theories of business cycles, it is fluctuations in expectations rather than preferences that provide the dynamic element. A prevalent economic model of the investor or producer involves anticipation of an uncertain future, and therefore its dynamic feature is due to expectations based on past events and their changes.[16] But this model of the consumer—on whose preferences the economic ethic is based—does not ordinarily involve rates of learning.

Thus if any learned behavior can be unlearned or extinguished rapidly enough, behavior may be seen as merely an instantaneous re-

expect the changes in preference produced by advertising to be noticed by economists in business schools. Economists do recognize that changes in tastes, fashions, or advertising may shift the demand curve; see Samuelson, *Economics,* p. 409; *Foundations,* pp. 17, 258, 280.

14. Policy recommendations are made for stabilization and growth of the economy, but the values that underlie them need to be systematically incorporated in a dynamic welfare economics.

15. See Samuelson, *Foundations of Economic Analysis,* p. 265; Keynes, *The General Theory of Employment, Interest and Money,* pp. 329–330.

16. Keynes (*ibid.,* p. 110) assumes that "short-period changes in consumption largely depend on changes in the rate at which income . . . is being earned and not on changes in the propensity to consume out of a given income." Another dynamic element "is to be sought in the influences which govern the recovery of the marginal efficiency of capital." (*ibid.,* p. 317).

sponse to the environment or situation, and the amount of a good purchased by a consumer can be seen as a single-valued function of price, income, and other simultaneous (rather than lagged) situational variables. Behavior then assumes an equilibrium value adjusted to the situation (price, stimuli, environment), and insofar as this single-valued functional relationship is seen to persist, "preferences" are considered not to change. A change of preferences would then correspond to a shift of the demand *curve,* but such a shift is more often seen as resulting from changes in income or in the supply of other goods. If we translate this approach into the situation of the experimental animal choosing between two branches of a maze, it is equivalent to assuming that he "knows" what lies at the end of each branch (the market situation) and that a change in behavior in response to this knowledge is *not* a "change in preference."

The "comparative statics" approach, as we have noted, treats human behavior (preferences) as either changing instantaneously in response to the situation or not changing at all. This distinction seems a convenience for the analysis of intervention in economic systems. A strength of economic analysis is its capacity to predict the directions of change of such systems in response to changes in exogenous variables such as supply, technology, taxes, subsidies, or regulations.[17] Some of these changes correspond to government policies that we wish to evaluate.

Even the effects of a change in demand due to advertising could be analyzed in this way; economists could predict directions of the resulting changes in price or shifts in consumption patterns of other goods. But what they *cannot* do with an ethic of preference satisfaction is to evaluate such changes in welfare terms. The welfare argument characteristically used to evaluate effects of specific (excise) taxes depends on the conclusion that a consumer finds himself on a lower indifference curve. But when preferences change, the indifference curves themselves move, and the welfare conclusion is indeterminate.

17. In analyses of this sort, many parameters that do not change may be conveniently ignored. Lindblom observes that policy analysis, as practiced by economists, "does not ask radical questions about fundamental features of the social structure." See his "Integration of Economics and the Other Social Sciences Through Policy Analysis," in Charlesworth, ed., *Integration of the Social Sciences Through Policy Analysis,* p. 1.

Those psychologists who study changes in behavior or personality are likely to see the problem, "What should we prefer?" more clearly.[18] They cannot limit themselves to ethics that treat the behavior tendencies of the organism in a given environment as fixed. Thus, insofar as they venture into the ethical realm, they must be concerned with desired changes in behavior or in its sources.

The alteration of behavior has not, of course, been the exclusive province of psychologists. Plato, when he assumed that only children aged ten or less would become citizens of his republic, recognized the possibility of change but saw it occurring primarily in youth.[19] Other utopias have also been concerned with the education as well as the selection of members, and some, looking beyond behavioral change, have considered changing even man's genetic characteristics.

Two major ethical approaches, emerging from the psychological study of changes in human behavior, are especially relevant to the interdisciplinary comparison we propose. One is the far-reaching ethic of B. F. Skinner, which considers the transformation of society by behavior technology; centered about behavior change, it also includes designs of social systems and their norms. The other embraces the ethics of therapy, which relate to a professional role dealing largely with individual patients in an existing society.[20]

The Ethics of B. F. Skinner

The ethics underlying the work of B. F. Skinner is of particular interest for our argument because it provides a sharply focused contrast with economic ethics. This contrast can be drawn without our considering the interrelation between ethics and complex models of personality; neither of the two approaches includes them. Moreover, both the economic ethic and Skinner's ethic are concerned with problems of

18. For a welfare analysis of preference changes due to advertising, one needs an external standard such as the economic notion of "merit goods"; see Hamilton, "The Demand for Cigarettes." The question of what we ought to prefer is raised explicitly in Joseph Margolis, *Psychotherapy and Morality,* pp. 38–39.

19. *The Republic of Plato,* p. 262 (VII.541).

20. Although there are therapeutic treatments based on Skinnerian principles, their goals are ordinarily specific and related to the patient's problems, rather than centering on reinforcement per se.

great generality, including the design of entire economies or societies. But in spite of these similarities, the two ethical systems differ somewhat in their notions of the good and differ radically in the alternative actions and policies they consider for realizing the good. Thus the contrast between these two "ethical hypotheses" can be focused on our rule of generality as regards the alternative actions to which they apply.

Skinner has been a leader in the psychological study of "operant conditioning," which he describes as follows:

> When a bit of behavior is followed by a certain kind of consequence, it is more likely to occur again, and a consequence having this effect is called a reinforcer. Food, for example, is a reinforcer to a hungry organism; anything the organism does that is followed by the receipt of food is more likely to be done again whenever the organism is hungry. Some stimuli are called negative reinforcers; any response which reduces the intensity of such a stimulus—or ends it—is more likely to be emitted when the stimulus recurs.[21]

Skinner is famous for experiments in which animal subjects are induced to behave in specified ways by the experimenter's control of the environment and the reinforcements it provides. His followers have applied these procedures not only to animal experiments, but also to teaching and to therapeutic behavior modification in which particular symptoms are changed.

Skinner's two chief ethical statements, written for popular consumption, have been *Walden Two* (1948), a fictional account of an ideal community in which desired behavior is reinforced, and *Beyond Freedom and Dignity* (1971), a more direct criticism of the widespread ethical concepts that figure in its title. Especially in the latter volume, he has developed what he considers to be the implications of an ethic stressing reinforcement as a standard or criterion.

Skinner's ethics, as a basis for ethical argument, is not merely the idiosyncratic product of a particular individual. It involves the central alternative that distinguishes psychological from economic ethics—

21. Skinner, *Beyond Freedom and Dignity,* p. 25.

consideration of change of preferences or of corresponding psychological variables. Few psychologists have extended concepts of their discipline into the construction of utopias or recommendations for social engineering, but those who do so are likely to propose changes in the ways in which human beings respond to, or cope with, the world.

The Skinnerian model (and ethic) considers the modification of discrete behavioral elements. It has been applied not only to the construction of utopias but also to therapy. Most therapeutic models, however, consider the preferences, or behavior tendencies, of an individual to be interrelated in his personality structure. In this prevalent therapeutic perspective, the alteration of a particular item of behavior may remove a symptom but not the underlying cause. Some readers will thus consider it strange that we group together Skinner and psychotherapists such as those in the Freudian tradition. Within psychology and psychotherapy, the proponents of these two approaches are at odds, and neither group wishes to be confused with the other. Nevertheless, for our purpose of developing discourse among the disciplines, they share a common criticism of economic ethics. We are not here concerned with stating the most effective means for producing desired changes in behavior or personality; this question may be left to the critical procedures of empirical science. We are, however, concerned with debate about what changes in behavior (or preferences) are *desirable,* and in raising this question the ethics of Skinner and of psychotherapy are potential allies rather than opponents.

The ethics of Skinner and of therapy differ not only in the complexity of their models of man, but also in the scope of the alternative policies they consider. From the therapist's perspective, the possibility of changing an individual's behavior or personality is constrained by the social structures and interpersonal relations in which the individual is involved; the design of utopias can consider these structures de novo, but the therapist must take many of them as given.

These two sorts of possible action—social transformation and therapy—are most important for our argument because of their means rather than their ends. The distinctive contribution of these psychological ethics to our argument is to highlight the lack of generality of economic ethics. Economists are not unaware that preference change is a

214 THE ETHICS OF THE SOCIAL SCIENCES

possible social policy,[22] but they cannot easily incorporate this possibility in their otherwise elegant ethical system. The various goals to which psychologists suggest that learning and therapy be directed are neither so uniform nor so precisely codified as those of welfare economics, but by selecting the work of one man we can more easily compare alternative consistent ethical systems.

Skinner's ethic considers society as a whole and is concerned with changing both its structure and the characteristics of its members. In contemplating such fundamental changes, it contrasts sharply with the value of satisfaction of given preferences, which economic ethics embodies and shares with major traditions of American society.[23] Concepts such as freedom and power, related to these traditions, tend to become ambiguous when we consider changes of preference that occur without coercion or punishment.

This ethic is not only distinct from that of economists; it is also distinct from Bentham's and Mill's conjunction of happiness and preference (desire). For Skinner writes, "Good things are positive reinforcers." This definition of the good differs from the assertion that things chosen are good, since learning and extinction take time. Behavior now being reinforced may not yet be fully learned; behavior reinforced in the past may not yet have been extinguished and may still be preferred (chosen) at the time in question when it produces harm.[24] Moreover, conflicts within ourselves can lead us to seek immediate and minor reinforcements instead of larger ones that would be available if we were able to act differently.

One similarity between Skinner's ethics and that of economists is that it aims at reducing the incidence of uncontrolled externalities. But while economists tend to see the remedies for these effects in collective action or quasi-market mechanisms, Skinner sees them in learning itself. Insofar as an organism is made "more sensitive to the conse-

22. See for example, Buchanan, *The Bases for Collective Action,* pp. 12–13; Arrow, "Gifts and Exchanges," pp. 354–355.
23. See Hartz, *The Liberal Tradition in America.*
24. *Beyond Freedom and Dignity,* pp. 98, 104–106. An ethic of reinforcement may also be more complex in its formulation because of the effectiveness of intermittent (rather than continuous) reinforcement in retaining learned behaviors. Skinner also considers cultural survival as a value (p. 130), but its potential conflict with reinforcement is pointed out by Stillman in "The Limits of Behaviorism," p. 207.

quences of its action," [25] externalities will be internalized—in both the economic and the psychological senses of the term. The term is now used in a double sense: individuals who incorporate ("internalize" in psychology) into their own personalities a concern for the welfare of others thus incorporate formerly external costs or benefits into their economic decisions ("internalize" in economics). But in addition, this learning can also reduce aggressive tendencies, which are not part of the economic model. It is interesting to note that among the economic categories of market failure, deliberate aggression or hostility is not usually included. Thus in psychology as well as in political science we find research reflecting ethical orientations to the reduction of aggression or the resolution of conflicts—a problem largely absent from economic ethics.

When we are concerned with the internalization of external effects, the remedies we choose may be different depending on whether the effects work through distant, impersonal processes or direct personal relations. When personal relations are involved, the economic remedy of market pricing or of exchange may be less appropriate and change of preferences or creation of norms more relevant. Thus it will be useful to try to distinguish between external effects resulting from consumption and those from production. Arrow's examples of the well-tended lawn, heathenism, homosexuality, and drug-taking, mentioned above in chapter 5, involve economies or costs impinging on one person as a result of another's consumption, broadly considered; his example of factory smoke involves production.

When these effects occur as a result of production, the economist's standard for judging them is to compare the resulting allocation of productive resources with that which would obtain if all effects *were* priced in competitive markets, that is, internal rather than external to the market. Equity and the producer's personal welfare are neglected.[26] But in consumption the problem seems different. Should the neighbor who tends his lawn be encouraged to exclude others from viewing it and to charge them for the privilege? He might thus be induced to devote more resources to lawn tending (now involving an ad-

25. *Beyond Freedom and Dignity*, p. 136.
26. See Coase, "The Problem of Social Cost." Producers' welfare may be reflected to some degree in the labor market.

ditional productive component), but in interpersonal relations, and in activities conducted for enjoyment rather than profit, this approach seems inappropriate. A particular problem arises, therefore, when we consider external economies or benefits from consumption. Whereas the economic approach suggests that these also be removed by introducing prices, in interpersonal relations we should perhaps try to increase the net benefits in other ways.

There are actually numerous social mechanisms that can encourage the internalization of external costs or benefits. The introduction of prices and exchange is only one of them; nor are they exhausted by the governmental economic interventions considered in chapter 6. The modification of preferences through learning, therapy, and the development of social norms is also a means of reducing what were previously external costs or encouraging external benefits [27] and thus is a means to the "internalization" of external effects. Similarly, the formation of a group or organization that acts as a unit in the market typically makes use of social norms (for internal decision) to transfer formerly external effects from market activities into group decision processes.

Skinner not only deals with the internalization of external effects through learning, but also provides for a system of continual reinforcement (social control) by other members of the social system, for the maintenance of the behavior tendencies in Walden Two. The likelihood of extinction of behavior (unlearning) is typically reduced by a system of intermittent reinforcement in most societies.[28]

The indignant criticism that Skinner's ethic has provoked suggests some of the normative limitations that our society imposes on the technology of behavior modification. These norms, which permit some such behavior changes and forbid others, are of several kinds.

First, it is widely considered, even in *Walden Two,* that within a certain range there is no disputing tastes. Provision is made for individual variation, without social efforts to control it. Huxley's *Brave*

27. See chapter 8 below; Skinner, *Beyond Freedom and Dignity,* p. 136.
28. On the "variable-ratio" schedule see *Beyond Freedom and Dignity,* pp. 151, 170. The inculcation of behavior tendencies is treated by sociologists as "socialization," and their maintenance is related to "social control." However, the same communications often perform both functions as they are received by different individuals.

New World required more homogeneous behavior within its genetic strata; Skinner permits variations in taste. The choices for which this latitude is allowed are ones that produce few external effects, and relatively little cost is involved in gratifying them; preferences among readily available foods, for example, are typically considered "matters of taste." Their differential effects on the individual's long-run welfare are also expected to be small. If all these conditions are met, even a Skinnerian ethic may provide some scope for individual behavioral variety over time and for diversity within society.

Second, there are widely assumed to be certain types of esthetic experiences which, if one is suitably prepared to appreciate them, are genuinely superior to others. "High culture" is the leading example. Here Bentham was skeptical, judging pushpin as good as poetry, but Scitovsky has argued to his fellow economists that the low patronage of the arts in America can be remedied only by a change in popular preferences.[29] If high culture is not merely an arbitrary cultural artifact—if the effort and opportunity to have certain experiences produce demonstrably superior results in terms of a specifiable ethic—then some collective action to shape preferences in this way may be justified.

Third, even within the economic framework of free and voluntary choices, we may imagine that individuals will choose to change their own preferences, without being entirely dependent on the environment for doing so. They may, for example, choose to develop their own esthetic tastes or change their preferences for food in the interest of either health or gastronomy.[30] To do this they may need the example of others (part of their environment) in order to anticipate their satisfaction after the change. But this sort of change is tolerated or esteemed more than is "behavioral engineering," because it is seen as a free choice by the person affected. Information, or access to environments, that promote such change may be sold on the market. Similar options in the form of therapy are available to private psychiatric patients, or to their families, if they can pay the price.

29. Scitovsky, "What's Wrong with the Arts Is What's Wrong with Society."
30. See James and Nordell, "Preference Transformations and Welfare Theory." Skinner goes further in suggesting "a world which will be liked not by people as they now are but by those who live in it." *Beyond Freedom and Dignity,* p. 156.

Fourth, there is a widespread concern with manipulation and with the infringement of freedom. Because of these norms, the shaping of preferences is limited to certain realms and certain means. Skinner objects to these limitations, which restrict nonaversive control to weak methods, but the conflict with his critics' values here runs deep.

The social roles within which preferences may legitimately be changed are thus restricted. In childhood, socialization of children by their parents and education chosen by the collectivity are permitted. As the recipients grow older (for example, college age) they are increasingly freed from direct influence of this type. When adults are the recipients, interpersonal modification of preferences is ideally expected to occur only in roles entered voluntarily. These include voluntary exposure to advertising or political campaigns, though normative limits are defined by complaints about "captive audiences." There are also the exceptional circumstances of involuntary therapy, penal institutions, or the military draft.

An especially significant set of roles is that of persons judged to be mentally ill and treated for this condition—whether voluntarily or involuntarily. These roles involve change of preferences, and the related ethics are close to the discipline of psychology. We therefore proceed to consider the ethics of therapy.

Ethical Criteria of Psychotherapy and Mental Health

Psychology, unlike most other social sciences, contains a major subfield that is directly concerned with professional practice: clinical psychology. The clinical psychologist is concerned with therapy or change in behavior; in a broad sense he works to bring about changes in human behavior analogous to those which the learning theorist or personality theorist studies disinterestedly. His measures of personality or behavior include psychological tests, interviews, and observation, and the concepts that organize them relate to personality and the diagnostic categories of mental illness. Superficially these aspects of human activity appear quite different from an animal's pressing a lever or its choice of a pathway in a maze. The analogy between the general processes studied in personality change and in learning theory never-

theless remains, as does that between economic choice and animal behavior.[31]

The clinical psychologist often pursues his practical work in collab-
oration with other closely related mental health professions, working
with psychiatrists and psychiatric social workers.[32] As professional
practice, this work is guided by norms of a different sort from those
that arise from academic science. The norms of a profession center
about the actual roles of its practitioners, while the ethics that arise on
the fringes of scientific disciplines (such as Skinner's) tend to be more
abstract and utopian. Thus the ethics of psychotherapy often ignore
many of the social processes that bring problems to the therapist, as
beyond his control.

Clinical psychologists, however, are more closely tied to the academic discipline of psychology than are engineers to natural science:
they are members of the same professional association and often the
same academic departments. These ties have encouraged a debate
about the goals of psychotherapy among professional colleagues who
study personality, social psychology, and related fields, as well as
among therapists themselves. From this combination of perspectives a
critical literature, transcending the immediate tasks of the practitioner,
has emerged.

This critical literature is of special interest for our ethical comparison for several reasons. First, the therapeutic role is more consciously
oriented to values and action than are many other aspects of psychology. Second, the limitations of that role have common features that
they share with other professional roles in which social science is
applied. And third, if we abstract from the specific goals and models
of personality that characterize particular therapeutic approaches, we

31. The relation is also expressed in forms of therapy based on learning theory; see
Dollard and Miller, *Personality and Psychotherapy;* Wolpe and Lazarus, *Behavior Therapy Techniques.*

32. These professionals engage in "therapy," defined as the alleviation of disease or,
by extension, as including treatment by professionals whose major role is to alleviate
disease. See Mechanic, *Mental Health and Social Policy,* pp. 6–7; Reisman, *The Development of Clinical Psychology.* Therapeutic work based on the role of the physician
often makes use of a naturalistic ethic; see Joseph Margolis, *Psychotherapy and Morality,* pp. 59–60.

can again see parallels with certain problems of economic ethics, notably that of coping with external costs.

This critical discussion, conducted largely by therapists and social psychologists, suggests that the therapist's role may be viewed in two principal ways. One is close to the conventional role of the physician, who diagnoses and treats diseases of individual patients who come to him. The other is similar in some ways to that of Skinner's system builder, though applied to smaller systems such as families, organizations, or communities rather than to entire societies. In this latter perspective "mental health," a goal of psychotherapy, can be seen as involving the modification of systems of interpersonal relations, aiming not simply at restoring the patient to normality but at broader ethical goals such as the general welfare. In the debate and criticism that relates these two perspectives to one another, we shall again see an analogy to the economic ethic, in consideration of problems of external cost. Through this analogy, we shall suggest not only that economic ethics are insufficiently general through their neglect of preference change, but that therapeutic ethics may fruitfully also be generalized by means of perspectives from welfare economics. We shall now trace the development of the social-system perspective and some of the debates that revolve about it.

When certain types of deviant or abnormal behavior came to be defined as "mental illness" and subject to treatment, the task of psychotherapy was defined, by analogy with that of medicine, as treatment of the *patient*. This definition implies that it is individuals, rather than social relationships or structures, that are treated. Individual patients come or are brought to the therapist. Some come voluntarily, because of complaints or symptoms from which they wish relief. Others are brought to the therapist by their families or associates or by processes of the law. In the latter case the goal of treatment may be the alleviation of difficulties or costs imposed by the patient on those about him. To some extent, society and its power relations define which members of a system are to be treated as "patients" who are expected to undergo treatment (or isolation from their previous environment) in order to reduce these costs. A norm supporting inequality—whether of class, race, or sex—may be used by a privileged group to direct social control at the less privileged. Reexamination of the power relations and choice processes that bring patients to treatment has not ordinarily been a major concern of the therapist's ethics, but an increasing number of critiques have been directed to this problem.[33] These critiques—whether of therapy or of society's treatment of crime—have tended to stress the use of these policies to favor one party's interest over another's. But the observation of such biases must go beyond an alienated opposition to all use of force in society and must return us to the problems of designing and controlling such processes for the general welfare.

Therapy is expected to begin with *problems*—imbalances or dissatisfactions felt by the patient or by those about him and brought to the therapist without his seeking them out. As in the case of medicine, therapy typically takes its start from the patient's complaint; in a free society the physician is not expected to take the initiative to tell people they are ill when they are not aware of it. If the patient ventures voluntarily into the consulting room, he may then be told that he has an illness he had not suspected; the physician has the prerogative of diagnosis. But even when the patient is brought to therapy involuntarily by others, the task of therapy is ordinarily limited to that of removing a problem or restoring an initial state of health.

The therapist then classifies problems into diagnostic categories, which ideally correspond to efficient choices among modes of treatment. Different types of therapy, hospitalization, or referral to specialists may be recommended. But the criterion of successful therapy normally remains the alleviation of the initial problem, as redefined by the physician.

This concern with problems resembles negative utilitarianism (the ethic of minimizing unhappiness) or the concern with poverty; it aims only to restore normality, not to improve the normal or to make saints or heroes. Speed reading, body building, sensitivity training, the cultivation of artistic skills, heightened esthetic appreciation, advanced sexual techniques, and other forms of self-improvement are outside the therapist's domain insofar as they transcend the restoration of normal-

33. See the work of Szasz, including *The Myth of Mental Illness;* Leifer, *In the Name of Mental Health;* Halleck, *The Politics of Therapy,* p. 27.

ity.[34] The ethics of restoring normality actually characterizes a wide variety of practical activities. In a society's dealing with personal dysfunctions or social problems, the restoration of the initial state is again the typical goal—though occasionally political action takes such an existing "social problem" or demand as an occasion to push for broader reforms.[35]

The tasks of psychotherapy thus begin with the alleviation of symptoms. For the patient who enters because of his own complaints, the initial problem of therapy is perhaps the removal of a compulsion or an inhibition, but psychotherapy provides wider latitude than other forms of medical practice for transformation of the complaint through diagnosis. The real problem may be seen by the therapist as that of rendering the unconscious conscious or as related to a general capacity to cope with the environment or the use of reason.[36] It may even involve the restructuring of motives so that they are mutually more consistent.

The problems that a patient brings to therapy may be his own or others' problems. He may be forced to enter therapy because he generates stress in others, or he may seek therapy because of stresses on him from others about him. Either the stressor or the stressed may enter therapy. And the stressor may not be a single individual but a social structure. It may be a structure (such as that of occupational mobility) that performs useful functions for society while generating psychic stress as an "externality." [37] The stress may also be generated by direct hostility or aggression, a cause not included in the economic model. The question as to who has to enter therapy may thus seem in-

34. This approach was challenged by Maslow, who stressed "peak experiences" in terms of self-actualization rather than normality; see for example his *The Farther Reaches of Human Nature*, ch. 12. The concept of normality itself requires scrutiny as to whether it is defined by the current normative expectations of a particular society or involves an ethic of perfectionism that may permit criticism of those norms.

35. Sociologists may redefine "social problems"; social scientists engaged by clients may attempt to redefine the client's problems; and psychotherapists may transform not only the meaning of symptoms, but also the range of symptoms considered relevant (Rieff, *Freud: The Mind of The Moralist*, p. 334). See also Mechanic, *op. cit.*, p. 31. In addition, the therapist may view the problem as extending beyond the patient to others in a social system in which he participates; see Laing, *The Politics of the Family*.

36. Rieff, *op. cit.*

37. Mechanic, *op. cit.*, p. 30. See also Hersch, "Social History, Mental Health, and Community Control."

determinate, as in Coase's example in which either the polluting factory or the nearby homeowner may pay for the reduction of pollution. We may thus consider social orders that are answers to the problem of "preventive mental health," but they risk presenting us with a great diversity of conceivable structures composed as in Skinner's *Walden Two*. Alternatively, we may try to work toward them piecemeal by devoting psychotherapy or learning to the restructuring of smaller social systems.[38]

By considering the relation between stressor and stressed, or social systems as wholes, we have possibly extended the definition of "therapy." The root definition of the term concerns the alleviation of disease. We may imagine someone who creates stress in others to have a "character disorder" and thus to require treatment, but he may also be selfish, inconsiderate, ambitious, or criminal, and thus deserving of nonpsychiatric social control rather than professional therapy. Similarly, apparently neurotic behavior may be reinterpreted as residing in a family configuration requiring treatment of the family as a whole. But if we consider a community, or part of a society, as susceptible to psychiatric interpretation and remedial action, our concept of disease or disorder has been extended. In this case it is the activities of a particular sort of professional, and of his categories of analysis, that we are using to define "therapy" in a broader and looser sense.

We thus enlarge our perspective on the range of problems brought to therapy from the alleviation of the patient's distress to include the reduction of costs (or the provision of benefits) to other members of a social system. The value guiding either of these activities may well be a general ethical system. If this system is negative utilitarianism, then they will be directed at the alleviation of felt suffering but not at the increase of happiness. The term "positive mental health" has sometimes been used to refer to such an enlargement of the concept beyond the mere alleviation of problems, but it remains ambiguous as long as it incorporates the term "health" without redefining it in a "positive" sense.

38. The possibility of incremental improvements has been challenged, however, by Gintis, who argues that the functional integration of American society militates against such change. See his "Neo-Classical Welfare Economics and Individual Development," applying Parsonian analysis to this problem.

The evaluation of the costs or benefits imposed on one person by another requires some of the same distinctions in therapy as in economics—in particular, the distinction between the recipient's personal welfare and his judgments of the general welfare. When those around a person define him as a potential patient, we must ask whether they do so because of pain, suffering, or stress that they themselves suffer (their own welfare) or because of judgments that the prospective patient's behavior is generally harmful. Conceivably some spectators will judge treatment necessary even though they experience little stress or pain themselves. Their "preferences" for treatment of the patient would not count, in the ethical hypothesis we proposed in chapter 5, in the aggregate of welfare used to evaluate the choice.

In actual situations of this sort, this conceptual distinction is often difficult to draw. An observer whose moral feelings are offended by deviant behavior may feel pain or unhappiness even if he is remote from the behavior itself. And personal stress or pain, if it is to be used to justify involuntary treatment, may be rationalized in terms of the general welfare. But the conceptual distinction is nevertheless important. In the ethic of preference satisfaction, as in Arrow's early writings, the distinction is not drawn, but the consequent amalgam of criteria is open to ethical criticism. One person's behavior may impose external costs on others, and therapy and other forms of social control are methods of alleviating them. But the very definition of an external cost must also be considered in at least two ways. Not only may our ethic define some preferences on the part of a person offended by another's behavior, as unrelated to that person's welfare, but a general practice of controlling behavior that offends others may lead to a conformity that jeopardizes values such as those of a free society or of innovation. In addition, both the existence of these "psychic externalities" and their removal may result from illusions, either of deviant behavior or of the conditions of its treatment.

If one person's activities impose an external cost on another and this situation can be ameliorated by exchange, then an economist would expect the exchange to take place, given enough time and sufficiently low transactions costs.[39] But when the reduction of a cost requires a

39. See for example Buchanan, *The Bases for Collective Action*. If, however, the cost is imposed intentionally, we might not expect the recipient to engage in exchange except under duress.

change in someone's behavior tendencies, we cannot so easily expect the change to occur by spontaneous voluntary action. Perhaps it could be induced by Skinner's nonaversive reinforcement, but in our present society coercion is often involved.

Between the cases of voluntary and involuntary submission to therapy, however, is an intermediate one in which therapeutic treatment is a condition for the patient's receiving some other good, just as the media viewer receives persuasive communication (advertising) as a condition for obtaining news or entertainment, or some students receive instruction as a condition for job opportunities. The practice of psychiatric social work, similarly, has sometimes been concerned with therapy for persons who do not seek it voluntarily. Rather, in order to be eligible for payments in money or in kind, clients may be required to submit to therapy.[40]

This combination of therapy with other goods depends, however, on an official social diagnosis of the situation. The client or patient is seen as deficient in resources; he may define himself in this way in order to receive certain benefits, or he may be included in such a definition by others affected by his behavior. But the alternative definition provided by the negative income tax (as contrasted with the "helping professions") is to assume that he lacks *only* resources and that once he receives them he may use them as well as the next person.

In these conditions for admission to therapy, we see three types of processes. First, the patient may enter on his own initiative, for relief of symptoms he himself defines. The physician may redefine the situation through his diagnosis but must in the end argue (if challenged) that his treatment is aimed at alleviating the symptoms. Secondly, the individual who enters may primarily want additional resources (goods and services) but may be required by the society's definition of his situation to enter therapy as a condition for receiving them. Third, the individual may be defined as in need of therapy even when he himself does not wish it and receives nothing in direct exchange. This last possibility includes referral by families or associates for "character disorders." It can extend by analogy, however, to societal judgments in which the poor are defined as requiring treatment for the "culture of poverty" or the Negro family structure is seen as in need of alter-

40. See Keith-Lucas, "The Political Theory Implicit in Social Casework Theory."

ation.[41] In recent years these last two definitions have been challenged by black political organizations.

A further distinction may be made in principle between entry into treatment for reasons of the patient's own welfare and entry for reasons affecting the welfare of others. In medical treatment, an unconscious patient may be brought into the emergency ward in order to save his life—even though his own wishes are not consulted. Even attempted suicides are treated in this way. Similarly, a neurotic who is apparently failing to accomplish his own goals may be induced to undergo treatment, though here the rationalization that treatment was undertaken "for his own good" can easily be a cloak for the motives of persons in the patient's environment. In contrast to this argument is the direct assertion that a patient is being treated because of his potential effects on "society" or on those about him.

The distinction between behavioral malfunctions affecting the patient himself, and those affecting others is brought out by Srole in the following way:

Intrapsychic Malfunction

		+	−
Interpersonal Malfunction	+	A	B
	−	C	D

In the middle and upper classes the group in cell C is accepted for outpatient treatment in no negligible numbers . . . [It] is regarded by the profession as on the whole satisfying its criteria of mental illness, including eligibility for and admission to the status of psychiatric patients. . . . [The] cell B disorders are not in practice regarded as satisfying the professions' criteria of mental illness or eligibility for patient status. . . . [The] two parameters [rows, columns above] must be regarded as of coordinate psychiatric significance, rather than as major and minor spheres, or central and peripheral areas of relevance and interest.[42]

41. See Srole, "Medical and Sociological Models in Assessing Mental Health," p. 48. See also articles by Clausen and Smith in the same volume. On the Negro family, see Rainwater and Yancey, *The Moynihan Report and the Politics of Controversy*.

42. Srole, *op. cit.*, pp. 49–50.

Assuming that it is "malfunctions" that are to be dealt with, rather than acts judged deviant on proper or improper grounds, Srole concludes that cell B has been improperly neglected by the mental health professions. Szasz, on the other hand, stresses the possible violation of individual rights, and subservience of psychiatrists to an existing power structure, in the forcible incarceration and treatment of persons in this same category.[43] Srole and Szasz, though they disagree on the relative desirability of these two types of therapy or professional intervention, agree on the distinction between them.

This dichotomy in the possible goals of therapy has also been emphasized by Mechanic as the distinction between "performance" and "personal distress." A diversity of goals is nevertheless concealed in a concept such as "performance." They relate in fact to the types of ethics held and the corresponding types of lives and societies to which the ethics lead. "Performance" can mean the effective production of various sorts of goods: for example, maximizing the national income, minimizing social conflict, or inducing maximal development of the potentialities of individuals (if we can specify which ones). The multiple meanings of this term in fact relate to the multiplicity of the ethics of therapy, or of mental health, generally.[44]

The criterion of "performance" in interpersonal relations also departs from the notion of "illness" by seeing problems in social systems rather than in individuals alone. These systems may be families, organizations, or communities. The concern with community mental health has led to stress on this difference. As Smith puts it,

> The community-centered approach to human effectiveness . . . requires emphasis on two relatively novel concepts. One is that human ineffectiveness or fulfillment cannot be usefully conceived or dealt with as a property of the isolated individual. It is rather a characteristic of behavior that the person shows as a participant in the small interpersonal systems that frame his daily life. . . . The . . .

43. Szasz, *The Myth of Mental Illness; Ideology and Insanity*. Robinson has also argued, in "Harm, Offense, and Nuisance," that compulsory therapy should be limited to cases involving potential harm to the patient himself.

44. On "performance" see Mechanic, *op. cit.*, p. 31. The multiplicity of criteria that have been used to define mental health is illustrated in Smith, *Social Psychology and Human Values*, p. 180.

concept . . . of social competence summarizes the person's own contribution to whether these "circles" are vicious or benign."

[Symptoms] require attention but, from the point of view of the *public interest,* rather less attention than might be given them in private psychotherapy.[45]

It is thus important, for intellectual and valuative clarity, to view the ethics of therapy in terms of the public interest or general welfare.[46] Both the patient and his role-partners in various social systems are involved in processes that may produce welfare or diswelfare, justice or injustice, or, in general, value-relevant consequences. Therapy of a particular patient is one among several conceivable ways of increasing the values realized in this interaction. Alternatives include therapy of *other* role-partners, either together with or instead of the initial patient; change in structural features or norms of those systems, including the approaches we discuss in other chapters; or removal of the individual (no longer a subject of therapy) from the system, as in incarceration or custodial care.

But in the domain of mental health, if we recognize the central involvement of notions such as "public interest" or "general welfare" we must also recognize that we have moved to an opposite pole from our previous economic and political approaches, as regards our means of furthering such values. In previous chapters we have stressed reasoned discussion among consumers, voters, or representatives. We have acknowledged that preferences might be changed by such discussion, but we have assumed in this discussion that the participants had reciprocal opportunities to influence one another. We have assumed (tacitly) that even "extremists" or "neurotics" might have such opportunities, unless the substance and form of their arguments led their fellow participants to judge them uninformed or irrational.

But if we go so far as to judge some citizens or consumers as "mentally ill," we are depriving them even more forcefully of their opportunity to argue their views than if we had listened to them and deemed them uninformed. We are then delegating that judgment to a special

---

45. Smith, "Competence and Mental Health," p. 113. My emphasis.
46. As Hartmann points out (*op. cit.,* pp. 69–70), health values cannot automatically be substituted for moral values.

group of psychotherapeutic professions. The possibilities of misuse of this judgment are quite clear when they are brought out explicitly, as by the writings of both Skinner and Szasz—even though these writers disagree in their recommendations. But these possibilities are far less clear when concealed in the terminology of medicine and justified simply in the name of science rather than of values or policy. Thus Clausen has warned us,

> Unless we can specify clearly the criteria for judging health, there is a danger that anything that differs from the conventionally established norms of some powerful segment of society will be labeled ill health or even disease, despite the lack of any scientific criterion by which disease can be assessed.[47]

A still more forceful warning of the political potentialities in therapy has been given in the writings of Szasz. He has no objection to the type of therapy received by patients who enter it voluntarily and are not hospitalized. But when psychiatry enters into the judgments of the courts, or the efforts of families or communities to have one of their members incarcerated, then the distribution of power in the use of this professional resource must be examined from a political perspective. When educational institutions—perhaps with the aid of psychology or psychiatry—become concerned with students' personality development, both the progress envisioned by Skinner and the controlled conformity feared by Szasz become possible.[48] But the problem involved in choosing policies that change the will is, Who shall debate these changes under what procedures? To restrict these choices to the therapeutic professions is to limit sharply the possibility of tempering science with democracy.[49]

In this connection, there is an interesting convergence between Smith's view of the public interest as a criterion for psychotherapy and the views of Srole, Skinner, and Szasz, even though their social philosophies differ. All these writers are concerned with societal intervention that claims to further the general welfare through behavioral

47. Clausen, "Values, Norms, and the Health called "Mental': Purposes and Feasibility of Assessment," p. 118. See also Keith-Lucas, *op. cit.*, pp. 1082–1083, 1091.
48. See Szasz, *Ideology and Insanity,* pp. 161–162.
49. See chapter 2 above and Hersch, *op. cit.*

change affecting social systems. All tend to ignore the diagnostic categories conventionally used by psychiatrists; as Smith puts it,

> The real and imagined needs of medical administration over patient populations defined as sick have created a nomenclature of essentially administrative illnesses that have little apparent relation to etiology, prognosis, or therapy. It may be the beginning of wisdom to regard many of the problems of diagnosis, the state of which few are content with, as artifacts of the historical social policy that has called these people sick, and therefore, has had to find illnesses for them.

And Szasz echoes this criticism emphatically.[50]

But even while these authors all see the problem as involving behavior alteration in social systems, their proposals for social policy are extremely diverse. Szasz is especially concerned with human freedom and sees this value in the legal system with its stress on rational argument and confrontation. He wishes to enhance personal responsibility by reducing the importance of psychiatric testimony in criminal trials. Smith and Srole frame their criticisms as efforts to enlarge and expand the activities of the mental health professions and to move beyond the notion of the patient who seeks help voluntarily for the relief of personal distress. They favor a greater concern with the general welfare, through treatment of persons who cause distress to others in social systems but who feel little distress themselves. Skinner, finally, goes far beyond the therapeutic treatment of persons; he considers the design of societies, or self-sufficient social systems, but without concern as to who implements these changes under what political decision procedures.[51] In rejecting the notions of freedom and dignity, he is thus at the opposite valuative pole from Szasz, even though both are concerned with the problems (and the desirability) of behavior alteration [52] in social systems. Szasz sees it actually occurring, and to

---

50. Smith, "Competence and Mental Health," p. 104; Szasz, *Ideology and Insanity,* pp. 51–68. The parallel is also pointed out in Goodall, "Shapers at Work," p. 60.

51. The inhabitants of Walden Two, however, enter it voluntarily, and presumably the reinforcement they receive there leads them to wish to stay.

52. In the economist's terms, preference change. Similar problems for the medical profession generally are discussed in Freidson, *Profession of Medicine,* pp. 253, 255, 375.

be resisted; Skinner sees it as occurring insufficiently, and to be fostered.

The Ethics and Politics of Preference Change

In our comparison of economic and psychological ethics, we have shown various ways in which economic ethics can be made more general by consideration of preference change as an available option. We have also suggested that economic notions such as "externality" are applicable to some issues related to change of preferences. The result of a comparison of this sort should be more general ethical hypotheses. Let us now consider what some of these hypotheses might be and how they might guide choices concerning preference change.

Suppose that a proponent of psychological ethics, through argument under our rules, has convinced an economist that change of preferences ought to be included among the alternatives to be considered. The participants in this discussion must then also agree on substantive criteria for evaluating the results, and they must raise the question as to who shall be entitled to change whose preferences, by what means. We consider first the substantive criteria regarding results of preference change and then procedural questions regarding power.

The question of when preferences should be changed may be approached within a general ethical framework, such as that of utilitarianism or perfectionism. Suppose at the start that we subscribe to an ethics defined in terms of "welfare" and that we know the welfare consequences of our acts.[53] What, then, should be our basis for choice when we have the possibility of changing the preferences of others?

The role of the parent provides a simple illustration of the way in which general ethical principles might be applied to changes of children's preferences. The parent, it is true, has special concern for his child's welfare, but when the child harms or pains others the parent

---

53. Ethics of justice or other nonwelfare ethics might incorporate analogous concepts. But even within the family of ethics of welfare, the diversity of goals possible must be recognized. Different ends for preference change would correspond to different notions of the good or to different "ethical hypotheses." Our assumption of perfect knowledge is of course restrictive, but it allows us to elaborate on Smith's notion of therapy in relation to the public interest.

may still try to correct the child in the interest of others' welfare as well as the child's. Note also that in the absence of diagnostic categories, the parent's therapeutic or instructional activities may not be limited to restoring normality; he may seek to surpass it. A parent might also consider the possible improvement in the general welfare that could be attained by bringing up different children in different ways.

The variety of goals that may possibly be served by changes of preferences may be clarified by the use of the notion of a "production function." Economists use this notion to refer to the possibilities of production of a firm or productive unit. The total amount or production or output of a given good is expressed as a function of each of the quantities of inputs—factors of production—that are used. If this function is known, then given factor and product prices the producer may choose the proper amounts of various factors of production in order to maximize profits. I introduce this notion to suggest a possible synthesis between economic and psychological ethics.

A corresponding notion in the realm of preference change would then be the "social production function" of the person deciding among alternative acts.[54] The dependent variable in such a function is a measure of social welfare according to some ethical system (though this cannot easily be a welfare function based on preferences). Welfare costs and benefits are assumed to be known for the corresponding acts. The choice whether to change preferences (or by analogy, the choice of therapeutic acts) would then be made so as to maximize net welfare. Such a notion would first permit some adjudication between acts that change preferences and acts that might increase welfare by other means. It would give especial attention to persons whose preference changes would have large and beneficial effects on the general welfare. Whether these changes occurred through restoring normality, or

54. See Schultze, *The Politics and Economics of Public Spending,* pp. 57ff. We set aside possible changes in the chooser's own preferences, but clearly his own "social production function" might be improved by reduction of internal conflicts. We assume that the chooser is deciding in terms of an ethical hypothesis and ignore the constraints on his choices, or the efforts required, that derive from his own personality. We likewise set aside therapeutic changes in the chooser that will lead him to consider others' welfare, assuming that his ethical hypothesis already leads him to do so.

raising their capacity above the norm, would be immaterial. A notion of this kind would provide a framework for guiding the longer-range development of preference-changing institutions. The development of institutions and norms for such guidance is vital because of the difficulties of leaving these choices entirely in the hands of particular individuals.

In this perspective, there need not be a single or uniform notion of the healthy personality, even within a given society. Therapy, like occupational choice, can consider the individual's capacities for contributing to welfare as defined by an ethical hypothesis. One might therefore consider that internalization of an ethical hypothesis, or adherence to values of the community,[55] is an aim of therapy. A "Protestant ethic" type of personality may be proper for those who are to serve as calculators (leaders, Guardians), while a greater capacity for spontaneous enjoyment may be more appropriate for the larger number who produce welfare primarily as a direct aspect of their own experiences. A neurotic dedication to scientific inquiry or social reform may likewise be more appropriate for a person whose primary ability can contribute to the solution of important technical or social problems. More generally, the scientist's "social responsibility" may thus be related to his capacities. A greater dedication than average to moral rectitude and self-abnegation—as well as a capacity to enjoy those experiences deemed worthy for the society to enjoy—may be proper for those who occupy roles of exemplars, such as teachers, religious and political leaders, or parents.

The perspective we have considered so far is aimed at illustrating that "therapy" can be a limited criterion for behavior or preference change—perhaps appropriately limited in view of the therapist's role but open to criticism as an ethical hypothesis. The broader perspective of Skinner reveals additional alternatives. But as soon as we consider these alternatives, we also encounter the problems raised by Skinner's critics or by Clausen or Szasz. Who is to decide? If it is an elite or a professional group, how is this group itself to be checked and controlled? And even if these questions could be solved, we must also ask

55. See Rieff, *The Triumph of the Therapeutic.*

how the many decisions we face can be brought within the range of our capacities through the creation of social institutions, simplifying categories, and standard procedures.

Even when we consider our role as that of an undifferentiated "person," without the advantages of leader or therapist, some of these questions still arise. By what means may we properly try to alter others' preferences? If we enhance another's welfare by fraud, do we not also risk the strengthening of an expectation of fraud and the weakening of norms that proscribe it? In discussing ethical argument (chapter 4), we assumed that each participant might try to influence the other's valuations by appeals to the interrelations among them. But this was a situation of reciprocal influence, and the rules governing it restricted it largely to the use of reason. The most rational of human institutions, of course, still contain overtones of emotion and personality, but ethical argument and persuasion can also be conducted by deeper appeals. The effect of seeing the life conditions of the poor, the sick, or the wounded; the opportunity to live in diverse cultures or subcultures; the connection of ethical judgments to strong interpersonal ties; the symbolic presentation of alternative life situations through the mass media or the arts; or therapy itself may well provide stronger motivations for change.

If one participant has especial access to these motivations for change—whether as a teacher, a political or moral leader, an organizational change agent, a psychotherapist, or a controller of mass communications—then the symmetry no longer exists. We must then ask how the occupants of these roles are themselves educated and chosen—and how, if at all, they are controlled.[56]

But as we confront the question of power, we must also notice that we have entered the realm of political persuasion—persuasion that affects others' judgments of what should be done rather than simply their welfare. The means that we have considered for influencing the general welfare may also be used to influence public decisions. Access to these means is thus regulated by controls related to particular roles (such as the roles of the professions) and to democratic control itself.

56. See Seeley, *Americanization of the Unconscious,* p. 60. On limitations on the role of the organizational change agent see White, *Psychic Energy and Organizational Change.*

In a political system that calls itself democratic, we may propose general principles for limiting the role of social science in preference-changing procedures. We assume, first, that the basis of democratic or representative government is conscious and informed choice by the citizens. We leave unanswered the question as to what proportion of the citizenry can attain this level of choice, but we wish institutions that will permit this proportion to expand.

A distinction then arises between the study by social scientists of *consequences* of alternative policies and the *processes* by which such policies are reached. Knowledge of consequences can be made available to citizens, who if properly trained may then evaluate the policies—and the facts and the communicators—critically in public debate. Specialized knowledge of processes, however, risks becoming the private possession of advertisers, public relations specialists, campaign managers, teachers, or therapists. It may also give advantages to parents, but these advantages are less clearly "problems."

When alternative decision processes or social structures are under consideration, the choice among them may still be presented so as to be conscious and informed. This choice may be individual, as when persons voluntarily leave one social system and enter another. It may be demographic, as when one system grows and another declines, but the motives for growth and decline are then less likely to come from reasoned comparison of the systems in question.

The choice may also be collective. Collective choice, as in the ratification of a constitution, may be preceded by debate on the merits of the proposal. *The Federalist Papers* represent one side of such a debate, which went deeper in its reasoning than mere political slogans.[57]

The central set of choices faced by a polity concerns the definition of its authority roles and choice of persons to fill them. In modern societies, many of these roles involve scientific competence, and the role of the psychotherapist is of especial importance because it involves preference change.

The definition of such a role includes the specification of role-partners (for example, patients) and how they are chosen. If the mar-

57. There is the logical possibility that revolution may be required to enhance the general welfare significantly. But the question still remains as to how the revolutionaries can be sure that their judgment of benefits and costs is correct.

ket for voluntarily chosen therapy, or the political allocation of involuntary therapy, is possibly subject to failure or inadequate performance, then the social policy in question needs to be widely debated beyond the ranks of the therapeutic profession. Szasz and others have taken a bold step in opening a formerly closed debate on professional ethics to a wider public. The disciplinary overlap between the roles of clinical psychologists and other social science roles has led to a related debate about "mental health."

The debate that surrounds such choices in a democratic polity assumes an ideal of equality and reciprocity. This ideal does not derive simply from the notion that each citizen votes for his private welfare and that all welfares are to count alike. It conflicts at times with the fact that some are more competent than others to discern the general welfare. But a fundamental source of support for such debate lies in the importance of participation and representation as a source of legitimacy for collectively binding decisions. In a world where traditional and religious authority have declined, and science and reason themselves are often questioned, there is more need for participation, consultation, and consent. It is to these processes, in the formation and change of social norms, that we now turn.

8 THE CHOICE OF SOCIAL NORMS

In the last three chapters we have analyzed ethical systems centering on individual preferences. The ethics we have considered from economics, political science, and psychology are different in important ways; their differences relate to different approaches by these disciplines to the study of individual behavior.

Sociology, on the other hand, is centrally concerned with social norms, which are properties of social systems rather than individuals. The notion of normative order, central to sociology, might be expected to lead to an ethic favoring social order.[1] But such an ethic is rarely explicitly advocated by sociologists today and seems unlikely to prevail in ethical argument even outside the university. Thus a more reasonable translation of sociological concepts into ethical discourse might concern the deliberate *choice* of norms, including their change through legislation or policy decisions. But a concern with choice of norms, as with change of preferences, cannot become part of an ethical hypothesis until the goal of that choice is specified.

An essential feature of the choice of norms in modern societies is that we cannot easily influence this choice without ourselves being subjected to the norms chosen. In contemporary democratic societies, reciprocity among citizens is of increasing importance. Thus the choice of social norms also relates to an important tradition of political philosophy—that of the social contract. Our previous argument has stressed individualistic ethical systems, but we also noted the possibility of relational ethics, involving values such as equality, justice, and freedom, and the disvalue of power. The valuative field of political philosophy has long been concerned with relational ethics, but some of the more recent developments in this field, which we have stressed for comparison with economics, are based on values associated with indi-

1. The functional analysis of social systems has been criticized on the ground that it tacitly favors such an ethic.

viduals. The relation between individual and relational approaches can be clarified by consideration of social norms, which will also bring out important contrasts between the ethical positions of economics, political science, and sociology. Sociology can thus make an important contribution to the enlargement of valuative discourse among the social sciences through its stress on the concept of normative order—social order that rests on the actions of individuals in view of shared notions of desirable ends.[2]

In stressing the study of norms and normative order, we must warn the nonsociologist reader that the study of these matters is quite distinct from asserting or espousing norms. The norms, customs, and laws of various societies constitute data for the sociologist, and the frequent stress by sociologists on the value-free character of their discipline results in part from the need to maintain this distinction. Sociologists, in their scientific investigations, seek to generalize about the norms of diverse social systems that may be either similar to, or divergent from, the norms under which they themselves live. In such research, they place the norms of science above allegiance to the norms of the particular systems or groups under study, but they may also study the norms of science with some detachment.

We therefore consider the study of social norms and normative order as a scientific domain that carries particular valuative implications—though not necessarily sympathy with particular sets of norms under study. I shall try to show, as for the other disciplines considered, that these valuative implications can be placed in a larger perspective—that they supplement, and are supplemented by, the perspectives of other disciplines.

Social Norms

The basic notion of norm and normative order that we shall employ is the one introduced by Parsons:

2. Parsons, *The Structure of Social Action,* pp. 74–76, 91ff. The creation of norms, in the form of "starting mechanisms," is discussed in Gouldner, "The Norm of Reciprocity," p. 176. Our treatment of sociology is admittedly selective, both in stressing norms and in deemphasizing the attendant notion of relational ethics.

The term normative will be used as applicable to an aspect, part or element of a system of action if, and only so far as, it may be held to manifest or otherwise involve a sentiment attributable to one or more actions that something is an end in itself. . . . An instance of a norm is the statement: "Soldiers should obey the orders of their commanding officers." [3]

The notion we shall consider differs from the predominant economic approach in that we shall be concerned with the collective aspect of "preferences," rather than regarding them as random or leaving their origins and interrelations unexamined. It also differs from the notion of benevolence; norms can support a variety of types of action, not all benevolent, and benevolence can be an individual or idiosyncratic tendency as well as a socially structured one.[4]

I shall use the term "norm" in an inclusive sense, ranging from general values that may permeate a society to particular regulations in organizations or the particular requirements that cluster to define a social role.[5] We also customarily include in the definition the collective aspects of norms; normatively oriented action involves the expectation that others in similar situations will and should act similarly. It is typically justified by the use of terms such as "ought" or "should," which carry the implication that the patterns of action in question bear in an obligatory fashion on others, including the persons addressed.

A norm is a property of a social system involving two or more individuals, not of individuals in isolation. When a norm exists in a given social system (and this existence is a matter of degree), several concomitant aspects or indicators of it may be observed in members of that system:

1. Conformity. Uniformities in behavior will be observed, in respects such as patterns of dress, language, and interpersonal grouping and association. Such uniformities are not sufficient conditions for the

---

3. Parsons, *The Structure of Social Action*, p. 75.
4. For a psychological approach to altruism see the essays in Wispé, ed., *Positive Forms of Social Behavior*.
5. These more and less general normative orientations have sometimes been distinguished through use of separate terms, e.g., "institutions" vs. "value patterns," in Parsons and Smelser, *Economy and Society*, p. 102.

existence of norms, as they can arise from physical and biological aspects of organism and environment, as well as from similarity in cognition.[6]

2. Expectations. Participants in the social system will be able to describe the behavior expected under given conditions. Although some expectations are taken for granted and will not be described in response to a direct inquiry, they can be revealed by the anxiety or moral indignation elicited by their disappointment.[7] An example is the norm concerning the distance between persons who are talking with one another in a given society or subculture.

3. Sanctions. Deviation from a norm typically elicits from members of the social system in question responses such as moral indignation, blame, censure, or punishment. Conversely, conformity with a norm for which special effort is required and not all are expected to conform, may elicit praise or other benefits. These actions normally serve as reinforcers.[8] Their effects on behavior include socialization and social control. In the economic approach, persons who may be recipients of sanctions are considered to calculate the likelihood of receiving them and to weigh this together with the severity of sanctions as an expected "cost" of particular actions. This approach similarly sees persons who administer sanctions as doing so because the satisfaction of their preferences is dependent on the behavior of others.

4. Internalization. A norm as defined here also involves a feeling on the part of members of the corresponding social system that conformity is desirable for its own sake—not merely because it will avoid

6. Sherif, in *The Psychology of Social Norms,* discussed similarities in cognition among members of groups. Similar processes were induced in the type of experiment initiated by Asch; see his *Social Psychology.* Uniformity of behavior is taken as a contingent feature of norms, rather than as part of the definition, in Gibbs, "Norms: The Problem of Definition and Classification." Nadel, on the other hand, noted three methods for investigating norms, based on "frequency distributions, codification, and maintenance processes"—*The Theory of Social Structure,* p. 25.

7. The learning of social expectations, and Mead's concept of the role of the other, are discussed in Berger, *Invitation to Sociology,* pp. 99ff. The conditionality of normative requirements on the performer's status is discussed in Parsons, "A Revised Analytical Approach to The Theory of Social Stratification," p. 394.

8. Skinner, *Beyond Freedom and Dignity,* ch. 3. Sanctions such as imprisonment may of course fail to change the motives or behavior of the prisoner.

punishment or attain some other goal of the actor. This feeling is shared by actors and observers.

Each of these aspects of norms may be present in particular situations to various degrees; the conditions under which they exist and develop constitute a major problem of sociological analysis. Central to these processes are verbal justifications, which we shall discuss further below.

The fourth aspect of norms—internalization—is most likely to be ignored by economists. The economic approach seems to require that persons act so as to maximize tangible rewards to themselves, such as amounts of goods and services or the opportunity to associate with certain types of people. Some economists have suggested, for example, that laws (and social norms in general) may be regarded as types of collective goods.[9] This may indeed be a useful perspective, insofar as we can assume that the response of citizens to laws is similar to their response to clean air. But insofar as their support for laws may also have components of internalized norms, then the economic approach may be misleading. Similarly, an economic approach is likely to treat crime as a calculated investment of time in order to maximize returns and the control of crime as using means to influence these returns and link them to the costs of punishment. The formation of groups or political parties is seen as a means to obtain returns or to economize information. And efforts are made to show that certain types of behavior, such as community mutual aid after disasters, could have been derived from a model of self-interest as well as by postulating norms. Altruism is seen as a resource in short supply.[10]

This approach has indeed been fruitful—especially in the domain in which economics itself has been fruitful: the prediction of ways in which a system will change under the influence of exogenous vari-

9. On maximization see Alchian and Kessel, "Competition, Monopoly, and the Pursuit of Money"; G. S. Becker, *The Economics of Discrimination*. On laws as collective goods see Buchanan, "The Bases for Collective Action," p. 2; and Riker, a political scientist, has considered "Public Safety as a Public Good."

10. See Douty, "Disasters and Charity: Some Aspects of Cooperative Economic Behavior"; Arrow, "Gifts and Exchanges," esp. pp. 354–355. Actually, both exchange and norms can be involved in the same situation; see Blau, *Exchange and Power in Social Life*, pp. 255–263.

ables. Nevertheless, it ignores the possibility of changing behavior by influencing the internalized aspect of norms. Some economists have recognized this possibility,[11] but most see it as a break with a fruitful conceptual scheme.

Sociologists have repeatedly called attention to the internalization of norms, changing a relation between persons from one of mere calculation and of means to one that is continued as an end in itself. Berger gives as an example the new army officer who receives salutes at first as an artificial convention but comes later to see them as part of a moral order. More relevant to economic analysis, Selznick describes the change from a newly formed organization to an "institution." [12] In its initial stage, an organization may be held together largely by material incentives. But with the passage of time, the members ordinarily become committed to certain goals and styles of operation, over and beyond the motivations provided by their salaries and working conditions. They can become reluctant to change their work styles and goals, even if this should be necessary to cope with changing market conditions. In this transition, a normative element has been added.

The possibility of gradual internalization of norms suggests a possible synthesis between the economic and normative perspectives. A norm or organization may indeed be initially based on exchange—within a more general normative framework—or on force. But it may later be internalized by the participants and thus acquire an additional basis of support. The degree of internalization, both at the introduction of the norm and later, is a matter to be determined empirically. The starting mechanisms for new norms, as Ellis points out, need not involve shared internalized values.[13] If a new form of ordered social interaction emerges without internalization, we might then call it a "norm without internalization," in view of our definition.

A major emphasis in sociological analysis has been on norms that the observer does not consider altering voluntarily. The terms "social

11. Boulding, "Human Betterment and the Quality of Life"; Tullock, *Toward a Mathematics of Politics,* ch. 1.

12. See Berger, *Invitation to Sociology,* p. 96; Selznick, *Leadership in Administration.*

13. Ellis, "The Hobbesian Problem of Order." A similar point is made by Stinchcombe in "Norms of Exchange."

structure" and "social organization" tend not to imply active intervention or choice. Systems of norms, whether functionally interrelated in a given social system or changing over time, are often seen as moving with all the immutability of the planets. And even though quantitative laws of normative change have not been discovered, this aspect of social science holds out hope of revealing underlying regularities not easily disturbed by human volition. Thus a frequent concern of sociologists has been to point out limits to our efforts at reform, unanticipated consequences that flow from them, or preconditions for voluntary action that are sometimes not clearly visible to the actor.

An example of this approach is the sociologist's reminder to the economist that even the market requires certain normative preconditions: the absence of force or fraud and the requirement that bargains will be kept. This includes the expectation that investments will continue to yield certain returns, property certain powers, and the like—giving rise to considerations of "equity" when property laws are changed and of compensation when there is expropriation.[14] The norms that underlie economic and political exchange are thus organized in systems that extend far beyond the obviously economic. The development of an occupational role distinct from that of home and family; the rationalization of law and administration; the acceptance of geographical mobility in relation to a job market—all are aspects of social structure related to the market.

Sociological Ethics: Normative Order, Science, and Opposition

Among the most persistent themes in the latent ethics of sociology has been the value of social order. Bramson has noted the importance in sociology of "the ideal of social order, the sociological focus on the group rather than on the individual, a legacy from sociology's most important historical source, 19th century European conservatism." [15] But seeing the importance of this value, he argues that sociologists can become more aware of it and free themselves from it.

14. But for an economist's analysis of such problems, see Hochman, "Rule Change and Transitional Equity."

15. Bramson, *The Political Context of Sociology,* p. 12. See also Nisbet, *The Quest for Community.*

One important avenue used for introducing values, related to the notion of social order, has been the study of "social problems." [16] An ingenious transition from the "is" to the "ought" can apparently be made by defining a social problem in terms of the disparity between an existing situation and widely held values or norms. Both the situation and the values or norms are factually observable.

But if we try to elevate this factual observation into an ethical hypothesis, its inadequacy is apparent in view of our rule of convictions. Should we always give priority to studying situations in which there is a disparity between reality and widespread normative expectations? Perhaps so, if social order is our goal, but this goal in turn requires justification. And even if we should study "social problems" in preference to major questions about which the public is not widely concerned, what should we do about them? Should we try to change the reality or the expectations? Surely there are some situations in which groups or societies entertain unreasonable, inconsistent, or harmful expectations. What then *should* we expect of the world? Questions of this kind follow directly from a consideration of "social problems" once we realize the possibility of rational valuative discourse and criticism. Indeed, the oppositional approach of many sociologists to conventional social values and authorities might seem to contribute to a "social problem" were it not for the fact that the expectations are generated within the discipline rather than in the society at large. The distinctive expectations of sociologists suggest the perverse possibility that we seek the "solution" of the problem in dealing with the expectations as well as with the reality. [17]

The stress within sociology on normative order, and the effort to develop valuative bases by supporting it, lead to formidable difficulties. Social order and functional analysis point to precisely the opposite values from those that many sociologists now wish to realize. Perhaps a sociological ethic of this sort would have been more appropriate to Eu-

16. The development of this approach has been summarized in Horowitz, *Professing Sociology,* pp. 80–100. We have discussed the problem of naturalistic ethics in chapter 3 above.

17. A possible arbitrariness in defining social problems is suggested by the "labeling" perspective, but this approach does not go on to propose criteria as to how problems *should* be characterized. The possible option of decreasing our expectations is proposed in Banfield, *The Unheavenly City.*

ropean conservatism of the nineteenth century, justifying the positions of traditional established strata.

Normative order, however, is by no means the only valuative focus of the discipline. Sociologists have been especially divided in recent years as to the proper relation of their discipline to the practical problems of society; this division has reflected the cleavage between science and valuation sketched in chapter 1. Arguments about the relation of sociology to the problems of society have been based not only on a valuation of normative order, but also on two other underlying values of the discipline: (1) an esteem for the procedures and status of science, and (2) an oppositional or critical approach associated with the "unmasking" of realities contrary to the conventional understandings of everyday life.[18] In recent years the last two values have been most conspicuous; the contemporary rise of radical or critical sociology represents a protest against the limitations of sociology as a allegedly value-free science. Neither of these two values, I shall argue, provides an adequate philosophical basis for ethical discourse, but such a basis may be possible if some sociologists can move away from the positivistic assumptions of the discipline and relate its concepts to ethical argument and to the role of chooser rather than observer.

Sociology has increasingly emulated the natural sciences in stressing verifiable, theoretically significant matters of fact and refining its techniques of investigation and analysis. It has followed a similar path to economics in setting aside the valuative concerns that occupied its founders. But this concern with "scientific maturity" [19] may have brought some of the disadvantages as well as the advantages of natural science. To emulate natural science in this sense implies either unconcern with policy applications or acceptance of the natural scientist's

18. See Shils, "The Calling of Sociology"; Berger, *Invitation to Sociology;* Berger, "Sociology and Freedom." The conceptual schemes of sociology also include those of social psychology and of human ecology, which are less closely connected with the valuation of normative order.

19. Among the founders' valuative concerns were Comte's "religion of humanity"; Durkheim's concern with ethical reasoning in *The Division of Labor in Society,* pp. 411–435; and Mead's concern with ethics in *Mind, Self, and Society,* pp. 379ff. For Weber's role see chapter 3 above. On "scientific maturity," see Smelser, "The Optimum Scope of Sociology," p. 5.

relation to policy—that of an employee (for example, an engineer) or an outsider (consultant) as regards fundamental valuative choices. Natural scientists, however, unlike sociologists, find a high demand for their technical knowledge and may sometimes make policy judgments while giving technical advice. Economists are likewise in demand but have the additional advantage of an ethic that appears simply to give others advice as to how efficiently to attain their own ends. Psychotherapists, like biological scientists in medicine, can intervene under the naturalistic ethic of "health," which if limited in application is nevertheless under some control from the profession as well as the market. In exchange for abandoning controversial valuative concerns, members of these other disciplines have been able to participate in policy formation in a way that sociologists have not.[20]

The engineering approach to applied sociology, associated with a primary emphasis on basic science, has involved selling of technical services in the market, with efforts to gain theoretically valuable byproducts. An aspect of this approach centering on consulting and contract research was developed in the Bureau of Applied Social Research at Columbia University. An example was Merton's "conversion of an applied into a theoretic research" when, studying a New Jersey community for *Time* magazine, he developed the notions of "local" and "cosmopolitan" influentials.[21]

Emulation of basic natural science can also lead, however, to efforts to discover invariant social processes or regularities that are not directly related to policy choices. Thus historical and comparative sociology deal with events that are treated as existing objectively and not modifiable by the sociologist's recommendations. Other research topics, such as social mobility and organizational decision making, can also be studied objectively even though they have potential policy applications. In this perspective, the sociologist studies existing normative orders rather than ones that might be created.

20. In 1970, among American Ph.D.'s in sociology, 75 percent were employed in educational institutions. For chemistry the proportion was 23 percent; physics, 50 percent; the biological sciences, 60 percent; economics, 59 percent; and psychology, 56 percent. See National Science Foundation, *American Science Manpower 1970*, p. 19.

21. See Merton, *Social Theory and Social Structure*, p. 442; Hyman, "Interviewing as a Scientific Procedure," p. 204. A recent extension of this approach is Lazarsfeld and Reitz, *An Introduction to Applied Sociology*.

A concern with intelligent policy choice has led some sociologists to criticize the natural science approach, including the positivistic notion that valuations are to be excluded from the discourse of the discipline. They have recognized that sociologists' adoption of the natural science model may gain objectivity but sacrifice their capacity to engage in reasoned valuative discourse. Thus twenty-five years ago Bendix asked, "Must we pay for the greater empiricism of modern social science with the unconscious and uncritical subordination of intellectual endeavor to the social and political forces of our time?" And Znaniecki asked, "Can we assume that, when sociologists decide to apply the results of scientific knowledge to the achievement of certain practical goals which conflict with other goals, they may simply follow their subjective preferences or conform with the requirements of the groups to which they belong?" [22]

Dissatisfaction with the detached role of the scientist has led some to propose other roles for the sociologist: an "enlightenment model" involving the sociologist in discourse and participation with subjects and other relevant publics; a "clinical model" involving interaction of the applied social scientist with the client and others affected; and a "pragmatistic model" stressing the interaction between expert and politician.[23] The roles of intellectual and humanist [24] have also been seen as involving the sociologist as a total person rather than in a segmented role and increasing his communication with the lay public rather than limiting it to expert colleagues.

These approaches stress the reciprocity between social scientists and those to whom they recommend policy. They deemphasize the distinction between basic and applied sociology and aim to improve policy advice through a heightened consciousness of the possibilities and limitations of applied roles. They do not, however, include explicit disciplinary discourse about the values to be served by applied sociology but expect the sociologist himself to introduce some of these values

22. Bendix, *Social Science and the Distrust of Reason,* p. 41; Znanlecki, "Should Sociologists Also be Philosophers of Values?," p. 81.

23. On the enlightenment model, see Janowitz, "Sociological Models and Social Policy," and Biderman, "Information $\neq$ Intelligence $\neq$ Enlightened Public Policy"; on the clinical model, Gouldner, "Explorations in Applied Social Science"; on the pragmatistic model, Habermas, *Toward a Rational Society,* p. 66.

24. See Horowitz, *Professing Sociology,* p. 201.

and to develop them further in the interactive process of applied work.

This questioning of the role of basic scientist or engineeer leads to a concern with values but not to particular valuative positions. It might lead back to a valuation of normative order, but sociologists have also sought to derive valuative criteria from other concepts of the discipline. "Social disorganization," like "social problems," seems to reflect valuations akin to that of normative order, and "extremism," as a concept of political sociology, relates to an existing political order. "Prejudice," "equality," "power structure," and "participation" all seem related to an underlying value of equality—whether in treatment, opportunity, or influence.[25]

An alternative effort at a naturalistic ethic[26] makes use of the observation that certain values are widespread or universal. It may consist in the justification that a journal concerned with social policy deal with "practical questions in the discussion of which there seems to be general agreement about the self-evident character of certain goals" or in the observation that "men everywhere prefer health to sickness and longevity to early death." [27] This sort of observation—like Arrow's postulates—may indeed permit some valuative discussion, but it excludes consideration of conflicting values.[28]

But sociology also contains a tradition as an "oppositional" science, concerned with social reform.[29] Sociologists have often chosen their discipline for reformist motives, drawn by the problems of their time and their society, as well as by the discipline's tendency to question official and accepted accounts of social institutions. An aspect of sociology that supports social criticism is its concern with

25. On secondarily evaluative terms see Hare, *Freedom and Reason*, pp. 24ff., and chapter 4 above. On the valuation of equality and its ad hoc character, see Coleman, "Inequality, Sociology, and Moral Philosophy," pp. 740–741.

26. G. E. Moore, *Principia Ethica*, p. 39; see also chapter 3 above. Etzioni, in *The Active Society*, pp. 622–628, advocates a naturalistic ethic based on needs.

27. Weber, *The Methodology of the Social Sciences*, pp. 55–56; W. E. Moore, "The Utility of Utopias," p. 771. The "quest for moral universals" is analyzed in Edel and Edel, *Anthropology and Ethics*, chs. 3–7.

28. Valuative discourse in sociology is not, however, precluded by the gap between fact and value; see Shils, "The Calling of Sociology," pp. 1422–1434; Friedrichs, *A Sociology of Sociology*.

29. The term "oppositional" is used in Shils, "The Calling of Sociology," pp. 1422ff., but the notion is closely related to the role of sociologist as "prophet" developed in Friedrichs, *A Sociology of Sociology*.

seeking out the informal substratum of normative order, as contrasted with the formal and manifest. Thus sociologists tend to study deviance rather than the formal requirements of the law or to set aside the formal structure of organizations to see how informal groups or external role relations affect the real behavior of men and women at work.

But this concern with informal substructure, while it fosters questioning of established ways, can also join with the scientific approach to drive sociology farther from examination of voluntary choices guided by ethical principles.[30] The study of informal norms and unintended consequences tends to show how human behavior resists influence and may discourage efforts at formation of new norms or organizations. It is important to know what we cannot do, but for voluntary choice we need to know whether policies achieve their intended results.[31]

In the late 1960s the oppositional aspect of sociology became especially important. Reformist recruitment to the discipline increased. The previous generation of American academic sociologists had often channeled their students' reformist motives into the pursuit of value-free science, but this channeling occurred less easily when leaders of the discipline also claimed to be useful to government and business and when the goals of these organizational clients were increasingly criticized.[32] There thus developed not only a radical movement within American sociology, but also an increasing concern among nonradical sociologists with the critical or oppositional aspects of the discipline.

The model of normative order had already been under criticism for some time as insufficiently concerned with social conflict. The study of social stratification has provided some expression for a concern with social opportunity and equality. And studies of community power

30. An oppositional perspective toward "rule creators" is taken in H. Becker, *Outsiders*, p. 147. Deliberate change of normative structures is analyzed, however, in Hopper, "Changing Social Roles as a Goal of Public Policy"; and the effects of legislation have been analyzed, e.g., in Ross, "Law, Science, and Accidents." See also Gouldner, "The Sociologist as Partisan."
31. On learning what we cannot do, see Gouldner, "Metaphysical Pathos and the Theory of Bureaucracy." Sumner distinguished between "crescive" and "enacted" norms in *Folkways*, p. 54; the tendency we here consider is to deal with the former.
32. In 1969 American sociology faculty members were farther to the left politically than those of any other discipline. See Lipset and Ladd, survey of faculty attitudes, reported in "The Profession: Faculty Opinion Survey."

structure had carried with them a latent opposition to the concentration of informal power.[33] The valuative themes of equality, conflict, and power were therefore solidly embedded in the sociological literature. The parallel themes of violence and revolution came also to be stressed by radical sociologists who were concerned with major changes in society and regime.

The central disciplinary literature of sociology has provided little place for the systematic discussion of the latent valuations in the discipline and their conflicts. Valuative discourse among sociologists, as among members of other disciplines, has found its greatest expression in parts of their literature other than articles in the major journals. Books, which need not pass the same type of screening as journal articles and depend in part for publication on profitable sales to nonspecialist readers, are one such outlet. Lectures, which also benefit from professorial autonomy, may be another; the authority of the lecturer in Germany led Weber to direct particular strictures against abuse of the lecture platform.[34] The founding of a special society and journal stressing social problems has been a compromise, unavailable to natural scientists, between professional publication and valuative concerns. The rare appearance of a frankly valuative article in a major journal may sometimes be credited to the privilege of a presidential address.[35]

Because of this lack of systematic valuative discourse, these latent values remain to be incorporated in general ethical systems. The valuation of equality might provide a useful supplement to the economic ethic, in which equity is at best a secondary theme. If it is equality of power, rather than condition, that is stressed, then the corresponding ethic would seem to be a relational one.[36] But a serious logical ob-

33. On conflict, see Dahrendorf, *Essays in the Theory of Society,* ch. 4; on the relation between stratification and equality, see Coleman, *op. cit.;* on community power, the valuative emphases of Hunter's *Community Power Structure* have been reflected in the subsequent literature.

34. Commentary on Rawls's *A Theory of Justice* has allowed some discussion of the issues he raised; see MacRae, "Justice, Normative Discourse, and Sociology," and Coleman, "Inequality, Sociology, and Moral Philosophy"; on organizations and power see Coleman, *Power and the Structure of Society;* on lectures, see Gerth and Mills, eds., *From Max Weber: Essays in Sociology,* p. 145.

35. See the discussion of fringe associations in chapter 3. The presidential address is W. E. Moore, "The Utility of Utopias."

36. A relational ethic of equality of power seems to be an important basis of Coleman's arguments in "Inequality, Sociology, and Moral Philosophy" and in *Power and the Structure of Society.*

stacle to incorporating values concerning power, conflict, violence, or revolution in an ethical hypothesis is that they appear to deal with means rather than ends. To oppose power or favor revolution is a temporary stance at best, for one is driven to ask, Power for what? Revolution for what? A risk of this perspective is that it may confound opposition to a particular normative order with opposition to normative order in general.

The Choice and Creation of Norms

Neither the value of normative order nor that of science or opposition appears to furnish an adequate basis for ethical discourse. But the *choice* among normative orders, while a logical extension of a central concept of sociology, does not restrict us to conservative choices and can occupy an important place in valuative discourse among the disciplines. This choice may relate to any of the four aspects of norms listed above.

Changes in norms have been studied as an aspect of "development," not only by sociologists but by other social scientists as well. The interrelation among these norms, and their immersion in larger complex social systems, makes it difficult to plan their change successfully, but the study of development is nevertheless often connected with evaluation and deliberate intervention.

This gradual change of norms is an important instance of the process known to sociologists as "social change." This process has been studied largely from the viewpoint of the detached scientific observer, rather than that of the policymaker who wishes to change or maintain social norms. Thus sociologists have observed and studied changes over time in frequencies of behavior such as migration or divorce, entry into new occupations, and the use of machines or contraceptives. But closely linked to this behavior are usually internalized moral beliefs about its rightness or wrongness. And as the behavior changes, prevalent characterizations of right and wrong conduct change with it.

Those who study contemporary social change may wish, however, to evaluate and influence it—to accelerate, divert, or retard it—as well as describe it. They may be drawn into a valuative or policy-oriented stance through involvement with sponsors, respondents, or partisans of alternative social orders, as well as through their own sense of problems. They may thus be led to ask ethical questions about alternative social orders.

A valuative perspective, arrived at in this way or some other, can lead sociologists to consider systematically the ways in which norms can and should be changed, as well as to reflect systematically on ethics. In this extension of the sociological concept of normative order, they can participate in valuative discourse that links the ethical perspectives of sociology, economics, and political philosophy. In this discourse, the concern of sociology with normative order would entitle it to deal with the vital problems of development and change of such orders and with their evaluation. Sociology could not, however, expect (even less than economics or political science) to derive ethical hypotheses from entirely within its own conceptual armory. The major contending ethical hypotheses that we might expect to arise derive from sources other than a valuation of normative order in itself. The participation of sociologists in this broader valuative discourse would enable them to supply an essential ingredient, but their special competence would lie in the analysis of particular *means*—the creation and change of social norms and structure—to more general social ends.[37]

We therefore center our discussion of sociological ethics on the notion of normative order because the *choice* of social norms is a major ethical and policy alternative related to our rule of generality, not because adequate ethics can be derived from that concept alone. The creation or change of rules, organizations, and constitutions involves choices among possible normative orders. Concern with social disorganization implies a valuation of increased social order; advocacy of anarchy, or of freedom, often implies that the degree of such order should be reduced.

The creation of norms, though we consider it as an extension of the sociologist's concerns, has been treated far more by political philosophers, such as Hobbes and Rousseau, who were able to ask when norms *should* be created—the problem to which we now turn. If soci-

37. In this respect the choice of norms is analogous to the possibility of changing preferences. The broadening of perspective that might result from combining sociology with economics has been suggested in Olson, "Economics, Sociology, and the Best of All Possible Worlds"; Barry, *Sociologists, Economists, and Democracy,* pp. 173ff.; and Ward, *What's Wrong with Economics?*

ology were able to incorporate valuative discourse, it might join this discussion and make important contributions.

Political philosophers have treated the creation of norms in connection with the notion of a social contract. This notion has often been invoked as a foundation for the legitimacy of political arrangements—by analogy with the process whereby one enters into a contract, or makes a promise, and is then obligated to act accordingly. The formation of such a contract is treated as subject to reasoned argument about its desirability—argument in which potential members participate on a footing of equality and not merely as objects of social engineering.

The formation of a social contract is more general than the process (real or hypothetical) whereby a constitution is formed. It includes legislation made through representative processes and a host of particular agreements by individuals to participate in organizations or engage in private transactions. The making of laws is a special case of the creation of norms—whether or not it results from a contractual or reciprocal process. Our reference in chapter 6 to the governmental function of making new laws, and thus possibly changing preferences, referred in part to this interrelation between citizen and government.

This approach to norms as contracts places special stress on reciprocity, which we shall discuss in more detail below. Some norms are indeed created de novo by persons interacting on an equal footing. The agreement of several private persons to join in a business partnership, or to play a game, may rest on no superior enforcement and draw only on the categories in which a society classifies such activities. But the creation of a role or organization may also derive some of its force from a hierarchy of normative orders that reach to the fundamental principles of organizations or of the state.

The Creation of Organizations

In addition to the study of norms and values, sociologists are centrally concerned with the ways in which these elements combine in social structures. A major type of social structure, especially important as a subject of valuative choices in modern societies, is the *organization*—a social structure deliberately formed for a specified purpose.[38]

38. Parsons, *Structure and Process in Modern Societies,* ch. 1.

Organizations are of importance to us because they are both possible instruments of deliberate action—from their definition—and sources of constraint on our choices.

The formation of organizations—like the founding of regimes, the writing of constitutions, and the establishment of rules or constituencies—is a major social alternative because it affects numerous subsequent choices. At its best, such a decision is expected to have lasting consequences; regimes when founded are expected to last. Yet the very persistence of these organizations also constrains subsequent choices and may impose the principles of the founding in new circumstances to which they are less appropriate. Thus an additional problem of choice is that of allowing organizations to go out of existence, or to adapt their structures and goals to new situations, as well as simply to persist under adversity.[39]

Economists, perhaps more than sociologists, have been concerned with evaluating the formation of organizations. In the realm of production, individuals join in the organization of firms. The question then rises why firms do, and should, come into existence, in contrast to the individual exchange relations that otherwise characterize the market economy. The formation of firms has been explained and justified as a device either to internalize external effects or to create a closed market with a central communications node. Olson has analyzed the creation of voluntary associations as sources of collective goods, but his analysis has been critical as well as justificatory, in that he concludes that certain groups are insufficiently organized.[40] The decision of an individual whether to join a group or remain in it has also been analyzed by Coleman, a sociologist, in terms of the utility gained from the individual's influence on the group and the group's external influence.[41] But these approaches cannot account for the devotion of a particular

39. Cf. Sills, *The Volunteers*. The persistence of organizations may be furthered not simply by members' learned normative commitment, but also by their investments in career prospects, skills, and interpersonal relations, and by selective processes of recruitment and advancement.

40. See Coase, "The Nature of the Firm"; Alchian and Demsetz, "Production, Information Costs, and Economic Organization"; Olson, *The Logic of Collective Action;* and chapter 6 above.

41. See Coleman, "Loss of Power." A modified economic approach, also considering loyalty to the organization, is Hirschman, *Exit, Voice, and Loyalty*.

member to a group when self-interest might dictate that he leave—
remaining in it dutifully even as its prospects decline, out of loyalty to
the organization, his fellow workers or members, and its symbols. In
this view, all marriages would be marriages of convenience.

A contract or coalition, in this perspective, is formed to further the
separate and private goals of those who enter into it. But if the actions
that constitute the contract are rendered in sequence, what is to prevent
the second party from breaching it once he has received what he
wants? (This indeed occurs in certain forms of organized crime.) The
authority of the state is invoked in support of contracts to increase the
likelihood that they will be kept. Without this authority, the force
behind private agreements may derive in part from the fear of future
private sanctions. But in addition, the contribution of an internalized
norm concerning the rightness of keeping one's word must not be ignored.

Thus while economic models can account fruitfully for aspects of
the formation of organizations, organizations can also long outlast
their original purposes. Exchange can be a fruitful model of some
aspects of social relations yet not exclude "organic *solidarity*" as a
basis of support for a differentiated role system which has become institutionalized. The formation and dissolution of coalitions among professional politicians may sometimes be accounted for in terms of rational calculations, but the formation of political parties may involve
more lasting ties.[42]

Newly formed groups have various degrees of durability. The study
of the conditions of durability involves elements from economics as
well as sociology: the environment of the group may alter the needs of
members to remain members. It may also involve elements of sheer
power: the Hobbesian bargain to convey power to a sovereign, in the
interest of the citizen's security, may be not only a promise but a giving of the means of power, subsequently enforceable whether the citizen wishes it or not. To sell oneself into slavery, or vote oneself into
totalitarian control, is a bargain of this sort. But beyond force and self-
interest, the creation and development of norms are important sources

42. On the persistence of political parties, see Lipset and Rokkan, eds., *Party Systems and Voter Alignments*.

of group stability and persistence. It is with these processes that we are
here concerned.

Economic analysis of the formation of organizations is useful not
simply for its explanatory contribution, but also for the valuative question it raises—whether it is desirable to form an organization. In an
ethic of preference satisfaction, it is preexisting preferences that constitute the justification for organization. To acknowledge that preferences may change further after an organization is created would appear
to undermine the initial assumption and relativize the problem. But the
development of these additional "preferences"—the internalization of
organizational norms—can be judged on grounds other than satisfaction of these new "preferences." We might then justify binding an
organization together with the additional cement of normative order
and overcoming disruptive influences such as result from the "free-
rider" problem.

The formation of norms and organizations may thus be seen as a
means of reducing external costs. It is one of a number of means of
dealing with externalities, which also include sheer compensation
without regard for obligation, the formation of coalitions, and psychotherapy. In any of these instances, there may be relative gainers; if
there is coercion, there may be losers as well.

But here again it is essential to distinguish preferences from welfare. The justification for the formation of norms or organizations lies
in a possibility of increased welfare, unrealizable through individual
action and exchange. If the new order thus formed is supported by internalized norms, the "preferences" to which they correspond need
not be included as elements of welfare. The same is true of the constraints imposed by the Hobbesian sovereign. The fact that participants
act out of a belief in the rightness of the order does not mean ipso
facto that they are enhancing their individual welfare.

The same distinction between preferences based on moral judgment
and the welfare of the person making that judgment was stressed in
chapter 5. There we considered the problem of external costs imposed
by one person who offends another's notions of proper religion or sexual behavior. We noted in Arrow's work an increasing willingness to
set these costs aside in welfare calculation. We need not do so in all
cases, for we may sometimes judge that a loss of welfare as well as an

unsatisfied preference is involved, but it is important that our categories *permit* the distinction. The reason for the distinction is the same here, where organizations are created to alleviate external costs or produce collective goods, as in Arrow's examples where norms produced external costs.

Reciprocity and Symmetry in the Choice of Norms

In analyzing ethics derived from economics, political science, and psychology, we have stressed actions or policies that may be chosen by social scientists using deterministic models of human behavior. In such choices, the social scientist or policymaker regards the consequences of his acts as scientifically predictable and evaluates them in terms of an ethical system applied to the expected consequences. The other human beings who may be influenced by the chooser's acts are viewed in terms of these predictions or expectations of consequences. None of these approaches ignores the fact that individuals relate to one another through valuing one another's welfare as well as through exchange. But in each case the policy alternatives that we considered were chosen by separate individuals. We have considered interaction between choosers to some extent in discussing coalition formation and legislative deliberation, but the perspective of participants in these processes needs to be considered in more detail.

A major condition for the formation of norms, insofar as we choose them voluntarily, is reciprocity—the "mutually contingent exchange of benefits" between the persons involved. This exchange often involves the particular case of symmetry, in which participants treat one another as occupying similar roles and grant each other benefits, or impose obligations on one another, of the same kind. A central aspect of the formation of norms in democratic societies involves this latter expectation and involves the possibility of taking the role of the other because that role is the same as one's own. The ideal social contract, Rawls's original position, and my proposed meta-ethics have this feature of symmetry.[43]

43. For this definition of reciprocity see Gouldner, "The Norm of Reciprocity," p. 164. An analogous relation is Habermas's "discursive formation of the public will"; see his *Theory and Practice*, p. 4.

We must recognize, of course, that not all norms place those whom they govern on an equal footing. Kings have ruled, and subjects have accepted their rule; slavery has found similar justification, as have modern systems of social stratification. Distinctions of privilege between the sexes have been accepted as right, and women have felt it was wrong for them to vote even when they had the opportunity.[44] It is difficult to imagine that the subject takes the role of the king, or the slave that of the master, symmetrically. But we must also note that where one human group has claimed the right to rule another, it has often evolved a justifying ideology that argued the other group was not fully human, denying the symmetry of the relation. In some agreements between superior and inferior, as the oath of feudal loyalty, there has been reciprocity in that the lord provided protection.[45]

The actual formation of norms depends on a variety of concrete conditions that place participants in different circumstances at the start. They may differ in power or resources. The preexisting normative structure will constrain their wishes and the categories in which they see the social world. Particular norms may be created as instances of more general norms: particular marriage contracts, economic contracts, acts of incorporation, laws under a constitution, and oaths of feudal loyalty are of this kind. New and more general norms may occasionally be created but none without a legacy from the past social systems in which its creators have lived.

When norms are created, the legitimacy with which they are endowed, or the support they receive, can thus rest on various bases other than social contracts. Weber referred to traditional, rational-legal, and charismatic types of authority.[46] Each of these types implies that new norms or commands may derive support from a larger preexisting normative structure, whether it be the notion of the divine right of kings, the existence of a legal system, or the esteem for certain personal qualities that are possessed by a leader.

But in situations where previous normative structures are less im-

44. Merriam and Gosnell, *Non-Voting*, ch. 5. On the general problem of hierarchical authority, see Macpherson, *The Political Theory of Possessive Individualism*, pp. 83, 294.

45. See Bendix, *Work and Authority in Industry;* Gouldner, "The Norm of Reciprocity," pp. 168–169.

46. See Weber, *The Theory of Social and Economic Organization*, pp. 386–392.

portant, social contracts can be more significant. As democracy and representation become more important bases of authority, greater importance is given to the reciprocal relations of consultation, consent, and participation. It is on this last basis that the authority of the representative rests in representative government. The notion of reciprocity connects the notion of the social contract to meta-ethical rules and to Mead's sociological notion of the "generalized other." [47] Thus in the consideration of social norms we find ourselves at a crossroads among several disciplines and at questions that concern the nature of ethics itself. The participation and deliberation involved in the choice of social norms can occur in small groups, group therapy, political deliberation, or ethical argument.

The contemporary social scientist who wishes to advocate the creation of norms may well find himself in a situation analogous to that of the social contract. As an advocate, he is likely to find himself in a reciprocal or participatory relationship with those whom he wishes to persuade. To persuade them he is required to listen to them as well. He has then departed from the role of the scientist, who engages in argument on an equal footing only with his expert colleagues; if his policies relate to laymen, he must now place himself in a reciprocal relationship with laymen.[48] This reciprocal relationship is important both because society requires it more now than in the past and because we must be concerned (regardless of the particular values of our time) with checking and controlling the policy advice given by experts. But it is important that the relationship be one of reciprocal reasoned argument. Reasoning is especially relevant because the claims of expertise must be heard and not simply compromised in terms of unreflective preferences.

Many norms involve not merely reciprocity, but symmetry among participants; in these cases there is an expectation that the social system will contain numerous participants similarly placed, subject to symmetrical requirements. The failure of some to abide by these

47. See Mead, *Mind, Self, and Society,* pp. 379ff., and for a more recent use of this concept in psychology, see Walster et al., "New Directions in Equity Research."

48. See Etzkowitz, "Institution Formation Sociology"; Janowitz, *Institution Building in Urban Education;* Friedrichs, "Dialectical Sociology"; White, *Psychic Energy and Organizational Change.*

requirements will be regarded by others as lessening the force of the same requirements on them—whether it is the "free-rider" problem considered by economists in decisions on collective goods or the persistent ethical argument, "What if everyone did that?" [49] The ubiquity of this feature in human ethical systems has in fact constituted an important argument against act-utilitarianism and for rule-utilitarianism or peremptory rules, which we shall consider below.

Conceivably this feature of norms derives from a more general property of the human mind—a tendency to see the diverse manifestations of the external world as reflecting real objects existing independent of our volition or imagination. The notion of real objects simplifies the flux of our perceptions by imposing a certain constancy on them. Reality can be attributed to a norm if it bears on all alike. This tendency to see norms as real and uniform—at least within "our" social system, whose members (as distinguished from outsiders) are really "people"—is manifested in many ways. Durkheim's reference to "social facts" as existing sui generis, apart from the attitudes and reactions of individuals, reflects this tendency. While this notion may be criticized by philosophers of science, it reflects precisely the status we give to material objects and events as more than a summary of individuals' reactions to them.[50] A parallel notion of the "group mind" was once held by social psychologists. Mead's notion of the "generalized other," denoting a perspective held by all who have learned to live in social groups, implies not only reciprocity with others but symmetry with them:

> To the degree that the self has taken the attitudes of others into itself through the language process, it has become the others, and the values of others are its own; to the degree that the self assumes the role of the generalized other, its values are the values of the social process itself.[51]

49. Broad, "On the Function of False Hypotheses in Ethics"; Singer, *Generalization in Ethics,* ch 1. The normative significance of the free-rider problem for collective goods, in contrast to mere externalities, may result from the symmetry involved.
50. Durkheim, *Rules of Sociological Method;* a similar reification of norms occurs in Rousseau's notion of the general will.
51. Morris, Introduction to Mead, *Mind, Self, and Society,* p. xxxiii. This process of role taking underlies many of our common sense notions of interpersonal comparison of welfare.

Thus in the wide normative domain of persons occupying similar positions in a social system, members of such a system expect others to act similarly and to see others' actions similarly, as though the system of actions were a "social fact." This basic assimilation of norms to the same perceptual categories as material facts may also underlie the appeal of naturalistic ethics purportedly derived from facts or, at an earlier stage in philosophy, of world-views that fused fact and value.[52]

The notion of reciprocity is also especially important in applied anthropology. The chief research method in anthropological field work is participant observation, which involves reciprocal interaction between the anthropologist and the people under study. Many anthropologists thus feel a particular responsibility toward the people they have studied.[53] The stress by anthropologists on understanding cultural diversity also militates against a social-engineering approach by one culture to another.

The essential feature of social norms, that they are expected to bear similarly on all who meet their defining conditions, is reflected in a special case of Kant's categorical imperative: "Act only on that maxim whereby thou canst at the same time will that it should become a universal law." [54] But actual norms, as distinguished from philosophical principles, typically apply only to persons who are members of a particular social system. Kant's principle is thus a generalization of ethical reasoning within social systems, but the maxims of a given society typically apply differently to outsiders. Some international social systems, such as scientific and religious groups, have norms that transcend national boundaries, but even these tend to treat outsiders distinctly. The problem of extending the effective application of norms, through ethical discourse, to outsiders, is closely associated with that of creating larger and more inclusive social systems.

The importance of symmetry in the formation of norms has contributed to the formulation of various symmetrical meta-ethics as well as relational systems of ethics. Treatment of others as similar to oneself is akin to the Golden Rule, to notions of the social contract, to Rawls's original position, and to Gewirth's Principle of Categorial

52. The separation between facts and values is criticized in Strauss, *Natural Right and History,* ch. 11.
53. See Weaver, ed., *To See Ourselves,* section 1.
54. Kant, *Fundamental Principles of the Metaphysic of Morals,* p. 43.

Consistency.[55] But our argument here stresses symmetry only in meta-ethics; the substantive ethical hypotheses we have considered are individualistic ethics, and reciprocity is seen as a condition for agreement or for support of norms but not as an end in itself.

The symmetry involved in social norms thus defines important conditions for ethical argument and applied social science. The meta-ethics I have proposed is one that provides for symmetrical persuasion in a quest for consensus. It is ill fitted for a unilateral contribution such as that made by the author of a scientific article or book. Such contributions are customary in science, where each member of a profession or discipline contributes his findings to the common fund and others may criticize or extend them. The relations among such scientific colleagues are symmetrical, but the contribution of each is a finding or a fact. A similar contribution in ethics risks appearing merely a personal opinion or statement, unworthy of serious consideration; a finding, on the other hand, claims to advance the common store of knowledge and requires scrutiny and recognition after it is published before it is genuinely accepted as part of that store.

The argument of this book is thus for a proposed social structure—a meta-ethics and a proposed communication structure relating it to the contemporary university—rather than merely for a personal ethics. One way to judge the desirability of such a structure is experimentally. Such an experiment may take place through the reciprocal argument of partisans of various ethical views, including the views prevalent or latent in various academic disciplines. Small-scale testing of the proposed social structure may constitute a step toward the creation of that or an alternative structure. But because others must take part in reciprocal discourse in order to institute such norms, I cannot present them as a "finding."

The reciprocity entailed in the normative dealings of human beings with one another is also a reason for the special inappropriateness of the "engineering model" of applied science in the social sciences. Those who are affected by the policies that social scientists propose are led to ask why social scientists should set themselves above other citizens. If they try to do so, they often encounter the claim that they

55. See Gewirth, "Categorial Consistency in Ethics."

are engaging in "manipulation"—that is, nonreciprocity—in their relations with their fellow human beings.

It is partly for this reason that an objective social science cannot easily be applied like natural science—indeed, that it cannot easily be formulated or discovered. The conditions of consent and the norms established in particular social systems can change the generalizations of social science, reinterpret them, incorporate or resist them. The task of the applied social scientist, in creating or changing norms in a democratic society, seems almost necessarily to involve participation in the debate about those norms rather than simply presenting blueprints.[56] Less free societies may well exclude many of their citizens from such debates, restricting discussion to a small group such as the inner circles of the ruling party. But in a democratic society, where the communications of applied science are public and those affected have access to their proposals, the debate about new norms can become a representative debate. Social scientists must in any regime discuss their proposals with those who hold power, but in a free regime this discussion must enter a legislative or rule-making process. Legislation is then an instance of the creation or change of norms, and its possibility and legitimacy rest on representation, participation, and deliberation—in which the arguments of applied social scientists constitute only a part.

Justification, Ethical Argument, and Change of Norms

An important aspect of norms—manifested in indications of conformity and of expectations, as well as in sanctions—is their verbal expression. In addition to the mere assertion or description of a norm, verbal forms can be used to justify it in terms of more general norms; for example, a particular contract may derive force from the general law of contracts and a particular law from the constitutional powers of the legislature. Words can also be used to justify a norm in terms of more general *values,* such as rationality, competitive opportunity, equality, self-realization, or obligation to authorities. Thus particular organizations may attempt to justify their activities on the ground that

56. See Friedrichs, "Dialectical Sociology." This necessity does not, however, imply that objective social science is impossible.

they contribute to more general societal values.[57] But values of this sort can also be invoked as reasons for deviation from a particular norm or for changing norms.

Reasoned ethical argument can involve drawing particular conclusions from the principles that express these values, but societal values themselves need not be taken as the ultimate foundations of ethical argument. Sartorius has suggested that the norms of existing legal systems may be studied in a quest for deeper principles embodied in them.[58] And the meta-ethics I have proposed carries this effort still farther, seeking not only to discover generality and consistency but to impose them on the principles that govern our actions. Thus an ethical hypothesis, or a notion of the common good, may be more general than the societal values that are used to justify particular norms or organizations.

Sociologists have studied the systems of justification that support normative behavior; when these systems stand in contrast to justification for routine and stable activities, they are sometimes called "ideologies." But the detailed verbal exchanges in which actions or rules are justified persuasively in terms of principles are less often studied.[59] The creation and change of norms are nevertheless open to reasoned discussion, which can involve either an application of an agreed-on ethical hypothesis or a test case in which ethical hypotheses are compared. Such discussion parallels the principled deliberation of judges, legislators, and informed citizens about the rightness of actions, laws, and regimes.

The study of incremental social change, as we have seen, can lead sociologists toward ethics and evaluation. But the evaluation of incremental changes in norms is also relevant to a philosophical debate concerning changes of rules. An ethical system known as rule-utilitarianism has been proposed, which separates the formation and change of rules from choices of acts falling within given rules. In this system, choices among norms or rules are to be made in terms of their expected consequences, but choices among acts falling under a given

57. See Parsons, *Structure and Process in Modern Societies,* chs. 1–2, esp. p. 19.

58. Sartorius, "The Justification of the Judicial Decision."

59. For a study of ideologies in everyday life see Dibble, "Occupations and Ideologies"; for a sociological study of verbal exchanges, see Scott and Lyman, "Accounts."

norm are to be made in terms of that norm itself. This ethical system has been proposed, in distinction to a more Benthamite "act-utilitarianism," in order to remedy some alleged defects of the latter.[60]

I shall argue, under the meta-ethical rule of consistency, that rule-utilitarianism contains a potential internal contradiction in view of the possibility of changing norms incrementally. But before doing so, I must explain the development of rule-utilitarianism, which relates to certain ethical convictions.

Social policies have often been compared on the basis of utilitarian considerations—especially if we consider utilitarianism as embracing that family of ethical systems that order alternatives in terms of their expected consequences. This broad usage of the term, which we shall now employ, has been customary in debates about rule-utilitarianism.

But the application of utilitarian considerations to particular choices among acts, as distinct from choices among norms, has encountered sharp criticism. A major line of critical argument has been that ethical theories or systems should correspond as far as possible with our moral convictions,[61] which often tell us to base our actions on considerations other than consequences. Braybrooke and Lindblom have summarized a number of these critical arguments:

> There are some moral judgments . . . that seem to have force independent of utilitarian considerations and that seem capable of withstanding utilitarianism in cases of conflict. . . . The judgments in question are all peremptory ones. . . . Among them are peremptory rules such as these: that one should keep promises, even when the consequences of doing so in a particular instance would be less happy than the consequences of breaking them; that however superior any person's capacity for happiness it would not be right to make the rest of the community miserable in order to make him happy; that one should not deliberately sacrifice the lives of some members of the community . . . in order to make gratuitous con-

60. The literature in which this distinction has been developed includes Toulmin, *The Place of Reason in Ethics*, ch. 11; Urmson, "The Interpretation of the Philosophy of J. S. Mill"; and Rawls, "Two Concepts of Rules," which also traces the earlier antecedents of the distinction.

61. In chapter 4 we noted that this type of argument often fails to derive from a consistent ethical system.

tributions to the happiness of other members; that the products of individual members of the community should not be taken from them
without compensation, when these have been produced on their own
time with resources that either belong to them or were hitherto free
for the taking; that people should not be incarcerated or executed for
crimes they have not committed; that people should not be con-
victed of crimes and punished on the basis of *ex post facto* legislation.[62]

Thus a Benthamite utilitarianism [63] applied universally to acts ("act-
utilitarianism") may specify certain choices as right that many
members of our society would consider wrong. These choices involve
departure from peremptory rules on the ground that the overall consequences of such departure, in particular cases, would be better than
those of conformity.

The problem thus posed is whether expected consequences should
indeed be the only criterion of the rightness of acts. These criticisms
have led some to reject ethical systems based solely on consequences.
But another response has been to compromise, retaining a concern for
consequences by applying it (in unqualified form) only to rules, or
classes of acts, rather than to acts in general. While conflicts between
an ethic of consequences and peremptory rules can easily be imagined
for particular acts, they seem less likely when we consider changes in
the rules themselves; the general prescription that promises be kept, or
murder not committed, would seem easily justifiable in terms of its
consequences. Thus if we chose only among rules, the dictates of our
preexisting moral convictions would better agree with calculation of
consequences, and conscience would be permitted to prevail over consequences when we chose among individual acts.

Rule-utilitarianism thus rests on a fundamental distinction between
two types of choices. In choices that fall within existing rules, we are
to judge the act as to whether it fits the rule, taking the rule itself for
granted. In choice among rules, however, we may compare one rule
with another in terms of their expected consequences.

62. Braybrooke and Lindblom, *A Strategy of Decision,* pp. 212–213.
63. Bentham, *Principles of Morals and Legislation,* p. 2.

This distinction encounters difficulties, however, when we consider the full range of choices open to us through the incremental change of norms in their various aspects, rather than the simple choices between rules or within them. We can show these difficulties by considering the methods proposed, under rule-utilitarianism, for distinguishing acts that change rules from acts that fall within existing rules. One example, suggested by Rawls, is the difference between the roles of legislator and judge.[64] The legislator's role is set above the existing laws he changes; voting for a new law does not constitute disobedience to the old. Rawls extends this notion of a distinct rule-making "office" to choices between rules more generally. On the one hand, someone who is simply a participant in a practice is not entitled to change it; for someone in this role, the rules defining the practice take precedence in particular cases. On the other hand, one can challenge a practice, and in this case "citing the rules (saying what the practice is) is naturally no avail." One must then assume another role: "If one seeks to question . . . rules, then one's office undergoes a fundamental change: one then assumes the office of one empowered to change and criticize the rules, or the office of a reformer, and so on." [65]

This distinction between roles, however, fails to apply to certain types of choices that involve gradual change of norms or changes in the degree to which a norm is effective. For norms can be changed in degree; a particular rule or norm can be more or less established or institutionalized in any of the aspects we have listed.[66] When we compare alternative rules or norms, we ordinarily have a wider range of choice than the simple choice between two norms; we may have to choose between a higher and a lower degree of social integration, social disorganization, or anomie, or the corresponding difference for a single norm.

The fact that norms can vary in degree renders it especially difficult to make a clear separation between choices within rules and choices

64. "Two Concepts of Rules," p. 7. The possibility of "judge-made law," however, can lead us to question the separability of the two roles.
65. *Ibid.*, pp. 27, 28. Toulmin makes a similar distinction in *The Place of Reason in Ethics*, pp. 150ff.
66. For this usage of the term "institutionalized," see Parsons and Shils, eds., *Toward a General Theory of Action*, pp. 20n., 40.

among rules.[67] While some rule-changing acts are set apart by definition of roles such as that of the legislator, others are not. A declaration
of one's intention to act as a reformer, or to create a test case,[68] may
affect the way in which an act is viewed and in turn affect its consequences. But any public deviant act can be expected to affect one or
more norms, whether it is intended to do so or not, and the same can
be said of acts that reaffirm or strengthen norms, such as rituals, sanctions, or education of the young. Whether we like it or not, we are
constantly engaged in choices that may affect norms. But the actor's
definition of his act should not impose a mandatory and exclusive classification of that act on the observer who judges it. An act aimed at
changing one rule or norm may affect others as well; a demonstration
in favor of minority rights may support the norm of equal treatment of
citizens of different groups, while weakening the norm of proceeding
through representative institutions. If acts that are intended to change
rules are evaluated exclusively in terms of the effects of the intended
change, some of their other consequences may be ignored; a reckless
neglect of means, relative to ends, might even result. The general
problem, which no version of utilitarianism can ignore, is to weigh indirect consequences operating through changes in norms, against
direct consequences.[69]

It might be argued that when important rules are at stake the indirect
consequences so outweigh the direct that only the effects of changing
the rules need be considered. But when we consider the smaller incremental changes in rules that may occur—changes in degree of institutionalization—and the various mixtures of direct and indirect consequences that exist, the distinction seems inadequate. Choices affecting
rules, if they are to be weighed in terms of their consequences, can be
made more universal and more consistent within the larger framework
of act-utilitarianism—a more consistent and general ethical hypothesis,
even though in conflict with important moral convictions.

67. A similar problem arises, it must be recognized, in the separation between ethics
and meta-ethics, e.g., between judging acts in terms of their promotion of happiness and
of rational discourse.

68. As in Toulmin, *op. cit.*, p. 151.

69. A similar combination of "primary" and "secondary" consequences was assumed by Bentham; see *Principles of Morals and Legislation*, ch. 12. This approach
was also followed in Sidgwick, *The Methods of Ethics*, pp. 475–495.

A second philosophical issue which is illuminated by a sociological approach to norms is that of how the general principles justifying acts are to be formulated. It has often been pointed out that ethical justifications are necessarily general; if acts are to be justified by reasons, they must exemplify general principles which are those reasons.[70] But not just any general principle will do. One can always construct fanciful ad hoc categories within which an act falls, placing it in some class that avoids embarrassing counterexamples. The mere requirement that justifications be general is not sufficient.

The possibility of an actor's defining a general justifying category is similar to his declaring himself a reformer and stating the new rule that he wishes to institute. But as we have seen, the actor's intention as to what rules or norms he will affect by his act cannot be the last word for an observer who evaluates the act. When leaders in new nations create political parties, for example, they may do so as means to national or personal power, but an important effect may concern national integration. Thus there is some uncertainty as to *how* an act should be generalized.

Singer has proposed to reduce this uncertainty by requiring that the principle be a *relevant* one. He gives examples relating to employment, in which universalistic standards determine relevance, and to sexual relations, in which the monogamous husband-wife relation determines it.[71] But implicitly he is saying that the preexisting normative structure of a society defines relevance. These norms would not be the same in every society, and therefore an argument or generalization that was relevant in one society would not be relevant in another. "Relevance" then centers on the norms of the society or social system and the relations among them. An ethical principle that can be used for serious justification would seem to be one that already finds support in a given society or can be developed from other such principles.

But if we define legitimate justifications in terms of the existing normative structure of a society, we limit our capacity to criticize that structure. In evaluating social change, we are appealing to an audience that places itself outside a changing society. We take this external stance even if our grounds of criticism are not utilitarian; as Gewirth

70. Singer, *Generalization in Ethics*, p. 25.
71. *Ibid.*, p. 23, and *passim;* pp. 29, 32.

has pointed out, relevance and moral propriety are not identical when we criticize a society that engages in discrimination.[72]

The normative structure of an existing society, while it must not limit us in our justifying principles, *is* relevant to our prediction of the consequences of acts. For as we have seen, the classification of acts depends in part on that structure; acts are relevant, in this sense, to some norms more than others, and they are more easily related to existing normative categories than to categories that do not currently exist. The question of which norms will be influenced is thus not entirely within the actor's or observer's choice. The classification is made by the society in which the actor is involved, in two senses: (a) the act is classified according to a preexisting array of normative categories; and (b) its further consequences affect a *system* of norms, a social *structure,* in which it is unlikely that one norm can be altered without affecting others. Thus the accurate description of social structure in these two senses is a necessary adjunct to predicting the consequences of acts.

Moreover, an existing normative structure need not be regarded as fixed; it can itself provide the basis for change. The norms of a society typically include partly institutionalized and conflicting principles. The actor retains some freedom to choose which of several social categories will be used by spectators to classify his act; its staging, its justification, and the manner in which it is carried out influence this classification. One of the most important modes of influencing categorization is the successful persuasion of the audience that a new category should be created.[73]

In this sense a major type of norm-changing act is that of the charismatic leader. Weber characterized this type of authority by Christ's words, "It is written . . . , but I say unto you." [74] The charismatic

---

72. Gewirth, "The Generalization Principle," pp. 237–238. The same question might also be raised about using the set of linguistic categories of a given society as a fundamental test of proper justifications. But a converse problem arises if we set ourselves above our own society in this way without acknowledging our own obligations within it.

73. This is analogous to de Jouvenel's assertion that the power to found new social aggregates is a major aspect of political influence. See Bertrand de Jouvenel, *Sovereignty,* p. 21.

74. Weber, *The Theory of Social and Economic Organization,* p. 361.

leader can thus be a giver of norms. The structure of norms that he enunciates, however, is not simply an assortment of disconnected principles. It derives from the preexisting normative structure of the society, from the specific grievances and strains that contributed to the charismatic movement, and from the personal characteristics of the leader. The problem here—one not stressed in Weber's work [75]—is one of ideological dynamics: how can these new ideological systems arise from previous structures?

But while it is of central importance for sociologists to try to predict changes in norms and their structure, the ethical problem is to evaluate these changes. Our predictions, if they are accurate, set limits on our alternatives, but they do not alone provide a basis for evaluation. For this purpose, the standard of "relevance" can no longer serve us.

The arguments by which we evaluate social change must therefore be distinguished from justification in terms of accepted norms. The status of these arguments thus requires discussion among qualified persons, including philosophers. Arguments that are intended to provide this sort of external point from which to view social change must look beyond the norms and values of a particular society for their justification. If they are to provide this sort of external point, they should presumably be derivable from a variety of prior ethical structures through the selective process of forming ethical hypotheses. In this sense our general criteria of judgment cannot be identical with those that are expressed in the norms of a particular society.

Valuative Discourse and the Social Sciences

We have now completed our simulated debate among ethical perspectives drawn from several social science disciplines. This comparison of ethical perspectives drawn from several disciplines has shown that each is incomplete; each is deficient, either in its lack of conformity to widely held convictions or in the limited generality with which it applies to possible alternative actions. Combinations of these ethics, however, might fare better in reasoned ethical argument.

The central focus of our argument has necessarily been the ethic of

75. Blau contends that Weber has no theory of revolution; see his "Critical Remarks on Weber's Theory of Authority," p. 309.

economics. This is so both because of the internal consistency of this ethic and because of its dominant place in the world today, especially in the United States. The economic ethic cannot be ignored; some of its deficiencies are also those of American policy formation. Yet we cannot take it merely as a target for indiscriminate criticism. We require that one ethical hypothesis, like a scientific paradigm, be replaced by another, and although we cannot easily replace the scientific paradigm of economics there is reason to believe that its ethical paradigm can and will be superseded.

In first examining some of the shortcomings of the economic ethic (chapter 5), I stressed the distinctions between preference and welfare and between one's own welfare and one's judgments of the general welfare. I also emphasized the possibility of policies regarding changes of preference, a point stressed further in chapter 7. I argued that the substantive concepts and procedural canons of a particular discipline, or of positivistic science generally, were too restrictive for rational ethical discourse. In this connection the characteristic insistence of welfare economics on ordinal description of preferences, and on the alleged impossibility of interpersonal comparison, are unnecessary restrictions.

In moving to the ethics of political science, I chose one particular approach to politics: that of "political economy," based largely on economics. This choice was made to stress the comparison of two similar ethical systems that differ only in a limited number of features. Some of the broader ethical considerations of political philosophy have, I hope, entered at other points. The analysis of political economy and its ethics naturally stressed criticisms similar to those made of economics: the importance of preference changes and of consideration of the general welfare, especially in legislative deliberation. At the same time I stressed an important advantage of the approach of political economy: a stress not simply on "democracy" as an encompassing class of political systems, but on the evaluation of small and precise differences among alternative democratic systems, such as changes in constituencies and electoral systems. Political economy asks what functions government should perform, and again in this connection it directs our attention to a host of detailed, solvable problems of some importance. It may indeed neglect some of the major issues involved in the founding of regimes and comparison among them, but in solving small problems it may provide a foundation for debate about the larger.

The ethics of learning and therapy stress the importance of change of preferences far more than does the internal debate in economics or even in politics. But they do not easily provide the basis for a complete ethical system. One reason for this incompleteness is that there are several alternative traditions latent in the ethics of psychology, including hedonism of a sort in Skinner, perfectionism in at least one ethics of therapy, and a type of negative utilitarianism in the ethic of health and illness. In addition, these ethics seem to ignore certain types of alternatives; one wonders whether a psychologist, faced with a policy problem, would consider a remedy such as that of effluent charges or whether a Skinnerian ethic could propose political institutions within which its rulers would be controlled.

The ethic I have selected from sociology is the least complete of all we have considered. The turmoil and division in this discipline may be related to the difficulty of developing an ethical hypothesis from disciplinary concerns. I suggested, therefore, that a major contribution of sociology might be to consideration of a special type of alternative: the choice of social norms. Choices of norms are important concerns of several disciplines: in economics, as a basis for exchange and a type of collective good; in psychology, as a process by which behavior and personality may be changed in social groups; and in political philosophy, in notions of the social contract as well as relational ethics.

Our discussion of internalization and reciprocity, in connection with the choice of social norms, also raises questions relevant to my proposed procedure for ethical argument. My meta-ethics requires that we alter our ethical system if it is shown to be inconsistent. But our ethical systems derive from convictions, some of which may have to be suppressed if they conflict with the system. These convictions, in turn, derive from our earlier learning and from our concurrent transactions with other persons. Some of these transactions may be contracts, carrying with them particular obligations; they may thus generate new particular convictions, in view of our previous internalization of general norms concerning such contracts. In choosing to enter into these obligations, we are presumably acting in terms of a general ethical system. But if these contracts evolve into institutionalized norms, we may also develop particular internalized convictions that come to conflict with that system. The tension between particular obligations and general principles of choice thus requires careful scrutiny.

Implicitly I have argued for some form of act-utilitarianism as a guide to social policy and the acts that affect policy. But the issues and alternatives raised by a debate among these disciplinary ethics are relevant to other ethics as well. Perfectionism, Rawls's theory of justice, and various forms of utilitarianism all must cope with markets, with preference changes, with political regimes, and with the choice of norms if they are to deal adequately with contemporary problems. Any other ethic, new or old, that would enter this debate must also face these challenges.

If this broad debate ensues, and finds an institutionalized place in the modern university, it may provide education, policy guidance, and an additional test of relevance beyond that of science alone. But in proposing this relationship between the university and society, I must now finally consider ways in which this debate might relate to both the university's disciplines and the institutions of the society at large.

PART THREE | SOCIAL FRAMEWORKS FOR VALUATIVE DISCOURSE

9 APPLIED SOCIAL SCIENCE, VALUATIVE DISCOURSE, AND DEMOCRACY

The preceding four chapters have shown the possibility of reasoned discourse among diverse valuative perspectives that can be found within the social sciences. But a mere exhortation to engage in this discourse is not enough. The social structures—disciplines and departments—that confer prestige, provide careers, and define problems as important in the social sciences do not necessarily foster this discourse. They stress factual research related to the theoretical structures of existing disciplines at the expense of value-guided and interdisciplinary work. Until alternative social structures are developed, valuative discourse by social scientists will be considered at best an amateur and dilettante activity.

I have also argued that the application of expert knowledge must be checked by controls of political responsibility. Voters and their representatives, as well as consumers, must exercise controls that go beyond the expression of untutored and unreflective preferences. They must therefore be well informed as to the expected consequences of policies, and in politics, if they are to deliberate in terms of the general welfare, they must argue from valuative principles by which policies may be judged. But the development of informed citizens and representatives, however desirable, cannot be expected to take place automatically. The discourse of citizens, like that of the university, is channeled by social structures and the motivations they induce. Thus we must suggest possible social institutions through which this guidance might work.[1]

The social institutions—or organizations if we form them deliberately—that are required must fulfill certain functions: the expertness of

---

1. My proposals are tentative and are relative to a particular situation. I take as given major features of the institutional structure of the modern democratic state and especially of American academic life. These may certainly be examined and questioned, but such problems lie beyond the compass of this book.

science and of disciplined valuative discourse must be transmitted to points of policy decision, but the trained persons who do so must be politically responsible, if possible, to those who are affected by their advice and decisions.

To relate technical discourse more closely to processes of public criticism, we may consider possible changes in both. I suggest them more confidently for the university than for the political system. On the one hand, universities and colleges may develop educational programs and personnel policies that encourage reasoned criticism of policy and the education of informed citizens; on the other, democratic and representative institutions may be developed that include expert information more effectively. I shall concentrate here on possible directions that might be taken in the administration of higher education, in disciplinary and professional associations, and in the critical functions of the legislature, which illustrate approaches to these problems.

Within the universities, many existing activities might provide bases for the institutions that are needed. Persons engaged in basic science— natural or social—might extend their activities to include valuation and choice *if* they could do so collectively within a recognized subspecialty in a discipline; this possibility is greater in the social sciences than in the natural. Philosophers who wished to deal with practical problems of policy might conceivably join together in a special field of applied philosophy. Persons in applied or professional schools might also develop general orientations toward applied social science—especially if those applied specialties included a broad range of particular policy areas, as planning, public administration, operations research, and systems analysis often do. Important contributions might also come from applied fields involving natural science.

Some of these possible bases for institutional development stress social science more than others. Operations research and philosophy, for example, seem relatively remote from social science, as well as from one another. Yet the contribution that each can make, in addition to the contribution of social science, is essential for the institutions we seek. The systematic and technical analysis of alternative decisions, represented by operations research and related fields, is an important advance in our understanding of many types of problems. But its philosophical bases, like those of policy choice generally, require deeper examination than is provided by assuming a criterion function or adapting economic ethics. And analysis of the human consequences of policy requires that operations research include contributions from social science as well.

Philosophy is of course central to the valuative discourse we have proposed. Yet philosophy, if it is to aid in policy choices, must extend its scope to include prediction of the consequences of our acts, as provided by science and particularly by social science. Deontological ethics that define the rightness of acts without regard for consequences may allow greater autonomy to philosophers, but most major policy choices involve ethical principles that call for the prediction of consequences.

The prediction of consequences of alternative policies also requires maximal use of the rigor and methods that the social sciences have developed. The need for valuative discourse does not imply that we should replace social science entirely by less rigorous and more "humanistic" approaches. We have stressed valuative discourse because without it applied science lacks intelligent guidance. But valuative discourse without a systematic and disciplined assessment of the consequences of our possible actions can also be sterile. In personal relations, the paraphernalia of social science may seem out of place in predicting these consequences, but in policy choices affecting large numbers of people they are vital. And even though we cannot aspire to know *all* these consequences, or to use the formal apparatus of social science in policy choice without the aid of prudent judgment, social science may nevertheless reduce our disagreements and our waste of resources in fruitless projects. We must therefore devise social structures within which the valuative discourse of philosophy and the social sciences can develop together with disciplined factual discourse about the consequences of our acts.

The Concepts of Applied Social Science [2]

We seek ways of organizing activity in the universities so as to combine science, valuation, application, and responsibility to those affected. This combination of features may conceivably arise in various

2. The general issues discussed in this section are also treated in Coleman, "Policy Research in the Social Sciences." A parallel argument for natural science is presented in Levins, "Fundamental and Applied Research in Agriculture."

ways. But an essential ingredient of all of them is social science; for this reason we have stressed the sources of such developments within existing social science disciplines.

There are nevertheless important difficulties in relating the social sciences to this task. Social science, insofar as it patterns itself on natural science, concentrates on problems defined by the internal discourse within groups of researchers. Even if these groups should introduce the valuative discourse I propose, they might still subdivide their *factual* discourse into compartments that did not fit the needs of policy choice. The closed character of individual disciplines can thus hinder the combination of specialties in application, even while it controls the quality of information supplied. This problem of compartmentalization is greatest when the fields to be combined are farthest from one another, such as natural and social science in problems of public health, the environment, or nuclear strategy. It is less when the disciplines in question have preexisting links resulting from cooperation on shared research problems. It may also be reduced by interdisciplinary training specifically related to the policy area in question or to policy problems more generally.

The problems and concepts of scientific investigation may be chosen in terms not only of the internal theoretical structure of a basic-science discipline, but also of practical concern with action in the world. These two criteria for guiding research may overlap; practical problems have at times generated significant theoretical questions, and basic science has made many discoveries with unanticipated practical applications. Thus it is widely believed by basic scientists (natural or social) that their problems are well chosen not only for the development of knowledge but also for its longer-run application.

I wish, however, to stress the insufficiency of basic science for purposes of application and the consequent conflicts between the criteria for choice of problems in basic and applied science. I shall therefore contrast two polar types: basic science, involving disciplinary criteria for choice of problems but no practical concern, and applied science, involving practical concern but no need to choose problems as the basic disciplines define them. I shall argue that the problems and concepts of basic science are not necessarily most useful in application— especially in the social sciences, where elegant and fundamental findings have been elusive. This argument might appear to lead to support for the existing applied disciplines and professions. But I shall also argue that *their* compartmentalization tends to underemphasize common factual and valuative problems that they share, which might be combined and studied in a more general field.

The concepts and variables of applied science differ from those of basic science in three ways. In applied science,

1. The dependent variable is a valuative one;

2. The independent variables, as they vary, are expected to relate to action that influences the realization of the value in question;

3. Applied research often involves a repeated alternation between action and the monitoring of a valuative dependent variable.

It is perhaps obvious that applied science aims at goals or values and that when we ask what should be done we are asking a *valuative* question. But we often conceal from ourselves the valuative status of our dependent variables by deriving them from clients' values, naturalistic ethics, or secondarily evaluative terms. As we become aware of the valuative status of our dependent variables, we must realize that the use of these variables can lead toward theoretical structures other than those of basic science. These variables, though general, may fail to enter into the general theories of a given discipline precisely because they are valuative.

The distinction between valuative variables and those of scientific theory was illustrated by our discussion of economic ethics in chapter 5. Economists have rejected cardinal welfare and interpersonal comparisons as unscientific concepts, but government officials engaged in cost-benefit analysis have had to ignore this limitation when faced with policy choices affecting large numbers of persons. Even these latter comparisons (or the analogous comparisons implied in GNP or national income) have in turn been criticized on the ground that increases in mere economic production and consumption do not guarantee improvement in the "quality of life." Whatever meaning we give to this phrase, it refers in at least some ethics to human experiences. Insofar as it does, its measurement would seem to take us away from economics into psychology, yet even then we cannot be sure that the variable measured will be one that is central to psychological theories of behavior.[3]

3. Land distinguishes between "social indicator models" and "social policy models," with only the latter involving valuative variables. The former, in the examples he

The connection between applied social science and valuative discourse lies in our choice of dependent variables. These variables cannot in general be chosen in terms of their theoretical significance for closed scientific communities that aim at abstract factual knowledge alone nor need they be chosen on the basis of particular applications. Not only must the dependent variables be valuative, but if policies in various areas are to be compared with one another these variables must derive if possible from *general* valuative systems. The particular and unrelated "secondarily evaluative terms" which we criticized in chapter 4 are not ordinarily interrelated in such systems. Neither are the valuative terms of the professions—for example, the delivery of health services, the durability of engineering structures, or the esthetic qualities of planned cities. These latter variables *are* valuative—and in this respect they depart from the concepts of the particular basic sciences—but they are not related to larger valuative systems. They do reflect a necessary factoring or suboptimization in the allocation of tasks. But the dependent variables in the most *fundamental* applied research must be derived from the ethical discourse we have proposed. The fact that they are not chosen for scientific reasons alone, but are derived from processes of discussion and consensus, does not prevent them from being either systematic or operational.

The interrelation of dependent variables through valuative discourse can then connect policy variables that derive from various disciplines or professions and that are means to related ends. For example, in policy choices concerning occupations and employment, welfare is likely to be affected by working conditions, opportunity for employment, and chances for advancement but also by the productivity of organizations and by the uncertainties and frustrations attendant on movement from one role to another. In addition, norms regarding rewards for productivity may affect welfare in the longer run. In choices affecting the equality of the sexes, equity and productivity must be weighed against the effects of equal employment on the socialization of chil-

---

gives, are more closely related to the concepts of sociology; the latter he considers to involve valuative variables on which there is no necessary consensus. See his "Social Indicator Models: An Overview," p. 20. But Schultze treats similar models more favorably, calling them "social production functions"; see *The Politics and Economics of Public Spending,* pp. 57–64.

dren. In international policy, effects on the security of nations that are expected to further particular values must be weighed against external effects on persons in other nations and against considerations of international equity. In each of these examples, the values of multiple outcomes must be related to one another by an ethical hypothesis—and some ethical systems would stress values other than those mentioned. Various policies affecting each outcome value must then be compared, all within a single causal model.

A second distinctive feature of applied research is its concern with variables related to action that *influences* the realization of the value in question. This feature is sometimes discussed as relating to "manipulable" variables, but such a characterization is too narrow. The study of national character in connection with wartime propaganda, or the forecasting of the weather, influence respectively the success of given propaganda strategies and the likelihood that people will become wet, hot, or cold or that crops will grow, yet the value-relevance of these studies does not depend on the manipulability of the variables in question. Rather, some act under consideration—sending a message, going outdoors, planting crops—will have different valued consequences, depending on the value of a nonmanipulated variable. In this case, the consequences of policy choice or of action depend in an *interactive* fashion on manipulated and nonmanipulated variables.[4] It is for this reason that unconditional prediction of the future, as is attempted in "futurology," may be relevant to policy choice if successful; it can not only improve our prediction of the difference in consequences among alternative acts, but also inform us about the feasibility of alternatives.

Insofar as we study nonmanipulable variables, we may be selecting problems analogous to those of basic science. But even if we are, we may nevertheless select among the variables of basic science a subset more relevant to valuative applications. There is a sense in which earlier historical times are less relevant. There is also a sense in which prediction of the future, if it is unaffected by our acts, may be irrelevant unless particular values may be realized in a way that depends on future states of affairs. A common phrase has been "understanding

4. See for example Fennessey, "Some Problems and Possibilities in Policy-Oriented Social Research," p. 372.

and control," sometimes with the addition of an intermediate stage of "prediction." But knowledge and understanding do not always lead to "control"—even on the part of the client, not to mention the social scientist, and prediction may lead not to control but to fatalism and indifference.

Some of the relations among manipulable and nonmanipulable variables, the "engineering model," and the service of organizational clients may be summarized by means of a simple symbolic notation. We wish to express the possibility that a valuative variable v may be affected (1) by changes in policy on the part of organizations, which in turn influence the situation s in which individuals find themselves; (2) by changes in the actions a by which affected individuals or actors adapt to the situation or to these organizational policies; and (3) by changes in nonmanipulable variables x_i. In these terms, if we use the symbol Δ to indicate the change in a variable, we may write

$$\Delta v = f(\Delta s, \Delta a, \Delta x_i)$$

This equation is a concise way of stating that there are two distinct modes of entry into a larger causal model [5] of the determinants of the valuative variable v. It also calls to our attention that we need be concerned only with *differences* in v among possible alternative acts or policies, not with actual values of v. It implies that we are comparing alternative possible acts or policies and not comparing the existing state of affairs with an unattainable standard.

In this formulation, the valuative variable v may be as specific as the expected net benefit from a proposed project or the incidence of a particular disease or as abstract as a general ethical desideratum—provided that it can be measured. A given policy choice may also involve more than one valuative variable, but we have argued that every effort should be made to reconcile multiple bases of valuation.

The problem of the applied social scientist, more generally, is simply that of an actor who wishes to maximize the value corresponding

5. In many applications of economic models to policy choices, Δa is considered as a function of Δs; the consumer or taxpayer is seen as reorienting his actions in a predictable way when the options open to him are changed. Moreover, the actor who engages in a may be an organization, as in the case of a firm adapting to governmental economic policy, and an organization may influence the situation of individuals by direct persuasive communication.

to a given ethical system. His first step must be one of exploration. What *are* his alternatives, in the most general sense? Before advising a particular client or organization, he must choose whether to work with that client, or another, or none.[6] He might join with others in setting up a new organization, try to change the leadership of existing organizations, or operate as an intellectual critic hoping in the longer run to effect structural changes. Still more general, he might choose not only his client or employer, but his occupation. The choice of alternatives is thus the broadest choice that may arise in "applied social science"—for the choice may extend outside the activities of science altogether. However difficult it may be to formalize this choice, we must recognize that it precedes any simple formulation such as the above equation implies. If one fails to see an important alternative, then the entire systematic procedure is of limited value.

The equation is intended to stress an alternative that has often been overlooked in applied social science—that of communication with actors (consumers, in a broad sense) whose choice of acts a influences v directly, rather than with organizations whose decisions influence the situation s. A frequent type of application of social science involves change in the situation s in order to alter a valuative variable (for example, by providing new products or policies) or alteration in the actions a by a change in the situation (for example, a change in an electoral law leading to a different number of parties). But the formulation of the equation reminds us that social research can also contribute directly to acts a.[7] It can supply information about products and opportunities available, government services, and political choices. If we are unable to modify the environment (as in the case of weather, at least until recently), we can provide information to individuals so that their actions a can take account of it—and similarly for traffic conditions, health conditions such as the possible spread of disease, or business conditions. As our knowledge increases we may be able to modify the environment as well and thus influence v through changes in s.

The situation s of an affected individual is in general defined in

6. See Dahrendorf, *Essays in The Theory of Society,* pp. 276–277.
7. We set aside the possibility that the social scientist will use information in personal production or consumption. On the use of knowledge to increase the efficiency of consumption, see G. S. Becker, *Economic Theory,* p. 47–48.

terms of his perception of it. This implies that the realization of a given value v can be influenced by socialization, education, advertising, propaganda, and the like, even without change in the situation as defined "objectively" by an observer. It also reminds us that the application of social science in direct communication to individuals may involve persuasion and can thus be criticized in the same terms as advertising. Fertility choices can be affected either by changes in social structure or by supplying information about birth control, and women's opportunities can be affected not only by social change but also by group discussion. In either example, the latter approach can involve persuasion and can have political overtones.

A major task of the applied social scientist working in a given problem area is to choose the general dependent variable that links together specific outcomes and specify (or seek to discover) the other variables and the nature of the functional relation f. This relation may be precise or vague, general or specific. It may be drawn from previous studies or developed de novo. The data on which it is based may already exist or may have to be gathered, depending on the state of knowledge and the exigencies of the decision required. But all these variants involve the effort to generalize from past experience and observation to new choices.

An extremely wide range of research activities is relevant to the discovery of the model or set of relationships involved in f. For policy alternatives that are effective in the long run, historical studies are relevant. For choices involving major structural changes in social institutions, comparison with the experience of other social systems may be required. The systematic measurement of specified welfare criteria is of course necessary and partly overlaps with studies of social indicators. Small-scale experiments on conditions affecting welfare indicators are essential if we are to propose policies confidently. And a particularly important and neglected field of study is the intentional alteration of norms.

In problems of system behavior such as economic prediction and traffic control, analysis is complicated by the fact that the systems consist of acting human beings whose choices produce the phenomena under consideration (though local intervention by private groups in weather modification could produce analogous effects). Economists can try to predict the trend of economic fluctuations and make this information available to individuals and firms for their decisions. If this information is widely enough used, however, it may influence the behavior of the system. As system behavior becomes more contingent on the choices of a few actors of comparable importance, the basis of their choices may come more nearly to resemble game strategies, as in the case of large firms, major interest groups, or great powers. As this contingent feature of interaction becomes dominant, we speak more of the political feasibility of actions than of determinate laws of behavior.[8] We may speak of possible coalitions and vetoes and of the need to formulate compromise proposals, rather than of power structure and elite behavior.

It is also possible to influence the operation of market and traffic systems by the creation of behavior-feedback systems such as we discussed in chapter 6, which may then act periodically to modify the parameters of the system. Thus in the economy the Federal Reserve Board or the Council of Economic Advisers may propose such action (though we do not now formulate scientific generalizations concerning *their* choices). In traffic control we may similarly use models of the traffic system or information-gathering devices such as traffic-flow monitors.[9]

These feedback systems remind us of the third distinctive feature of applied social science: that it requires *repeated measurement over time*. Such measurements are involved in the scientific study of systems in motion, from astronomy to electronics. They are also available to economists, being compiled by governments at the urging of both business firms and academic researchers. But in the other social sciences, either basic or applied, they are less generally available. In applied science, outside the laboratory, they are particularly necessary. A single policy choice may be accompanied by a single evaluation measurement or study, but uncontrolled variables fluctuating over time usually need to be taken into account by continuous or periodic moni-

8. See for example Meltsner, "Political Feasibility and Policy Analysis."
9. If these procedures are to be generalized, we must recall some of their limits as well. The time that elapses in them between policy decision and information feedback is short relative to a human lifetime. They do not consider the interests, or the socialization, of new generations. And they use information generated from relatively public sources.

toring. The use of this approach for economic indicators has led to increasing discussion of analogous "social indicators," which might well be related to ethical hypotheses and to the models, or social production functions, that predict the corresponding valuative variables.

Repeated observation may also be required, not merely to take account of uncontrolled external influences, but to perfect an engineeering design. Even though "prototypes of social programs, unlike hardware systems, cannot be evaluated and tested in the laboratory or wind tunnel," [10] an approximation to this repeated testing is desirable in order to see whether anticipated values have actually been realized when a decision is put into effect.

The conceptual schemes and procedures of applied science are thus distinct from those of basic science, even though they can draw on the resources of basic science. A central difference between the two lies in the valuative character of the dependent variables of applied science. If these variables are disparate and fragmented, like our initial ethical convictions or our secondarily evaluative terms, then applied science will be similarly fragmented, but if they are connected by ethical hypotheses, a more general applied science may be possible.

The goals of the basic social science disciplines lead to choice of problems and concepts that are not always the same as those needed for practical choice. The possible conflict between the two paths leads often to statements that "as economists," "as sociologists," or among natural scientists, "as scientists," we cannot deal with certain problems, because they involve valuative concepts and thus do not conform to the standards of existing disciplines. At the same time,the applied disciplines or professions, while they combine the skills of basic disciplines, may sometimes cleave too narrowly to the question as to what they should do "as physicians," "as engineers," "as social workers," or "as lawyers." [11]

10. Schultze, *The Politics and Economics of Public Spending*, p. 60. The evaluation of social programs is also complicated by political influences in indicators themselves by persons or groups affected; see Henriot, "Political Questions about Social Indicators"; Biderman, "Information ≠ Intelligence ≠ Enlightened Public Policy."

11. Relations between the social sciences and existing professions are discussed in *Knowledge Into Action*, ch. 3.

The specificity of values of existing applied fields may be illustrated by noting the diversity and separateness of the applied sciences and professions. Those that make use of the physical sciences include the engineering specialties (civil, chemical, electrical, mechanical, nuclear, aerospace, etc.). For the biological sciences the chief examples are the medical and paramedical professions. Other applied biological sciences include agronomy, forestry, animal breeding, and veterinary science. Corresponding specialties utilizing the social sciences include education, social welfare, community organization, business administration, journalism, public administration, international affairs, industrial sociology and psychology, and clinical psychology. In addition there are specialties combining natural and social science, such as architecture, public health, and city planning. Each of these specialties typically has its own societies, its own literature, and its own occupational market.

These fields perform essential functions in the application of scientific knowledge but are insufficient in themselves. Fields of this kind develop only when predictable occupational markets have arisen and supply personnel to these markets. Their professional concerns often center not about variables such as v, but about means to the attainment of valued ends that work through the profession in question. Thus the profession of medicine is less concerned with prevention of illness than with the delivery of health services.

For skills that are more general and more adaptable in the anlaysis of policy choices, it is desirable to supplement these applied fields. New problems that have potentially large effects but that do not require entire new profesions for their study may require the rapid recruitment of generalists in policy analysis together with relevant specialists from existing fields. And the programs of training in existing specialties may well share common elements that these generalists can develop further.

Policy Analysis as an Applied Discipline

The possibility of creating new roles within the university can easily be overlooked. When an academic or professional person judges that action is required, he may consult with colleagues in his field to consider what members of that group can do, or he may consult with persons who are not colleagues and speak to them as citizens or "intellectuals." Pressing problems may not allow time for the creation of new fields or roles to deal with them, and the creation of these fields may not seem to be the responsibility of persons in existing specialties. If the action proposed lies outside the listener's role—or worse, if it appears to threaten his group by transferring some of its functions to others—it is unlikely to be welcomed.[12] Thus a phrase such as "the scientist's social responsibility" tacitly assumes that "the scientist" is a role defined in terms of technical competence by the mutual judgments of scientific colleagues, in relation to theoretically significant problems. An important potential contribution of the university, however, lies in the creation of *new* roles with new criteria for their performance. For democratic evaluation and control of decisions involving expertise, universities must place greater stress on the education of the informed public and on the participation of their own faculties as well as their graduates in this evaluation.

A particularly promising new role may be provided by the emerging field of policy analysis, which combines many of the requisite skills and may evolve into an applied discipline. If enlarged to include the valuative discourse I have proposed as well as undergraduate education for informed citizenship, it might fulfill many of the functions I have discussed. A number of graduate schools of public policy analysis, overlapping with existing disciplines but defining a new domain of expertness, have been organized in the United States in the past few years. This development has been stimulated by an increasing expectation that social science will be relevant to policy, together with increasing doubt as to whether policies enacted have produced the intended results. The curricula of these schools share many common elements, including decision criteria, such as cost-benefit analysis; statistical decision theory; social indicators, evaluation research, and the measurement of desired outcomes; construction of models (for example, economic models) linking policy variables to outcomes; organizational politics; and case studies, internship, and contact with prac-

---

12. A basic principle for assessment of the political feasibility of policy advice is that advice threatening to the career expectations or constituency base of the advisee is to be avoided. This is well-known in politics but not always part of scientists' training.

titioners to connect general principles with concrete situations and develop interpersonal skills.[13] Joint degree programs between policy analysis and professional training, including law, engineering, and medicine, are also being developed. The extension of this field so as to relate to applied natural science is particularly desirable.

The field of policy analysis has a natural affinity with interdisciplinary ethical discourse. It needs this discourse so that its practitioners can intelligently define both their own ends and the relation of their specialty to democratic political responsibility. Wide-ranging ethical discourse will be facilitated by the education of undergraduates, whose responsibilities as citizens may enlarge their view relative to the occupational concerns, career channels, and employment constituencies of applied graduate schools. A program of instruction and research in policy analysis would not center exclusively on either basic scientific disciplines or on particular occupational outlets but would deal with a domain relevant both to conventional applied occupations and to their critics. Such a program might define a general sphere of competence shared by advisers employed in organizations and informed citizens in voluntary associations.

Although policy analysis also has an obvious affinity with social science, it can also draw on other fields within the university and experience outside the university. Natural science is obviously involved in a great many policy choices; we have dealt with this relation in chapter 2. The study of cases of political decision can also involve instances from history and literature, from Thucydides and Shakespeare to the present. Students' experience in employment or internship may be interpreted in the classroom. Mid-career training of civil servants in "reverse sabbaticals" can educate both the civil servants and the students with whom they associate. Journalists who make use of scientific knowledge may be intermediaries in this process, serving to educate the public. For all these sorts of activities, a unified notion of training in policy analysis may be useful.

13. The specificity of policy choice has been stressed by C. E. Lindblom, who recommends, "Adapt your calculation to your social and political role." Lecture at Duke University, April 9, 1973. Since the goal of training in this field is choice in actual situations without laboratory-type control, practice with specific materials and situations is essential.

This developing specialty might gain support and stability by developing reward structures similar to those of the existing disciplines—in effect, by becoming a new applied discipline. Universities with schools or departments of policy analysis could give career advancement credit to faculty members for publishing reasoned evaluations and criticisms of policies on which they are expert—in the same way as credit is given for research publications. Not only the individual university, but also the university system may provide career motivations for expert policy analysis as a form of public service, if alternative policies can be compared critically and expertly through published work, and if a national market exists for faculty members who are judged in terms of their analyses.[14] Similar motivations can of course be provided by professional schools. In this way, university faculty members might be induced to supply more information for informed public debate, which would also include contributions from other sources. The basis of this criticism must be kept heterogeneous in terms of ethical hypotheses and clients' interests; valuative discourse implies diversity and argument, not professional unity, in debates on specific policy choices. Particular care is necessary in view of the interests of universities and disciplines themselves.

Three streams of graduates must be provided by such a discipline if it is to contribute to democratic policy choice, train new teachers, and be securely based. One is the stream of expert practitioners who would move into nonacademic positions as either advisers or (if they acquire the needed skills) as policymakers. These graduates would typically hold the master's degree, often in conjunction with a professional degree. A second is the stream of undergraduate majors, who would carry the knowledge they have acquired into the professions (though without the master's degree), into business, into voluntary associations, and into their roles as individual citizens.

Persons trained in graduate schools of policy analysis would expect

14. These suggestions are not intended to devalue the teaching function, which must also be assessed and rewarded more than at present. Policy-related research may be general as well as specific; see *Knowledge Into Action*, ch. 8. On national markets and publication see Ben-David, *The Scientist's Role in Society*, ch. 8. Policy advising also requires skills in personal relations, which are not so easily rewarded in this sort of national market.

to go largely into nonacademic employment and to conform somewhat to the engineering model, supplying technical advice and skill to large organizations or for otherwise given ends. In this respect graduate policy training would resemble training in engineering, medical, or law schools or the training of students for conventional professional roles in the medieval universities.[15] But undergraduate training would be designed for the informed citizen, and not simply for those expecting employment by a large organization or professional practice. The informed citizen, especially if he is to judge policies in terms of the general welfare, must choose his own system of values rather than accept it from an employer or profession. A central feature of such a discipline must therefore be reasoned valuative discourse. The policy adviser who works for a large organization may be governed by his employment contract, and not simply by his own system of values, but having formulated his ethics clearly he may have chosen better among employers in the first place. Thus for both undergraduates and graduate students in policy analysis, the conventional aspect of the engineering model would be modified to include reasoned discussion of the ends of policy and critical evaluation of the goals of large organizations.

A third significant stream consists of those earning the doctorate in policy analysis, many of whom would become university teachers. Some of those receiving the doctorate would also move into nonacademic employment, but they would be able to move back and forth between practice and academia, and much of their research would be published for expert scrutiny by their peers in the new discipline. This publication would provide both a forum for public review and expert criticism of policy proposals and a basis for assessment of the authors' qualifications.

Such a discipline requires all three ingredients—graduate training for practical work, undergraduate teaching, and academic training for teaching and publication. It is possible to combine any two of the three ingredients, but each such combination would provide something less. Omission of graduate teaching that prepared students for practical

15. Ben-David, *op. cit.*, p. 46.

work would fail to provide a needed output of technical skills to society. Omission of undergraduate teaching would leave a "graduate school of public policy" that risked training its students too much for specific job outlets, had too little valuative discourse, and did not contribute sufficiently to the preparation of informed citizens and critics. Finally, omission of academic training for teaching and publication would give rise to isolated policy schools but could not easily provide the academic careers and national market of a discipline. It is also possible for policy analysis to be provided by private consulting organizations or "think tanks." These organizations do not formally perform the teaching functions but may serve both as outlets for university training in policy analysis and as stimulating competition if these university programs should fail to maintain the necessary types of competence.[16]

In combining these ingredients, policy analysis should avoid developing a structure like that of the medical or legal profession. If it came to resemble medicine, it might become *too* influential and too little susceptible to expert-aided dissent. A deliberate stress is necessary, therefore, on maintaining internal bases of dissent. Such a combination of expertness and diversity is better illustrated by the coexistence of competing schools of policy advice in economics than by the external appearance of harmony that has often characterized the medical profession. For this reason I propose the structure of an "applied discipline," whose graduates move into diverse occupational roles, rather than a profession. Diversity of ethical hypotheses can be fostered by diversity of occupational outlets.

Table 9.1 presents some of these features more systematically. The extreme "ideal" type of pure science involves no intervention by the scientist in policy advising, private or public; no professional or policy-related degrees that qualify him to give practical advice; and no collective decisions by scientists as a group on "science in policy." [17]

16. Bernal proposed the organization of research in governmentally sponsored academies and technico-scientific institutes; see *The Social Function of Science*, pp. 280–286.

17. Actual associations of basic scientists have been concerned with "policy for science," as regards research support, but insofar as their advocacy relates to the presumed consequences of research for society it is not usually based on expert research regarding these consequences.

TABLE 9.1

Alternative Models of Disciplines or Professions

Discipline or Profession	Research Degree (doctorate)	Under-graduate Teaching	Professional Degree Given?	Professional Degree Includes Basic Science Training	Professional Practice Consulting or Jobs in Private Sector	Professional Practice Public Policy Advice	Does Group Take Collective Stands on Public Policy?
Pure Science	+	+	0		0	0	0
Chemistry	+	+	0		(+)	(+)	0
Engineering	(+)	+	+	+	+	(+)	0
Economics	+	+	0		+	+	0
Business Administration	(+)	+	+	+	+	(+)	0
Public Administration	(+)	(+)	+	(+)	0	(+)	(+)
Medicine	(+)	0	+	+	+	0	+
Law	(+)	0	+	0	+	(+)	+
Policy Analysis	+	+	+	+	(+)	+	0

+: indicates that element in question is present
(+): sometimes present
0: absent
blank: not applicable

Chemistry and economics depart from this model in that their members do advise both public officials and private firms on practical matters; other sciences in actuality do so as well. Engineering, business administration, public administration, medicine, and law give professional degrees qualifying the practitioner to give practical advice. But whereas the medical and legal professions take collective stands on public policy that involves their expertise (and their professional interests), and public administrators as a group may take stands on how government should be administered, neither engineering nor business administration appears to do so. Perhaps the organizational nature of their practice makes the latter groups "professions without community." [18]

I propose for policy analysis a structure that combines the research, undergraduate teaching, and professional practice aspects of all the other specialties listed but excludes collective stands on public policy. In the categories of table 9.1, this structure resembles that of engineering or business administration, but these professions follow the "engineering model" and are less concerned with either public policy or valuative discourse. Policy analysis is primarily concerned with public policy, but the proposed structure provides only for individual, rather than collective, stands on such questions. The training of policy analysts can draw on the basic social sciences, just as medical training draws on basic medical and biological science. But policy analysis differs from medicine in involving undergraduate education as well as in avoiding collective positions on public policy.

A central requirement for attracting able people to policy analysis is the existence of predictable careers. Many of these careers must be outside the universities, and some will be less predictable than others. But for the detachment, the generality, and the systematic expert criticism that any such field requires, the possibility of university careers is essential. For this purpose the participants require research training, an extensive communications system (for example, periodicals) for published analyses, and a national job market including university positions—in short, one or more disciplines or subdisciplines.

18. Perrucci and Gerstl, *Profession Without Community: Engineers in American Society.*

Politicization and Autonomy of the University

I have proposed the development of policy analysis as an applied discipline in the university, in close connection with the social sciences. This connection is intended to increase the relevance of social science to fundamental valuative problems and to public policy, but it raises perennial problems concerning the possible politicization of the university.

When information is introduced into a political arena in support of one policy as against others, it can be expected to provoke reactions from the opponents of that policy. Such reactions are understandable, since proponents of the policy may wish to present information selectively. The most obvious reaction by opponents is to question the validity of the information advanced or the qualifications or motives of those who supply it. This questioning may be beneficial if it leads to more diverse expert criticism, but if it subjects scientific information to inexpert appraisal it undermines the value of science and expertness.

If a particular source of information is seen as a threat to a vital policy position, however, the partisans of the threatened policy may go farther. If they can prevent the discussion of the policy, or later prevent its implementation, and thus attain their ends, they are likely to do so. If not, they may level accusations at the advisers who oppose them. Even scientists, especially if arguing before a lay audience, may resort to such appeals. Accusations of disloyalty, subservience to foreign influences, or religious or ideological heterodoxy, as well as racism or subservience to financial or military interests, have been directed at academics who took positions on major policy questions. Not only individual advisers, but the institutions with which they are connected, may be the targets of such criticism.[19] These institutions may, in turn, be called on to purify themselves by controlling or expelling the individuals in question.

The claim to pursue knowledge freely and autonomously can thus conflict with the claim to advocate policies based on that knowledge,

19. A discipline may also receive such criticism, as when policy analysts take the role of social scientists and social science is held responsible for their advice; see Benveniste, *The Politics of Expertise,* p. 19.

when those policies threaten significant interests. The basic sciences have been protected from this conflict through the separation of facts and values and the separation of the roles of scientist and citizen. The applied sciences have largely avoided it through their service to clients and interests in society who themselves take the responsibility for policy choices; this relation is symbolized by the anonymous adviser sitting beside a responsible official who testifies before a congressional committee. The problem can also be moved away from the university itself by locating policy-related research outside the university. Individuals or institutions who advocate policy may then be held politically responsible, but attacks on them may be diverted from the university.[20]

Established professions such as medicine and law can take stands on some political questions without risking internal fragmentation or external attack. But even these professions may lose some of their influence if they carry their prerogatives too far: the American Medical Association's long opposition to federal aid for health care, and the American Bar Association's disapproval of certain Supreme Court nominations, have caused political reactions that led to either a change of stand or a loss of influence by the profession.

The proposed field of policy analysis, however, is a new one, and includes valuative discourse about matters as fundamental as the good life and the best political regime. Such a discipline may encounter particular political resistance, even if its policy stands are taken by individuals rather than collectively. Some of these individuals may be protected by institutions that support their values. For those in universities, the relevance of the discipline to debates in the outside society may depend particularly on academic freedom in relation to policies that appear to threaten powerful interests. But this freedom depends, in the last analysis, on the willingness of others to grant it and on the institutionalization of the underlying norms in society. Only if the results of this intervention are viewed on balance as clearly benefical by the relevant constituencies can such a discipline expect to retain a place in the university.

20. The possibility of insulating policy-related institutes from basic sciences in the universities for this reason is discussed in Easton, *The Political System* (2nd ed.), p. 356.

The valuative discourse we have proposed will also be more heterogeneous in its basic assumptions than is the discourse of any existing
basic or applied science. Distinct philosophical views may become
sharply separated by the effort to formulate precise and consistent
valuative positions. Particular philosophies might become implanted in
certain institutions or subdisciplines. The representation of one or
another of these views in a policymaking or advising position might
make more difference, as regards the advice given, than the employment of persons with various political affiliations. The apparent consensus on values in fields such as cost-benefit analysis or the design of
social indicators might be much less if the philosophies of Aristotle,
Plato, Rousseau, Nietzsche, deontologists, and act-utilitarians were
sources for alternative approaches to policy.

In view of this heterogeneity, the policy analyst guided by a particular philosophy may sometimes find it easier to stress citizen education
rather than direct policy advice. The educator can allow his students to
choose among diverse ethical hypotheses, while as policy adviser he
must choose one ethical position. If he is seen as introducing a personal or sectarian philosophy into his advice on public policy, especially if he does so covertly or in conflict with clients' or employers'
goals, he is open to attack.

The potential relations between valuative topics in the university
and clients or opponents in the outside society depend on the configuration of values in both. If there should be a large consensus on certain
values, then valuative discourse might rest on assumed agreed principles. Thus in the medieval universities the dominance of the Church
and its values was matched by university education for major roles in
the "establishment" of that time. A similar uniformity of views may
also exist in a modern state based on a single religion or in the contemporary USSR, where Marxism-Leninism is both a subject in the
philosophical faculties and the official philosophy of the state.

But in a pluralistic society this "official" relationship cannot so easily exist. Organizations dominated by one valuative position (for example, universities supported by a single religious group) may choose
simply to express that one position. The radical "free university" or
the academic department "captured" by partisans of one viewpoint
may also try this strategy, but unless that viewpoint is also strongly

held outside the strategy is less likely to succeed. In a pluralistic political system, however, the dominance of a particular philosophy may vary with time. Thus the political influence of a particular institution may also fluctuate if it is committed to one viewpoint; political action organizations must take this risk, but organizations guaranteeing continuity of functions (such as teaching) and employment may not be able to afford it. There may be a realm, defined by prudence, within which the university should maintain contact with all tendencies, and a realm beyond, which threatens the values that the institution serves, where this pluralism ceases.

The reconciliation of institutional interests and the need for criticism is in part a matter of political prudence. Policy recommendations may be couched in nonpartisan terms, so as not to threaten directly the officeholding chances of one or another party. The policy adviser may attempt to play the role of the therapist,[21] if he is also politically accountable. A limitation of the range of policy judgment, or of its connection with specific current choices, may have to be accepted as a condition for the survival of the discipline.

More important, we must ask whether research on policy problems, done within one nation and regime, can gain support and respectability regardless of the dissonance of its conclusions with the values of various "establishments." The diversity of such "establishments" is one crucial factor. What Shils has called the "concentration of charisma" in new nations,[22] depriving governments of independent sources of information and criticism, is a problem for old nations as well. One remedy might lie in the maintenance of an international policy-oriented social science,[23] with diversity encouraged by various national positions as well as within nations.

Policy Analysis and Democracy

If policy analysis is not only to provide advice to decision centers, but also to aid in the intelligent control of these centers by informed

---

21. An example of advice aimed at conduct of a policy of this type is Parsons, "The Problem of Controlled Institutional Change."

22. Shils, "Concentration and Dispersion of Charisma."

23. See Easton, *op. cit.,* p. 347.

citizens, then we must develop political institutions that encourage citizens to seek and use information. We have considered the motivation of university teachers to teach policy analysis and to engage in reasoned public evaluation of policies. The motivation of informed citizens generally, however, is not assured by education alone. The dissemination of technical information to citizens has often been a goal of undergraduate education, but we cannot be sure whether citizens thus trained will later inform themselves and participate in the making of public decisions. Persons who are paid to do so will do so. Scientists who are aroused by social problems related to their expert fields will spend some time on these problems—but often in a spirit of "doing good" together with colleagues, rather than in the spirit of rigorous criticism that would guide their professional work. A few experts may work on the staffs of voluntary organizations, whether public health specialists working for labor unions or economists for consumer organizations.

To design and appraise institutions that encourage informed citizen participation is a large and complex task. One reason for its complexity is that various notions of the good and of democracy lead to advocacy of various types and degrees of participation; in chapter 6 we left unanswered the question as to when citizens should vote for personal welfare and when for the general welfare. A second source of its complexity is that it involves extensive analysis of alternative social structures and their consequences. This analysis has been an important concern of political scientists and political sociologists, but the results are far from definitive. We take up the problem, not in hope of solving it, but in order to stress its integral connection with our previous argument.

One institution that can foster informed participation is the legislature. The legislative process, in contrast to executive decisions, involves public debate. Judicial processes also involve reasoned public argument, but their justifications derive from the interpretation of existing laws, rather than the principles on which new laws must be based. In chapter 6 we discussed deliberation and judgment of the general welfare as especially necessary in the legislature. On those issues that the public should judge in terms of the general welfare, perhaps informed deliberation in the legislature can foster informed deliberation among citizens generally. If there are other issues that the public should judge in terms of personal welfare, legislative debate can still inform that judgment, even though deliberation is then less relevant.

A valuable source of technically informed public debate might be the infusion of expertise into the legislative function of "oversight of administration." [24] One function of the legislature is the review and criticism of Executive action, but the reviews performed by congressional committees, or by the General Accounting Office, in the United States have in the past often centered on whether the terms of the law were faithfully carried out. These reviews have been increasingly extended, however, to expert study of whether the *purposes* of legislation were accomplished. Increasing attention is being given by Executive departments and agencies to evaluation studies, but studies by researchers attached to Congress can provide a more independent criticism, less closely tied to the interests of the agencies administering the policies. Either committee staffs, the Office of Technology Assessment, or possibly a Social Accounting Office analyzing the contribution of legislation and administration to changes in social indicators might fulfill this function. Congress itself can thus increase the technical component of its reviews of agency performance by examining whether organizations charged with producing health or education, or with alleviating poverty, actually did so. Such questions are at least as important as whether every penny of the budget has been spent in accordance with the provisions of the law. And in this context social science is of special importance because of its relation to the measurement of valuative variables.

The evaluation of administrative actions—and of the laws under which they took place—can also make use of the published reviews of policy that might come from the universities and from policy analysts elsewhere. Possibly the published versions of these reviews may become available too slowly to meet deadlines for decision on new legislation, but for review of past policies the delays of published in-

24. The importance of this legislative function for training leaders was stressed by Weber; see his *Economy and Society,* vol. 3, pp. 1381–1469. A related argument for policy analysis in state legislatures is Wheeler, "Evaluating Social Programs: The Case for a State GAO."

terchanges may be more tolerable. These delays may also be more consonant with the pace of legislative deliberation than with the faster pace of executive action.

The development of these capacities on the part of Congress requires not only extensive technical staffs for both political parties, but also an increased appreciation of technical problems on the part of congressmen themselves. The general competence required to supervise technical staffs must therefore be developed further among potential political leaders through their training in college and in their professions, must be appreciated by their constituents, and must be rewarded by advancement within Congress. If public issues come to be debated more in terms of the measurable consequences of policies, the demand for technical competence in assessment of these consequences may increase. Journalists, leaders of voluntary associations, public spokesmen for policymaking organizations, and committees appointed by professional associations to study problems of public policy may all be informed for this debate by policy-related technical training.

The relation between knowledge and interest is an inevitable problem for the institutions that channel expert knowledge into political choices. Congressional committees, though ideally formed to provide expertness and close study of legislation, have come to represent producer interests as well as the general interest. Augmented committee staffs might conceivably strengthen a partisan or interest-oriented view as well as provide expertise. Controversies between economists representing labor and management may indicate the degree of expert consensus that can be expected.

Legislative review of policy may thus utilize the contributions of policy analysis and encourage informed public debate. But these advantages might be imagined to obtain without valuative discourse, which is our central concern. The widespread ethic of preference satisfaction, for example, largely ignores the enlightenment or change of those preferences. In one form this ethic regards the voter's choice, however arrived at, as an automatic expression of his preferences and thus of his welfare. A second form, akin to Raiffa's decision analysis, would require the citizen to systematize his notions of personal welfare.[25] In this perspective, information such as legislative debate could supply would have value.

But if public debate on at least some issues should involve deliberation about the general welfare, then it will include important valuative components. Parties, factions, and interest groups may articulate their philosophies more clearly—if their clienteles and alliances do not encourage obscurity. Criteria such as cost-benefit analysis can be scrutinized as regards not only their accuracy and feasibility, but also their desirability. Groups that claim to represent the public interest may be required to state more clearly and consistently what notion of that interest they claim to further. Possibly philosophically trained legislators or staff members will help to clarify these issues publicly. Issues such as the subsidy or regulation of communications, the setting of the social discount rate, the preservation of natural and cultural heritages, the guarantee of justice and of rights may come to be debated in larger terms.

We have come to focus attention on the informed citizen, who debates questions of values and means to them, from two distinct starting points. In part I, analyzing the scientific discourse of the university, we stressed the need for valuative discourse in order to transcend the specialized and positivistic aspects of science. This valuative discourse was intended to contribute to the citizen's education for the problems and responsibilites he faces in an increasingly technological society.

But in part II, we analyzed alternative notions of the good and alternative criteria for public policy. We stressed the inadequacy of the economic ethic as a guide to political life or even to informed consideration of the consumer's choices. Central to this criticism was the distinction between an individual's social welfare function and the choices he makes for his personal welfare. We saw deliberation in terms of notions of the general welfare as especially necessary in the legislature. But parallel debate among citizens is a likely concomitant

25. As we noted in chapter 5, Raiffa sees systematization of values, even in private interest, as foreign to economic notions of consumer or firm behavior; see his *Decision Analysis,* pp. 127–128, 255. G. S. Becker sees the educated consumer as making more efficient choices in service of his more basic values but does not relate this effort to reasoned consistency; see his *Economic Theory,* pp. 47–48.

of this sort of legislative debate. Thus the importance of the informed citizen emerges not only from an initial critique of the relation between university and society, but also from a more refined analysis based on relations among the ethics of the social sciences.

The Social Function of Social Science

The role that applied social science, or policy analysis, must play—fulfilling its social function or its social responsiblity—must be in part a reflexive one.[26] These fields must be able to analyze their own activities, both in proposing directions for development and in evaluating the effectiveness of their own work. This book is intended to exemplify the approach of policy analysis, in applying the general findings of the sociology of science to assessing this possible new discipline; in proposing discussion aimed at the development of new norms and roles; and in placing these arguments in the specific context of the social sciences in the contemporary United States.

The discipline of policy analysis, like other disciplines, must continually examine whether it is effectively carrying out its tasks. Not merely the advancement of knowledge, nor reasoned ethical discourse, but the values that they mean to realize in *society* must be examined to see whether they have been furthered. Is social welfare—on any of several definitions—increasing or being maximized? Are citizens becoming, and remaining, informed? No mere myths of the success of education will do, nor can we replace the myth of beneficent science by another untested myth of beneficent ethical discussion. These judgments of effectiveness are especially difficult for the enterprise proposed in this book, however, because the enterprise has no single common goal. Particular policies may be judged (at least in principle) in terms of particular ethical systems, and diverse judgments may be made of them depending on the ethical starting points. But the discourse we have proposed may be a prerequisite even for these diverse judgments of the "success" of the enterprise. Suffice it to say that success cannot be judged in terms of persons involved, budgetary

26. This has been argued in Gouldner, *The Coming Crisis of Western Sociology,* and Friedrichs, *A Sociology of Sociology;* and Easton has made a similar critique of Weber's value-free stance (*op. cit.,* p. 359).

allocations, or acceptance of a new specialty and its familiarity to the public. These accomplishments, though perhaps necessary, measure the attainment of organizational goals but not of any philosophical notion of the general welfare.

It should also be obvious that reflexive analysis, though desirable, is not the central activity of the proposed discipline. The major concern of policy analysis must be with choices concerning the outside society. Concern for the organization of the academic world is a necessary condition for the development of policy analysis as a discipline, but a more important condition in the long run is the constructive analysis of concrete policy choices through research and effective policy advice.

These concrete policy choices must be diverse in several ways. They must include both the small and the large.[27] They must include proposals derived from various political and philosophical viewpoints. They must deal not only with the problems currently deemed urgent by society, but also with others that are anticipated by expert foresight.

The social function of social science is thus not simply to serve the interest of any particular class in a given period of history, nor is it to serve the interests of academics themselves. Rather, it is to provide guidance to society, through research, reasoned discourse, and education as to what interests should be served in particular circumstances and as to the means to do so.

Social science—both as it is and as it may develop—can provide clarity and objectivity in our anticipation of the consequences of a wide range of possible policies. It has made slow but steady progress toward the development of methods and findings that will be useful for the choice between policies—perhaps more readily useful in this choice than in the quest for laws parallel to those of Newton or Einstein. Thus applied social science requires not methodological revolution so much as guidance.

The guidance that social science requires must derive from both reasoned valuative discussion and the development of supportive social structures. But even if these features are established, the diversity of valuative discourse may be difficult to maintain. The analytic categories and valuative indices formed are likely to become reified. The

27. See Braybrooke and Lindblom, *A Strategy for Decision,* ch. 4.

professional groups that deal with these categories may find that careers and world-views depend on their maintenance. Thus as we strive to build these social structures, we must hope that they will do more than support new vested interests or another established priesthood.

Our proposals for a new discipline and new legislative functions are intended to illustrate a major practical problem for social scientists. The systematic discussion of goals, and the effort to design social structures that will further these goals, are a central task involving social science and philosophy in the guidance of public policy. At the heart of this problem is the design and evaluation of educational, economic, and governmental institutions. The value of expertness which science embodies, and its relations with the values of democracy, impel us to try to improve these institutions. If we can do so, we may then choose more intelligently among public policies through the combined application of social science and systematic ethics.[28]

28. This chapter has been adapted in part from Duncan MacRae, Jr., "Policy Analysis as an Applied Social Science Discipline, "*Administration and Society,* Vol. 6, No. 4 (February 1975), pp. 363–388, by permission of the publisher, Sage Publications, Inc.

BIBLIOGRAPHY

Abelson, Robert P., and Rosenberg, Milton J., "Symbolic Psycho-Logic."
Behavioral Science 3, no. 1 (January 1958) : 1–13.

Albert, Hans. *Plädoyer für Kritischen Rationalismus.* Munich: Piper, 1971.

———. *Traktat über Kritische Vernunft.* Tübingen: J.C.B. Mohr, 1968.

Alchian, Armen A., and Kessel, Reuben A. "Competition, Monopoly, and
the Pursuit of Money." In National Bureau of Economic Research, *Aspects
of Labor Economics.* Princeton, N.J.: Princeton University Press, 1962.

———, and Demsetz, Harold. "Production, Information Costs, and Economic Organization," *American Economic Review* 62, no. 5 (December
1972) : 777–795.

Alexander, Sidney S. "Comment." In Julius Margolis, ed., *The Analysis of
Public Output.*

———. "The Impersonality of Normative Judgments." In Walter A. Eltis,
F. G. Scott, and J. N. Wolfe, eds., *Induction, Growth and Trade: Essays in
Honor of Sir Roy Harrod.* Oxford: Clarendon Press, 1970.

———. "Social Evaluation through Notional Choice." *Quarterly Journal of
Economics,* 88, no. 4 (November 1974).

Almond, Gabriel A., and Coleman, James Smoot, eds. *The Politics of the Developing Areas.* Princeton, N.J.: Princeton University Press, 1960.

———, and Verba, Sidney. *The Civic Culture.* Princeton, N.J.: Princeton
University Press, 1963.

Arrow, Kenneth J. "Gifts and Exchanges." *Philosophy and Public Affairs* 1,
no. 4 (Summer 1972) : 343–362.

———. "Little's Critique of Welfare Economics." *American Economic Review* 41, no. 5 (December 1951) : 923–934.

———. "Political and Economic Evaluation of Social Effects and Externalities." In Julius Margolis, ed., *The Analysis of Public Output.*

———. "Public and Private Values." In Sidney Hook, ed., *Human Values
and Economic Policy.* New York: New York University Press, 1967.

———. *Social Choice and Individual Values.* 2d ed., New Haven, Conn.:
Yale University Press, 1963.

———. "Social Responsibility and Economic Efficiency." *Public Policy* 21,
no. 3 (Summer, 1973) : 303–317.

Arrow, Kenneth J., and Scitovsky, Tibor, eds. *Readings in Welfare Economics*. Homewood, Ill.: Richard D. Irwin, 1969.

Asch, Solomon E. *Social Psychology*. Englewood Cliffs, N.J.: Prentice-Hall, 1952.

Ayer, Alfred J. *Language, Truth and Logic*. 2d ed., London: Gollancz, 1946.

Bachrach, Peter. *The Theory of Democratic Elitism*. Boston: Little, Brown, 1967.

Banfield, Edward C. *The Unheavenly City*. Boston: Little, Brown, 1970.

Barber, Bernard. *Science and the Social Order*. New York: Free Press, 1952.

———. "Some Problems in the Sociology of the Professions." In Kenneth C. Lynn and the editors of Daedalus, eds., *The Professions in America*. Boston: Beacon, 1964.

Baritz, Loren. *The Servants of Power*. New York: Wiley, 1965.

Barry, Brian. *The Liberal Theory of Justice*. Oxford: Clarendon Press, 1973.

———. *Political Argument*. London: Routledge, 1965.

———. *Sociologists, Economists, and Democracy*. London: Collier-Macmillan Ltd., 1970.

Bator, Francis M. "The Anatomy of Market Failure." *Quarterly Journal of Economics* 72, no. 3 (August 1958) : 351–379.

———. "The Simple Analytics of Welfare Maximization." *American Economic Review* 47, no. 1 (March 1957) : 22–59.

Baumgardt, David. *Bentham and the Ethics of Today*. Princeton, N.J.: Princeton University Press, 1952.

Baumol, William. "Community Indifference." *Review of Economic Studies* 14(1), no. 35 (1946–47) : 44–48.

———. "On the Social Rate of Discount." *American Economic Review* 58, no. 4 (September 1968) : 788–802.

Bay, Christian. "Politics and Pseudopolitics." *American Political Science Review* 59, no. 1 (March 1965) : 39–51.

———. *The Structure of Freedom*. Stanford, Calif.: Stanford University Press, 1958.

Becker, Gary S. *Economic Theory*. New York: Knopf, 1971.

———. *The Economics of Discrimination*. 2d ed. Chicago: University of Chicago Press, 1971.

Becker, Howard S. *Outsiders*. New York: Free Press of Glencoe, 1963.

Ben-David, Joseph. *The Scientist's Role in Society*. Englewood Cliffs, N.J.: Prentice-Hall, 1971.

Bendix, Reinhard. *Social Science and the Distrust of Reason, University of California Publications in Sociology and Social Institutions*. Berkeley, Calif.: University of California Press, 1951.

———. *Work and Authority in Industry*. New York: Wiley, 1956.

Benham, Lee K. "The Effect of Advertising on the Price of Eyeglasses." *Journal of Law and Economics* 15, no. 2 (October 1972) : 337–352.

Bentham, Jeremy. *An Introduction to the Principles of Morals and Legislation*. New York: Hafner, 1948.

Benveniste, Guy. *The Politics of Expertise*. Berkeley, Calif.: Glendessary, 1972.

Berelson, Bernard R., Lazarsfeld, Paul F., and McPhee, William N. *Voting*. Chicago: University of Chicago Press, 1954.

Berger, Peter L. *Invitation to Sociology: A Humanistic Perspective*. Garden City, N.Y.: Doubleday, 1963.

———. "Sociology and Freedom." *American Sociologist* 6, no. 1 (February 1971) : 1–5.

Bergson, Abram. "A Reformulation of Certain Aspects of Welfare Economics." *Quarterly Journal of Economics* 52, no. 2 (February 1938) : 310–334.

———. *Essays in Normative Economics*. Cambridge, Mass.: Harvard University Press, 1966.

Bernal, John D. *The Social Function of Science*. Cambridge, Mass.: M.I.T. Press, 1967; first edition London: Routledge & Kegan Paul, 1939.

Biderman, Albert D. "Information ≠ Intelligence ≠ Enlightened Public Policy: Functions and Organization of Societal Feedback." *Policy Sciences* 1, no. 2 (Summer 1970) : 217–230.

Birch, Anthony H. *Representative and Responsible Government*. London: G. Allen and Unwin, 1964.

Bish, Robert L. *The Public Economy of Metropolitan Areas*. Chicago: Markham, 1971.

Bittner, Egon. "Radicalism and The Organization of Radical Movements." *American Sociological Review* 28, no. 6 (December 1963) : 928–940.

Black, Duncan. "On Arrow's Impossibility Theorem." *Journal of Law and Economics* 12, no. 2 (October 1969) : 227–248.

Blau, Peter M. "Critical Remarks on Weber's Theory of Authority." *American Political Science Review* 57, no. 2 (June 1963) : 305–316.

———. *Exchange and Power in Social Life*. New York: Wiley, 1964.

Boulding, Kenneth E. "Human Betterment and the Quality of Life." In Strumpel et al., eds., *Human Behavior in Economic Affairs*.

———. "The Network of Interdependence." Paper presented at the Public Choice Society, Chicago, February 19, 1970.

Bradburn, Norman. *The Structure of Psychological Well-Being*. Chicago: Aldine, 1969.

Bramson, Leon. *The Political Context of Sociology*. Princeton, N.J.: Princeton University Press, 1961.

Brandt, Richard B. "Personal Values and the Justification of Institutions." In Sidney Hook, ed., *Human Values and Economic Policy*.

Braybrooke, David. "From Economics to Aesthetics: The Rectification of Preferences," *Noûs* 8, no. 1 (March 1974), 13–24.

——. *Three Tests for Democracy*. New York: Random House, 1968.

——, and Lindblom, Charles E. *A Strategy of Decision*. New York: Free Press, 1970.

Brecht, Arnold. *Political Theory*. Princeton, N.J.: Princeton University Press, 1959.

Broad, C. D. "On the Function of False Hypotheses in Ethics." *Ethics* 26 (April 1916) : 377–397.

Brooks, Harvey. "The Scientific Adviser." In Robert Gilpin and Christopher Wright, eds., *Scientists and National Policy Making*. New York: Columbia University Press, 1964.

Buchanan, James M. *The Bases for Collective Action*. Morristown, N.J.: General Learning Press, 1971.

——. "Individual Choice in Voting and the Market." *Journal of Political Economy* 42, no. 4 (August 1954) : 334–343.

——. "The Institutional Structure of Externality." *Public Choice* 14 (Spring 1973) : 69–82.

——, and Tullock, Gordon. *The Calculus of Consent*. Ann Arbor: University of Michigan Press, 1962.

Bühler, Charlotte, and Allen, Melanie. *Introduction to Humanistic Psychology*. Monterey, Calif.: Brooks/Cole, 1972.

Burenstam Linder: *see* Linder.

Carnap, Rudolf. "The Elimination of Metaphysics Through Logical Analysis of Language." Translated by Arthur Pap. In Alfred J. Ayer, ed., *Logical Positivism*. New York: Free Press, 1959.

Carroll, James D. "Participatory Technology." *Science* 171, no. 3972 (February 19, 1971) : 647–653.

Cavell, Stanley. "Must We Mean What We Say?" *Inquiry* 1, no. 3 (Autumn 1958) : 172–212. Reprinted in Chappell.

Chappell, Vere C., ed. *Ordinary Language*. Englewood Cliffs, N.J.: Prentice-Hall, 1964.

Charlesworth, James C., ed. *Integration of the Social Sciences Through Policy Analysis*. Philadelphia: American Academy of Political and Social Science, 1972.

Chase, Edward T. "Politics and Technology." *Yale Review* 52, no. 3 (March 1963) : 321–339.

Chase, Samuel B., ed. *Problems in Public Expenditure Analysis.* Washington, D.C.: Brookings, 1968.

Clapp, Charles L. *The Congressman: His Work as He Sees It.* Washington: Brookings, 1963.

Clausen, John A. "Values, Norms, and the Health Called 'Mental': Purposes and Feasibility of Assessment." In S. B. Sells, ed., *The Definition and Measurement of Mental Health.*

Coase, R. H. "The Nature of the Firm." *Economica,* New Series 4, no. 16 (November 1937) : 386–405.

―――. "The Problem of Social Cost." *Journal of Law and Economics* 3 (1960) : 1–44.

Coleman, James Samuel. "Collective Decisions." *Sociological Inquiry* 34, no. 2 (Spring 1964) : 166–181.

―――. "Inequality, Sociology, and Moral Philosophy." *American Journal of Sociology* 80, no. 3 (November 1974) : 739–764.

―――. "Internal Processes Governing Party Positions in Elections." *Public Choice* 11 (Fall 1971) : 35–60.

―――. "Loss of Power." *American Sociological Review* 38, no. 1 (February 1973) : 1–17.

―――. *Policy Research in the Social Sciences.* Morristown, N.J.: General Learning Press, 1972.

―――. "Political Money." *American Political Science Review* 64, no. 4 (December 1970) : 1074–1087.

―――. "The Possibility of a Social Welfare Function." *American Economic Review* 46, no. 5 (December 1966) : 1105–1122.

―――. *Power and The Structure of Society.* New York: Norton, 1974.

―――, et al. *Equality of Educational Opportunity.* Washington, D.C.: U.S. Government Printing Office, 1966.

Converse, Philip E. "The Nature of Belief Systems in Mass Publics." In David E. Apter, ed., *Ideology and Discontent.* New York: Free Press, 1964.

Cropsey, Joseph. "Conservatism and Liberalism." In Robert A. Goldwin, ed., *Left, Right, and Center.* Chicago: Rand McNally, 1967.

―――. "The Moral Basis of International Action." In Robert A. Goldwin, ed., *America Armed.* Chicago: Rand McNally, 1963.

―――. *Polity and Economy.* The Hague: Martinus Nijhoff, 1957.

―――. "Radicalism and Its Roots." *Public Policy* 18, no. 3 (Spring 1970) : 301–319.

―――. "What Is Welfare Economics?" *Ethics* 55, no. 2 (January 1955): 116–125.

Curry, R. L., Jr., and Wade, L. L. *A Theory of Political Exchange*. Englewood Cliffs, N.J.: Prentice-Hall, 1968.

Curtis, Richard M. "Decision Rules and Collective Values in Constitutional Choice. In Richard G. Niemi and Herbert Weisberg, eds., *Probability Models of Voting Bodies*. Columbus, Ohio: Charles E. Merrill, 1972.

Cyert, Richard M., and Hedrick, Charles M. "Theory of the Firm: Past, Present, and Future: An Interpretation." *Journal of Economic Literature* 10, no. 2 (June 1972) : 398–412.

Dahl, Robert A. *A Preface to Democratic Theory*. Chicago: University of Chicago Press, 1956.

Dahrendorf, Ralf. *Essays in the Theory of Society*. Stanford, Calif.: Stanford University Press, 1968.

————. *Society and Democracy in Germany*. New York: Doubleday, 1967.

Dallmayr, Fred R. "Toward a Critical Reconstruction of Ethics and Politics." *Journal of Politics* 36, no. 4 (November 1974) : 926–957.

Daniels, George H. "The Pure-Science Ideal and Democratic Culture." *Science* 156, no. 3783 (June 30, 1967) : 1699–1705.

Davis, Otto A., and Hinich, Melvin. "A Mathematical Model of Policy Formation in a Democratic Society." In Joseph L. Bernd, ed., *Mathematical Applications in Political Science II*. Dallas, Texas: Arnold Foundation Monograph XVI, Southern Methodist University, 1966.

Daudt, H. *Floating Voters and the Floating Vote*. Leiden: Steinfert Kroese, 1961.

De Meyer, Frank, and Plott, Charles R. "The Probability of a Cyclical Majority." *Econometrica* 38, no. 2 (March 1970) : 345–354.

————, and ————. "A Welfare Function Using 'Relative Intensity' of Preference." *Quarterly Journal of Economics* 85, no. 1 (February 1971) : 179–186.

De Santillana: *see* Santillana.

Dewey, John. *The Public and Its Problems*. Chicago: Gateway, 1946.

————. *Theory of Valuation*. International Encyclopedia of Unified Science 11, no. 4. Chicago: University of Chicago Press, 1939.

Dibble, Vernon K. "Occupations and Ideologies." *American Journal of Sociology* 68, no. 2 (September 1962) : 229–241.

Diesing, Paul. *Reason in Society*. Urbana, Ill.: University of Illinois Press, 1962.

Dolbeare, Kenneth M. "Public Policy Analysis and the Coming Struggle for the Soul of the Postbehavioral Revolution." In Philip Green and Sanford Levinson, eds., *Power and Community*. New York: Random House, 1970.

Dollard, John, and Miller, Neal E. *Personality and Psychotherapy*. New York: McGraw-Hill, 1950.

Douty, Christopher M. "Disasters and Charity: Some Aspects of Cooperative Economic Behavior." *American Economic Review* 62, no. 4 (September 1972) : 580–590.

Downs, Anthony. *An Economic Theory of Democracy*. New York: Harper & Row, 1957.

———. "In Defense of Majority Voting." *Journal of Political Economy* 69, no. 2 (April 1961) : 192–199.

Duncan, Otis Dudley. "Path Analysis: Sociological Examples." *American Journal of Sociology* 72, no. 1 (July 1966) : 1–16.

Dupuit, Jules. "De la Mesure de l'utilité des travaux publics." *Annales des Ponts et Chaussées* 8 (1844). Reprinted in translation in Arrow and Scitovsky, eds., *Readings in Welfare Economics,* as "On the Measurement of the Utility of Public Works."

Durkheim, Émile. *The Division of Labor in Society*. Translated by George Simpson. New York: Free Press, 1947.

———. *Rules of Sociological Method*. Translated by Sarah A. Solovay and John H. Mueller. Chicago: University of Chicago Press, 1938.

Easterlin, Richard A. "Does Money Buy Happiness?" *The Public Interest* 30 (Winter 1973) : 3–10.

Easton, David. *The Political System*. 2d ed., New York: Knopf, 1971.

———. *A Systems Analysis of Political Life*. New York: Wiley, 1965.

Eckert, Roland. *Wissenschaft und Demokratie*. Tübingen: J.C.B. Mohr, 1971.

Edel, Abraham. *Science and the Structure of Ethics*. In *International Encyclopedia of Unified Science,* 11, no. 3. Chicago: University of Chicago Press, 1961.

Edel, May, and Edel, Abraham. *Anthropology and Ethics*. Rev. ed. Cleveland: Case Western Reserve Press, 1968.

Edelman, Murray. *The Symbolic Uses of Politics*. Urbana, Ill.: University of Illinois Press, 1964.

Edgeworth, Francis Y. *Mathematical Psychics*. London: London School of Economics and Political Science, 1881.

Einstein, Albert. *Relativity—A Richer Truth*. Boston: Beacon, 1950.

Ellis, Desmond P. "The Hobbesian Problem of Order: A Critical Appraisal of the Normative Solution," *American Sociological Review* 36, no. 4 (August 1971) : 692–703.

Ellul, Jacques. *The Technological Society*. Translated by John Wilkinson. New York: Vintage Books, 1964.

Erikson, Erik H. *Insight and Responsibility.* New York: Norton, 1964.

Etzioni, Amitai. *The Active Society.* New York: Free Press, 1968.

Etzkowitz, Henry. "Institution Formation Sociology." *American Sociologist* 5, no. 2 (May 1970) : 120–124.

Farquharson, Robin. *Theory of Voting.* New Haven, Conn.: Yale University Press, 1969.

Federal Inter-Agency River Basin Committee. *Proposed Practices for Economic Analysis of River Basin Projects.* Washington, D.C.: U.S. Government Printing Office, 1950.

Feibleman, James K. *An Introduction to Peirce's Philosophy.* New York: Harper, 1946.

Feinberg, Gerald. *The Prometheus Project.* Garden City, N.Y.: Doubleday, 1969.

Fennessey, James. "Some Problems and Possibilities in Policy-Oriented Social Research." *Social Science Research* 1, no. 4 (December 1972) : 359–383.

Fenno, Richard F., Jr. *The Power of the Purse.* Boston: Little, Brown, 1966.

Ferber, Robert. "Consumer Economics: A Survey." *Journal of Economic Literature* 11, no. 4 (December 1973) : 1303–1342.

Ferejohn, John A. *Pork Barrel Politics.* Stanford, Calif.: Stanford University Press, 1974.

Fishburn, Peter C. "The Theory of Representative Majority Decision." *Econometrica* 39, no. 2 (March 1971) : 273–284.

———. *The Theory of Social Choice.* Princeton, N.J.: Princeton University Press, 1973.

Flathman, Richard E. *The Public Interest.* New York: Wiley, 1966.

Fleming, J. Marcus. "A Cardinal Concept of Welfare." *Quarterly Journal of Economics* 66, no. 3 (August 1952) : 366–384.

Foster, C. D., and Beesley, M. E. "Estimating the Social Benefit of Constructing an Underground Railway in London." *Journal of the Royal Statistical Society,* Series A, 126, part I (1963) : 46–92. Reprinted in Arrow and Scitovsky, eds., *Readings in Welfare Economics.*

Frankena, William K. *Ethics.* Englewood Cliffs, N.J.: Prentice-Hall, 1963.

Freidson, Eliot. *Profession of Medicine.* New York: Dodd, Mead, 1970.

Freud, Sigmund. *New Introductory Lectures on Psycho-Analysis.* Translated by W. J. H. Sprott. New York: Norton, 1933.

Friedrichs, Robert W. "Dialectical Sociology: Toward a Resolution of the Current 'Crisis' in Sociology." *British Journal of Sociology* 23, no. 3 (September 1972) : 263–274.

————. *A Sociology of Sociology.* New York: Free Press, 1970.
Frohlich, Norman, Oppenheimer, Joe A., and Young, Oran R. *Political Leadership and Collective Goods.* Princeton, N.J.: Princeton University Press, 1971.
Fromm, Erich. *Man for Himself.* New York: Rinehart, 1947.
————. *The Sane Society.* New York: Rinehart, 1955.
Galbraith, John K. *The New Industrial State.* New York: Houghton Mifflin Co., 1967.
————. "Power and the Useful Economist." *American Economic Review* 63, no. 1 (March 1973) : 1–11.
Garfinkel, Harold. *Studies in Ethnomethodology.* Englewood Cliffs, N.J.: Prentice-Hall, 1967.
Gerth, Hans H., and Mills, C. Wright, eds. *From Max Weber: Essays in Sociology.* New York: Oxford, 1946.
Gewirth, Alan. "Categorial Consistency in Ethics." *Philosophical Quarterly* 17, no. 69 (October 1967) : 289–299.
————. "The Generalization Principle." *Philosophical Review* 73, no. 2 (April 1964) : 229–242.
————. "Positive 'Ethics' and Normative 'Science'." *Philosophical Review* 69 (July 1960) : 311–330.
Gibbs, Jack P. "Norms: The Problem of Definition and Classification." *American Journal of Sociology* 70, no. 5 (March 1965), 586–594.
Gilpin, Robert. *American Scientists and Nuclear Weapons Policy.* Princeton, N.J.: Princeton University Press, 1962.
Gintis, Herbert M. "Alienation and Power: Towards a Radical Welfare Economics." Doctoral dissertation, Harvard University, 1969.
————. "Neo-Classical Welfare Economics and Individual Development." *Occasional Papers of the Union of Radical Political Economists* No. 3 (July 1970).
Goldworth, Amnon. "Bentham's Concept of Pleasure: Its Relation to Fictitious Terms." *Ethics* 82, no. 4 (July 1972) : 334–343.
Goodall, Kenneth. "Shapers at Work." *Psychology Today* 6, no. 6 (November 1972) : 53–138.
Goodman, Leo A., and Markowitz, Harry. "Social Welfare Functions Based on Individual Rankings." *American Journal of Sociology* 58, no. 3 (November 1952) : 257–262.
Goodwin, Leonard. "The Historical-Philosophical Basis for Uniting Social Science with Social Problem-Solving." *Philosophy of Science* 29, no. 4 (October 1962) : 377–392.
Gottlieb, Gidon. *The Logic of Choice.* New York: Macmillan, 1968.

Gouldner, Alvin W. *The Coming Crisis of Western Sociology.* New York: Basic Books, 1970.

———. "Explorations in Applied Social Science." *Social Problems* 3, no. 3 (January 1956) : 169–181.

———. "Metaphysical Pathos and the Theory of Bureaucracy." *American Political Science Review* 49, no. 2 (June 1955) : 496–507.

———. "The Norm of Reciprocity: A Preliminary Statement." *American Sociological Review* 25, no. 2 (April 1960) : 161–178.

———. "The Sociologist as Partisan: Sociology and the Welfare State." *American Sociologist* 3, no. 2 (May 1968) : 103–116.

Graaff, J. de V. *Theoretical Welfare Economics.* Cambridge: University Press, 1967.

Greene, Kenneth V., Neenan, William B., and Scott, Claudia D. *Fiscal Interactions in a Metropolitan Area.* Lexington, Mass: Lexington Books, 1974.

Grofman, Bernard. "Some Notes on Voting Schemes and the Will of the Majority." *Public Choice* 7 (Fall 1969) : 65–80.

Gunnell, John G. "Reason and Commitment." In his *Philosophy, Science and Political Inquiry.* Morristown, N.J.: General Learning Press, 1974.

Haberer, Joseph. *Politics and the Community of Science.* New York: Van Nostrand Reinhold, 1969.

Habermas, Jürgen. *Theory and Practice.* Translated by John Viertel. Boston: Beacon Press, 1973.

———. *Toward a Rational Society.* Translated by Jeremy J. Shapiro. Boston: Beacon Press, 1970.

Hagstron, Warren O. *The Scientific Community.* New York: Basic Books, 1965.

Halévy, Elie. *The Growth of Philosophic Radicalism.* Translated by Mary Morris. Boston: Beacon Press, 1955.

Halleck, Seymour L. *The Politics of Therapy.* New York: Science House, 1971.

Hallowell, John H. *The Moral Foundation of Democracy.* Chicago: University of Chicago Press, 1954.

Halperin, Morton H. *Bureaucratic Politics and Foreign Policy.* Washington, D.C.: Brookings, 1974.

Hamilton, James L. "The Demand for Cigarettes: Advertising, the Health Scare, and Perspectives on the Cigarette Advertising Ban," *Review of Economics and Statistics* 54, no. 4 (November 1972) : 401–411.

Hansen, Thomas J., and Prince, Barry L. "The Paradox of Voting." *Public Choice* 15 (Summer 1973) : 103–117.

Harberger, Arnold C. "Three Basic Postulates for Applied Welfare Economics: An Interpretive Essay." *Journal of Economic Literature* 9, no. 3 (September 1971) : 785–797.

Hare, R. M. *Freedom and Reason.* New York: Oxford University Press, 1965.

Harsanyi, John C. "Cardinal Welfare, Individualistic Ethics, and Interpersonal Comparisons of Utility." *Journal of Political Economy* 63, no. 4 (August 1955) : 309–321.

Hart, Herbert L. A. *The Concept of Law.* Oxford: Clarendon Press, 1961.

Hartmann, Heinz. *Psychoanalysis and Moral Values.* New York: International Universities Press, 1960.

Hartz, Louis. *The Liberal Tradition in America.* New York: Harcourt Brace and World, 1955.

Haveman, Robert H., and Margolis, Julius, eds. *Public Expenditures and Policy Analysis.* Chicago: Markham, 1970.

Haveman, Robert H., and Weisbrod, Burton A. "Defining Benefits of Public Programs: Some Guidance for Policy Analysts," *Policy Analysis* 1, no. 1 (Winter 1975) : 169–196.

Heidenheimer, Arnold J., ed. *Political Corruption.* New York: Holt, Rinehart, and Winston, 1970.

Helle, Horst J. "Knowledge and Action in Sociological Theory." *Mens en Maatschappij* 42, no. 3 (May–June 1967), 196–205.

Henriot, Peter J. "Political Questions about Social Indicators." *Western Political Quarterly* 23, no. 2 (June 1970) : 235–255.

Hersch, Charles. "Social History, Mental Health, and Community Control." *American Psychologist* 27, no. 8 (August 1972) : 749–854.

Hicks, John R. "The Foundations of Welfare Economics." *Economic Journal* 49, no. 4 (December 1939) : 696–712.

———. *Value and Capital.* Oxford: Clarendon Press, 1939.

Hildreth, Clifford. "Alternative Conditions for Social Orderings." *Econometrica* 21, no. 1 (January 1953) : 81–94.

Hinich, Melvin J., and Ordeshook, Peter C. "Social Welfare and Electoral Competition in Democratic Societies." *Public Choice* 11 (Fall 1971) : 73–87.

Hirschman, Albert O. *Exit, Voice, and Loyalty.* Cambridge, Mass.: Harvard University Press, 1970.

Hitch, Charles J., and Roland N. McKean. *The Economics of Defense in the Nuclear Age.* New York: Atheneum, 1969.

Hochman, Harold M. "Rule Change and Transitional Equity." In H. M. Hochman and George E. Peterson, eds., *Redistribution Through Public Choice.* New York: Columbia University Press, 1974, chapter 2.

Hochman, Harold M., and Rodgers, James D. "Pareto Optimal Redistribution." *American Economic Review* 49, no. 4, part 1 (September 1969) : 542–557.

Hook, Sidney, ed. *Human Values and Economic Policy*. New York: New York University Press, 1967.

Hopper, Janice H. "Changing Social Roles as a Goal of Public Policy: Use of an Evolving Model for Analyzing the Processes of Role Change." *American Sociologist* 6 (Supplementary issue, June 1971) : 48–54.

Horowitz, Irving L. *Professing Sociology*. Chicago: Aldine, 1968.

Hughes, Everett C. "Professions." In Kenneth C. Lynn and the editors of *Daedalus*, eds., *The Professions in America*. Boston: Beacon, 1964.

Hume, David. *A Treatise of Human Nature*. Edited by L. H. Selby-Bigge. Oxford: Clarendon Press, 1896.

Hunter, Floyd, *Community Power Structure*. Chapel Hill, N.C.: University of North Carolina Press, 1953.

Hunter, J.F.M. "The Possibility of a Rational Strategy of Moral Persuasion," *Ethics* 84, no. 3 (April 1974) : 185–200.

Huxley, Aldous L. *Brave New World*. Garden City, N.Y.: The Sun Dial Press, 1932.

Hyman, Herbert H. "Interviewing as a Scientific Procedure." In Daniel Lerner and Harold D. Lasswell, eds., *The Policy Sciences*.

International Encyclopedia of Unified Science. Chicago: University of Chicago Press, 1938–1969. Two vols., issued in separate parts.

James, Estelle, and Nordell, Lawrence P. "Preference Transformations and Welfare Theory." Working Paper No. 22A. Department of Economics, State University of New York at Stony Brook, 1971.

Janowitz, Morris. *Institution Building in Urban Education*. New York: Russell Sage Foundation, 1969.

————. "Sociological Models and Social Policy." *Archiv für Rechts- und Sozialphilosophie* 55, no. 3 (August 1969) : 305–321. Reprinted in his *Political Conflict*. Chicago: Quadrangle Books, 1970.

Jencks, Christopher, and Riesman, David. *The Academic Revolution*. Garden City, N.Y.: Doubleday, 1968.

Joergensen, Joergen. *The Development of Logical Empiricism*. *International Encyclopedia of Unified Science* II, no. 9. Chicago: University of Chicago Press, 1951.

Johnson, Harry G. "The Economic Approach to Social Questions." *Economica* 35, no. 137 (February 1968) : 1–21.

Jouvenel, Bertrand de. *Sovereignty*. Chicago: University of Chicago Press, 1957.

Jouvenel, Robert de. *La République des camarades*. Paris: Grasset, 1914.

Kaldor, Nicholas. "Welfare Propositions of Economics and Interpersonal Comparisons of Utility." *Economic Journal* 49, no. 3 (September 1939) : 549–552.

Kant, Immanuel. *Fundamental Principles of the Metaphysic of Morals.* Chicago: Regnery, 1949.

Kaplan, Abraham. *The Conduct of Inquiry.* San Francisco: Chandler, 1964.

Katona, George. "What Is Consumer Psychology?" *American Psychologist* 22, no. 3 (March 1967) : 219–226.

Keith-Lucas, Alan. "The Political Theory Implicit in Social Casework Theory." *American Political Science Review* 47, no. 4 (December 1953) : 1076–1091.

Kemeny, John G. "A Philosopher Looks at Political Science." *Journal of Conflict Resolution* 4, no. 3 (September 1960) : 292–302.

Kemp, Murray, and Asimakopolos, A. "A Note on Social Welfare Functions and Cardinal Utility." *Canadian Journal of Economics and Political Science* 18, no. 2 (May 1952) : 195–200.

Kendall, Willmoore. "The Open Society and Its Fallacies." *American Political Science Review* 54, no. 4 (December 1960) : 972–979.

————, and Carey, George W. "The 'Intensity' Problem and Democratic Theory." *American Political Science Review,* 62, no. 1 (March, 1968) : 5–24.

Key, V. O., Jr. *The Responsible Electorate..* Cambridge, Mass.: Belknap Press, 1966.

Keynes, John Maynard. *The General Theory of Employment, Interest and Money.* London: Macmillan, 1936.

Kingsley, J. Donald. *Representative Bureaucracy.* Yellow Springs, Ohio: Antioch, 1944.

Knight, Frank H. "The Ethics of Competition." *Quarterly Journal of Economics* 37 (1923) : 579–624. Reprinted in his *The Ethics of Competition and Other Essays.* New York: Harper, 1935.

————. "Some Fallacies in the Interpretation of Social Cost." *Quarterly Journal of Economics* 38, no. 4 (August 1924) : 582–606.

Knowledge into Action: Improving the Nation's Use of the Social Sciences. Report of the Special Commission on the Social Sciences of the National Science Board. Washington, D.C.: U.S. Government Printing Office, 1969.

Kohlberg, Lawrence. "Development of Moral Character and Moral Ideology." In *Review of Child Development Research,* vol. I. New York : Russell Sage Foundation, 1964.

Kolakowski, Leszek. *The Alienation of Reason.* Translated by Norbert Guterman. Garden City, N.Y.: Doubleday, 1968.

Kornhauser, William. *The Politics of Mass Society*. New York: Free Press, 1959.

―――. *Scientists in Industry*. Berkeley, Calif.: University of California Press, 1963.

Kramer, Gerald H. "On a Class of Equilibrium Conditions for Majority Rule." *Econometrica* 41, no. 2 (March 1973) : 285–297.

―――. "A Dynamical Model of Political Equilibrium." Cowles Foundation Discussion Paper No. 396. New Haven, Conn., 1975.

Kress, Paul F. "The Web and the Tree: Metaphors of Reason and Value." *Midwest Journal of Political Science* 13, no. 3 (August 1969) : 395–414.

Krislov, Samuel, *Representative Bureaucracy*. Englewood Cliffs, N.J.: Prentice-Hall, 1974.

Kruskal, William H., ed. *Mathematical Sciences and Social Sciences*. Englewood Cliffs, N.J.: Prentice-Hall, 1970.

Kuhn, Thomas S. *The Structure of Scientific Revolutions*. 2d ed. Chicago: University of Chicago Press, 1970.

Laing, Ronald David. *The Politics of the Family and Other Essays*. New York: Random House, 1972.

Lancaster, Kelvin. "A New Approach to Consumer Theory." *Journal of Political Economy* 74, no. 2 (April 1966), 132–157.

Land, Kenneth C. "Social Indicator Models: An Overview." In Kenneth C. Land and Seymour Spilerman, eds., *Social Indicator Models*. New York: Russell Sage Foundation, 1975.

Landauer, Carl. "On the Social Rate of Discount: Comment." *American Economic Review* 59, no. 5 (December 1969) : 917–918.

Lasswell, Harold D. "The Garrison State." *American Journal of Sociology* 46, no. 4 (January 1941) : 455–468.

―――. "Policy Sciences." In David L. Sills, ed. *International Encyclopedia of Social Science*. New York: Free Press, 1968.

Lazarsfeld, Paul F., and Reitz, Jeffrey G. *An Introduction to Applied Sociology*. New York: Elsevier, 1975.

Leifer, Ronald. *In the Name of Mental Health*. New York: Science House, 1969.

Lenk, Hans. "Der 'Ordinary Language Approach' und die Neuträlitatsthese der Metaethik." In Hans-Georg Gadamer, ed., *Das Problem der Sprache*. Munich: Wilhelm Fink Verlag, 1967 : 183–206.

Lerner, Daniel, and Lasswell, Harold D. eds. *The Policy Sciences*. Stanford, Calif.: Stanford University Press, 1951.

Levi, Edward H. *An Introduction to Legal Reasoning*. Chicago: University of Chicago Press, 1961.

Levins, Richard. "Fundamental and Applied Research in Agriculture." *Science* 181, no. 4099 (August 10, 1973) : 523–524.

Lewis, Clarence I. *An Analysis of Knowledge and Valuation.* La Salle, Ill.: Open Court, 1946.

Lindblom, Charles E. "Intergration of Economics and the Other Social Sciences Through Policy Analysis." In James C. Charlesworth, ed., *Integration of the Social Sciences Through Policy Analysis.*

————. *The Intelligence of Democracy.* New York: Free Press, 1965.

Linder, Staffan Burenstam. *The Harried Leisure Class.* New York: Columbia University Press, 1970.

Lindsay, A. D. *The Modern Democratic State.* New York: Oxford University Press, 1962.

Lippmann, Walter. *The Phantom Public.* New York: Harcourt, Brace, 1925.

————. *The Public Philosophy.* New York: Mentor, 1956.

Lipset, Seymour M. *Political Man: The Social Bases of Politics.* Garden City, N.Y.: Doubleday, 1960.

————, and Ladd, Everett M. "The Profession: Faculty Opinion Survey." *P.S.* 3 (Summer 1970) : 382–386.

———— and Rokkan, Stein, eds. *Party Systems and Voter Alignments.* New York: Free Press, 1967.

Lipsey, R. G., and Lancaster, Kelvin. "The General Theory of Second Best." *Review of Economic Studies* 24 (1956) : 11–32.

Little, Ian Malcolm David. *A Critique of Welfare Economics.* Oxford: Clarendon Press, 1950.

Lowi, Theodore J. "American Business, Public Policy, Case-Studies, and Political Theory." *World Politics* 16, no. 4 (July 1964) : 677–715.

————. *The End of Liberalism.* New York: Norton, 1969.

Luce, R. Duncan, and Raiffa, Howard. *Games and Decisions.* New York: Wiley, 1957.

Maass, Arthur A. "Benefit-Cost Analysis: Its Relevance to Public Investment Decisions." *Quarterly Journal of Economics* 80, no. 2 (May 1966) : 208–226.

Machlup, Fritz. "Are the Social Sciences Really Inferior?" *Southern Economic Journal* 27, no. 3 (January 1961), 173–184.

MacKaye, James. "Convictionism vs. Non-convictionism." *International Journal of Ethics* 39, no. 1 (October 1928) : 15–40.

Macpherson, C. B. *The Political Theory of Possessive Individualism: Hobbes to Locke.* New York: Oxford University Press, 1964.

MacRae, Duncan, Jr. "Careers, Science, and Politics." *Bulletin of the Atomic Scientists* 22, no. 2 (February 1966) : 26–28.

MacRae, Duncan, Jr. "A Dilemma of Sociology: Science Versus Policy." *American Sociologist* 6 (Supplementary issue, June 1971) : 2–7.

———. *Dimensions of Congressional Voting, University of California Publications in Sociology and Social Institutions* 1, no. 3. Berkeley, Calif.: University of California Press, 1958.

———. "Justice, Normative Discourse, and Sociology." A review of John Rawls's *A Theory of Justice. Contemporary Sociology* 2, no. 2 (March 1973) : 129–132.

———. *Parliament, Parties and Society in France 1946–1958*. New York: St. Martin's, 1967.

———. "Science and the Formation of Policy in a Democracy." *Minerva* 11, no. 2 (April 1973) : 228–242.

———. "Scientific Communication, Ethical Argument, and Public Policy." *American Political Science Review* 65, no. 1 (March 1971) : 38–50.

———. "Social Science and the Sources of Policy: 1951–1970." *P.S.* 3, no. 3 (Summer 1970) : 294–309.

———. "Sociology in Public Policy Analysis." In Stuart S. Nagel, ed., *Policy Studies and the Social Sciences*. Lexington, Mass.: Lexington-Heath, 1975.

———. "Some Political Choices in the Development of Communications Technology." In H. Sackman and Norman Nie, eds., *The Information Utility and Social Choice*. Montvale, N.J.: AFIPS Press, 1970.

———. "Utilitarian Ethics and Social Change." *Ethics* 78, no. 3 (April 1968) : 188–198.

Mannheim, Karl. *Ideology and Utopia*. New York: Harcourt, Brace, 1936.

Marcuse, Herbert. *One-Dimensional Man*. Boston: Beacon Press, 1964.

Margenau, Henry. *Ethics and Science*. Princeton, N.J.: Van Nostrand, 1964.

Margolis, Joseph. *Psychotherapy and Morality*. New York: Random House, 1966.

Margolis, Julius, ed. *The Analysis of Public Output*. New York: Columbia University Press and National Bureau of Economic Research, 1970.

Marschak, Jacob. "Towards an Economic Theory of Organization and Information." In R. M. Thrall, C. H. Coombs, and R. L. Davis, *Decision Processes*. New York: Wiley, 1954.

Maslow, Abraham H. *The Farther Reaches of Human Nature*. New York: Viking Press, 1971.

———. *Toward a Psychology of Being*. New York: Van Nostrand, 1968.

Mates, Benson. "On the Verification of Statements about Ordinary Language." *Inquiry* 1, no. 3 (Autumn 1958) : 161–171. Reprinted in Vere C. Chappell, ed. *Ordinary Language*.

Mayhew, David R. *Congress: The Electoral Connection.* New Haven: Yale University Press, 1974.

Mayo, Henry B. *An Introduction to Democratic Theory.* New York: Oxford University Press, 1960.

McConnell, Grant. *Private Power and American Democracy.* New York: Knopf, 1966.

McDermott, John. "Technology, The Opiate of the Intellectuals." *New York Review of Books* 13, no. 2 (July 31, 1969) : 25–35.

McPhee, William N. *Formal Theories of Mass Behavior.* New York: Free Press, 1962.

Mead, George H. *Mind, Self, and Society,* edited by Charles W. Morris. Chicago: University of Chicago Press, 1934.

Meade, James E. "External Economies and Diseconomies in a Competitive Situation." *Economic Journal* 62, no. 1 (March 1952) : 54–67.

Mechanic, David. *Mental Health and Social Policy.* Englewood Cliffs, N.J.: Prentice-Hall, 1969.

Meehan, Eugene. *Value Judgment and Social Science.* Homewood, Ill.: Dorsey, 1969.

Melnik, Constantin, and Leites, Nathan. *The House Without Windows.* Evanston, Ill.: Row, Peterson, 1958.

Meltsner, Arnold. "Political Feasibility and Policy Analysis." *Public Administration Review* 32, no. 6 (November–December 1972) : 859–867.

Merriam, Charles E., and Gosnell, Harold F. *Non-Voting.* Chicago: University of Chicago Press, 1924.

Merton, Robert K. *Social Theory and Social Structure.* Enlarged ed. New York: Free Press, 1968.

Michels, Robert. *Political Parties.* Translated by Eden and Cedar Paul. New York: Free Press, 1949.

Mill, John Stuart. *Utilitarianism, Liberty, and Representative Government.* London: Dent, 1910.

Mishan, E. J., *Economics for Social Decisions.* New York: Praeger, 1973.

———. "The Postwar Literature on Externalities: An Interpretative Essay." *Journal of Economic Literature* 9, no. 1 (March 1971) : 1–28.

———. "A Survey of Welfare Economics, 1939–59." *Economic Journal* 70, no. 278 (June 1960) : 197–265.

Misiak, Henryk, and Sexton, Virginia S. *History of Psychology: An Overview.* New York: Grune & Stratton, 1966.

Moore, George Edward. *Principia Ethica.* Cambridge: University Press, 1903.

Moore, Wilbert E. "The Utility of Utopias." *American Sociological Review* 31, no. 6 (December 1966) : 765–772.

Morison, Robert S. "Science and Social Attitudes." *Science* 165, no. 3889 (July 11, 1969) : 150–156.

Moynihan, Daniel P. *The Politics of a Guaranteed Income.* New York: Vintage, 1973.

Musgrave, Richard A. *Fiscal Systems.* New Haven, Conn.: Yale University Press, 1969.

————. *The Theory of Public Finance.* New York: McGraw-Hill, 1959.

Myrdal, Gunnar. *An American Dilemma.* New York: Harper, 1944.

Nadel, S. F. *The Theory of Social Structure.* London: Cohen & West, 1957.

Nader, Ralph. "The Scientist and His Indentured Professional Societies." *Bulletin of The Atomic Scientists* 28, no. 2 (February 1972) : 43–46.

Nagel, Ernest. *The Structure of Science.* New York: Harcourt, Brace and World, 1961.

National Science Foundation. *American Science Manpower 1970.* Washington, D.C.: U.S. Government Printing Office, 1971.

Neumann, John von, and Morgenstern, Oskar. *The Theory of Games and Economic Behavior.* Princeton, N.J.: Princeton University Press, 1944.

Nisbet, Robert A. *The Quest for Community.* New York: Oxford, 1953.

Niskanen, William A., Jr. *Bureaucracy and Representative Government.* Chicago: Aldine-Atherton, 1971.

Nordhaus, William, and Tobin, James. "Is Growth Obsolete?" National Bureau of Economic Research's *Fiftieth Anniversary Colloquium Series, Economic Research: Retrospect and Prospect,* General Series 96, vol. 5, *Economic Growth.* New York: Columbia University Press, 1972.

Okun, Arthur M. *The Political Economy of Prosperity.* New York: Norton, 1970.

Olsen, Edgar O. "A Normative Theory of Transfers." *Public Choice* 6 (Spring 1969) : 39–58.

Olson, Mancur, Jr. "The Economics of Integrative Systems." In Bernhard Külp and Wolfgang Stützel, *Beiträge zu einer Theorie der Sozialpolitik.* Berlin: Duncker & Humbolt, 1973.

————. "Economists, Sociologists, and the Best of All Possible Worlds." *The Public Interest* 12 (Summer 1968) : 96–118.

————. *The Logic of Collective Action.* Cambridge, Mass.: Harvard University Press, 1965.

————. "The Principle of 'Fiscal Equivalence.' " *American Economic Review* 59, no. 2 (May 1969) : 479–87.

———— and Richard J. Zeckhauser. "The Efficient Production of External Economies." *American Economic Review 60,* no. 3 (June 1970) : 512–517.

Ostrom, Vincent. *The Intellectual Crisis in American Public Administration.* University, Ala.: University of Alabama Press, 1973.

Owen, John D. "Education for Majority Voting?" *Public Choice* 6 (Spring 1969) : 59–70.

Pareto, Vilfredo. *Cours d'Économie Politique*. Lausanne: Rouge. Tome I, 1896; Tome II, 1897.

———. *Manuel d'Économie Politique*. Paris: Giard and Brière, 1909. Translated by Ann S. Schwier as *Manual of Political Economy*. New York: Kelley, 1971.

Parsons, Talcott. "The Problem of Controlled Institutional Change: An Essay on Applied Social Science." *Psychiatry* 8, no. 1 (February 1945) : 79–101. Reprinted in his *Essays in Sociological Theory*. New York: Free Press, 1954.

———. "The Professions and Social Structure." In his *Essays in Sociological Theory*. New York: Free Press, 1954.

———. "A Revised Analytical Approach to the Theory of Social Stratification." In his *Essays in Sociological Theory*. New York: Free Press, 1954.

———. *The Social System*. New York: Free Press, 1951.

———. *Structure and Process in Modern Societies*. New York: Free Press, 1960.

———. *The Structure of Social Action*. New York: McGraw-Hill, 1937.

———, and Platt, Gerald. "Considerations on the American Academic System." *Minerva* 6, no. 4 (Summer 1968), 497–523.

———, and Shils, Edward A., eds. *Toward a General Theory of Action*. Cambridge, Mass.: Harvard University Press, 1951.

———, and Smelser, Neil J. *Economy and Society*. New York: Free Press, 1956.

Pateman, Carole. *Participation and Democratic Theory*. Cambridge: University Press, 1970.

Pattanaik, Prasanta K. *Voting and Collective Choice*. Cambridge: University Press, 1971.

Pauly, Mark V. "Optimality, 'Public' Goods and Local Governments: A General Theoretical Analysis." *Journal of Political Economy* 78, no. 3 (May/June 1970) : 572–585.

Peirce, Charles S. *Collected Papers*. Cambridge, Mass.: Belknap Press, 1960.

Perrucci, Robert, and Gerstl, Joel E. *Profession Without Community: Engineers in American Society*. New York: Random House, 1969.

Perrucci, Robert, and Rothman, Robert A. "Obsolescence of Knowledge and the Professional Career." In Robert Perrucci and Joel E. Gerstl, eds., *The Engineers and the Social System*. New York: Wiley, 1969.

Piaget, Jean. *The Moral Judgment of the Child*. Translated by Marjorie Gabain. New York: Free Press, 1948.

Pigou, Arthur C. *The Economics of Welfare.* 4th ed., London: Macmillan, 1932.

Pitkin, Hanna. *The Concept of Representation.* Berkeley, Calif.: University of California Press, 1967.

Plato. *The Republic of Plato.* Translated by F. M. Cornford. New York: Oxford, 1945.

Poincaré, Henri. *Science and Method.* Translated by F. Maitland. New York: Dover, 1952.

Polanyi, Michael. *Personal Knowledge.* Chicago: University of Chicago Press, 1958.

————. "The Republic of Science: Its Political and Economic Theory." *Minerva* 1, no. 1 (Autumn 1962) : 54–73.

Pomeranz, John E., and Weil, Roman L. "The Cyclical Majority Problem." *Communications of the Association for Computing Machinery* 13, no. 4 (April 1970) : 251–254.

Popper, Karl R. *The Logic of Scientific Discovery.* New York: Harper & Row, 1968.

————. *The Open Society and Its Enemies.* 4th ed., New York: Harper & Row, 1963.

Price, Don K. *The Scientific Estate.* Cambridge, Mass.: Harvard University Press, 1965.

Rae, Douglas W. "Decision-Rules and Individual Values in Collective Choice." *American Political Science Review* 63, no. 1 (March 1969) : 40–56.

————, and Taylor, Michael. *The Analysis of Political Cleavages.* New Haven, Conn.: Yale University Press, 1970.

Raiffa, Howard. *Decision Analysis.* Reading, Mass: Addison-Wesley, 1968.

Rainwater, Lee, and Yancey, William L. *The Moynihan Report and the Politics of Controversy.* Cambridge, Mass.: M.I.T. Press, 1967.

Rawls, John. "Outline of a Decision Procedure for Ethics." *Philosophical Review* 60, no. 2 (April 1951) : 177–197.

————. *A Theory of Justice,* Cambridge, Mass.: Belknap Press, 1971.

————. "Two Concepts of Rules." *Philosophical Review* 44, no. 1 (January 1955) : 3–32.

Reagan, Michael D. "R & D: Suggestions for an Allocations Framework." *Public Administration Review* 27, no. 2 (June 1967), 104–111.

Reichenbach, Hans. *The Rise of Scientific Philosophy.* Berkeley, Calif.: University of California Press, 1951.

Reisman, John M. *The Development of Clinical Psychology.* New York: Appleton-Century-Crofts, 1966.

Rescher, Nicholas. *Distributive Justice*. Indianapolis: Bobbs-Merrill, 1966.

Rheinstein, Max, ed. *Max Weber on Law in Economy and Society*. Translated by Edward A. Shils and Max Rheinstein. Cambridge, Mass.: Harvard University Press, 1954.

Ribich, Thomas I. *Education and Poverty*. Washington, D.C.: Brookings, 1968.

Riecken, Henry W. "Social Sciences and Social Problems." *Social Science Information* 8, no. 1 (February 1969) : 101–129.

Rieff, Philip. *Freud: The Mind of the Moralist*. Garden City, N.Y.: Doubleday, 1961.

————. *The Triumph of the Therapeutic*. New York: Harper & Row, 1966.

Riker, William H. "Public Safety as a Public Good." In Eugene V. Rostow, ed., *Is Law Dead?* New York: Simon and Schuster, 1971.

————. "Voting and the Summation of Preferences." *American Political Science Review* 55, no. 4 (December 1961) : 900–911.

————, and Stephen J. Brams. "The Paradox of Vote Trading." *American Political Science Review* 67, no. 4 (December 1973) : 1235–1247.

————, and Ordeshook, Peter C. *An Introduction to Positive Political Theory*. Englewood Cliffs, N.J.: Prentice-Hall, 1973.

Robbins, Lionel. *An Essay on the Nature and Significance of Economic Science*. London: Macmillan, 1937.

Robinson, Daniel N. "Harm, Offense, and Nuisance: Some First Steps in the Establishment of an Ethics of Treatment." *American Psychologist* 29, no. 4 (April 1974) : 233–238.

Rogin, Michael P. *The Intellectuals and McCarthy*. Cambridge, Mass.: M.I.T. Press, 1967.

Ross, H. Laurence. "Law, Science, and Accidents: The British Road Safety Act of 1967." *Journal of Legal Studies* 2, no. 1 (January 1973) : 1–78.

Rossi, Peter H. "Researchers, Scholars, and Policy-Makers." *Daedalus* 93, no. 4 (Fall 1964) : 1142–1161.

Roszak, Theodore. *The Making of a Counter Culture*. Garden City, N.Y.: Doubleday, 1969.

Rothenberg, Jerome. *The Measurement of Social Welfare*. Englewood Cliffs, N.J.: Prentice-Hall, 1961.

Rousseau, Jean-Jacques. *The Social Contract and Discourses*. London: J. M. Dent, 1913.

Russell, Bertrand. *A History of Western Philosophy*. New York: Simon and Schuster, 1945.

Sabine, George H. "The Two Democratic Traditions." *Philosophical Review* 61, no. 4 (October 1952) : 451–474.

Samuelson, Paul A. *Economics*. New York: McGraw-Hill, 1970.
————. "Evaluation of Real National Income." *Oxford Economic Papers,*
N.S., 2, no. 1 (January 1950) : 1–29.
————. *Foundations of Economic Analysis*. New York: Atheneum, 1965.
————. "The Pure Theory of Public Expenditure." *Review of Economics and
Statistics* 36, no. 4 (November 1954) : 387–389.
————. "Social Indifference Curves." *Quarterly Journal of Economics* 70,
no. 1 (February 1956) : 1–22.
————. "The Two-Part Golden Rule Deduced as the Asymptotic Turnpike of
Catenary Motions." *Western Economic Journal* 6, no. 2 (March
1968) : 85–93.
Santillana, Giorgio de. *The Crime of Galileo*. Chicago: University of Chicago
Press, 1955.
Sartorius, Rolf. "The Justification of the Judicial Decision." *Ethics* 78, no. 3
(April 1968) : 171–187.
Schelling, Thomas. "The Life You Save May Be Your Own." In Samuel B.
Chase, ed., *Problems in Public Expenditure Analysis*.
Scherhorn, Gerhard and Wieken, Klaus. "On the Effect of Counter-Informa-
tion on Consumers." In Strumpel et al., eds., *Human Behavior in Eco-
nomic Affairs*.
Schick, Allen. "The Road to PPB: Stages of Budget Reform." *Public Ad-
ministration Review* 26, no. 4 (December 1966) : 243–258.
————. "Systems Politics and Systems Budgeting." *Public Administration
Review* 29, no. 2 (March/April 1969) : 137–151.
Schlick, Moritz. *Problems of Ethics*. Translated by David Rynin. New York:
Prentice-Hall, 1939.
Schmid, A. Allan. "Public Appropriations Structure and Performance: The
Case of PPBS in Water Resources." *Michigan State University Agricultural
Economics Report* no. 153 (January 1970).
Schultze, Charles L. *The Politics and Economics of Public Spending*. Wash-
ington, D.C.: Brookings, 1968.
————. "The Reviewers Reviewed." *American Economic Review* 61, no. 2
(May 1971) : 45–52.
Schumpeter, Joseph A. *Capitalism, Socialism, and Democracy*. New York:
Harper, 1950.
Schutz, Alfred. "The Well-Informed Citizen: An Essay on the Social Dis-
tribution of Knowledge." *Social Research* 13, no. 4 (December 1946),
463–472.
Scitovsky, Tibor. "A Note on Welfare Propositions in Economics." *Review
of Economic Studies* 9 (1941) : 77–88.

———. "What's Wrong with the Arts Is What's Wrong with Society." *American Economic Review* 62, no. 2 (May 1972) : 62–69.

Scott, Marvin B., and Lyman, Stanford M. "Accounts." *American Sociological Review* 33, no. 1 (February 1968) : 46–62.

Seeley, John R. *Americanization of the Unconscious*. New York: International Science Press, 1967.

Sells, S. B., ed. *The Definition and Measurement of Mental Health*. Washington, D.C.: National Center for Health Statistics, 1968.

Selznick, Philip. *Leadership in Administration*. Evanston, Ill.: Row, Peterson, 1957.

———. *The Organizational Weapon*. New York: Free Press, 1960.

Sewell, William H. "Inequality of Opportunity for Higher Education." *American Sociological Review* 36, no. 5 (October 1971), 793–809.

Sherif, Muzafer. *The Psychology of Social Norms*. New York: Harper, 1936.

Shils, Edward A. "The Calling of Sociology." In Talcott Parsons, Edward A. Shils, Kaspar D. Naegele, and Jesse R. Pitts, eds., *Theories of Society*. New York: Free Press, 1961.

———. "Concentration and Dispersion of Charisma: Their Bearing on Economic Policy in Underdeveloped Countries." *World Politics* 11, no. 1 (October 1958) : 1–19.

———. "The Intellectuals and the Future." *Bulletin of the Atomic Scientists* 23, no. 8 (October 1967) : 7–14. Reprinted in his *The Intellectuals and the Powers and Other Essays*. Chicago: University of Chicago Press, 1972.

———. *The Torment of Secrecy*. New York: Free Press, 1956.

Shryock, Richard H. "American Indifference to Basic Science during the Nineteenth Century." *Archives Internationales d'Histoire des Sciences* 28, no. 5 (October 1948) : 50–65.

Shubik, Martin. "Voting, or a Price System in a Competitive Market Structure." *American Political Science Review* 64, no. 1 (March 1970): 179–181.

Sidgwick, Henry. *The Methods of Ethics*. New York: Dover, 1966.

Sills, David L. *The Volunteers*. New York: Free Press, 1957.

Simon, Herbert A. "Theories of Decision-Making in Economics and Behavioral Science." *American Economic Review* 54, no. 3 (June 1959) : 253–283.

Simon, Julian L., "Interpersonal Welfare Comparisons Can Be Made—and Used for Redistribution Decisions." *Kyklos* 27, fasc. 1 (1974) : 63–98.

———. "Some Principles of Practical Welfare Economics." *Management Science* 13, no. 10 (June 1967) : B-621-630.

Simpson, Richard L. "Imperative Control, Associationism, and the Social

Order." In Herman Turk and Richard L. Simpson, eds., *Institutions and Social Exchange*. Indianapolis: Bobbs-Merrill, 1971.

Singer, Charles. *A Short History of Science to the Nineteenth Century*. Oxford: Clarendon Press, 1941.

Singer, Marcus G. *Generalization in Ethics*. New York: Knopf, 1961.

Skinner, Burrhus F. *Beyond Freedom and Dignity*. New York: Bantam/Vintage, 1972.

———. *Walden Two*. New York: Macmillan, 1948.

Skura, Barry. "SSSP, Valuative Discourse and the Ambivalence of Sociologists." Center for Social Organization Studies, paper no. 167. Chicago: University of Chicago, 1970.

Sloss, Judith. "Stable Outcomes in Majority Voting Games." *Public Choice* XV (Summer 1973) : 19–48.

Smart, J.J.C. "The Methods of Ethics and the Methods of Science." *Journal of Philosophy* 62, no. 13 (June 24, 1965) : 344–349.

Smelser, Neil J. "The Optimum Scope of Sociology." In Robert Bierstedt, ed., *A Design for Sociology*. Philadelphia: American Academy of Political and Social Science, 1969.

Smith, M. Brewster. "Competence and Mental Health: Problems of Conceptualizing Human Effectiveness." In S. B. Sells, ed., *The Definition and Measurement of Mental Health*.

———. *Social Psychology and Human Values*. Chicago: Aldine, 1969.

Smolensky, Eugene, Burton, Richard, and Tideman, Nicolaus. "The Efficient Provision of a Local Non-Private Good." *Geographical Analysis* 2, no. 4 (October 1970) : 330–342.

Solow, Robert M. "The Economics of Resources or the Resources of Economics." *American Economic Review* 64, no. 2 (May 1974) : 1–14.

Somit, Albert, and Tanenhaus, Joseph. *The Development of American Political Science*. Boston: Allyn & Bacon, 1967.

Srole, Leo. "Medical and Sociological Models in Assessing Mental Health." In S. B. Sells, ed., *The Definition and Measurement of Mental Health*.

Steiner, Jürg. *Amicable Agreement Versus Majority Rule*. Chapel Hill, N.C.: University of North Carolina Press, 1974.

Stigler, George J. "The Economics of Information." *Journal of Political Economy* 69, no. 3 (June 1961) : 213–225.

———. *Essays in The History of Economics*. Chicago: University of Chicago Press, 1965.

———. "The Theory of Economic Regulation." *Bell Journal of Economics and Management Science* 2, no. 1 (Spring 1971) : 3–21.

———. *The Theory of Price*. New York: Macmillan, 1946; 3d ed., 1966.

Stillman, Peter G., "The Limits of Behaviorism: A Review-Essay on B. F. Skinner's Social and Political Thought." *American Political Science Review* 69, no. 1 (March 1975) : 202–213.

Stinchcombe, Arthur L. "Norms of Exchange." In William Starbuck, ed., *Handbook of Organizational Design*. Amsterdam: Elsevier, in press.

Storer, Norman W. *The Social System of Science*. New York: Holt, Rinehart, & Winston, 1966.

Strauss, Leo. "Epilogue." In Herbert J. Storing, ed., *Essays on the Scientific Study of Politics*. New York: Holt, Rinehart, and Winston, 1962.

⸺. *Natural Right and History*. Chicago: University of Chicago Press, 1953.

Strumpel, Burkhard, Morgan, James N. and Zahn, Ernest, eds. *Human Behavior in Economic Affairs: Essays in Honor of George Katona*. San Francisco: Jossey-Bass, 1972.

Subramaniam, V. "Representative Bureaucracy: A Reassessment." *American Political Science Review* 61, no. 4 (December 1967): 1010–1019.

Sumner, William G. *Folkways*. Boston: Ginn, 1907.

Sutton, Francis X., Harris, Seymour E., Kaysen, Carl, and Tobin, James. *The American Business Creed.* Cambridge, Mass.: Harvard University Press, 1956.

Szasz, Thomas S. *Ideology and Insanity*. Garden City, N.Y.: Doubleday, 1970.

⸺. *The Myth of Mental Illness*. New York: Hoeber-Harper, 1961.

Tarascio, Vincent J. *Pareto's Methodological Approach to Economics*. Chapel Hill, N.C.: University of North Carolina Press, 1968.

Taylor, Michael. "Proof of a Theorem on Majority Rule." *Behavioral Science* 14 (1969) : 228–231.

Telser, Lester G. "Some Aspects of the Economics of Advertising." *Journal of Business of the University of Chicago* 41, no. 2 (April 1968) : 166–173.

Theil, Henri. *Optimum Decision Rules for Government and Industry*. Chicago: Rand McNally, 1964.

Toulmin, Stephen E. *An Examination of the Place of Reason in Ethics*. Cambridge: University Press, 1950.

Tullock, Gordon. "Entry Barriers in Politics." *American Economic Review* 55, no. 2 (May 1965) : 458–466.

⸺. "The General Irrelevance of the General Impossibility Theorem." *Quarterly Journal of Economics* 81, no. 2 (May 1967) : 256–270.

⸺. *Private Wants, Public Means*. New York: Basic Books, 1970.

⸺. "A Simple Algebraic Logrolling Model." *American Economic Review* 60, no. 3 (June 1970) : 419–426.

Tullock, Gordon. "The Social Rate of Discount and the Optimum Rate of Investment: Comment." *Quarterly Journal of Economics* 78, no. 3 (May 1964), 331–336.

———. *Toward a Mathematics of Politics*. Ann Arbor, Mich.: University of Michigan Press, 1967.

Tussman, Joseph. *Obligation and the Body Politic*. New York: Oxford, 1960.

Urmson, J. O. "The Interpretation of the Philosophy of J. S. Mill." *Philosophical Quarterly* 3, no. 10 (January 1953) : 33–40.

Von Neumann, John, and Morgenstern, Oskar: *see* Neumann.

Walsh, V. C. "Axiomatic Choice Theory and Values." In Sidney Hook, ed., *Human Values and Economic Policy*.

Walster, Elaine, Berscheid, Ellen, and Walster, G. William. "New Directions in Equity Research," *Journal of Personality and Social Psychology* 25, no. 2 (February 1973) : 151–176.

Ward, Benjamin. *What's Wrong with Economics?* New York: Basic Books, 1972.

Ward, Lester F. *Applied Sociology*. Boston: Ginn, 1906.

Watson, James D. *The Double Helix*. New York: New American Library, 1969.

Weaver, Thomas, ed. *To See Ourselves*. Glenview, Ill.: Scott, Foresman, 1973.

Weber, Max. *Economy and Society*. Edited by Guenther Roth and Claus Wittich. New York: Bedminster, 1968.

———. *The Methodology of the Social Sciences*. Translated and edited by Edward A. Shils and Henry A. Finch. New York: Free Press, 1949.

———. "Politics as a Vocation." In *From Max Weber: Essays in Sociology*, translated and edited by Hans H. Gerth and C. Wright Mills. New York: Oxford University Press, 1946 : 129–156.

———. *The Theory of Social and Economic Organization*. Translated by A. M. Henderson and Talcott Parsons, edited by Talcott Parsons. New York: Oxford University Press, 1947.

Weber, Max: *see also* Gerth and Mills.

Weinberg, Alvin M. *Reflections on Big Science*. Cambridge, Mass.: M.I.T. Press, 1967.

Weisbrod, Burton A. "Income Redistribution Effects and Benefit-Cost Analysis." In Samuel B. Chase, ed. *Problems in Public Expenditure Analysis*.

Wertheimer, Max. *Productive Thinking*. New York: Harper, 1945.

Wheeler, Gerald R. "Evaluating Social Programs: The Case for a State GAO." *Policy Studies Journal* 3, no. 4 (Summer 1975): 390–397.

White, Orion, Jr. *Psychic Energy and Organizational Change*. Beverly Hills, Calif.: Sage, 1973.

Whitehead, Alfred N. *Science and the Modern World*. New York: Mentor Books, 1948. Originally published 1925.

Wicksell, Knut. "A New Principle of Just Taxation." Translated by J. M. Buchanan. In Richard A. Musgrave and Alan T. Peacock, eds., *Classics in the Theory of Public Finance*. New York: St. Martin's, 1967.

Wicksteed, Philip H. *The Common Sense of Political Economy*. London: Macmillan, 1935.

Williams, Walter. *Social Policy Research and Analysis*. New York: American Elsevier, 1971.

Windham, Douglas M. *Education, Equality and Income Distribution*. Lexington, Mass.: D. C. Heath, 1970.

Wispé, Lauren G., ed. "Positive Forms of Social Behavior: An Overview." *Journal of Social Issues* 28, no. 3 (1972) : 1–19.

Wittgenstein, Ludwig. *Tractatus Logico-Philosophicus*. Translated by C. K. Ogden and F. P. Ramsey. London: Routledge and Kegan Paul, 1922.

Wolff, Robert Paul. *The Poverty of Liberalism*. Boston: Beacon Press, 1968.

Wolin, Sheldon. "Political Theory as a Vocation." *American Political Science Review* 63, no. 4 (December 1969), 1062–1082.

Wolpe, Joseph, and Lazarus, Arnold A. *Behavior Therapy Techniques*. Oxford: Pergamon, 1966.

Zeckhauser, Richard J. "Optimal Mechanisms for Income Transfer." *American Economic Review* 61, no. 3, part 1 (June 1971) : 324–334.

———. "Processes for Valuing Lives." Discussion Paper No. 29D, Public Policy Program, Kennedy School of Government. Cambridge, Mass.: Harvard University, January 1975.

———, and Schaefer, Elmer. "Public Policy and Normative Economic Theory." In Raymond A. Bauer and Kenneth Gergen, eds., *The Study of Policy Formation*. New York: Free Press, 1968.

Ziman, John. *Public Knowledge: The Social Dimension of Science*. Cambridge: University Press, 1968.

Znaniecki, Florian. "Should Sociologists Also Be Philosophers of Values?" *Sociology and Social Research* 37, no. 1 (September–October 1952) : 79–84.

INDEX